Marguerite Patten's
BEST BRITISH DISHES

Marguerite Patten's
BEST BRITISH DISHES

Grub Street | London

This edition first published in 2008 by
Grub Street
4 Rainham Close
London
SW11 6SS
Email: food@grubstreet.co.uk
www.grubstreet.co.uk

Design by Lizzie B Design
Photography by Michelle Garrett
Food preparation and styling by Jayne Cross
Edited by Hannah Stuart
Indexing by Amy Davies Dolamore

This is a revised and updated edition of *Classic British Dishes* published by Bloomsbury in 1994

A CIP record for this book is available from the British Library

ISBN 978- 1-906502-23-2

Printed and bound in Malta

Mixed Sources
Product group from well-managed
forests, and other controlled sources
www.fsc.org Cert no. TT-CoC-002424
© 1996 Forest Stewardship Council
FSC

The paper used for this book is FSC-certified and totally
chlorine-free. FSC (the Forest Stewardship Council) is
an international network to promote responsible
management of the world's forests.

Contents

Introduction

Throughout my career I have enjoyed travelling abroad and learning about the cuisine of various countries. At the same time I have used every opportunity to tell the people I meet overseas about the splendour of British food and cooking, of which I am extremely proud. I think most people would agree that the success of good cooking depends on the skill of the cook but also on the availability of first class ingredients.

This is where we are so fortunate in Britain; we have some of the finest produce in the world. The quality and wide selection of our fish, meat, poultry and game is outstanding and so are our dairy products.

During the Second World War British farmers worked tirelessly to ensure we had adequate supplies of homely vegetables to augment the sparse rationed foods. Nowadays the role of many farmers has changed. They still produce well known vegetables and fruits but, in addition, a wide range of more exotic produce, which until recently, could only be grown abroad.

Do visit one of the many farmers' markets held throughout Britain. Marvel at the wonderful selection of vegetables. Why do they look so fresh? Because the journey from the farm to the market is so short. Admire the splendid range of meat and meat products – some of which are a speciality of one farm or one area – and the interesting British cheeses and baked goods.

For many years British chefs and cooks have shown the world just how skilful they are at producing imaginative dishes from every cuisine, including the finest British fare. We have a wealth of national dishes, some of which have survived for generations; they are part of our British heritage. I have selected the best for this book. It is fascinating that within these relatively small islands, there is such a diversity of food and cooking. The English, Irish, Scots and Welsh all have their specialities. British menus should never be dull.

For centuries cooks have filled their store cupboards with home-made jams and jellies. I have not included a selection in this book, for I give a comprehensive collection in my popular book *The Basic Basics Jams, Preserves and Chutneys Handbook* (also published by Grub Street).

In this book, I have selected the very best of British recipes. Some are famous, others less well known. They reflect the fine flavours that are typical of our dishes. I have made sure that many of these are ideal for our busy life-style today. Many of the savoury dishes in the opening chapter, some of the soups, fish dishes and salads, are ideal when you are short of time.

A good proportion of British fare is based upon economical food. Sometimes people forget that less expensive fish, cuts of meat and poultry and vegetables have just as much good flavour as the more costly food. Home baking is both delicious and economical too.

Just why have we such a wealth of traditional recipes? As far back as the sixteenth century, it was acknowledged that the Tudor banquets were the most exciting and exotic in Europe. Even during those days, our merchant seamen roamed the world and brought back spices and other exotic foods to enhance our home-produced ingredients. Herbs were grown extensively as they were considered an essential part of cooking as well as being used for medicinal purposes. Today's British cooks are using generous amounts of fresh herbs again. Our involvement in India in the days of the British Empire, and growth of the East India Company, meant we learned something about Indian food – and some of those dishes became incorporated into our national cuisine. Our use of spices has also increased recently.

I am proud to compile this British book and I hope readers enjoy using it to prepare the best of British food.

Marguerite Patten

Starters

In the past British menus have used the French term 'hors d'oeuvre' to describe the first course of a meal. Today's more relaxed style means that in many restaurants this is now given as Starters. For family and less formal meals this extra course is often omitted and the meal begins with the main course or a small bowl of soup.

When you do decide to have a starter there is a wealth of food from which to choose. This chapter begins with a selection of potted foods, a delicious speciality of Britain. You could serve small portions of the fish or vegetable dishes in the book, as well as those in this section.

Colourful salads, as on pages 210 to 211, are a modern favourite, refreshing and low-calorie. Do not be conservative in your choice of ingredients, add seasonal British fruits to enhance both the flavour and health value of your starter salad.

▣ Potted Foods

For centuries good cooks have produced these from a wide variety of ingredients, as this is an excellent way of using surplus food. The recipes are far less complex than European pâtés and terrines, but that does not impair their flavour. In fact, the relatively few extra ingredients added to the basic food means you have a very definite taste. In the past potted foods were topped, and thus sealed, with a thick layer of melted fat, to exclude the air. This method can still be used, although with today's efficient refrigeration and the current desire to use the minimum of fat in recipes, it can be omitted and the potted food topped with a thick layer of foil.

The method of making potted foods is a simple one – the ingredients are pounded with butter and a clever choice of flavourings. Cooks of the past made good use of herbs, spices and even nuts and dried fruits to enhance the taste of the smooth savoury mixture. To achieve the correct texture the foods can be pounded in the traditional manner with a pestle and mortar or with less effort in a food processor. Use this appliance carefully as over-processing results in a sticky texture.

The selection of potted foods in this book ranges from various fish and meats to cheese. Country recipes are often based upon a local cheese and potted cheese is an ideal way of using a mixture of left-over cheeses (see page 16).

To serve potted foods

Either arrange neat portions, or small individual containers filled with the food, on individual plates with a suitable salad garnish. Hot toast is the usual accompaniment. A sauce is not essential with potted foods but it does make for a more unusual dish. Choose a refreshing Cucumber Sauce (see page 106) or salad dressing, such as those on page 212, with potted fish, one of the fruit sauces on pages 191 and 192 with potted meat and game or cheese. Potted foods also make excellent sandwich fillings.

Fish

Small portions of most of the fish dishes in this book could be served for a first course but some fish are particularly suitable for this purpose (see pages 17 to 27). Oysters are included for, to the majority of British gourmets, these are a perfect start to the meal when they are in season, i.e. from September to April. It is strange to think that in the nineteenth century oysters were so inexpensive that they were regarded as a poor man's dish, as described by Sam Weller in *Pickwick Papers* by Charles Dickens.

> 'It's a wery remarkable circumstance sir,' said Sam
> 'that poverty and oysters always seem to go together.'

Do not despise the more humble shellfish, such as cockles, winkles, whelks and mussels, as they each have an interesting flavour. Good supplies are caught in many parts of the British Isles, and the stalls piled high with these fish were welcome and familiar sights at the horse and amusement fairs of the past. An interesting salad is made by combining these fish (see page 26).

Vegetables

Various salads, such as those on page 28 to 30 make good starters. One of the finest vegetables for this course is asparagus. There are few flavours to compare with fresh asparagus and this is a vegetable which is grown to perfection in England. Because it has such a delicious taste elaborate methods of cooking and serving are unnecessary, but I am indebted to that wonderful cook of the nineteenth century, Eliza Acton, for the unusual asparagus recipe you will find on page 28.

In the past globe artichokes were grown in abundance in Britain, for they are an eye-catching plant as well as appetising vegetable. After years of having to import these you will be able to buy home-grown artichokes in farmers' markets when they are in season.

It is interesting how a realization of the value of mushrooms of all kinds has suddenly become the vogue and whether you buy these, or go on a mushroom-picking expedition, you have a fungi which has endless uses. Recipes for mushroom starters are on page 29.

◙ Making Potted Food

To produce potted foods that are full of flavour, make sure the cooked fish or meats are not over-cooked and dry. Use these ingredients as soon after cooking as possible.

Most recipes mention clarified butter. While this is not essential and ordinary fresh or salted butter can be used, the result is better if the butter is first treated in this way. The method of clarifying butter is given on page 12. The amount of butter used in the recipes will appear very generous; this is because it is used to blend the ingredients together and to cover the potted food. The purpose of covering the food with a layer of melted butter is to form an airtight seal and exclude the air, so the potted food will keep for several days in the refrigerator.

When melting the butter to blend with the ingredients, take care this does not darken in colour as this will spoil the appearance of the potted food.

To serve potted foods, turn out of the container(s) on to a bed of crisp salad.

◉ Potted Shrimps

Cooking time: few minutes ◉ Serves 4

British shrimps look like miniature prawns. They have a particularly sweet taste but sadly they are quite difficult to obtain. The best shrimps are considered to come from Morecambe Bay on the coast near the beautiful Lake District. You can buy shrimps straight from the boat, boil them yourself or buy them already cooked. You may be fortunate enough to catch a few shrimps in the rock pools in other parts of Britain's coastline. Shrimps are also caught in Norfolk around the Wash. Small prawns could be substituted when shrimps are unavailable.

Metric Imperial { **Ingredients** } American
1.2 litres/2 pints { **shrimps or prawns, cooked**} (see page 83 } 2¹/2 pints
100 g/4 oz { **clarified butter, see page 12** } ¹/2 cup
to taste { **cayenne pepper** } to taste
to taste { **freshly ground white pepper** } to taste
pinch { **grated or ground nutmeg** } pinch
pinch { **salt, if desired** } pinch

Peel the shrimps or prawns while warm. If they have become cold, put them into a container of boiling water for a few seconds and peel while warm.

Heat the butter, do not allow it to darken. Blend half the butter with the shrimps or prawns and the remainder of the ingredients. Spoon into individual dishes.

Pour the remaining butter over the fish. Allow to cool. Serve with hot toast.

Potted Salmon

Cooking time: few minutes ◉ Serves 4

Metric Imperial { **Ingredients** } American
350 g/12 oz { **fresh salmon, cooked** } {see page 98} 3/4 lb
175 g/6 oz { **clarified butter** } {see below} 3/4 cup
to taste { **ground or grated nutmeg** } to taste
to taste { **ground mace** } to taste
to taste { **salt and freshly ground black pepper** } to taste
2 teaspoons { **lemon juice** } 2 teaspoons

Finely flake the cooked fish. Melt the butter. Blend half the butter with the fish either by pounding until smooth or by placing in a food processor for a few seconds. Add the rest of the ingredients.

Spoon into individual containers. Cover with the remaining melted butter.

Variations:
- ◉ This recipe is equally good made with cooked fresh trout or kippers, or uncooked smoked trout.
- ◉ Add 1 to 2 tablespoons dry sherry to the potted mixture.
- ◉ Flavour the mixture with finely chopped fennel or dill leaves.

To Clarify Butter

The purpose of clarifying butter is to remove the milk solids (whey) and any liquid from the fat. Clarified butter is used in curries (it is called 'ghee') and when clarified it becomes a better fat for frying. It makes an excellent seal over potted foods. These are the two simple ways to clarify butter.

1. Place a double thickness of muslin or gauze (from a chemists) over a basin. Heat the butter carefully in a saucepan, do not allow it to become dark in colour. When the butter begins to foam, pour through the muslin. Any impurities are trapped in the fabric and the clarified butter will set in the basin.
2. Place the butter in a pan with water to cover. Heat until the butter has melted then leave until cold and set once more. Lift the butter off the water. Any impurities are within the water. This is also the basic method for clarifying dripping.

Potted Crab

Cooking time: few minutes ◉ Serves 4 to 6

Information about cooking and dressing crab and other dishes using crab are on pages 98 and 100. Potted crab makes an excellent starter served with hot toast and a crisp green salad. The flavour of crab is so good that you need few additional ingredients.

Metric Imperial { **Ingredients** } American
1 { **large cooked crab** } 1 lb
100 g/4 oz { **clarified butter** } {see page 12} 1/2 cup
2 tablespoons { **lemon juice, or to taste** } 3 tablespoons
good pinch { **ground mace** } good pinch
good pinch { **English mustard powder** } good pinch
to taste { **salt and freshly ground white pepper** } to taste

Remove all the flesh from the body and claws of the crab and pound this until smooth. You can mix the dark and white crabmeat together. Do not over-process fish if using a food processor, for it becomes sticky. Melt the butter. Blend half with the crabmeat, then add the required amount of lemon juice, mace, mustard powder and seasoning. Spoon into individual containers, then cover with the remainder of the melted butter.

◉ Potted Lobster

The method of making this dish is similar to that used for crab above. Lobster has a firmer, and less moist, flesh than crab and it is advisable to use 150 g/5 oz (5/8 cup) butter plus 2 tablespoons (3 tablespoons) of dry white wine. The potted lobster has a most attractive colour if you select a female lobster with coral. Page 99 gives details about choosing and cooking lobster.

Remove the flesh from the body and claws of a large lobster. Chop finely then pound until smooth. A food processor can be used but take care that the fish is not overprocessed. Blend the lobster with 75 g/3 oz (3/8 cup) of the melted butter and the wine. Allow to stand for 10 minutes to soften the flesh. Add the coral (if using), lemon juice, mace, mustard and seasoning as in the recipe above. Put into small containers and cover with the rest of the melted butter.

◉ Potted Veal and Ham

Cooking time: 1 hour 20 minutes ◉ Serves 6 to 8

This is ideal for a starter or a sandwich filling. The same ingredients are used as part of a filling in a raised pie (see page 149). In this case the veal and ham mixture is not cooked first. It is not essential to use clarified butter as one of the ingredients for the meat mixture; ordinary salted or fresh butter is satisfactory. Tender veal fillet is ideal for the potted meat mixture but as a filling in a raised pie you could use less expensive shoulder or breast.

Metric Imperial { **Ingredients** } American
350 g/12 oz { **uncooked veal** } 3/4 lb
225 g/8 oz { **cooked ham** } 1/2 lb
100 g/4 oz { **bacon rashers** } 1/4 lb
50 g/2 oz { **butter** } 1/4 cup
good pinch { **ground mace** } good pinch
4 tablespoons { **veal stock** } 6 tablespoons
2 tablespoons { **dry sherry** } 3 tablespoons

to taste { **salt and freshly ground black pepper** } to taste

To coat the mixture: 75 g/3 oz { **clarified butter** } {see page 12} 3/8 cup

Put the veal, ham and de-rinded bacon through a mincer at least twice to give a smooth mixture. A good processor can also be used. Melt the 50 g/2 oz (1/4 cup) of butter, add to the meats together with the mace, stock, sherry and seasoning.

Put into 6 to 8 small containers, cover with foil and stand in a roasting tin of hot water, which should come half way up the containers. Preheat the oven to 160°C/325°F, Gas Mark 3 and cook for 1¼ hours. Allow to cool, then top with the melted clarified butter.

◉ Potted Beef and Ham

Substitute lean beef for the veal in the recipe above. Topside of beef or good quality chuck steak could be used. Substitute beef stock for veal stock and red wine for sherry. As beef has a more robust flavour than veal, add a finely chopped medium onion and a garlic clove. Heat the 50 g/2 oz (1/4 cup) butter and cook the onion and garlic for 5 minutes then blend with the minced beef, ham and bacon and the other ingredients. Continue as for Potted Veal and Ham but allow 1½ hours cooking time.

◉ Potted Pheasant

Cooking time: 3 minutes ◉ Serves 4 to 6

Metric Imperial { **Ingredients** } American

350 g/12 oz { **cooked pheasant, weight without skin and bone**} (see page 168) 3/4 lb

100 g/4 oz { **clarified butter** } (see page 12) 1/2 cup

1½ tablespoons { **port or Madeira wine** } 2 tablespoons

to taste { **ground mace**} to taste

to taste { **ground cinnamon**} to taste

to taste { **salt and freshly ground black pepper** } to taste

Cut the flesh from the pheasant. Put through a mincer twice to give a fine mixture or chop in a food processor. Heat the butter and blend half with the pheasant. Add the port or Madeira wine, spices and seasoning. Put into individual containers and top with the remaining butter. This can be served as a pâté with toast or as a light main meal with mixed salad. It also makes an excellent sandwich filling.

Variations:
- ◉ Use grouse or pigeon or other game birds or roast venison instead of pheasant.
- ◉ Use a mixture of game birds or equal quantities of game bird flesh and cooked ham.
- ◉ Use clarified dripping from roasting the bird(s) instead of butter.
- ◉ Old recipes often include finely chopped walnuts or blanched almonds as these give a pleasant change of texture. Allow approximately 100 g/4 oz (1 cup).

Potted Beef

Follow the recipe above but use lightly cooked roast beef or steak instead of the pheasant. Omit the mace and cinnamon and flavour the mixture with English mustard and brandy, rather than port or Madeira wine.

Potted Chicken

Follow the recipe above but use chicken instead of pheasant. The mixture has a better flavour if equal quantities of breast and leg meat are used. It is better to flavour the poultry with dry sherry rather than with port or Madeira wine.

Turkey or guinea fowl are equally good in the recipe.

Potted Ham and Tongue

Cooking time: few minutes ◉ Serves 4 to 6

Metric Imperial { **Ingredients** } American
225 g/8 oz { **cooked ham** } 1/2 lb
225 g/8 oz { **cooked ox tongue** } 1/2 lb
100 g/4 oz { **clarified butter** } (see page 12) 1/2 cup
3 tablespoons { **port or red wine** } 41/2 tablespoons
good pinch { **ground mace** } good pinch
small pinch { **ground or grated nutmeg** } small pinch
to taste { **cayenne pepper** } to taste
to taste { **freshly ground black pepper** } to taste
1/2 teaspoon { **English mustard powder** } 1/2 teaspoon
to taste {**salt, if required**} to taste

Mince the ham very finely and the tongue a little less finely and mix together (the mixture looks more interesting if the small pieces of tongue are seen). Melt the butter and add half to the meat, together with the wine, spices, pepper and mustard.

Blend the ingredients together, add salt if desired. Spoon into small pots or one container and cover with the rest of the butter.

This is excellent served with hot toast or as a sandwich filling or with salad.

Potted Hare

Cooking time: few minutes ◉ Serves 6 to 8

This is an excellent way of using the cooked flesh from part of the back (saddle) of the hare.

Omit both the ham and tongue in the recipe above, but retain all the other ingredients plus 50 g/2 oz (1/4 cup) extra butter for the topping.

Use 450 g/1 lb cooked hare, the weight when removed from the bones, plus the cooked liver of the hare and 50 g/2 oz (generous 1/2 cup) pistachio nuts. The hare can be roasted, as in the recipe on page 171.

Mince the flesh of the hare and the liver finely, blend together. Melt the 100 g/4 oz (1/2 cup) butter then continue as in the recipe above. Hare has very lean flesh and needs plenty of butter in the mixture. Blanch the pistachio nuts by placing in boiling water for 1 to 2 minutes then removing the skins. Add to the hare mixture. Spoon into small pots or one container. Melt the 50 g/2 oz (1/4 cup) butter and spoon over the mixture.

◉ Potted Cheese

No cooking ◉ Serves 4 to 6

This is one of the oldest pâtés or potted mixtures. When the cheese is well pounded and the mixture has stood for a while, it is possible to cut this into neat slices. It can be served with hot toast, biscuits or bread and it is excellent with various salads or with fruit, fruit chutney or fruit sauce.

The choice of cheese is entirely a personal matter. I think a white Cheshire is best of all but, for a really strong flavour, a Lancashire is excellent or one can use a mature Cheddar. Try mixing several different cheeses together.

Various communities often made a feature of using local cheeses for this dish.

Metric Imperial { **Ingredients** } American

150 g/5 oz { **clarified butter** } (see page 12) 5/8 cup
350 g/12 oz { **Cheshire white cheese, or see above** } 3/4 lb
1 to 2 teaspoons { **mustard powder** } 1 to 2 teaspoons
2 tablespoons { **dry sherry** } 3 tablespoons
75 g/3 oz { **fresh, dried or pickled walnuts, depending on flavour required** } 3/4 cup

Cream 75 g/3 oz (6 tablespoons) of the butter until very soft. Grate the cheese finely, then put it into a bowl and work well until like butter. A pestle and mortar is ideal for this purpose, but a wooden spoon, used with energy, will give somewhat the same effect. Add the cheese to the creamed butter. Blend the mustard (the amount depends upon personal taste) with the sherry, then gradually mix this with the cheese and butter.

If using fresh walnuts remove the skins; in my opinion fresh nuts are the best, since they do not detract from the colour or flavour of the cheese, but many people enjoy the 'bite' of black pickled walnuts. Chop the walnuts finely. Blend with the cheese mixture. Put into small pots. Melt the remaining butter, allow to cool, then spoon over the top of each pot. Allow adequate time for the cheese mixture to become firm.

Potted Stilton

Follow the recipe for Potted Cheese above, but omit the nuts. Crumble and then beat the Stilton before blending with the butter. Port wine could be used instead of sherry. A good pinch of ground mace can be added for extra flavour.

A more unusual taste is given by adding a few raisins, soaked in port wine.

Oysters

No cooking

To many people, oysters are the ultimate luxury as a starter.

To serve oysters:
These should be opened carefully so none of the delicious liquor inside is wasted. Either 6 or 12 oysters are required for each portion.

The raw oysters are left on the bottom (rounded) shells with their liquor and served on large plates, on a bed of ice if possible so they are kept very cold. Wedges of lemon and cayenne pepper or Tabasco sauce and thin brown bread and butter are the usual accompaniments.

Oyster Patties

Cooking time: 6 minutes ⊚ Serves 4

Lift 24 small oysters from their shells. Coat in a little seasoned flour, then beaten egg and fine crisp breadcrumbs.

Heat 50 g/2 oz (1/4 cup) of butter and 1 tablespoon olive oil in a large frying pan. Add the coated oysters and fry for 1 minute, then turn and fry quickly on the second side for 1 minute. Lower the heat and cook for another 1 or 2 minutes. Drain on absorbent paper and serve at once with lemon and cayenne pepper.

Scalloped Oysters

Cooking time: 10 minutes ⊚ Serves 4

Do not over-cook the oysters as they would become tough. A little grated cheese can be added to the crumb topping, if you wish. (Pictured on page 19.)

Metric Imperial { **Ingredients** } American
12 { **large oysters** } 12
75 g/3 oz { **butter** } 3/8 cup
100 g/4 oz { **soft breadcrumbs** } 2 cups
pinch { **cayenne pepper** } pinch
To garnish: { **lemon wedges** }

Preheat the oven to 220°C/425°F, Gas Mark 7. Remove the oysters from the shells, saving any oyster liquid. Melt the butter and add to the crumbs. Mix the crumb mixture and sprinkle half on the bottom shells of the oysters. Add the fish with the liquid and a pinch of cayenne, then top with the rest of the buttered crumbs. Heat for 10 minutes or until the topping is brown. Serve with lemon wedges.

▣ Smoked Fish

Smoking has been a common form of food preservation in Britain for centuries. The food would be hung over an outdoor wood fire or placed under a smoke-hole in the chimney. Larger homes frequently had a separate smoke-house. Many fish are smoked, the most popular being haddock, Finnan Haddie is famous, and herrings. The most popular form of smoked herrings are kippers. The fish is split before smoking; the Isle of Man claims to produce the best kippers. Bloaters are lightly salted herrings, left ungutted before smoking, sadly these are less available today. Yarmouth, on the east coast was noted for these fish. Buckling is another kind of smoked herring, the head is removed and the fish gutted before being smoked. Mackerel, sprats and trout are other economical varieties of fish that are smoked by many firms. Some of these are ideal for a starter; others more suitable for breakfast or main dishes.

Products to be eaten raw or cooked afterwards are cold-smoked at around 24°C/75°F. This does not cook the food. This temperature is used for smoked salmon and haddock. Hot-smoking at temperatures of 82°C/180°F is used for most other fish. Today a variety of foods are smoked professionally and expertly, ranging from selections of fish, meat, poultry and game to cheese.

▣ **Arbroath Smokies:** These are produced in Scotland from very small, delicately flavoured haddock. The method of smoking means that little heating is necessary before serving the fish. Although a favourite breakfast dish in Scotland, they can be served at the start of a meal.

Grilled Smokies: top the fish with butter and grill for a few minutes only, serve with hot toast or oatcakes and butter.

Potted Smokies: the uncooked flesh can be flaked then pounded and used as in Potted Salmon (see page 12). Use exactly the same proportions of fish, butter, etc., as in that recipe. If it is difficult to remove the skin, simply pour boiling water over the smokies, leave for a minute then drain well and remove the skin and bones.

▣ **Smoked Eel:** Whether this is sold as fillets or slices, make quite sure the fish looks oily and feels soft; if dry and hard it is very unappetizing. Serve with Horseradish Cream (see page 111) or with scrambled eggs flavoured with chopped chives (see page 219). Garnish with lemon and serve with brown bread and butter.

▣ **Smoked Mackerel and Trout:** These fish should be soft and oily, not hard and dry. Serve as for smoked eel.

- **Smoked Salmon:** Scottish smoked salmon is superb. Take care to buy only from good sources. Select carefully to make sure it is freshly smoked, i.e. bright in colour and pleasantly moist. Buy freshly sliced if possible. Serve with lemon and cayenne pepper.
- **Smoked Oysters and Sprats:** Oysters should look firm but not hard; sprats soft and oily. Serve as for smoked eel.

◉ Kipper Pâté

Cooking time: few minutes ◉ Serves 4 to 6

Metric Imperial { **Ingredients** } American
4 { **large kippers** } 4
2 { **garlic cloves** } 2
50 g/2 oz { **butter** } 1/4 cup
1 tablespoon { **lemon juice** } 1 1/4 tablespoons
little { **single cream** } little
to taste { **freshly ground black pepper** } to taste

Put the kippers in a dish and pour boiling water over them, cover the dish and leave for a few minutes. Drain and then flake the fish, discarding the skin and bones. Peel and crush the garlic. Melt the butter, then add to the kippers with the garlic, lemon juice and enough cream to make a soft mixture. Add pepper to taste. Serve with hot toast and butter.

◘ Smoked Poultry and Game

No cooking

Although these smoked foods have been relatively unknown in Britain until recently, they are becoming more and more popular and companies throughout Britain are producing them with great success. Undoubtedly they will become classic British foods of the future.

Serve thin slices of smoked chicken, turkey or venison as a starter. These foods are a particularly good choice when the main course is fish. The flesh of the birds and game has a delicious taste, especially served with Cranberry Sauce (see page 192) and a crisp salad.

◘ Smoked Cheeses

Cheese was once considered a fitting ending to a meal but nowadays many menus begin with cheese and salad. The cheeses are often imported but quite a number of individual British farmers, who pride themselves on producing cheese, are smoking small quantities which are becoming very popular.

The most pleasing way to serve the smoked cheese as a starter is heated. Cut slices of firm smoked cheese, such as Cheshire or Cheddar, place these on foil on the grill pan, top with a very little butter and grill for a short time, until the surface of the cheese begins to bubble. Serve at once with a colourful mixed salad, which should include slices of crisp dessert apple, dipped in lemon juice to preserve the colour. The contrast between hot cheese and cold salad is very pleasant. Portions of soft smoked cream cheese can be heated in the same way.

⊡ Serving Crab and Lobster

Both cooked crab and cooked lobster make excellent starters. Serve small portions of Dressed Crab (see page 100) or Lobster (see page 99).

The salads to serve with these fish can be made more interesting and refreshing by including suitable fruits, such as avocado slices (a modern British classic) dipped in an oil and lemon dressing, orange segments or even slices of ripe melon.

⊡ Shellfish Mimosa

A colourful way of garnishing any shellfish salad is to rub cooked egg yolks through a coarse sieve, so the golden yolk falls over the fish like mimosa balls.

◉ Devilled Crab

Cooking time: 6 to 8 minutes ◉ Serves 4

Metric Imperial { **Ingredients** } American
1 large or 3 small { **crab(s), dressed** } (see page 100)   1 large or 3 small
50 g/2 oz { **butter** } 1/4 cup
50 g/2 oz { **soft breadcrumbs** } 1 cup
1 to 2 teaspoons { **curry powder, or to taste** } 1 to 2 teaspoons
1 teaspoon { **Worcestershire sauce, or to taste** } 1 teaspoon
to taste { **salt and freshly ground black pepper** } to taste
1 to 2 tablespoons { **double cream** } 1 1/2 to 3 tablespoons
To garnish: { lemon and lettuce}

Remove the crabmeat from the shells, place in a basin and mix dark and light together. Add half the butter and half the breadcrumbs to the fish. Blend the remaining butter and breadcrumbs together in another basin.

Stir the curry powder, sauce, seasoning and cream into the crabmeat and spoon the mixture into 4 clean crabshells or flameproof dishes. Top with the buttered crumbs.

Preheat the grill at a medium heat and cook for 6 to 8 minutes or until the topping is golden brown and the fish piping hot. Serve with lemon and a border of lettuce.

◉ Crab au gratin

This dish is made in very much the same way as Devilled Crab, page 21, but the curry powder and Worcestershire sauce should be omitted. Instead, blend a little extra cream with the crabmeat, crumbs and seasoning or replace the cream with soft cream or curd cheese.

Blend the buttered crumbs with several tablespoons of finely grated Cheddar or Cheshire cheese; cover the crabmeat mixture with this topping. Grill as before.

▣ Serving scallops

Scallops are one of the best shellfish caught in British waters. They are at their best from October to March and they are equally suitable for a light meal or a more sustaining main course (see pages 64 and 84).

Really fresh scallops have bright orange roes. The very small scallops, mostly caught around the Channel Islands and the Isle of Man, are known as 'queenies'. Try to buy scallops in closed shells and either get the fishmonger to open them for you or heat them for a few minutes in a saucepan until the shells open.

Never over-cook scallops, they are ready to serve when the white flesh turns opaque. Cooking for too long a period makes them extremely tough and unpalatable.

◉ Fried scallops

Cooking time: 5 to 6 minutes ◉ **Serves 4**

Metric Imperial { **Ingredients** } American
8 medium { **scallops** } 8 medium
to taste { **lemon juice** } to taste
little { **plain flour** } little
to taste { **salt and freshly ground black pepper** } to taste
To fry: { **butter or oil** }
To garnish: { **lemon slices and salad** }

Dry the scallops well and flavour with a little lemon juice. Blend the flour and seasoning and coat the fish. Heat a little butter or oil in a frying pan and cook the scallops for 5 to 6 minutes. Serve at once with the lemon and salad.

Variation:
- ◉ Coat the fish with egg and breadcrumbs or batter (see page 63) and then fry.
- ◉ A modern classic way of serving very fresh scallops is simply to marinate them in lemon juice or a lemon and olive oil dressing and serve without cooking.

⊙ Whitebait

Cooking time: 2 to 3 minutes for each batch ⊙ Serves 4

Whitebait are the fry (the young) of herrings and sprats. When the fresh fish is unavailable you can buy frozen whitebait. If a generous amount of cayenne pepper is used in the coating the dish is often called Devilled Whitebait. The fish are very small, just about 5 cm/2 inches in length. Some of the best whitebait are caught at Southend, the popular seaside resort on the east coast. Another source is off the coast in Norfolk.

Metric Imperial (**Ingredients**) American
450 g/1 lb (**whitebait**) 1 lb
to taste (**salt and freshly ground black pepper**) to taste
to taste (**cayenne pepper**) to taste
50 g/2 oz (**plain flour**) 1/2 cup
To fry: (**oil**)
To garnish: (**lemon quarters**)

Whitebait are a highly perishable fish, so store them carefully. If frozen, allow to defrost sufficiently to separate the fish then dry them well.

Blend a little salt, black pepper and cayenne pepper with the flour. To coat the fish either put the seasoned flour into a large bag, add the fish and shake the bag gently until the fish are well coated, or put the seasoned flour on to a large dish and turn the fish around in this until coated. Shake off the surplus flour before frying.

Heat the oil to 185°C/365°F. To test the temperature without a thermometer see information on page 62.

Put some of the coated fish into the heated frying basket, lower into the oil and fry for 2 to 3 minutes or until brown and crisp, then remove to absorbent paper to drain. Keep hot in the oven while frying another batch. Garnish the cooked fish with lemon.

Whitebait are generally served with brown bread and butter and extra cayenne pepper.

⊙ Fried Herring Roes

Cooking time: 5 to 6 minutes ⊙ Serves 4

Although often served as a savoury at the end of a meal or a breakfast dish, hard herring roes make an excellent snack.

Coat 450 g/1 lb hard herring roes with plain flour, mixed with a little salt, freshly ground black pepper and a pinch of cayenne pepper, as whitebait, above. Either fry in hot oil in exactly the same way and for the same time as whitebait, or fry in hot butter in a frying pan for 5 to 6 minutes. Garnish with lemon and parsley. Serve with hot toast and butter.

◉ Fried Eels

Cooking time: 10 to 15 minutes ◉ **Serves 4**

Eels in various forms have always been a favourite in England, particularly with Londoners. Young eels (elvers) should be selected for this dish.

Metric Imperial { **Ingredients** } American
550 g/1¼ lb { **elvers** } 1¼ lb
4 to 8 { **bacon rashers** } 4 to 8
25 g/l oz { **butter** } 2 tablespoons
To garnish: { **sliced lemon, parsley sprigs** }

As elvers are so young it is not essential for these to be skinned but the fish is more tender if this is done. Cut the fish into 2.5 cm/1 inch slices. De-rind the bacon. Put the bacon rinds and bacon into a large frying pan and cook until bacon is tender. Remove the bacon to absorbent paper and keep hot while frying the fish. Remove the bacon rinds, add the butter to the pan, heat this and fry the fish for 5 to 8 minutes until it becomes tender and opaque in appearance.

Serve the fish with the bacon and garnish with lemon and parsley.

◉ Sprat Fritters

Cooking time: 3 to 4 minutes each batch ◉ **Serves 4**

These small fish are extremely inexpensive but they were once so highly prized that they were taken to London to serve as a first course at the Lord Mayor's official banquet. They can be coated with flour as whitebait and fried (see page 24) or coated with very fine oatmeal and cooked on a bed of salt, as herrings (see page 67), or prepared as below.

Metric Imperial { **Ingredients** } American
450 g/l lb { **sprats** } 1 lb
{ **coating batter** } (see page 64)
To fry: { **oil** }
To garnish: { **sliced lemon** }

Wash the fish, remove the heads and intestines. Dry well then coat as instructions on page 63. Heat the oil to 185°C/365°F. Put some of the fish into a frying basket and cook until golden and crisp. Drain on absorbent paper. Keep hot while frying another batch. Serve with lemon, brown bread and butter and cayenne pepper.

◉ shellfish salad

Cooking time: as individual fish ◉ **Serves 4**

It is sad, but true, that some of our most interesting shellfish are unknown to many people simply because these are not displayed and sold as often as they should be. Also the fact that cockles, mussels and whelks are relatively inexpensive often makes people fail to realize their interesting flavour. Fortunately supermarkets and fishmongers are starting to display much more varied and lavish displays of fish.

A wonderful starter or main dish is made by serving some of these lesser-known varieties of fish. These can be bought ready-cooked or cooked at home. They can be served cold or while still warm from cooking, with the salad.

Metric Imperial { **Ingredients** } American
900 ml/1½ pints { **cockles in shells** } scant 4 cups
900 ml/1½ pints { **mussels in shells** } scant 4 cups
24 { **whelks in shells, as small as possible** } 24
350 g/12 oz { **unpeeled prawns** } ¾ lb
To garnish: { **mixed salad** }

Cook the fish as below.
◉ **Cockles:** wash well as they can be very full of sand. Discard any fish where the shells remain open. To give extra flavour cook as mussels below, or simply cook in a pan with enough water to cover. Place a lid or tea-cloth over the pan and cook steadily for a few minutes until the shells open. Discard any that are closed.
◉ **Mussels:** wash well, discard any where the shells remain open. Put into a pan with a little chopped parsley and chopped onion. Add enough water or white wine to cover, plus a little seasoning. Put on the lid and cook steadily for a few minutes until the shells open. Discard any mussels where the shells do not open completely.
◉ **Whelks:** soak in cold water for several hours. Put into lightly salted water and simmer for 1 hour if small or 1¼ hours if large.
◉ **Prawns:** put into lightly salted boiling water and cook for 4 to 6 minutes or until the shells turn pinkish-red. Do not over-cook.

Remove the cockles and mussels from their shells, leave the whelks in their shells, but provide strong pins to tackle these. Peel the prawns, unless using very large ones which can be served in their shells with individual finger bowls.

Arrange the fish in groups on individual plates and serve with mayonnaise or salad dressing but do provide vinegar too, for this is the traditional British accompaniment to cockles and whelks.

Soused Herrings

Cooking time: 1¹/₂ hours ⊙ Serves 6

This method of cooking herrings makes them ideal for salads and starters. They are not unlike the European rollmop herrings in flavour. Pickling spices vary a great deal in strength so use the smaller amount the first time you make this dish. You will find recipes similar to the one that follows in many areas where herrings are plentiful. Fresh mackerel can be cooked in the same way.

Metric Imperial { **Ingredients** } American

6 { **large herrings, with soft or hard roes**} 6
2 to 3 { **medium onions** } 2 to 3
6 { **fresh bay leaves** } 6
250 ml/8 fl oz { **brown malt vinegar** } 1 cup
250 ml/8 fl oz { **water** } 1 cup
1 to 2 teaspoons { **mixed pickling spices, or to taste** } 1 to 2 teaspoons
to taste { **salt and freshly ground black pepper** } to taste

Preheat the oven to 140°C/275°F, Gas Mark 1.
Cut the heads from the fish, split them along the stomachs, then open out flat. Remove and discard the intestines, except the roes. Wash and dry these. Lay the herrings on a board with the skin side uppermost, run your finger or thumb down the centre of the back of each fish, then turn them over; you will find you can lift away the backbone and most of the other bones. Any small bones left can be removed with tweezers or fingers.

Peel the onions and cut into thin rings. Place 1 or 2 rings, a bay leaf and herring roes on each herring. Roll the fish from the head ends to the tails; allow the tails to stand upright. Secure the rolls with wooden cocktail sticks. Place the herrings in a casserole dish with the remaining onion rings. Blend the vinegar, water, pickling spices and seasoning. Pour over the herrings. Cover the casserole and cook the herrings for 1¹/₂ hours.

Although these herrings are generally served cold, they are also very good hot, served with a crisp green salad. Lift the fish from the liquid, strain this and use a little in the salad dressing.

Spiced Herrings

Follow the recipe above, but use only half the amount of pickling spices and add ¹/₂ to 1 teaspoon allspice to the vinegar and water. Core, but do not peel, 2 dessert apples, cut into rings and add to the other ingredients.

Variations:
⊙   Use pilchards, a slightly smaller fish than herrings, in either of these recipes.

▣ Vegetable Starters

Serve the portions of asparagus or globe artichokes on individual plates; provide finger bowls of cold water decorated with small flower heads as most people like to eat both these vegetables with their fingers. The hot or cold stems are dipped into hot melted butter or a sauce; the cold stems are dipped in the dressing.

▣ Asparagus

Asparagus should have firm stems and perfect tips. If the stems show any signs of wrinkling the vegetable is stale. Asparagus should be kept in the salad drawer of the refrigerator until required, or placed with the base of the stems in a bowl of cold water in a cool place. British asparagus is in season from late May to July.

Cut away the base of the stems and gently scrape the lower half of the stems, taking care not to damage the tender tips. Wash in cold water.

The ideal way to cook asparagus is in an asparagus basket placed in a saucepan, thus enabling the stems to stand upright. If this is not possible, tie the asparagus in bunches of 6 to 8 stems to make them less likely to fall.

Place in boiling salted water, tips uppermost. The cooking time depends upon the thickness of the stems. Thick young asparagus takes about 18 to 20 minutes; thin stems, often called 'sprue' asparagus, about 12 to 15 minutes. To test if cooked, insert the tip of a knife in the thickest part of a stem, it should feel just tender. Lift the asparagus out of the pan and drain well.

To serve asparagus hot: arrange 6 to 8 stems on hot plates and serve with melted and lightly seasoned butter, English Butter Sauce (see page 104) or Hollandaise Sauce (see page 105).

To serve asparagus cold: remove from the pan, drain well and cool, then serve with a garnish of lemon and vinaigrette dressing (see page 212).

◉ Eliza Acton's Asparagus and Egg

This is based upon a nineteenth century recipe, but I have used rather longer parts of the asparagus stems. Cook the asparagus as above; do not over-cook. Cut off the tips with about 5 cm/2 inches of stem. Use the remainder of the stems in soup (see page 35). I have altered the next stage of Eliza Acton's recipe to ensure a shorter cooking time so the asparagus keeps firm.

To 350 g/12 oz (3/4 lb) cooked tips and stems, allow 50 g/2 oz (1/4 cup) butter. Heat the butter in a large frying pan, dry the portions of asparagus well, add to the butter. Turn in this for several minutes, then stir in 1 teaspoon flour, 1/2 teaspoon sugar and 3 well beaten and seasoned egg yolks. Stir over a low heat until the egg sauce adheres to the asparagus and serve at once. This makes a starter for 4.

Country-style Mushrooms

Cooking time: 10 minutes ⊙ **Serves 4**

Metric Imperial { **Ingredients** } American
4 { **bacon rashers** } 4
225 g/8 oz { **large mushrooms, or a mixture of types** } 1/2 lb
50 g/2 oz { **butter** } 1/4 cup
150 ml/1/4 pint { **double cream** } 2/3 cup
3 tablespoons { **white wine or dry cider** } 41/2 tablespoons
to taste { **salt and freshly ground black pepper** } to taste
For the topping: { **little grated cheese** }

De-rind the bacon and chop the rashers into small pieces. Wipe and slice the mushrooms. Heat the butter with the bacon rinds, fry the bacon and mushrooms for a few minutes, then discard the rinds. Spoon the bacon and mushrooms into 4 individual heated flameproof dishes. Preheat the grill.

Whip the cream, blend in the wine or cider and season lightly. Spoon over the mushroom mixture and top with a little grated cheese. Heat under the grill for several minutes until golden brown. Serve with brown bread and butter.

Mushroom Ramekins

Cooking time: 10 minutes ⊙ **Serves 4**

Metric Imperial { **Ingredients** } American
225 g/8 oz { **mushrooms** } 1/2 lb
50 g/2 oz { **butter** } 1/4 cup
2 tablespoons { **beef or chicken or vegetarian stock** } 3 tablespoons
4 { **eggs** } 4
150 ml/1/4 pint { **double cream** } 2/3 cup
2 to 3 teaspoons { **chopped chives, or to taste** } 2 to 3 teaspoons
2 to 3 teaspoons { **chopped parsley, or to taste** } 2 to 3 teaspoons
1/4 teaspoon { **chopped thyme, or to taste** } 1/4 teaspoon
to taste { **salt and cayenne pepper** } to taste

Wipe the mushrooms, remove the stalks and chop these finely. Heat the butter in a frying pan, add the mushroom stalks and caps. Cook steadily for 4 minutes.

Remove the caps, keep warm on a plate over hot water or on a dish in the oven. Beat the stock and eggs, add the cream, herbs and seasoning. Pour over the mushroom stalks. Stir over a low heat until the consistency of thick cream. Spoon into individual ramekin dishes and top with the mushroom caps. Serve with crisp toast.

◉ Hot Globe Artichokes

Cooking time: 25 to 40 minutes ◉ Serves 4

It is a joy to know that globe artichokes are once again growing in Britain – where they belonged a century ago. Look out for these in farmers' markets when in season. Really fresh artichokes should be bright green in colour and very firm in texture; avoid any that have brown leaves. The small or medium-sized artichokes have a more delicate flavour than the outsize ones.

Metric Imperial { **Ingredients** } American
4 { **globe artichokes** } 4
to taste { **salt and freshly ground back pepper** } to taste
To serve: { **hot butter** }

Pull away any tough outer leaves; this may not be necessary with young vegetables. Cut away the stalk so the artichokes will stand upright when cooked. It is quite usual to trim the rounded leaves at the top to make them straight and level, but not essential.

If possible choose an enamel saucepan in which to cook the artichokes as this helps to keep them a good colour. Wash the artichokes in cold water. Fill a saucepan with plenty of water, add salt to taste and bring the water to the boil. Put in the artichokes, cover the pan and boil steadily. The timing varies a great deal. Young artichokes take about 25 minutes but more mature ones can take up to 40 minutes.

To test if cooked, lift an artichoke from the pan and try to pull away an outer leaf; if the vegetable is ready to serve the leaf comes away easily and the fleshy base is tender. Drain the artichokes. Cut out and discard the centre part, known as the choke. Heat and lightly season a generous amount of butter. Serve each artichoke with hot butter. This can be heated in a saucepan or bowl in a microwave.

It is important to provide finger bowls as it is usual to dip the leaves in the butter with your fingers. The base of the artichoke, known as the heart, is cut with a knife and fork.

◉ Cold Globe Artichokes

Cook 4 artichokes, remove the chokes and allow the vegetables to become cold. Fill the centre cavities with oil and vinegar or oil and lemon dressing (see page 212).

◉ Stuffed Globe Artichokes

Cook 4 artichokes, remove the centre chokes and allow the vegetables to become cold. Blend 100 g/4 oz (1/2 cup) soft cream cheese with enough single cream to give the consistency of thick cream. Season to taste and spoon into the centre cavities of the vegetables.

Soups

'Soup of the evening, beautiful soup'

Most British people would agree with the words above, taken from *Alice in Wonderland*, when they taste a really good home-made soup. Soups of many different kinds have been a feature of British meals for generations; the selection is almost endless. Each part of Britain has its own traditional, and very individual, recipes. For the most part the soups and broths are fairly sustaining, as they were created to keep families warm and satisfied during rather cold weather. They were often made with very economical ingredients, for a bowl of soup would be the major part of a meal when money was scarce.

Soups have always been included in the menu at formal dinners and grand banquets and the dishes served on these occasions are lighter and more subtly flavoured.

Recipes for all these kinds of soups are in the pages that follow.

▣ Stock for soup

The stock, or liquid, used in making a soup is very important. In many of the vegetable soups you can use water or milk and water but in some of these, such as the Dried Pea Soup and Green Pea Soup (see pages 39 and 40), a really well-flavoured bacon stock is the secret of a rich flavour, although chicken stock can be substituted.

On the occasions when you have boiled a joint of bacon for a family meal, as page 138, cherish any stock left and use it to add flavour to soups.

Fish stock is recommended for some of the fish soups. You can buy this quite readily. The method of making this at home is on page 88. Good chicken and other poultry stock recipes are on page 126 but commercially made chicken stock is good.

There are good stock (often called bouillon) cubes available today. These are added to liquid to make stock. Choose those that are lowest in salt content.

Vegetable Soups

We are very fortunate in Britain in that we have an excellent selection of vegetables that can be used to produce interesting soups. If you compare the cooking times, in this book and other modern cookery books, you will find that these are much shorter than in older books, for one of the lessons we have learned is that vegetables, whether to be part of a soup or a vegetable dish, are so easily spoiled by prolonged heating. To retain the maximum goodness and the true taste of individual vegetables, cook the soup for the shortest possible time.

Fish Soups

There is no doubt that fish soups are served far less frequently in Britain than in many other countries, which is surprising, for as an island we have a wonderful selection of fish from which to make the soups. The fish soups that have become classic dishes are excellent; you will find them on pages 44 to 49. These soups are based upon various kinds of fish, including smoked haddock, crab, fresh salmon and mussels, which are extremely popular in many parts of Britain.

Meat Soups

Several of the meat soups form complete and very satisfying meals. It used to be the custom to remove the cooked meat from the liquid and vegetables and serve this as the second course of the meal.

Poultry and Game Soups

A home-made chicken soup, rich and creamy, is delicious. Two of the chicken soups in this book, on page 58, remind one of the way stock was thickened a long time ago. Flour was not used; instead the cooks would grind up almonds and use these. Obviously the nuts impart a most unusual and very pleasant taste to the soup. Modern ground almonds give the same result. A Cock-a-Leekie soup is one of the great family soups from Scotland, here again an unexpected flavour is given by including prunes among the other ingredients (see page 57). Game abounded in Britain and the game soups, on pages 58-9, are based upon very old recipes.

Garnishes for Soups

Modern cooks have discovered the important part that various herbs can play in cooking and in garnishing dishes and these are used in many of the recipes in this chapter. A favourite garnish is croûtons. The method of preparing these, plus hints on storing the crisp, diced bread, is given on page 53.

⊙ Country Vegetable Soup

Cooking time: 30 minutes ⊙ Serves 6

Recipes for mixed vegetable soups vary a great deal as the soup is made with whatever vegetables are available. It is important to choose a good blending of flavours, and not to allow one particular vegetable to be over-powering. Include some carrots and/or tomatoes which ensure that the soup has an attractive colour and some potatoes or starchy vegetables that will thicken the soup.

Metric Imperial { **Ingredients** } American
2 { **medium onions** } 2
3 { **medium carrots** } 3
1 { **very small parsnip or portion of a swede** } 1
2 { **medium potatoes** } 2
2 { **medium tomatoes** } 2
2 { **garlic cloves, optional** } 2
2 { **medium leeks** } 2
a few { **shelled green peas** } a few
40 g/1½ oz { **butter** } 3 tablespoons
1.2 litres/2 pints { **water** } 5 cups
to taste { **salt and freshly ground black pepper** } to taste
To garnish: { **chopped parsley or watercress** }

Peel all the vegetables, skin the tomatoes, skin and crush the garlic, cut away the tough green part of the leeks.

This soup can be served without sieving or liquidizing it so either cut the vegetables into very small even-shaped dice or grate them. The tomatoes should be finely chopped. Heat the butter in a large saucepan, add the onions and garlic, if using, and gently cook for 5 minutes, taking care that the onion does not discolour. Pour in the water, bring this to the boil, then add all the vegetables with seasoning to taste. Cover the saucepan and cook fairly briskly until the vegetables are just tender, then serve with the garnish. You can make a smooth puréed soup by sieving or liquidizing the vegetables, reheating the soup before serving.

Variation:
⊙ This soup becomes a light meal if topped with a thick layer of grated cheese or small balls of cream cheese, just before serving.

⊙ Cream of Vegetable Soup

Use only 900 ml/1½ pints (3¾ cups) water. Sieve or liquidize the soup and reheat with 300 ml/½ pint (1¼ cups) single cream or half milk and half cream.

Cream of Asparagus Soup

Cooking time: 30 minutes ◎ Serves 4 to 6

Metric Imperial { **Ingredients** } American
350 g/12 oz { **asparagus** } 3/4 lb
1 { **small onion** } 1
25 g/1 oz { **butter** } 2 tablespoons
300 ml/1/2 pint { **chicken stock or water** } 11/4 cups
to taste { **salt and freshly ground white pepper** } to taste
300 ml/1/2 pint { **milk** } 11/4 cups
150 ml/1/4 pint { **single cream** } 2/3 cup
To garnish: { **fried croûtons** } (see page 53)

Trim the asparagus and peel and chop the onion. Heat the butter in a saucepan and cook the onion very gently for 5 minutes, take care it does not darken in colour. Add the asparagus to the pan with the chicken stock or water and seasoning. Bring to the boil, cover the pan and simmer for 10 minutes, then add the milk and cook for a further 5 to 10 minutes, or until the asparagus is just soft. When the asparagus is almost tender, remove several stems and cut off a few tips, reserve these to garnish the soup. Either sieve or liquidize the soup, then return to the pan with the cream and reheat. Top with the croûtons just before serving.

Variations:
◎ Top the soup with sieved hard-boiled egg yolks to give a contrast in colour.

Cream of Watercress Soup

Cooking time: 15 minutes ◎ Serves 4

The value of watercress as a healthy vegetable has been appreciated for several centuries. According to Alexis Soyer in his book *The Pantropheon* both the Romans and the Greeks granted to this cruciform plant a host of beneficient qualities. The main growing areas are in Hampshire and other Home Counties. Clean pure water is essential for healthy watercress. Do not overcook this soup once the watercress has been added for much of the flavour will be lost.

This particular recipe has many variations as the basic ingredients blend so well with a variety of different foods. (Pictured page 37.)

Metric Imperial { **Ingredients** } American
100 g/4 oz { **watercress leaves** } 2 cups
150 ml/1/4 pint { **milk** } 2/3 cup
50 g/2 oz { **butter** } 1/4 cup
25 g/1 oz { **cornflour** } 1/4 cup
750 ml/11/4 pints { **chicken stock** } generous 3 cups
150 ml/1/4 pint { **single cream** } 2/3 cup

1 { **egg yolk** } 1
1 tablespoon { **lemon juice** } 1¼ tablespoons
to taste { **salt and freshly ground white pepper** } to taste
To garnish: { **small watercress sprigs** }

Chop the watercress leaves finely just before making the soup. This can be done with a sharp knife or in a food processor or liquidizer. It is easier if a small quantity of the milk is added to the leaves when using these appliances.

Heat the butter in a saucepan, stir in the cornflour, then gradually blend in the milk, stock and cream. Stir or whisk as the mixture comes to the boil and thickens slightly, then allow it to simmer steadily for 10 minutes. Add the watercress leaves.

Blend the egg yolk with the lemon juice, whisk a few spoonfuls of the very hot, but not boiling, watercress soup into this mixture then return to the pan. Simmer, but do not allow to boil, for 2 to 3 minutes. Season to taste and serve, topped with the sprigs of watercress.

◉ Cheese and Watercress Soup

Follow the recipe above but stir 75 g/3 oz (¾ cup) finely grated Cheddar or Cheshire cheese into the soup immediately after adding the egg and lemon mixture.
Garnish the soup with watercress sprigs and a light dusting of grated cheese.

◉ Egg and Watercress Soup

Follow the recipe for Cream of Watercress Soup on page 35 but use 2 egg yolks. Hard-boil 2 eggs and chop the yolks very finely. Add to the soup just before serving.

◉ Ham and Watercress Soup

Follow the recipe for Cream of Watercress Soup on page 35 but substitute stock from boiling bacon or ham for the chicken stock. Add 100 g/4 oz (½ cup) finely diced cooked ham to the soup just before serving.

◉ Seafood and Watercress Soup

Follow the recipe for Cream of Watercress Soup on page 35 but substitute fish stock for the chicken stock. Increase the amount of lemon juice in the recipe to 1½ tablespoons (2 tablespoons). Add 100 g/4 oz (¼ lb) flaked cooked salmon, chopped prawns and other cooked fish to the soup just before serving.

Irish Milk Soup

Cooking time: 20 minutes, plus time to cook potatoes ⊚ Serves 4

Kale is one of the vegetables that grows vigorously in Ireland and this is combined with the creamy butter and milk to make an unusual but excellent soup.

Metric Imperial { **Ingredients** } American
350 g/12 oz { **very young kale** } 3/4 lb
3 { **medium potatoes, boiled** } 3
50 g/2 oz { **butter** } 1/4 cup
50 g/2 oz { **plain flour** } 1/2 cup
1.2 litres/2 pints { **milk** } 5 cups
to taste { **salt and freshly ground black pepper** } to taste

Wash and shred the kale very finely. Dice the cooked potatoes. Heat the butter in a pan, stir in the flour, then add the milk and stir or whisk as the mixture comes to the boil and thickens slightly. Add the kale to the sauce, with a little seasoning. Cover the pan and cook steadily for about 6 minutes, or until the kale is tender. Add the potatoes and heat for a few minutes.

Cauliflower Milk Soup

Follow the recipe above but use a small cauliflower instead of kale. Remove the tender green leaves from the cauliflower, slice these finely, and cook for 5 minutes in 250 ml/8 fl oz (1 cup) boiling water. Make the sauce as above but with only 1 litre/1 3/4 pints (4 1/4 cups) milk.

Divide the cauliflower into small florets then add to the sauce, with the lightly cooked stalks and liquid. Proceed as the recipe above, cooking for 6 minutes then adding the diced potatoes. Garnish with chopped chervil.

Cream of Tomato Soup

Cooking time: 45 minutes ⊚ Serves 4

This soup is certainly not an old established classic dish in this country as tomatoes are a relatively modern taste. Research indicates that tomato soup is the favourite of a great many people, so it may be termed a twentieth century classic. Cornflour is used, in preference to flour, for thickening; it shortens the cooking time and therefore the possibility of the soup curdling.

Metric Imperial { **Ingredients** } American
450 g/1 lb { **tomatoes, preferably plum type** } 1 lb
1 { **small onion** } 1
1 { **small carrot** } 1
1 { **bacon rasher, optional** } 1
25 g/1 oz { **butter** } 2 tablespoons

450 ml/3/4 pint { **chicken or vegetable stock** } 2 cups
few { **borage or thyme leaves** } few
to taste { **salt and freshly ground black pepper** } to taste
1 teaspoon { **soft light brown sugar** } 1 teaspoon
2 level teaspoons { **cornflour** } 2 level teaspoons
300 ml/1/2 pint { **milk** } 1 1/4 cups
To garnish: { **little cream** }

Skin the tomatoes, halve and remove the pips, if you are liquidizing the soup and want the purée to be absolutely smooth. This is unnecessary if the soup is to be sieved. Peel and chop the onion and carrot. De-rind the bacon and chop the rasher, saving the rind. Put the rind into a saucepan with the butter, heat until the butter has melted then add the onion and carrot and cook gently for 5 minutes. Add the bacon and cook for a further 5 minutes, taking care the bacon and onion do not discolour. Remove the bacon rind.

Add the stock, tomatoes, herbs, a little seasoning and the sugar. Cover the pan and simmer for 30 minutes then sieve or liquidize the mixture. The herbs can be removed or left with the other ingredients.

Return the soup to the pan. Blend the cornflour with the milk, add to the tomato mixture and stir or whisk continually until the mixture thickens. Do not allow to boil briskly. Adjust the seasoning and serve the soup topped with cream.

Variation:
⊙ Omit the cornflour and milk and use more stock to make a clear soup, this is excellent served cold or even lightly frosted to become an iced soup.

⊙ Dried Pea Soup

Cooking time: 1 3/4 to 2 hours ⊙ **Serves 4 to 6**

This is a very old recipe. Country people often dried vegetables, such as peas, as a way of preserving them for winter use. This is the kind of soup that is so satisfying it makes a complete light meal.

Dickens called dried pea soup a 'London Particular' in one of his novels, since he felt the colour of the soup bore a resemblence to the thick 'pea soup' fogs that were a feature of London in the old days.

Stock from cooking bacon is the perfect liquid for this soup but chicken stock could be substituted.

Metric Imperial { **Ingredients** } American
225 g/8 oz { **dried peas** } 1/2 lb
1.8 litres/3 pints { **bacon or chicken stock** } 7 1/2 cups
2 { **bacon rashers** } 2
2 { **medium onions** } 2
2 { **large carrots** } 2

to taste { **freshly ground black pepper** } to taste
to taste { **salt, optional** } to taste
1 to 2 sprigs { **fresh mint, or a little dried mint** } 1 to 2 sprigs
to taste { **milk, optional, see method** } to taste
To garnish: { **fried croûtons** } (see page 53)

Soak the peas in the stock overnight. De-rind the bacon and chop the rashers into small pieces. Peel and slice the onions and carrots. Heat the bacon rinds with the diced bacon in a pan and cook steadily until crisp. Discard the rinds and lift the chopped bacon out of the pan to add to the soup before serving. Add the onions to the pan and cook gently for 5 minutes then add the peas and stock. Add pepper to taste and the carrots. Omit the salt if using bacon stock but add a little with chicken stock. Put in the mint. Cover the pan and simmer gently for 1¹/₂ to 1³/₄ hours or until the peas are very tender. Sieve or liquidize the soup, return to the pan and add a little milk if the mixture is rather thick. Season to taste and reheat. Top with the fried bacon and add the croûtons immediately before serving.

◉ Green Pea Soup

Cooking time: 35 minutes ◉ Serves 4 to 6

If the fresh peas are beautifully young and tender you can cook the whole pods for this soup.

Metric Imperial { **Ingredients** } American
2 { **small onions** } 2
675 g/1¹/₂ lb { **peas in pods** } 1¹/₂ lb
  or 350 g/12 oz { **shelled green peas** } ³/₄ lb
25 g/1 oz { **butter** } 2 tablespoons
750 ml/1¹/₄ pints { **chicken stock** } generous 3 cups
1 to 2 sprigs { **fresh mint** } 1 to 2 sprigs
to taste { **salt and freshly ground black pepper** } to taste
300 ml/¹/₂ pint { **single cream** } 1¹/₄ cups
To garnish: chopped { **chives and mint** }

Peel and slice the onions. Wash the pods and remove all stalks. Heat the butter in a saucepan, add the onions and cook gently for 5 minutes, do not allow them to colour. Add the stock, bring to the boil then put in the peas with the mint and a little seasoning. Cover the pan and simmer for 15 minutes if using young green peas but for 20 to 25 minutes if cooking the whole pods.

   If using shelled peas: sieve or liquidize the soup. If using peas in pods: you must rub the pods and peas through a fine sieve. Return the soup to the pan, add the cream and heat very gently. Garnish with the chopped chives and mint.

Variation:
◉ Use stock from cooking a bacon joint instead of chicken stock and be sparing with the salt.

⊙ Chilled Green Pea Soup

Follow the recipe above but instead of 750 ml/1/4 pints (generous 3 cups) of stock use only 450 ml/3/4 pint (2 cups) and 300 ml/1/2 pint (11/4 cups) dry white wine.

Sieve or liquidize the soup when the peas are tender and chill it well. Whisk in the cream just before serving and serve in well-chilled soup cups. Top with the chopped herbs.

⊙ Sorrel Soup

Cooking time: 30 minutes ⊙ Serves 4 to 6

Sorrel is a herb that has been used for generations in soups and sauces and as a vegetable. It grows well in all parts of Britain, as well as throughout Europe (see page 106).

Metric Imperial { **Ingredients** } American
450 g/1 lb { **sorrel** } 1 lb
1 { **medium onion** } 1
50 g/2 oz { **butter** } 1/4 cup
2 teaspoons { **rosemary leaves, finely chopped** } 2 teaspoons
1.2 litres/2 pints { **boiling water** } 5 cups
to taste {**salt and freshly ground black pepper** } to taste
2 teaspoons { **lemon juice** } 2 teaspoons
2 { **egg yolks** } 2
150 ml/1/4 pint { **single cream** } 2/3 cup
To garnish: { **fried croûtons** } (see page 53)

Wash the sorrel very well in cold water then shred with a stainless steel knife to avoid spoiling the flavour of the vegetable. Peel and chop the onion. Heat the butter in a saucepan, add the onion and cook gently for 5 minutes. Do not allow it to discolour.

Add the sorrel and rosemary, blend with the onion. Pour the boiling water into the saucepan, then add a little seasoning and the lemon juice. Cover the saucepan and cook steadily for 15 to 20 minutes, or until the sorrel is very tender. Sieve or liquidize the soup and return to the saucepan.

Blend the egg yolks and the cream, add a little of the very hot, but not boiling, sorrel soup then tip back into the saucepan and simmer gently for 5 minutes. Do not allow the soup to boil. Adjust the seasoning. Garnish with croûtons.

⊙ Cabbage Soup

Follow the recipe for Sorrel Soup but use a small cabbage instead of the sorrel. Since this vegetable has less flavour use chicken stock instead of water and 2 onions. Cook the vegetable mixture for 10 minutes instead of 15 to 20 minutes.

Spinach Soup

Follow the recipe for Sorrel Soup but use young spinach leaves instead of sorrel and substitute finely chopped tarragon leaves for rosemary.

Welsh Leek and Potato Soup

Cooking time: 30 minutes ⊙ Serves 4

The flavour of this soup is not unlike the French Vichyssoise, especially if made with chicken stock and served cold. Leeks are used in so many Welsh dishes and this soup is one of the most successful of their classic recipes. The Welsh name for this soup is Cennin a Thatws Cawl.

Metric Imperial { **Ingredients** } American
4 { **medium leeks** } 4
2 { **small onions** } 2
2 { **medium potatoes** } 2
450 ml/3/4 pint { **lamb, mutton or chicken stock** } 2 cups
to taste { **salt and freshly ground black pepper** } to taste
50 g/2 oz { **butter** } 1/4 cup
50 g/2 oz { **plain flour** } 1/2 cup
600 ml/1 pint { **milk** } 21/2 cups
To garnish: { **little cream, chopped parsley** }

Clean and neatly slice the leeks; reserving a little of the tender green part. Peel and finely dice the onions and potatoes. Put the vegetables, except the reserved green part of the leeks, into a saucepan with the stock and a little seasoning and cook for 20 minutes, adding the shredded part of the leeks towards the end of this time.

In a separate pan heat the butter, stir in the flour, then blend in the milk and stir or whisk as the sauce comes to the boil and thickens slightly. Season to taste. Blend this with the soup and heat for a few minutes. Top with cream and parsley.

Variations:
- Liquidize or sieve the soup and reheat or serve cold.
- To make a lighter textured soup use the same amount of leeks, onions and potatoes as above; cook in chicken stock. Sieve or liquidize the ingredients, then blend with 300 ml/1/2 pint (11/4 cups) single cream and 150 ml/1/4 pint (2/3 cup) dry white wine. Serve cold or heat carefully, do not allow to boil. Top with chopped chives.

Leek and Green Pea Soup

Use chicken stock as previous recipe but with 1 potato plus 100 g/4 oz (1/4 lb) peas. Cook the vegetables with a sprig of fresh mint. Serve hot or cold and garnish with finely chopped mint.

⊙ Mustard Soup

Cooking time: 20 minutes plus 1 hour infusion time ⊙ **Serves 4**

Mustard plants have been cultivated in Britain for over 2000 years and are mentioned in a number of ancient writings. The Romans and other nations fermented the seed in new sweet wine. There are many kinds of mustard plants, some giving white seeds and others black seeds. English mustard is prepared from the white seeds.

This creamy soup is quickly made. The amount of mustard powder can be adjusted to suit personal taste. When making this soup for the first time it is wise to use only half the mustard powder at the beginning then taste the soup and add more mustard later if the flavour is not sufficiently strong. If adding more mustard to the finished soup, blend it to a smooth paste with milk rather than adding it as a dry powder.

Metric Imperial { **Ingredients** } American
1 { **medium onion** } 1
600 ml/1 pint { **chicken stock** } 2¹/2 cups
25 g/1 oz { **butter** } 2 tablespoons
25 g/1 oz { **plain flour** } ¹/4 cup
1 to 2 tablespoons { **English mustard powder** } 1¹/2 to 3 tablespoons
300 ml/¹/2 pint { **milk** } 1¹/4 cups
to taste { **salt and freshly ground white pepper** } to taste
2 { **egg yolks** } 2
225 ml/7¹/2 fl oz { **double cream** } 1 cup

Peel and halve the onion. Heat the stock, add the onion halves. Remove from the heat, cover the pan and leave the onion to infuse in the stock for an hour.

Melt the butter in a saucepan, stir in the flour and mustard powder and then blend in the milk. Stir as the sauce slowly comes to the boil and thickens. Add a little seasoning. Whisk the chicken stock into the sauce, add the onion and heat thoroughly.

Blend the egg yolks with half the cream, whisk a little of the hot, but not boiling, soup into this mixture then whisk it into the other ingredients. Simmer for about 10 minutes, taking care the mixture does not boil. Remove the onion just before serving. Top each portion of soup with the remaining cream.

Variation:
⊙   Stir a selection of lightly cooked and finely diced vegetables into the soup just before adding the egg yolk and cream mixture.

Oatmeal Soup

Cooking time: 50 minutes ⊙ Serves 4 to 6

Oatmeal has been one of the basic foods in Britain for generations and is particularly popular in Scotland. This is a wonderfully satisfying and inexpensive soup with a good flavour. The vegetables may be changed, you can add finely diced celery, celeriac, young turnips or swede (known in Scotland as 'neeps').

Metric Imperial { **Ingredients** } American
2 { **medium onions** } 2
2 { **medium carrots** } 2
25 g/1 oz { **butter or margarine** } 2 tablespoons
2 tablespoons { **medium or fine oatmeal** } 3 tablespoons
600 ml/1 pint { **chicken or ham stock** } 2¹/2 cups
300 ml/¹/2 pint { **milk** } 1¹/4 cups
to taste { **salt and freshly ground black pepper** } to taste
150 ml/¹/4 pint { **single cream** } 2/3 cup
2 tablespoons { **chopped parsley** } 3 tablespoons
To garnish: { **fried croûtons** } (see page 53)

Peel and finely dice the onions and carrots. Heat the butter or margarine in a large saucepan, add the onions and cook gently for 5 minutes; do not allow to colour.

Blend the oatmeal with the onions, then pour in the stock. Bring to the boil and stir as the mixture thickens slightly. Lower the heat, add the carrots, cover and simmer gently for 20 minutes, stirring from time to time. Pour in the milk, add seasoning to taste, cover the pan once again and continue simmering for another 20 minutes. Stir frequently during this time. Blend the cream and half the parsley into the soup and heat for a few minutes. Serve topped with the croûtons and the rest of the parsley.

Quick Cooking Oatmeal Soup

Use rolled oats instead of oatmeal. Reduce the amount of stock to 450 ml/3/4 pint (2 cups) and cook for 5 minutes only before adding the milk and carrots. Simmer at this stage for 10 to 15 minutes, to make certain the carrots are tender.

Cullen Skink

Cooking time: 20 minutes ⊙ Serves 4 to 6
This is an excellent Scottish soup made with smoked haddock (Finnan haddie). The soup has a more delicate flavour if made with the smaller Arbroath Smokies. Pages 74, 75, 90 and 92 give more recipes using haddock.

Metric Imperial { **Ingredients** } American

2 { **eggs** } 2

675 g/1½ lb { **smoked haddock on the bone**} 1½ lb
  or 350 g/12 oz { **smoked haddock fillet** } ¾ lb

1.2 litres/2 pints { **milk** } 5 cups

to taste { **freshly ground white pepper** } to taste

to taste { **salt, if required** } to taste

To garnish: { **chopped parsley** }

Hard-boil the eggs, shell and chop finely. Remove the fins and tail from the haddock and cut the fish into several pieces. Put into a pan with the milk and pepper and poach for 10 minutes, or until the fish is tender. Remove the fish from the liquid, discard all bones and skin then flake the fish. Strain the milk.

Either pound the fish with the chopped eggs or put these into a food processor with a little milk and process until very smooth. Return to the pan with the milk and heat. Taste and adjust the seasoning. Top with the parsley.

Variations:
- For a richer flavour use a little less milk in the soup and add some single cream with 25 g/1 oz (2 tablespoons) butter just before serving; heat for 5 minutes.
- A more sustaining soup is made by pounding or liquidizing 2 or 3 cooked potatoes or a small amount of mashed potatoes with the fish and hard-boiled eggs.
- Use other smoked fish, such as cod or trout instead of haddock.

◉ Salmon Soup

Substitute the same quantity of fresh salmon for the haddock fillet in the recipe above. Poach in well-seasoned milk, or use half milk and half fish stock. A good-sized sprig of fennel and a peeled, halved onion can be added to the liquid to give extra flavour. Pound or liquidize the cooked salmon with the hard-boiled eggs as in the recipe above. Reheat the fish and eggs in the strained liquid with the addition of a little single cream and small knob of butter. Top with chopped fennel leaves.

◉ Mussel Brose

Cooking time: 25 minutes ◉ Serves 4

Musselburgh has a fine mussel bed at the mouth of the river Esk and gave its name to this brose (soup).

Metric Imperial { **Ingredients** } American

2 litres/3½ pints { **mussels** } 9 cups

2 { **medium onions** } 2

300 ml/½ pint { **water** } 1¼ cups

1 { **small bunch parsley** } 1
25 g/1 oz { **oatmeal** } 1/4 cup
25 g/1 oz { **butter** } 2 tablespoons
600 ml/1 pint { **milk** } 2½ cups
to taste { **salt and freshly ground black pepper** } to taste
To garnish: { **chopped parsley** }

Wash the mussels well, discard any that do not close when sharply tapped. Pull away any small growth from the sides. Peel and chop the onions. Put the mussels into a large saucepan with the onions, water and parsley. Heat steadily for a few minutes until the shells open. Discard any mussels where the shells have not opened properly. Remove the fish from the shells, strain the liquid and put on one side.

Meanwhile preheat the oven to 180°C/350°F, Gas Mark 4; place the oatmeal on a flat baking tray and place in the oven for 8 to 10 minutes, or until golden brown.

Heat the butter in a saucepan, add the onions and cook gently for 10 minutes, or until soft. Add the milk and mussel liquid, bring to the boil then stir in the oatmeal. Continue stirring as the liquid boils and thickens slightly, add the mussels with seasoning to taste and heat for a few minutes. Top with parsley and serve.

⊙ Cream of Mussel Soup

Cooking time: 25 minutes ⊙ Serves 4 to 6

Buy the same quantity of mussels as above, but use half water and half wine as the cooking liquid with only 1 small chopped onion. Strain the liquid and remove the mussels from their shells.

Wipe and thinly slice 100 g/4 oz (1/4 lb) button mushrooms. Heat 25 g/1 oz (2 tablespoons) butter and cook these until soft, put on one side.

Heat 50 g/2 oz (1/4 cup) butter in a pan, then stir in 50 g/2 oz (1/2 cup) plain flour. Blend in 600 ml/1 pint (2½ cups) milk and 150 ml/1/4 pint (2/3 cup) single cream and stir until the mixture thickens. Remove from the heat, add the mussel liquid, the mussels and seasoning to taste. Heat gently, without boiling, for a few minutes. Serve the soup topped with a little more cream and the mushrooms.

⊙ Oyster Soup

Cooking time: 1½ hours ⊙ Serves 4 to 6

This interesting soup is a speciality of Wales, where it is known as Cawl Wystrys. The partnership of meat stock and oysters may seem unusual but it gives a perfect blending of flavours.

Metric Imperial { **Ingredients** } American
2 { **medium onions** } 2
225 g/8 oz { **scrag end of lamb** } 1/2 lb
few { **lamb bones** } few

1.8 litres/3 pints { **water** } 7$\frac{1}{2}$ cups
to taste { **blade of mace or pinch ground mace** } to taste
to taste { **cayenne or freshly ground black pepper** } to taste
50 g/2 oz { **butter** } $\frac{1}{4}$ cup
50 g/2 oz { **plain flour** } $\frac{1}{2}$ cup
24 { **small oysters** } 24
To garnish: { **shredded leek, lemon wedges** }

Peel the onions and leave whole. Put into a saucepan with the meat, bones, water, mace and a little pepper. Bring the liquid to the boil, remove any grey scum, cover the pan and simmer for 1$\frac{1}{2}$ hours then strain carefully. You can clarify the liquid as explained on page 50. If necessary return to a pan and boil briskly until reduced to 750 ml/1$\frac{1}{2}$ pints (3$\frac{1}{3}$ cups) or 900 ml/1$\frac{1}{2}$ pints (4 cups) for a thinner soup. Adjust the seasoning but remember oysters are very salty so avoid extra salt.

Heat the butter in a pan, stir in the flour, then add the stock and whisk or stir as this comes to the boil and thickens slightly, add any liquor from the oyster shells. Either heat the oysters for 2 minutes in the soup or place the raw oysters in soup plates and top with the very hot soup. Garnish with the raw leek and lemon.

◉ Lobster Soup

To make a soup for 4 people remove all the flesh from the body and claws of a cooked medium-sized lobster. Dice the meat and set aside. Put the clean shells into a pan with a sprig of chervil or parsley, 1 small onion, 600 ml/1 pint (2$\frac{1}{2}$ cups) water and seasoning. Simmer for 15 minutes then strain the stock.

Make a thick sauce with 50 g/2 oz ($\frac{1}{4}$ cup) butter, 50 g/2 oz ($\frac{1}{2}$ cup) plain flour, 300 ml/$\frac{1}{2}$ pint (1$\frac{1}{2}$ cups) milk, as on page 103. When this has thickened add the lobster stock, 300 ml/$\frac{1}{2}$ pint (1$\frac{1}{2}$ cups) single cream, the diced lobster meat and a few tablespoons of dry sherry. Heat gently, without boiling, and serve hot. Garnish each portion of soup with lemon wedges.

◉ Partan Bree

Cooking time: 30 to 35 minutes ◉ Serves 4 to 6

The word 'partan' is Scottish for crab. This easily-made soup retains all the flavour of fresh crab but is also a good way to use frozen crabmeat.

Metric Imperial { **Ingredients** } American
1 { **large cooked crab** } 1
75 g/3 oz { **long grain rice** } $\frac{1}{2}$ cup
600 ml/1 pint { **fish stock** } 2$\frac{1}{2}$ cups
600 ml/1 pint { **milk** } 2$\frac{1}{2}$ cups
$\frac{1}{2}$ teaspoon { **anchovy essence** } $\frac{1}{2}$ teaspoon
to taste { **salt and freshly ground white pepper** } to taste

150 ml/¼ pint { **single cream** } ⅔ cup
To garnish: { **chopped parsley, fried croûtons** } (see page 53)

Remove all the flesh from the body of the crab and the claws (see page 100). Save a little white and dark crabmeat to garnish the soup.

Put the rice and stock into a large saucepan, simmer for 20 minutes or until the rice is nearly tender. Add the milk towards the end of the cooking time, when there is less possibility of the liquid boiling over. Stir in the anchovy essence and crabmeat and add seasoning to taste. Do not use too much salt.

Simmer for a few minutes only until the crab is really hot (overcooking makes all shellfish very tough). Stir the cream into the soup just before serving and heat gently. Garnish with the reserved crabmeat, parsley and croûtons.

Variation:
- Use 350 to 450 g/¾ to 1 lb frozen crabmeat instead of the fresh crab.

◉ Cornish Crab Soup

A very similar soup to the one above is served in Cornwall, where crabs are plentiful and extremely popular for sustaining Cornish 'high-teas'.

The liquid used in Cornwall is often half milk and half chicken or fish stock but the soup is enriched by blending a generous amount of Cornish cream into the mixture just before serving. Whisk or stir the soup vigorously to make sure the cream is well-blended with the rest of the ingredients.

◉ Salmon Broth

Cooking time: 1 hour ◉ **Serves 4 to 6**

This dish is typical of soups that can be served as a complete light meal. It is an ideal dish to make now salmon is plentiful and relatively inexpensive. It is a Scottish recipe and one that reflects the hearty soups enjoyed in that country. The use of a variety of herbs gives it a most subtle taste.

Metric Imperial { **Ingredients** } American
1 { **salmon head** } 1
225 g/8 oz { **fresh salmon, weight when skin and bone removed**} ½ lb
225 g/8 oz { **cod** } ½ lb
1.5 litres/2½ pints { **water** } 6¼ cups
to taste { **sprigs of thyme, tarragon, chervil or parsley and chives** } to taste
to taste { **salt and freshly ground black pepper** } to taste
2 { **small onions** } 2
2 { **medium carrots** } 2
2 { **medium potatoes** } 2

25 g/1 oz { **butter** } 2 tablespoons
150 ml/1/4 pint { **double cream** } 2/3 cup
To garnish: { chopped parsley, coarse brown breadcrumbs }

Put the salmon head into a large saucepan, remove the skin and bones from the fresh salmon, add these to the salmon head together with the cod, water, herbs and seasoning. Cover the pan and simmer for 30 minutes, then strain the stock.

Cut the fresh salmon into 1.5 cm/1/2 inch dice. Peel, then finely dice the onions, carrots and potatoes. Heat the butter in a saucepan, add the onions and cook gently for 5 minutes, do not allow these to brown. Add the strained fish stock, together with the carrots and bring to the boil. Cook briskly for 5 minutes, then put in the diced salmon and potatoes and cook steadily for 10 to 15 minutes, or until fish and vegetables are tender. Stir in the cream and heat, without boiling, for a few minutes. Adjust the seasoning and top each portion of soup with the parsley and a good layer of brown breadcrumbs.

Variation:
◉ Cook the diced vegetables in the strained fish stock, and, when soft, sieve or liquidize the mixture. Add the diced salmon and cook for 10 minutes then add the cream and heat. Garnish as the soup above.

◉ Mock Turtle Soup

Cooking time: 3 hours ◉ **Serves 8**

Real turtle soup is a delicacy reserved for ceremonial occasions, such as the Lord Mayor's official banquets at the Guildhall, London. Turtles are not obtainable in Britain, so the only turtle soup one can have is sold in cans. This soup has much the same flavour and sticky texture as the true turtle soup, hence the name.

Metric Imperial { **Ingredients** } American
1 { **calf's head** } 1
few drops { **vinegar** } few drops
1 { **large onion** } 1
2 { **medium carrots** } 2
2 to 3 { **celery stalks** } 2 to 3
2.4 litres/4 pints { **veal stock** } 10 cups
to taste { **sprigs of basil, chives, marjoram** } to taste
2 { **fresh bay leaves or 1 dried bay leaf** } 2
to taste { **salt and freshly ground black pepper** } to taste
150 ml/1/4 pint { **dry sherry** } 2/3 cup
To garnish: { lemon wedges }

Ask the butcher to split the calf's head. The brains and tongue can be removed and used for savoury dishes (see pages 156 and 158). Wash the head then place in a saucepan with cold water to cover. Add the vinegar then bring the water to boiling point and remove the head from the pan. Discard this water.

Peel and chop the onion and carrots, dice the celery. Put the head back into a clean pan, add the stock, herbs and a little seasoning. Cover the pan and simmer steadily for almost 3 hours or until the meat is tender. Strain the stock. For a very clear stock clarify the liquid, as described below.

Remove the meat from the bones and cut into small neat dice. Return to the clear stock with the meat, heat thoroughly. Add the sherry and any extra seasoning required. It is quite usual to add a little more sherry to individual portions of this soup and each serving is accompanied by wedges of lemon.

▣ To Clarify Clear Soups

Strain through a fine sieve to remove herbs or any vegetables, then strain through muslin to extract tiny particles of food. For extra clarity return the soup to the pan. Add 2 egg whites to each 1.8 litres/3 pints (7¹/2 cups) of liquid. Boil for 25 minutes. Tiny particles will adhere to the whites. Strain through fresh muslin.

◉ Clear Beef Soup

Cooking time: 1¹/4 hours plus time to make the beef stock ◉ Serves 6 to 8

'Clear Soup' is exactly the same recipe as 'Consommé'. The use of egg shells makes doubly sure the liquid becomes clear. The egg white adhering to the shells collects any small pieces of food in the liquid.

Beef tea was considered to be a panacea for minor ailments and a great 'pick-me-up'. It was said that good beef tea would make a hale man envy the sick.

Metric Imperial { **Ingredients** } American
675 g/1¹/2 lb { **shin of beef** } 1¹/2 lb
2.25 litres/4 pints { **very good beef stock** } (see page 126) 11 cups
to taste { **salt and freshly ground black pepper** } to taste
1 { **onion, optional** } 1
1 { **carrot, optional** } 1
2 { **fresh bay leaves or 1 dried bay leaf** } 2
3 { **egg whites with their shells** } 3
300 ml/¹/2 pint { **dry sherry** } 1¹/4 cups
To garnish: see method

Dice or coarsely mince the beef. Put into a large saucepan with the stock and a little seasoning. Peel the onion and carrot and leave them whole. Add to the stock with the bay leaves. Cover the pan and simmer for 1 hour. Strain the soup and return to the saucepan. Bring to boiling point, add the egg whites and their shells and simmer for a further 20 minutes then strain through several thicknesses of muslin. Return to the pan and reheat, add the sherry and any extra seasoning required and heat, without boiling, then garnish and serve.

Garnishes: chopped herbs, finely diced, or matchsticks of freshly cooked mixed vegetables, cooked rice or shredded almonds.

Variation:
◉   Use good game or poultry stock and flesh instead of beef (see page 126).

◉ Beef Tea

Cut 675 g/1½ lb lean shin or neck of beef into small dice; put into a deep casserole with 1.2 litres/2 pints (5 cups) water and a little seasoning. Do not add vegetables. Cover the casserole tightly and cook for 4 to 5 hours in an oven preheated to 150°C/300°F, Gas Mark 2. Strain the liquid and serve.
The beef can be minced then pounded with butter and served as Potted Beef.

◉ Clear Brown Windsor Soup

Cooking time: 2½ hours ◉ **Serves 4 to 6**
Sadly many an indifferent brown soup is given the title above and in consequence this soup has not had the regard it deserves. When made properly, it is quite the most delicious of all meat soups. There are two versions, one is an elegant clear soup and the other a sustaining thickened soup, both are given here.

Metric Imperial { **Ingredients** } American
1 { **calf's foot** } 1
225 g/8 oz { **stewing beef** } ½ lb
2 to 3 { **beef bones** } 2 to 3
1.8 litres/3 pints { **water** } 7½ cups
to taste { **sprigs of parsley, thyme and rosemary** } to taste
2 { **fresh bay leaves or 1 dried bay leaf** } 2
to taste { **salt and freshly ground black pepper** } to taste
150 ml/¼ pint { **Madeira wine** } ⅔ cup
To garnish: see method

Wash the calf's foot, dice the meat and put both into a saucepan with the beef bones, water, herbs and seasoning. Cover the pan and simmer steadily for 2¼ hours. Strain and clarify the soup as on page 50. Return the soup to the pan with the Madeira and any extra seasoning required. Heat thoroughly and serve.

The garnishes for this soup vary. The simple ones are parsley and fried croûtons but small pieces of lobster or anchovy fillets were quite usual in the past.

Thick Brown Windsor Soup

A good brown stock is required for this, it can be made with the calf's foot and beef bones with herbs and seasoning, as in the recipe above. The stewing beef is not used to make stock, but diced and added to the soup later.

Peel and chop 1 large onion, 2 medium carrots and 2 celery sticks. Heat 50 g/2 oz (¼ cup) beef dripping or butter in a pan, add the stewing beef and onions and cook steadily for 10 minutes. Pour in 1.5 litres/2½ pints (6¼ cups) of the brown stock, add the carrots and celery with seasoning and extra herbs, as in the recipe above. Simmer for 2 hours. Sieve or liquidize the ingredients then return to the pan and heat with a little Madeira wine.

Another version of this soup adds about 50 g/2 oz (⅓ cup) cooked long grain rice with the Madeira wine.

Kidney Soup

Cooking time: 30 minutes ◉ Serves 4

Kidneys are a favourite offal in Britain and this soup retains the good flavour of the meat. Do not overcook the kidneys, they should be just tender.

Metric Imperial { **Ingredients** } American
2 { **bacon rashers** } 2
225 g/8 oz { **lambs' kidneys** } ½ lb
1 { **medium onion** } 1
25 g/1 oz { **butter** } 2 tablespoons
1 tablespoon { **plain flour** } 1¼ tablespoons
900 ml/1½ pints { **brown stock** } 3¾ cups
to taste { **salt and freshly ground black pepper** } to taste
3 to 4 tablespoons { **port wine, optional** } 4 to 5 tablespoons
To garnish: { **fried croûtons** } (see page 53)

De-rind the bacon and cut the rashers into small pieces, saving the rind to give extra fat. Skin and halve the kidneys, remove any gristle and fat. Peel and chop the onion. Heat the butter and bacon rinds, add the onion and chopped bacon; cook for 5 minutes, remove the bacon rinds. Coat the kidneys in the flour, then add to the pan and stir over the heat for 5 minutes. Pour in the stock, season lightly. Bring to the boil, cover the pan, lower the heat and cook for 15 minutes.

Remove a halved kidney from the soup and chop very finely. Sieve or liquidize the rest of the ingredients. Return to the pan with the diced kidney, port wine and any extra seasoning required. Heat thoroughly. Garnish with croûtons.

To Make Fried Croûtons

White bread is generally used for this purpose but brown or wholemeal can be substituted.

Cut the crusts off the bread and then cut the crumb into small dice. If preparing croûtons as an accompaniment to soup they should be approximately 6 mm/1/4 inch in size. Larger croûtons are made to garnish many savoury dishes.

The croûtons can be shallow fried in clarified butter, or a combination of butter and oil, or deep fried in hot oil or fat. They should be just golden brown in colour. Always drain the fried croûtons on absorbent paper.

A large supply can be prepared and frozen. Freeze on flat trays, so the small dice do not stick together, than pack in bags or boxes.

Oxtail Soup

Cooking time: 2½ to 3 hours ● Serves 4 to 6

This is one of the favourite meat soups in Britain. The following is the classic way to make it but you could take meat, stock and vegetables left from Oxtail Ragoût (see page 135) and turn that into an excellent soup. The variation in cooking time depends upon the quality of the meat. It is a good idea to make the soup, allow it to become cold, then remove any excess fat before reheating.

Metric Imperial { **Ingredients**} American
1 { **oxtail** } 1
1 { **large onion** } 1
1 { **small turnip**} 1
3 { **medium carrots**} 3
50 g/2 oz { **beef dripping or butter** } 1/4 cup
1.8 litres/3 pints { **beef stock** } 7½ cups
to taste { **sprigs of parsley, rosemary, sage and thyme, tied with string or in muslin** } to taste
to taste { **salt and freshly ground black pepper** } to taste
50 g/2 oz { **plain flour** } 1/2 cup
3 tablespoons { **port or red wine, optional** } 4 tablespoons
To garnish: { **chopped parsley** }

Cut the oxtail into neat pieces, if this has not been done by the butcher. Soak for about 30 minutes in cold water then drain. Peel and finely dice the onion, turnip and carrots. Heat the dripping or butter in a pan, add the vegetables and cook steadily for 10 minutes until a pale golden colour. Add most of the stock together with the herbs, oxtail and a little seasoning. Cover the pan and simmer steadily for 2 to 2½ hours, or until the meat is tender. Remove the oxtail and the herbs.

Cut all the meat from the bones. Blend the flour with the remaining stock, whisk or stir into the hot liquid and continue stirring until the soup thickens. Return the meat to the soup and add the wine. Heat thoroughly then adjust the seasoning and serve topped with the parsley.

Variations:

- The soup can be sieved or liquidized after adding the boned meat to the liquid.
- For a more colourful soup garnish with a selection of lightly cooked, diced mixed vegetables.

 Mulligatawny Soup

Cooking time: 1 hour ◎ Serves 4

Agents from the East India Company brought both spices and recipes to Britain during the seventeenth century. A charter was first given by Elizabeth I in 1600 for direct trade with India. By 1624 some 24 British ships were used for trading with India. This recipe is one of the best known they brought back to Britain. Some recipes use beef stock, but lamb or mutton stock gives a better flavour. In the past this was obtained by boiling a sheep's head.

Metric Imperial { **Ingredients** } American
1 { **medium dessert apple** } 1
1 { **large carrot** } 1
2 { **medium onions** } 2
50 g/2 oz { **lamb or mutton dripping or butter** } 1/4 cup
25 g/1 oz { **plain flour** } 1/4 cup
1 tablespoon { **curry powder, or to taste** } 1 1/4 tablespoons
1.2 litres/2 pints { **lamb or mutton stock** } 5 cups
1 tablespoon { **sweet chutney** } 1 1/4 tablespoons
25 g/1 oz { **sultanas** } 3 tablespoons
1 teaspoon { **sugar, or to taste** } 1 teaspoon
to taste { **salt and freshly ground black pepper** } to taste
1 to 2 teaspoons { **lemon juice or vinegar** } 1 to 2 teaspoons

Peel and neatly dice the apple, carrot and onions. Heat the dripping or butter and fry these ingredients gently for 5 minutes. Stir in the flour and curry powder and cook for 2 minutes, stirring well. Blend in the stock, stirring as it comes to the boil and gives a slightly thickened mixture.

Add the chutney, sultanas, sugar and seasoning to taste. Simmer gently for 45 minutes. The soup can be served either as it is or sieved or liquidized to make a smooth mixture. Add the lemon juice or vinegar and heat.

Variations:

- An interesting addition is to add 1 tablespoon (1 1/2 tablespoons) long grain rice when the stock comes to the boil and the mixture thickens slightly.
- For a more sustaining soup do not sieve or liquidize the mixture. Add a little finely diced cooked lamb or mutton just before serving and heat for a short time.

⊙ Scotch Broth

Cooking time: 2 to 2¼ hours ⊙ Serves 4 to 6

This provides a wonderfully satisfying meal made with inexpensive meat. It is one of the most famous of all Scottish soups. It is reported in Boswell's *Journal* that Dr Johnson, on a visit to Aberdeen, ate several helpings of the soup and expressed his enjoyment of the dish. In Scotland you may find it referred to as Barley Broth.

Metric Imperial { **Ingredients** } American
50 g/2 oz { **pearl barley** } generous ¼ cup
675 g/1½ lb { **scrag end of lamb** } 1½ lb
1.5 litres/2½ pints { **water** } 6¼ cups
to taste { **salt and freshly ground black pepper** } to taste
to taste { **faggot of herbs** } to taste
450 g/1 lb { **mixed root vegetables** } 1 lb
¼ { **small cabbage heart** } ¼
To garnish: { **chopped parsley** }

Put the barley into a saucepan with enough cold water to cover it. Bring the water to the boil, then strain and discard the water. This process is known as 'blanching' – it whitens the barley and gives it a better texture.

Cut away the surplus fat from the lamb. Put the meat into a saucepan with the measure of water given above, the barley, seasoning and herbs. Bring the water to the boil. Remove any scum that comes to the surface, then cover the pan and lower the heat. Simmer for 1¼ hours. Lift the meat from the liquid and cut it into small pieces. Return to the pan or, if very tender, add with the cabbage later.

Peel and finely dice the root vegetables, add to the pan and cook steadily for 25 to 30 minutes. Shred the cabbage, add to the rest of the ingredients and cook for 5 to 10 minutes only. Remove the herbs and top the soup with the parsley.

⊙ Welsh Cawl

Cooking time: 1¼ hours ⊙ Serves 4 to 6

This, like Scotch Broth, is a meal in a soup. Place 675 g/1½ lb best end of neck lamb chops in a saucepan with 1.5 litres/2½ pints (6¼ cups) of water and a little seasoning. Cover the pan and simmer for 45 minutes, then allow to get cold. Remove all the fat from the top of the liquid.

Peel and slice 2 medium onions, 4 medium potatoes, 1 small parsnip and 2 medium carrots. Wash and slice 2 medium leeks. Add the vegetables to the meat and stock and continue cooking for a further 25 minutes. Thinly slice another leek and add to the soup; cook for 4 to 5 minutes so this vegetable keeps firm.

Traditionally the vegetable soup is served first and the meat afterwards. You could also serve the complete soup. Top with chopped parsley.

Cock-A-Leekie

Cooking time: 1½ hours ⊚ **Serves 4 to 6**

This is one of the best known Scottish soups and is satisfying and economical. If only a light soup is required then a small amount of the chicken is used; the remainder can be saved for another meal. For a satisfying 'meal in a soup' use the whole bird. The cooking time is fairly short as today's chickens are tender. In the old days this dish would have been made with an elderly boiling fowl, which needed several hours cooking.

Metric Imperial { **Ingredients** } American
12 { **large prunes** } 12
450 g/1 lb { **leeks** } 1 lb
1.2 litres/2 pints { **chicken stock or water** } 5 cups
1 { **small chicken** } 1
to taste { **sprigs of parsley and thyme** } to taste
to taste { **salt and freshly ground black pepper** } to taste
To garnish: { **chopped parsley** }

Cover the prunes with cold water and allow to soak overnight or for several hours. If the prunes are the tenderized variety, then soaking is unnecessary and they need a short cooking time only.

Cut the leeks into thin rings. Put the chicken stock or water into a saucepan, add the chicken with the herbs and seasoning to taste. Cover the pan and cook steadily for 1 hour, or until the chicken is tender. Lift the bird out of the pan. Strain the stock, measure and, if necessary, boil rapidly in an open pan until reduced to 900 ml/1½ pints (3¾ cups).

Add the leeks to the stock together with the prunes. Cover the pan and cook for 20 to 30 minutes or until the leeks and prunes are tender. Either cut approximately 225 g/8 oz (½ lb) breast meat from the chicken or use all the chicken flesh. Dice finely, add to the pan. Heat the soup and garnish with chopped parsley.

Variations:
- ⊚ There are a number of variations on this dish. If you like the prunes very soft then cook these separately and add to the soup towards the end of the cooking period.
- ⊚ To give a stronger flavour to the soup use beef stock instead of chicken stock.
- ⊚ A few chopped leeks, an onion and diced bacon can be cooked with the chicken. These are not served in the soup but they add an excellent flavour to the stock.

Almond and Chicken Soup

Cooking time: 20 minutes ◦ Serves 4 to 6

This is known also as La Reine Soup, for it is believed that the mother of Mary, Queen of Scots brought the recipe to Scotland from France. It was quite usual to thicken soups with almonds in the past. These give a good flavour and are easily incorporated into the mixture as they thicken without fear of the liquid becoming lumpy. For an outstanding soup the chicken stock must be strongly flavoured (see page 126).

Metric Imperial { **Ingredients** } American
2 { eggs } 2
50 g/2 oz { **almonds** } generous 1/2 cup
225 g/8 oz { **cooked chicken breast** } 1/2 lb
900 ml/1 1/2 pints { **chicken stock** } 3 3/4 cups
25 g/1 oz { **soft breadcrumbs** } 1/2 cup
150 ml/1/4 pint { **single cream** } 2/3 cup
to taste { **salt and freshly ground white pepper** } to taste
To garnish: { **chopped parsley** }

Hard boil the eggs, shell and remove the yolks. Chop the yolks and whites separately. Save the egg whites for a garnish. Blanch and finely chop the almonds, unless you are using a liquidizer or food processor when they can be left whole.

Cut the cooked chicken into very small dice. To prepare the soup by hand put the egg yolks, almonds and chicken breast into a bowl, add a little chicken stock then pound the mixture until smooth. Alternatively, the ingredients can be put into a liquidizer or food processor with some of the stock and emulsified to a smooth purée.

Pour the remaining chicken stock into a saucepan, add the chicken purée with the breadcrumbs, cream and seasoning. Heat thoroughly but do not allow the soup to boil. Garnish each portion with the chopped egg whites and parsley.

Grouse Soup

Cooking time: 1 1/2 hours ◦ Serves 4

This recipe can be used with pigeons, pheasants or other game birds as well as grouse. It is an ideal way of using older birds that are not sufficiently tender to roast.

Metric Imperial { **Ingredients** } American
1 { **large grouse** } 1
2 { **medium onions** } 2
2 { **medium carrots** } 2
2 { **celery sticks from the heart** } 2
50 g/2 oz { **butter or game or beef dripping** } 1/4 cup

1.5 litres/2¹/2 pints { **brown stock** } 6¹/4 cups
5 to 6 { **juniper berries** } 5 to 6
to taste { **salt and freshly ground black pepper** } to taste
2 { **fresh bay leaves or 1 dried bay leaf** } 2
150 ml/¹/4 pint { **sweet sherry or sweet Madeira wine** } ²/3 cup
1 tablespoon { **redcurrant jelly** } 1¹/2 tablespoons

Cut the grouse into joints. Peel and slice the onions and carrots. Chop the celery into small pieces. Heat the butter or dripping in a large saucepan, add the grouse and brown on all sides, remove from the pan, put in the vegetables and cook for 5 minutes in any fat remaining in the pan. Add the stock, the grouse, juniper berries, seasoning and bay leaves. Cover the pan and simmer for 1 hour, or until the grouse is nearly tender. Remove the joints of game and cut the meat from the bones. Save a little of the breast meat but return the remainder to the pan and simmer for a further 15 minutes then sieve the ingredients. If liquidizing instead then the juniper berries and bay leaves must be removed first.

Return the purée to the pan, add the sherry or wine and the jelly, heat thoroughly, taste the soup and season to taste. Mince or finely chop the small portion of breast meat, add to the soup just before serving.

◉ Hare Soup

The recipe above can be used with about 450 g/l lb hare, or venison or rabbit. Both hare and venison need definite sweetness to balance the flavour so add 25 g/1 oz (3 tablespoons) raisins to the ingredients and double the amount of redcurrant jelly.

When returning the purée to the pan add 40 g/1¹/2 oz (good ¹/3 cup) ground almonds and a few blanched pistachio nuts. Rabbit soup can be made in the same way as Grouse Soup. A little double cream can be stirred into this, and all game soups, just before serving.

Fish Dishes

As no part of Britain is far from the sea we are fortunate in having access to many fishing grounds. In addition, the British Isles abounds with rivers and lakes, where enthusiastic anglers catch freshwater fish such as salmon, eel, trout and the very special, and somewhat scarce, smelts.

From ports in Cornwall in the south-west of England, to the very north of Scotland our fishing fleets have sailed throughout the centuries. It is recorded that in the 1300s English fishermen first ventured as far as Iceland. There they caught great shoals of fish. Much of the fish caught at that time was salted and dried, principally for use during Lent. The church's ruling that no meat must be eaten during the period of Lent was strictly followed in those days. Although many European countries esteem bacalao (the name by which salt cod is known) very highly, it has not been popular in our country for some time. It made a brief appearance during the war years and just afterwards, in the late 1940s, when fresh fish was difficult to obtain as many British ships and sailors, including fishermen, were engaged on other duties. Even then, it was treated with some disdain.

Since the days of the early journeys by our fishermen, who even sailed as far as Newfoundland, the fleet has had varying fortunes. Quotas have been imposed as to the amount of fish that can be caught in certain waters. Although the present day fishing fleet is small, compared to that of a few decades ago, it is extremely efficient and well-equipped. Refrigerated ships, and those that can freeze fish while at sea, mean that catches reach ports and markets in good condition.

Certain fish become scarce due to over-fishing and it is up to the general public to respect the advice given by the Ministry of Agriculture.

During the 1950s and 1960s we were urged to eat herrings (and other fish based on these such as kippers, bloaters and buckling). The people willingly obliged, for herrings are an economical, as well as especially healthy, fish. In consequence we depleted the amount of herrings in the sea and we were instructed NOT to buy them as the stocks were so low. After decades of shortage, herrings are now plentiful again - because of wise fishing.

Recently cod and haddock became very scarce and once again we had to avoid buying them and our fishermen had to observe strict quotas. Gradually these fish are becoming more plentiful again.

Today luxurious halibut, turbot and monkfish are all becoming scarce, so we must look for alternatives. Skate is another fish we must avoid at the moment.These restrictions do not mean we cannot buy fish but rather that we should be adventurous and try newer alternatives.

▣ Fried Fish

Cooking time: varies, see method

There is no doubt that fried fish and chips is still one of the favourite dishes in Britain and it is not difficult to prepare this at home. If the cooking is done well, the dish is delicious. For this method of frying the fish is given a coating which could consist of a thin layer of batter, or breadcrumbs, or oatmeal, as used for herrings (see page 67). After cooking the coating should be crisp and golden, without a hint of greasiness, and the fish inside moist and tender.

Most white fish are suitable for frying, the most popular types today being cod, fresh haddock, hake, monkfish and plaice. If shallow frying, the fish should be coated with seasoned flour, egg and breadcrumbs (see page 63); a batter coating is less suitable. If deep frying, either use this coating or the batter given under the Isle of Man Platter (see page 64).

Whether shallow or deep frying, it is essential to make sure that the oil is thoroughly heated before adding the fish. Temperatures to which the oil should be heated are given on page 62, together with ways of testing the temperature without using a thermometer.

▣ Shallow Frying of Fish

Coat the fish as the method given on page 63.

Heat 2 to 3 tablespoons of oil in a large frying pan, test to see if it is really hot with a cube of day-old bread (see page 62). Add the fish and fry quickly on the under side, then turn over and fry quickly on the second side. If frying thick portions of fish, lower the heat and cook for a little longer. If frying thinner fillets of fish, quick frying on both sides should be adequate. Drain the fish on paper towel after frying.

  ◉ Thin fillets of fish take approximately 5 to 6 minutes total cooking time.
  ◉ Thick fillets of fish take approximately 8 to 10 minutes total cooking time.

◎ Deep frying of Fish

Coat the fish as the method given on page 63 or with batter as page 64.

Heat the oil in a deep pan or an electric fryer. You need a temperature of 180°C/356°F (or the nearest on the thermometer) for cooking most types of fish or 185°C/365°F for small or very thin portions. Always heat the frying basket in the oil, so the fish will not stick to that. Place the coated fish in the frying basket and lower into the hot oil.

- ◎ Thin fillets of fish take approximately 3 minutes cooking time.
- ◎ Thick portions of fish take approximately 5 minutes cooking time.
- ◎ There is no need to turn the fish over when deep frying.
- ◎ Drain the fish on absorbent paper after deep frying.

▣ Temperatures for Deep Frying

Frying in a good depth of oil is a method used to cook fish, and many other foods. It should achieve an excellent result with a crisp brown dry – not greasy – coating to the food. Although the food is fried in a large amount of oil, the fat content of the cooked dish is lower than when food is shallow fried as the high temperatures and quick cooking prevents the food absorbing oil. Always drain the fried food on absorbent paper after frying. Strain the oil after use and do not continue to use this when it darkens in colour or smells in any way.

These are the temperatures recommended for various types of frying and the way to judge the temperature without a thermometer. Use a cube of day-old bread (fresh bread does not react in the same way). The precise Fahrenheit conversion is given first then the temperature recorded on most thermometers given in brackets.

- ◎ **170°C/338°F (340°F)** – the bread should take a good minute to turn golden. Use for solid pieces of food that need long cooking.
- ◎ **175°C/347°F (350°F)** – the bread should turn golden within 55 to 60 seconds. Use for thick portions of food that need steady cooking.
- ◎ **180°C/356°F (360°F or 355°F)** – the bread should turn golden within 50 to 55 seconds. Use for medium-sized portions of food that need some minutes frying.
- ◎ **185°C/365°F (365°F)** – the bread turns golden within 45 seconds. Use for thin or small portions of food that are cooked within a short time.
- ◎ **190°C/374°F (375°F)** – the bread turns golden within 30 to 35 seconds. Use for second frying of potatoes.

Always preheat the frying basket in the hot oil or fat so the food will not stick to it. Never fill the pan of oil or fat too full or it could boil over. Do not leave a pan of hot oil or fat unattended – it is a source of danger. Electric fryers are thermostatically controlled, so should be safe to leave.

◘ Choice of Fats

Oil is recommended for deep frying, as pure lard is no longer used a great deal. In various recipes, where food is shallow fried, the kind of fat to use is given in the recipe. A little oil is often included with butter for it helps to prevent the butter overheating. Choose polyunsaturated fats and oils.

When shallow frying ensure the oil or fat is well heated before adding the food. If using a silicone (non-stick) frying pan you can reduce the oil or fat by 50 per cent.

◘ Fish and Chips

It may sound difficult to fry both the fish and the potatoes at one time, but as explained on page 197, the right way to fry potatoes is to cook them until softened then remove from the pan and fry them again just before serving.

This means that you can do the first frying of the potatoes before cooking the fish. Fry the fish and drain, then place on a heated dish in the oven to keep hot for a short time. Reheat the oil to the higher temperature required for the final frying of the potatoes, cook these for the final 1 to 2 minutes, drain and serve. In this way you have perfectly fried fish and chips.

Many people would say the classic accompaniment to fish and chips are vinegar and plenty of salt and a newspaper wrapping adds to the flavour.

◉ Breadcrumb Coating of Fish

Cooking time: as pages 61-2 ◉ Serves 4

Metric Imperial { **Ingredients** } American
4 { **portions of fish** } 4
To coat the fish:
to taste { **salt and freshly ground black pepper** } to taste
1 to 2 tablespoons { **plain flour** } 1 to 2 tablespoons
1 { **egg** } 1
50 g/2 oz { **crisp breadcrumbs, or as required** } ½ cup

Dry the fish thoroughly, especially if using defrosted frozen fish. Blend a very little salt and pepper with the flour and dust this over the fish: this helps to give a good surface for the egg and crumbs.

Break the egg on to a plate and beat with a fork, then brush over all sides of the first portion of fish. Continue with the other portions. Place the crisp breadcumbs on a flat dish or sheet of greaseproof paper, turn the egg-coated fish in the crumbs until evenly coated. Pat the crumbs into the fish with a flat-bladed knife. If time permits, chill for a short period before frying as this helps the crumbs adhere to the surface. Always shake off surplus crumbs before frying.

Either shallow or deep fry as instructions on pages 61-2.

Variations:

◉   Add chopped herbs to the crumbs or flavour these with a very little finely grated lemon zest. Blend a small amount of finely grated Parmesan or other good cooking cheese with the crumbs. Use oatmeal or rolled oats instead of breadcrumbs.

◉ Isle Of Man Platter

Cooking time: 6 to 7 minutes ◉ Serves 4

All around the coast in Britain you will be able to get locally caught white fish and some shellfish but no area takes more pride in serving such a splendid selection of fried fish than the Isle of Man.

Metric Imperial { **Ingredients** } American
See method { **mixed fish** } See method
little { **flour** } little
to taste { **salt and freshly ground black pepper** } to taste
For the coating batter:
100 g/4 oz { **self-raising flour or plain flour sifted with 1 teaspoon baking powder** } 1 cup
2 { **eggs** } 2
150 ml/1/4 pint { **milk** } 2/3 cup
2 tablespoons { **water** } 3 tablespoons
2 teaspoons { **oil** } 2 teaspoons
To fry: { **oil** }
To garnish: { **lemon and parsley** }

The selection of fish may vary a little but ideally you should have:

◉   4 small fillets of sole or plaice; 1 small cooked lobster; 16 to 20 cooked mussels; 8 small oysters; 8 Dublin bay (large) peeled prawns; 16 to 20 queenies (the very small scallops obtainable in the Isle of Man). Shell all the fish.

Blend a little flour with seasoning and coat the fish. Divide the lobster into neat pieces. Blend the ingredients for the coating batter together, adding the small amount of oil just before coating the food, and whisk briskly.

Heat the oil to 185°C/365°F. Fry the white fish for 2 minutes, add the oysters and queenies and cook for a further 2 minutes. Drain on absorbent paper and keep hot. Reheat the oil and fry the remaining fish for 2 to 3 minutes. Drain well.

Arrange on the hot platter so everyone has a good selection of the various kinds of fish. Garnish with lemon wedges or slices and sprigs of fresh or fried parsley.

◉ To Fry Parsley

Wash and dry sprigs of parsley very thoroughly. Heat the oil as above and put in the parsley. Fry for about 3 seconds only, drain and serve at once.

⊙ Fried Skate with Capers

Cooking time: 15 minutes ⊙ **Serves 4**

We are advised to avoid buying skate at the present time, due to the shortage of the unique fish but I have retained the recipe in the hope that skate will be readily available soon.

Also the method of cooking is suitable for other fish. The flavour will not be the same as skate but the dish will still be delicious if cooked in the method given below. Try using economical coley, or less well known pollock portions or fresh mackerel fillets. For a luxury use shelled, but uncooked, large Dublin Bay prawns. Although skate can be fried without steaming it first, this step is advisable for the flesh becomes more succulent. Skate is a particularly perishable fish, so store it carefully. Dried nasturtium seeds are a good alternative to capers. Pickle these in vinegar to make sure they keep well.

Metric Imperial { **Ingredients** } American
4 { **skate wings** } 4
75 g/3 oz { **butter** } 3/8 cup
to taste { **salt and freshly ground black pepper** } to taste
3 teaspoons { **caper** } 3 teaspoons
3 teaspoons { **lemon juice** } 3 teaspoons
1 tablespoon { **chopped parsley** } 1 1/2 tablespoons
To garnish: { **parsley sprigs** }

Wash the skate in plenty of cold water then put into a steamer over a pan of boiling water and cook for 5 minutes. If more convenient, place the fish on a large plate or dish, cover with foil and steam for 10 minutes.

Heat the butter in a large frying pan, add the skate and a little seasoning. Cook steadily, turning the fish over once or twice, until tender. Remove from the pan to a heated dish, add the capers, lemon juice and parsley to the butter remaining in the pan. Heat for 1 minute, or until the butter turns a dark golden colour, then spoon over the fish. Garnish with parsley.

⊙ Fried Smelts

Cooking time: 8 to 10 minutes ⊙ **Serves 4**

Many new foods have appeared in Britain during the last two or three decades but sadly some of our traditional ones have almost disappeared. Smelts are a case in point, largely due to pollution in our rivers. If you are fortunate enough to obtain any then follow the recipe above for frying the fish. There is no need to steam smelts before frying. Allow 2 or 3 per person. Wash the fish well, remove the fins then season the fish. Fry in hot butter, as given for skate, then add the capers, lemon juice and parsley. Alternatively, wash the fish well, remove the fins, coat in flour, then egg and breadcrumbs and shallow or deep fry for 5 to 7 minutes.

☉ Trout with Almonds

Cooking time: 10 to 15 minutes ☉ **Serves 4**

Both trout and almonds have always been plentiful in this country and they make a very pleasing and easily prepared dish.

Metric Imperial { **Ingredients** } American
50 g/2 oz { **almonds** } scant 1/2 cup
4 { **large trout** } 4
75 g/3 oz { **butter** } 3/8 cup
to taste { **salt and freshly ground black pepper** } to taste
2 to 3 teaspoons { **lemon juice** } 2 to 3 teaspoons
To garnish: { **lemon wedges and parsley** }

Blanch the almonds by putting them into boiling water for a few seconds, then removing them and pulling away the skins. Cut the almonds into strips.

   Slit the trout, remove and discard the intestines but leave the heads and tail intact. Heat the butter in a large frying pan and add the fish, with a little seasoning. Cook steadily on both sides until the fish is tender. Lift from the butter on to a heated dish. Add the almonds to the pan and heat steadily until both the almonds and the butter have turned a golden brown. Add the lemon juice, heat for a few seconds then spoon over the trout and serve. Garnish with the lemon and parsley.

☉ Trout in Parsley

Cooking time: 10 to 15 minutes ☉ **Serves 4**

Metric Imperial { **Ingredients** } American
4 { **trout or 2 salmon trout** } 4
little { **plain flour** } little
to taste { **salt and freshly ground black pepper** } to taste
75 g/3 oz { **butter** } 3/8 cup
2 to 3 tablespoons { **finely chopped parsley** } 3 to 4 tablespoons
To garnish: { **lemon halves** }

Fillet the fish and halve the salmon trout fillets. Dust with flour and seasoning. Heat the butter in a frying pan, add the fish and cook on both sides. Lift out of the pan, coat with parsley. Add any butter left in the pan. Garnish and serve.

⊙ Fried Cod's Roe

Cooking time: 3 to 4 minutes ⊙ **Serves 4**

Cod's roe is a highly nutritious food. It makes an excellent breakfast dish if fried with bacon, but it is equally good served for a light dish with salad.

Metric Imperial { **Ingredients** } American
450 g/1 lb { **cooked cod's roe** } 1 lb
50 g/2 oz { **butter** } 1/4 cup
2 teaspoons { **oil** } 2 teaspoons
To garnish: { **lemon and parsley sprigs** }

Skin the roe and cut into 1.5 cm/1/2 inch slices. Heat the butter and oil and fry the roe on either side for 11/2 to 2 minutes. Drain on absorbent paper and serve.

Variation:
⊙ Buy uncooked cod's roe, place in a steamer and cook over boiling water for approximately 10 minutes per 450 g/1 lb until the fish turns creamy white.

⊙ Herrings in Oatmeal

Cooking time: 10 minutes ⊙ **Serves 4**

This is one of the Scottish methods of cooking this excellent fish. It has the reputation of being one of Edward VII's favourite breakfast dishes.

Metric Imperial { **Ingredients** } American
4 large { **herrings, with roes** } 4 large
little { **milk** } little
40 g/11/2 oz { **fine or medium oatmeal** } 1/2 cup
to taste { **salt and freshly ground black pepper** } to taste
To fry: little { **butter, oil or salt** }
To garnish: { **lemon wedges** }

Bone the herrings (see page 94), remove the heads and cut each fish into 2 fillets. Brush with a little milk. Blend the oatmeal with salt and pepper and coat the fish and the roes. Omit the salt if frying the fish in salt.

There are two methods of cooking the herrings. Either heat a little butter or fat in a large frying pan, add the fish and fry for 5 minutes on either side, or the second, and more traditional method, is to heat a thin layer of salt in the pan and cook the fish in this for about the same time.

⊙ Shellfish Fritters

Cooking time: 5 minutes ⊙ Serves 4

This is a delicious way of cooking a mixture of shellfish. The fish is actually mixed with the batter which is given an interesting flavour by the addition of chopped herbs and cayenne pepper.

Metric Imperial { **Ingredients** } American
225 g/8 oz { **peeled prawns** } 1/2 lb
100 g/4 oz { **crabmeat** } 1/4 lb
For the batter:
100 g/4 oz { **plain flour** } 1 cup
to taste { **cayenne pepper** } to taste
2 { **eggs** } 2
150 ml/1/4 pint { **milk, or milk and water** } 2/3 cup
1 to 2 tablespoons { **finely chopped mixed herbs** } 1 to 2 tablespoons
To fry: { **oil** }
To garnish: { **lemon wedges** }

Chop the prawns and mix with the crabmeat. Blend the flour and a very little cayenne pepper. Separate the eggs, add the yolks to the flour with the milk, or milk and water, the herbs and fish. Whisk the egg whites and fold into the batter just before frying the fritters.

Heat the oil to 185°C/365°F and fry small spoonfuls of the mixture for 5 minutes or until crisp and golden brown. Drain on absorbent paper and serve with lemon.

⊙ Fried Dublin Bay Prawns

Cooking time: 8 to 9 minutes ⊙ Serves 4

The area around the East Coast of Ireland, like the Isle of Man, is rich in shellfish, including the very large prawns which bear the name of Dublin Bay.

Metric Imperial { **Ingredients** } American
1 { **medium onion** } 1
2 { **sticks from the celery heart** } 2
16 to 20 { **Dublin Bay prawns, cooked** } 16 to 20
50 g/2 oz { **butter** } 1/4 cup
1 to 2 tablespoons { **finely chopped parsley** } 11/2 to 21/2 tablespoons

Peel and finely chop the onion, slice the celery into very small pieces. Peel the prawns. Heat the butter in a frying pan, add the onion and celery and cook for 5 minutes. Put in the prawns and parsley and heat for 3 to 4 minutes then serve.

⊙ Salmon Patties

Cooking time: 6 to 7 minutes ⊙ Serves 4 to 6

This recipe is an excellent way of serving salmon. The fish must be cooked first, but take care it is not over-cooked for it must retain its moist texture.

The patties are generally deep-fried in oil, but can be baked instead.

Metric Imperial { **Ingredients** } American
For the puff pastry:
225 g/8 oz { **flour, etc.** } (see page 296) 2 cups
For the filling:
350 g/12 oz { **cooked salmon** } 1½ cups
1 teaspoon { **finely grated lemon zest** } 1 teaspoon
1 tablespoon { **lemon juice** } 1¼ tablespoons
2 teaspoons { **chopped fennel or dill leaves** } 2 teaspoons
3 tablespoons { **double cream** } 4 tablespoons
to taste { **salt and freshly ground white pepper** } to taste
To fry: { **oil** }

Make the pastry and roll out until just 3 mm/⅛ inch in thickness; it can be a little thicker if baking rather than frying the patties. Cut into rounds about 12.5 cm/5 inches in diameter.

Flake the salmon and blend with the other ingredients for the filling. Place a good spoonful of the filling over just half of each pastry round. Dampen the edges of the pastry and fold the pastry over the filling. Seal the edges by pressing together very firmly. Chill the patties before frying as this encourages the pastry to rise well.

Heat the oil in a deep fryer to 185°C/365°F. See page 62 for ways of testing the heat without a thermometer. Put in some of the patties, and cook for 6 to 7 minutes, until golden in colour and well-risen. Drain on absorbent paper and keep warm while frying the rest of the patties. Serve hot or cold with salad.

Variations:
- The patties can be baked instead of being fried. Roll out the pastry as above. Add the filling and seal the edges of the pastry. Place on a baking tray and brush with a little beaten egg. Chill for at least 30 minutes.
- Preheat the oven to 220°C/425°F, Gas Mark 7 and bake the patties for 20 minutes. Lower the heat slightly after 15 minutes if the pastry is turning brown too quickly.

⊙ Fish Cakes

Cooking time: 5 minutes ⊙ **Makes 8**

Make sure the fish is only lightly cooked, or see the method of using uncooked fish at the bottom of the page. The secret of really good fish cakes is to have a soft mixture of fish and potato with a really crisp brown coating on the outside.

Metric Imperial { **Ingredients** } American
225 g/8 oz { **cooked white fish or salmon, weight when cooked** } 1/2 lb
225 g/8 oz { **cooked old potatoes** } 1/2 lb
To bind the mixture:
25 g/1 oz { **butter** } 2 tablespoons
25 g/1 oz { **plain flour** } 1/4 cup
150 ml/1/4 pint { **milk** } 2/3 cup
to taste { **salt and freshly ground black pepper** } to taste
To flavour the mixture: see method
To coat the fish cakes:
1 tablespoon { **plain flour** } 11/4 tablespoons
1 { **egg** } 1
50 g/2 oz { **fine crisp breadcrumbs** } 1/2 cup
To fry the fish cakes:
50 g/2 oz { **fat or butter** } 1/4 cup

Flake the fish and mash the potatoes, blend the two ingredients together. Heat the butter in a saucepan, stir in the flour then add the milk and stir briskly as the mixture comes to the boil and makes a thick binding sauce (known as a panada).

Add the sauce to the fish and potatoes, together with a little seasoning. Mix thoroughly and add any desired favouring. This could be a little chopped parsley or mixed herbs, a few drops of anchovy essence or chopped gherkins. Divide into 8 portions, then allow to cool and stand for 1 to 2 hours until the mixture stiffens.

Form into neat cakes then coat in flour, beaten egg and crisp breadcrumbs. Heat the fat or butter and fry the cakes until crisp and brown on both sides. Drain on absorbent paper and serve.

Variations:
⊙   Use an egg to bind the mixture instead of the sauce.
⊙   Use finely minced raw fish and cook the fish cakes for a slightly longer period.
⊙   Use cooked risotto (medium grain) rice instead of potatoes.
⊙   Make miniature-sized fish cakes to serve for a hot appetiser.

▣ Baked Fish

Cooking time: varies, see method

A wide variety of fish can be baked in the oven. With the exception of Soused Herring and similar dishes where longer and slower cooking allows the flavour of the vinegar to penetrate the fish, it is wise to use a moderately hot oven (see below). Fish needs to be cooked in the shortest possible time to retain texture and flavour.

If you want the fish to brown slightly on top do not cover the dish but if you want it to keep very moist put a lid on the dish or cover it with foil.

Put the fish into a well-buttered ovenproof dish, top with a little melted butter, seasoning and a squeeze of lemon juice. To give more flavour add finely chopped herbs – the most suitable are chives, dill, fennel leaves, parsley, tarragon (use this sparingly) and thyme (lemon thyme is particularly good). Preheat the oven to 190°C/375°F, Gas Mark 5, or as directed in any specific recipe.

- Thin fillets of fish take approximately 12 to 15 minutes cooking time. If the fillets are not skinned, place the fish with the flesh side uppermost. Long fillets can be folded or even rolled. This will increase the cooking time slightly.
- Thicker fillets of fish take approximately 20 to 25 minutes cooking time.
- Really thick fish portions take approximately 30 to 40 minutes cooking time.
- Whole fish need approximately 12 minutes per 450 g/1 lb cooking time.

Where other ingredients and/or liquid are added to the dish, the cooking time may be a little longer.

▣ Baked Salmon

Salmon is known as the 'king of fish'. Its monetary value has changed over the years. In Victorian times it was so plentiful and cheap that it was given to servants, who complained about having it so frequently. The fish subsequently became expensive but today salmon farms have made this kind relatively inexpensive. The flavour of farmed salmon is not considered as fine as that of wild salmon.

Scottish salmon is the best known, and has the highest reputation, but excellent salmon is caught in other parts of Britain too.

Although salmon is an oily fish it can become dry very easily. When baking the fish wrap it in foil. The foil should be coated with oil if serving the cooked fish cold, as butter makes a film on the fish, but use melted butter when having the fish hot. A little seasoning and lemon juice can be added. Wrapping in foil means a slightly longer cooking time is needed than given above.

- Thick salmon steaks take approximately 25 minutes cooking time and whole salmon approximately 14 minutes per 450 g/1 lb at 190°C/375°F, Gas Mark 5.

▣ Roast Fish

Cooking time: see under Baked Fish, page 72

When one describes roasting any food you really mean it should be put on to a turning spit and cooked over a fire. If you have these conditions then you can roast fish the proper way. If you roast in a tin in the oven then you are really baking the food in fat. Most fish can be roasted in the traditional, and correct way, or 'roasted' in a tin in the oven. Either method is suitable for whole fish, such as cod, turbot and smaller pike. Very large pike reach a size of almost 1 metre/a generous 3 feet.

Whichever method you choose the cooking time is similar to that given for baking whole fish on page 72.

Prepare the fish, wash and dry it well and clean out the intestines. Freshly caught pike should be lightly salted and left like this for 12 hours before rinsing in cold water and cooking. Weigh the fish to calculate the total cooking time.

If roasting on a spit over heat, brush the fish with a generous amount of oil and continue doing this throughout the cooking period. If cooking in a tin in the oven, heat several tablespoons of oil in the tin, roll the fish in this so all sides are coated, and continue to baste the fish with hot oil during the whole of the cooking period. The oven should be preheated at 190°C/375°F, Gas Mark 5.

The oil can be flavoured with salt and pepper, spices, such as paprika or chilli pepper, or chopped herbs such as dill or fennel leaves.

The cooked fish can be served with any of the accompaniments to be found on pages 82 and 103-6. Be very careful when serving cooked pike, for the bones are exceptionally sharp and hard. Remove these if possible after cooking.

◉ Trout and Bacon

Cooking time: 12 to 15 minutes ◉ Serves 4

This is not just a British favourite but a European one too. Trout and bacon are a splendid combination cooked over a barbecue.

Metric Imperial { **Ingredients** } American
4 { **trout** } 4
4 to 8 { **bacon rashers** } 4 to 8

Clean the fish and remove the heads. If baking in the oven leave whole but if cooking on a spit or on metal skewers cut each fish into several chunky pieces.

Preheat the oven to 190°C/375°F, Gas Mark 5. De-rind the bacon and halve the rashers lengthways then cut in smaller pieces. Twist the strips around the fish. Either place on the spit, on long skewers or in a dish. Cook for 12 to 15 minutes.

◉ Fish Bake

Cooking time: 1 hour ◎ **Serves 4**

This dish, based on white fish and an egg custard, is often included in recipes for invalids as it is easy to digest. It is given more flavour by adding herbs and mushrooms.

Metric Imperial { **Ingredients** } American
100 g/4 oz { **button mushrooms** } 1/4 lb
25 g/1 oz { **butter** } 2 tablespoons
4 { **fillets of whiting, plaice or fresh haddock** } 4
2 { **eggs** } 2
2 { **eggs yolks** } 2
450 ml/3/4 pint { **milk** } 2 cups
to taste { **salt and freshly ground black pepper** } to taste
2 tablespoons { **mixed fresh herbs, such as fennel or dill,** } 2 1/2 tablespoons
        { **tarragon, parsley and thyme** }

Preheat the oven to 150°C/300°F, Gas Mark 2. Wipe the mushrooms and slice very thinly. Heat the butter and cook the mushrooms for 3 minutes. Place in the bottom of a deep 1.5 litre/2 1/2 pint (6 1/4 cup) oblong casserole. Skin the fish. Arrange on top of the mushrooms.

Beat the eggs with the yolks, add the milk and seasoning to taste; strain over the fish, then add the herbs, sprinkling them evenly over the egg custard.

Stand the casserole in a tin of warm water (a bain-marie) and bake for just 1 hour or until the custard is set. Serve with crisp toast or mixed vegetables.

◪ To Skin Fish

Sprinkle a little salt on a chopping board, dip the blade of a sharp knife into the salt. Make a cut at the tail end of the fish then gradually cut away the flesh from the skin. Turn the fish over and repeat this on the second side.

Fillets of fish have only the one side from which to cut the skin.

◉ Coley and Mushroom Casserole

Cooking time: 35 minutes ◎ **Serves 4**

The mixture of mushrooms and herbs in this dish adds an interesting flavour to the fish. Different types of mushrooms, or a mixture of mushrooms, could be used instead of the cultivated button mushrooms. This is a combination of many old recipes for a fish casserole.

Metric Imperial { **Ingredients** } American
450 g/1 lb { **fresh coley, weight without skin** } 1 lb
225 g/8 oz { **button mushrooms** } 1/2 lb

2 { **medium tomatoes** } 2
75 g/3 oz { **butter** } 3/8 cup
1 tablespoon { **chopped parsley** } 1 1/4 tablespoons
1 teaspoon { **chopped thyme** } 1 teaspoon
to taste { **salt and freshly ground black pepper** } to taste

If you have bought fresh coley fillets, skin them (see page 74), then divide the fish into 4 portions. Cut away the skin from coley cutlets if you have purchased them instead. Wipe the mushrooms and thinly slice the cups and chop the stems. Skin and slice the tomatoes. Heat 50 g/2 oz (1/4 cup) of the butter and toss the mushrooms in this, then add the herbs and a little seasoning. Preheat the oven to 190°C/375°F, Gas Mark 5.

Place half the mushroom mixture into a casserole, top with the fish and another layer of the mushroom mixture, then the sliced tomatoes. Melt the remaining butter and spoon over the food. Cover the dish and bake for 30 minutes.

This is excellent served with creamed potatoes and a green vegetable.

Variation:
◉ Use cod, haddock or hake portions instead of fresh coley.

◎ Fish Crumble

The casserole can be given an interesting crumble topping.

Rub 50 g/2 oz (1/4 cup) butter into 100 g/4 oz (1 cup) plain flour. Add 50 g/2 oz (1/2 cup) grated Cheddar, Cheshire or Lancashire cheese to the flour mixture together with a little seasoning. Bake the casserole as above for 20 minutes only. Remove the lid, sprinkle the crumble mixture over the ingredients. Return the dish to the oven, lower the heat to 180°C/350°F, Gas Mark 4 and bake for a further 20 minutes.

◎ Plaice in Raisin Sauce

Cooking time: 25 minutes ◎ **Serves 4**

Plaice has fine flakes so it cooks quickly. It is therefore important to check the baking carefully. It is advisable to start making the sauce before removing the fish from the oven, so that is not kept hot for too long a period.

Many historical records use dried fruits with fish, as well as with meat, it gives an interesting taste and texture.

Metric Imperial { **Ingredients** } American
4 { **medium plaice** } 4
50 g/2 oz { **raisins** } 1/3 cup
300 ml/1/2 pint { **dry white wine** } 1 1/4 cups
to taste { **salt and freshly ground black pepper** } to taste
25 g/1 oz { **butter** } 2 tablespoons

25 g/1 oz { **plain flour** } 1/4 cup
150 ml/1/4 pint { **single cream** } 2/3 cup
3 teaspoons { **chopped fennel leaves** } 3 teaspoons

Fillet the fish as described below, if the fishmonger has not already done this. The fish can be skinned if desired (see page 74). Fold the fillets and place into a casserole with the raisins, wine and a little seasoning. Cover the dish. Preheat the oven to 190°C/375°F, Gas Mark 5.

Bake for 15 to 18 minutes, then lift the fish on to a heated dish. Meanwhile, heat the butter in a saucepan, stir in the flour and then gradually add the cream. Stir as the sauce comes to the boil and thickens, remove from the heat and add the wine and raisins from the casserole to the sauce. Stir over a low heat until the ingredients are well blended, do not allow the sauce to boil. Season to taste and add the chopped fennel then pour over the plaice.

▣ To Fillet Flat Fish

Make a deep incision down the centre of one side of the fish. Cut all around the edge of the fish. Insert the knife under the centre of the fish. Gently cut the first fillet away from the bone, then repeat with the second fillet. Turn the fish over and repeat this process. Information on skinning fish is on page 74.

◉ Baked Whiting

Cooking time: 20 to 25 minutes, see method ◉ Serves 4

Whiting is one of the less expensive white fish. It is in season throughout the year and it has a particularly fine texture and delicate flavour. It is often recommended as a dish for invalids, for it lends itself to simple ways of cooking, like poaching or steaming. Filleted whiting can be served in place of more expensive sole fillets. In this particular recipe the mushrooms and onions give a good flavour to the fish. Use spring onions, not ordinary onions.

Metric Imperial { **Ingredients** } American
4 { **large whiting or 8 small ones**} 4
8 to 12 { **spring onions** } 8 to 12
100 g/4 oz { **button mushrooms** } 1/4 lb
50 g/2 oz { **butter** } 1/4 cup
2 teaspoons { **finely chopped parsley** } 2 teaspoons
to taste { **salt and cayenne pepper** } to taste
150 ml/1/4 pint { **dry white wine** } 2/3 cup
To garnish: { **fried croûtons** } (see page 53)

Remove the heads from the fish and clean them well. Chop the spring onions finely, include a little of the tender part of the green stems. Wipe and slice the mushrooms.

Put the fish with the onions and mushrooms into an ovenproof dish. Melt the butter and spoon over the ingredients. Add the parsley, a little salt and cayenne pepper together with the wine.

Preheat the oven to 190°C/375°F, Gas Mark 5. Cover the dish and bake for 20 minutes if cooking small fish but 25 minutes for larger whiting. Do not over-cook the fish. The dish is more interesting if the onions retain a little of their crisp texture. Serve the fish with a topping of crisp croûtons.

Variations:
- **Saffron Whiting:** follow the recipe above but flavour the wine with a pinch of saffron powder or a few saffron strands.
- **To use saffron strands:** these can be infused in any liquid for about 15 minutes then the liquid strained. It will have absorbed both the colour and flavour of the saffron. In mixtures where little, if any, liquid is used simply add the strands; these look attractive after being cooked and they are edible.

◉ Baked Cod and Bacon

Cooking time: 25 to 30 minutes ◉ Serves 4

The combination of fish and bacon is a popular one with trawlermen at sea and the definite flavour of cod makes it an ideal choice for this dish.

Metric Imperial { **Ingredients** } American
4 { **cod steaks, each about 225 g/8 oz (½ lb)**} 4
to taste { **salt and freshly ground black pepper** } to taste
4 { **bacon rashers** } 4
1 to 2 teaspoons { **lemon juice** } 1 to 2 teaspoons
For the stuffing:
50 g/2 oz { **butter** } ¼ cup
100 g/4 oz { **soft breadcrumbs** } 2 cups
1 teaspoon { **finely grated lemon rind** } 1 teaspoon
1 to 2 tablespoons { **chopped parsley** } 1 to 2 tablespoons
1 { **egg** } 1
To garnish: { **lemon slices** }

Place the cod steaks on a board, season lightly. De-rind the bacon and stretch the rashers with the back of a knife. Wrap a bacon rasher around each cod steak and secure with a wooden cocktail stick. Place the fish into an ovenproof dish. Preheat the oven to 200°C/400°F, Gas Mark 6. Melt the butter, add to the other ingredients in the stuffing. Spoon over the top of each portion of cod and spread out evenly. Cover the dish with foil and bake for 25 to 30 minutes. Remove the foil for the last 10 minutes so the stuffing browns. Garnish with lemon slices.

Variation:
- Use 50 g/2 oz (½ cup) shredded suet instead of the butter. Substitute other fish, such as fresh haddock, hake portions or halibut for the cod.

☉ Cod Kedgeree

This is a variation on the traditional kedgeree recipe (see page 90).

Omit the bacon and stuffing from the recipe. Top two lightly seasoned steaks of cod, each weighing approximately 225 g/8 oz (1/2 lb), with a little melted butter. Cover the dish and bake for 20 to 25 minutes at the setting given above. Make sure the fish is not over-cooked. Break into large flakes.

Heat 25 g/1 oz (2 tablespoons) butter and fry a finely chopped onion; add 350 g/12 oz (generous 2 cups) cooked long grain rice, the cod, a pinch of curry powder and enough single cream to moisten the dish. Heat thoroughly, form into a pyramid shape. Top with cooked chopped bacon rashers and 1 or 2 chopped hard-boiled eggs.

☉ Eels in Madeira Wine

Cooking time: 45 minutes ☉ Serves 4

Eels are caught in very large quantities in various rivers throughout Britain as well as in the sea. Conger eels are reasonably plentiful in the coastal waters around southern England. Eels used to be extremely popular but over the years the well-known classic ways of cooking this interesting fish have been forgotten which is a pity for the flesh has a good flavour. There are more recipes using eel on pages 25 and 92.

This particular dish is suitable for larger eels, for the slices need to have a reasonable diameter to insert the stuffing in the centre of the slices.

Madeira wines have always been very popular in this country and their rich flavour is excellent with this particular fish. The same wine could be served with the dish.

Metric Imperial { **Ingredients** } American
900 g/2 lb { **eel, weight before skinning** } 2 lb
For the stuffing:
100 g/4 oz { **peeled prawns** } 1/4 lb
25 g/1 oz { **butter** } 2 tablespoons
1 tablespoon { **chopped parsley** } 11/4 tablespoons
50 g/2 oz { **soft breadcrumbs, preferably brown** } 1 cup
1 { **egg** } 1
to taste { **salt and freshly ground black pepper** } to taste
For the sauce: 300 ml/1/2 pint { **Madeira wine (choose a drier variety)** } 11/4 cups
To garnish: { **few unpeeled prawns** }

Skin the eel, or ask the fishmonger to do this for you. Cut the eel in slices approximately 5 cm/2 inches thick. Insert the blade of a knife in the centre of each slice to make a good sized cavity.

Chop the prawns very finely. Melt the butter, mix with the prawns and all the other ingredients in the stuffing. Insert some in the centre of each slice and spread any of the stuffing left over the top of the slices. Place the fish into a large shallow casserole, with the stuffing uppermost. Pour the Madeira wine over and around the fish. Cover the casserole.

Preheat the oven to 190°C/375°F, Gas Mark 5 and bake for 45 minutes. Lift the fish on to a heated dish, strain the wine and serve with this. Garnish with the prawns.

▣ Baking Fish in Foil

The method of enclosing fish in greaseproof paper is extremely satisfactory. Today this idea can be extended to cook fish in foil parcels. It is particularly good for cooking salmon and firm fish such as turbot or halibut.

Cut squares of foil sufficiently large to wrap around the fish. Each portion should be individually wrapped. If you intend to serve the fish hot, coat the foil with melted or softened butter. If the fish is to be served cold use olive oil or other salad oil instead, for this prevents a film forming over the fish. Add the fish, top with more butter or oil with seasoning, a little lemon juice and finely chopped fennel, dill or parsley, skinned and sliced tomatoes and/or sliced unpeeled mushrooms.

To avoid using too much fat, add 2 to 3 tablespoons of white wine, cider or fish stock instead of the butter or oil.

Fold the foil around the fish. Follow the baking times on page 72 but either use a slightly hotter oven, i.e. 200°C/400°F, Gas Mark 6 instead of 190°C/375°F, Gas Mark 5 or increase the cooking time at the original heat by 5 minutes.

◉ Mullet in Paper

Cooking time: 20 minutes ◉ Serves 4

There are both grey and red mullet. The latter has a far better flavour than the larger grey mullet. Red mullet are small fish, only about 15 cm/6 inches in length. The flesh is very delicate which is why baking in paper is an ideal method of cooking the fish. Red mullet is both expensive and rare, and is mostly caught in the south of England.

Metric Imperial { **Ingredients** } American
8 to 12 { **red mullet** } 8 to 12
little { **oil** } little
to taste { **salt and freshly ground black pepper** } to taste
50 g/2 oz { **butter** } 1/4 cup
2 tablespoons { **lemon juice** } 3 tablespoons

Wash the fish and gently scrape away the scales. Split it and remove all the intestines, except the liver which should be kept in the fish. Lightly oil 8 to 12 greaseproof paper bags or sheets. Season the fish and insert in the bags and seal these or wrap the fish securely in the sheets of paper. Preheat the oven to 190°C/375°F, Gas Mark 5 and bake the fish for 20 minutes. Open the bags or wrappings carefully and pour any liquid that comes from the fish on to the plates then add the fish.

Heat the butter with the lemon juice and pour over the fish.

Red Herrings

Cooking time: 8 minutes ◦ **Serves 4**

Metric Imperial { **Ingredients** } American
4 { **large herrings** } 4
300 ml/¹/₂ pint { **light or dark beer** } 1¹/₄ cups
to taste { **salt and freshly ground black pepper** } to taste
40 g/1¹/₂ oz { **butter** } 3 tablespoons
To garnish: { **lemon wedges** }

Bone the herrings as described on page 94. Leave them flat and retain the roes. Place the fish in a dish and add the beer with a little seasoning. Marinate for 1 hour then lift the herrings and roes out of the liquid and drain well. Melt the butter.

   To grill the fish: preheat the grill; place a piece of foil over the grid of the grill pan and brush with some of the melted butter. Put the herrings, with the cut side uppermost, and the roes on the foil. Brush with the rest of the butter and cook for about 8 minutes, or until tender.

   To bake the fish: preheat the oven to 190°C/375°F, Gas Mark 5. Place the fish in a shallow ovenproof dish, top with the melted butter and bake for 20 minutes.

   Serve the fish garnished with lemon. A little of the beer in which the fish was marinated can be heated and spooned over the herrings and the roes.

Stuffed Cornish Sardines

Cooking time: 20 minutes ◦ **Serves 4**

Metric Imperial { **Ingredients** } American
8 { **sardines** } 8
For the stuffing:
as under Eels in Madeira Wine (see page 78)
25 g/1 oz { **butter** } 2 tablespoons

Split the fish and remove the intestines. Sardines can be boned in the same way as herrings (see page 94). Make the stuffing and place in the fish together with the roes. Put into a dish. Melt the butter and pour over the fish. Preheat the oven to 190°C/375°F, Gas Mark 5. Cover the dish and bake the fish for 20 minutes.

Cornish Herrings

Cooking time: 30 to 35 minutes ◦ **Serves 4**

Although this dish is made with herrings, it is quite likely that you would be given it made with pilchards instead if you were in Cornwall for these are plentiful around that coast. They are slightly smaller than herrings. Sweet eating (dessert) apples are recommended in both the dishes that follow.

Metric Imperial { **Ingredients** } American
4 { **large herrings or 8 smaller herrings or sardines** } 4
4 { **small onions** } 4
4 { **small dessert apples** } 4
25 g/1 oz { **butter** } 2 tablespoons
to taste { **salt and freshly ground black pepper** } to taste

Cut the heads off the fish and bone them (see page 94). Peel the onions and slice them very thinly. Core, but do not peel the apples and cut into thin rings. Melt the butter in a pan, add the onions and cook for 5 minutes. Blend with the apple rings. Preheat the oven to 190°C/375°F, Gas Mark 5.

Fill the herrings with the onions and apples and place in an ovenproof dish. Season the fish and cover the dish. Bake for 25 to 30 minutes. The lid or foil can be removed after 15 minutes so the herrings become slightly crisp on top.

◉ Fruit Stuffed Mackerel

Cooking time: 30 minutes ◉ Serves 4

Metric Imperial { **Ingredients** } American
4 { **medium mackerel** } 4
2 { **large dessert apples** } 2
2 to 3 tablespoons { **sultanas or raisins** } 3 to 4 tablespoons
to taste { **salt and freshly ground black pepper** } to taste
2 teaspoons { **lemon juice** } 2 teaspoons

Prepare the mackerel by removing the heads and boning them. Peel and grate the apples, blend with the sultanas or raisins, seasoning and lemon juice. Fill the mackerel with this mixture. Put in an ovenproof dish. Preheat the oven to 190°C/375°F, Gas Mark 5. Cover the dish and bake for 30 minutes.

▣ Grilled Fish

This is a method of cooking where the minimum of fat needs to be used, although it must be remembered that many types of fish do need a certain amount of fat in cooking to prevent the flesh becoming dry.

Always preheat the grill before cooking. If the fish is to be placed directly on the rack of the grill pan then brush this with a little oil or melted fat to prevent the fish sticking. You can cover the rack with foil, which makes it easy to remove the fish.

White fish and oily fish like herrings, mackerel and salmon can all be grilled. The following recipes give an idea of the versatility of grilled fish.

When grilling fillets of fish there is no need to turn these over. When grilling thicker portions of fish these need quick grilling on either side and then slightly slower cooking, with the heat of the grill reduced, to complete the cooking. Thin fillets of fish take approximately 5 to 6 minutes cooking time.Thick portions of fish take approximately 8 to 10 minutes total cooking time.Whole fish take about the same total cooking time as thick fillets, but this varies according to the thickness of the fish. Grilled fish do not need draining on absorbent paper after cooking.

◎ Flavoured Butters

No cooking ◎ Serves 4

These butters are particularly suitable for topping grilled or poached fish. The mixture should be prepared ahead, then chilled so it can be cut into neat pats. Allow approximately 25 g/1 oz (2 tablespoons) of butter for each person for poached fish, but less if the fish has been brushed with butter during cooking.

◎   **Anchovy Butter:** add a squeeze of lemon juice and a little freshly ground white pepper to the butter then gradually add a few drops of anchovy essence. Do not use salt, for the anchovy essence provides that, as well as colour and flavouring.

◎   **Herb Butter:** the recipe for Parsley Butter is on page 121. Other herbs can be used, particularly fennel and dill, which blend so well with fish. Add a little lemon juice and seasoning and the amount of finely chopped herbs required.

◎   **Shrimp Butter:** use approximately the same weight of cooked peeled fish as butter. Chop and then pound the fish until smooth. Blend with the butter and a little lemon juice. Prawns or crab or lobster can be used also. Lobster Coral Butter is on page 100.

◎ Grilled sole

Cooking time: 10 minutes ◎ Serves 2

Dover sole is one of the finest of all white fish. While it is used in a wide variety of dishes, the classic British ways of cooking the fish are to grill or fry it. Lemon sole is smaller than Dover sole and the flavour is less good.

Grilled sole can be rather dry, even when well-basted with butter. To make sure the fish is beautifully moist, marinate it in creamy milk for at least 30 minutes before cooking. Grilled sole is generally served whole. The tail and head can be removed before cooking or left on. Fried sole can be cooked whole or divided into fillets.

Metric Imperial { **Ingredients** } American
2 { **Dover sole** } 2
150 ml/¼ pint { **full cream milk** } 2/3 cup
75 g/3 oz { **butter** } 3/8 cup
to taste { **salt and freshly ground white pepper** } to taste
To garnish: { **lemon slices** }

Pour the milk into a dish, put the sole into the milk. Leave for 15 minutes, then turn the fish over. Drain well before cooking.

Melt the butter, add a little seasoning. Preheat the grill on full heat. Brush the rack of the grill pan with a little butter so the fish does not stick to it, or place foil over the rack and brush with butter. Brush the top side of the fish with butter and grill for 5 minutes. If the fish is very thick turn over, brush with more butter and cook for 5 minutes. Thinner fish do not need turning, but after 5 or 6 minutes you can lower the heat slightly. Brush with butter several times during the cooking period. Garnish with lemon.

It is difficult to accommodate more than two sole under the grill at one time. If serving this fish for more than two people cook in batches and keep the cooked fish well covered with melted butter and foil in the oven.

Variations:
◉   Flavour the melted butter with a little lemon or lime juice.
◉   Top the fish with Parsley Butter (see page 121), Anchovy Butter (see page 82) or Lobster Coral Butter (see page 100).

◉ Fried Sole

Either coat the whole fish or fillets of sole with seasoned flour or egg and breadcrumbs or batter, then fry as page 62. If frying the whole fish, the batter coating is less usual or suitable.

◉ Salmon with Shrimp Sauce

Cooking time: 15 minutes ◉ Serves 4

Although one thinks of salmon as coming from Scotland, many parts of Britain produce this splendid fish. Shrimps make an excellent sauce; small prawns could be substituted.

Metric Imperial { **Ingredients** } American
25 g/l oz { **butter** } 2 tablespoons
4 { **salmon cutlets** } 4
1 to 2 teaspoons { **lemon juice** } 1 to 2 teaspoons
to taste { **salt and freshly ground white pepper** } to taste
For the Shrimp Sauce:
225 g/8 oz { **shrimps, weight before peeling** } 1/2 lb
150 ml/1/4 pint { **water** } 2/3 cup
25 g/1 oz { **butter** } 2 tablespoons
25 g/1 oz { **flour** } 1/4 cup
300 ml/1/2 pint { **milk** } 11/4 cups

Melt the butter for cooking the fish. Cover the grid of the grill pan with foil and brush with a little melted butter. Arrange the salmon on the foil and coat with half the butter and half the lemon juice, add a little seasoning.

Preheat the grill and cook the fish for 5 to 6 minutes, depending upon the thickness of the portions. Turn over and brush the second side with more butter and lemon juice and cook for 5 to 6 minutes. Serve with the sauce.

For the Shrimp Sauce: wash then peel the shrimps. If cold drop into boiling water for a few seconds to facilitate peeling, then drain. Put the shells into the 150 ml/1/4 pint (2/3 cup) water and simmer for 10 minutes, then strain the liquid. You should have about 4 tablespoons (5 tablespoons) left. Heat the butter, then stir in the flour and add the milk. Stir or whisk as the liquid comes to the boil and the sauce thickens, add the shrimp stock with a little seasoning. Simmer gently for a few minutes, add the shrimps and heat for 2 minutes, do not over-cook, otherwise the fish become tough.

Variation:
- Use small prawns instead of shrimps.

◎ Anchovy Sauce

Omit the shrimps and the shrimp stock. Make the sauce with the butter, flour and milk, add a few drops of anchovy essence or 1 teaspoon anchovy sauce, stir into the sauce with freshly ground pepper and a little cream.

◎ Lobster Sauce

Use several tablespoons of finely chopped lobster flesh plus the coral of a hen lobster instead of the shrimps in the recipe above.

◎ Scallops and Bacon

Cooking time: 6 minutes ◎ **Serves 4**

Traditionally the combination of fish and bacon was not unusual and it was much appreciated by trawlermen when at sea. Care must be taken not to over-cook scallops.

Metric Imperial { **Ingredients** } American
8 large or 16 small { **scallops** } 8 large or 16 small
2 tablespoons { **lemon juice** } 3 tablespoons
to taste { **freshly ground black pepper** } to taste
8 { **rashers of long streaky bacon** } 8
To garnish: { **lemon wedges** }

If the scallops are still on their shells remove these, but save any liquid from the shells. Halve large scallops. Put the fish and liquid from the shells into a basin with the lemon juice and pepper. Leave for 30 minutes.

De-rind the bacon and stretch each rasher to make it longer (see page 85), then halve these. Wrap each portion of bacon around a scallop. Secure with wooden cocktail sticks. Preheat the grill. Place the bacon-wrapped fish under the grill and cook for 4 minutes then turn over and cook on the other side for 2 minutes. Serve with lemon.

Variation:
- Thread the bacon rolls on to 4 long metal skewers and grill as above.

▣ To Stretch Bacon

Remove the rinds of the bacon. Place the rashers on a board and stroke firmly with a blunt knife or back of a knife until they become longer and more pliable.

◉ Devilled Prawns

Use 16 large peeled prawns instead of scallops in the recipe above. Marinate the prawns for about 30 minutes in 150 ml/1/4 pint (2/3 cup) white wine or cider, with 1/2 teaspoon curry paste (smoother than curry powder) and a few drops of Worcestershire sauce. Drain the fish, and put on to long metal skewers with small bacon rolls between each prawn. Brush the prawns with the marinade before cooking.

Grill as in the recipe above but turn the skewers over after 2 to 3 minutes cooking time. Never try and eat the fish and bacon straight from the skewers; these are too hot. Pull the food off the skewers with the prongs of a fork.

◉ Herrings with Mustard Sauce

Cooking time: 15 minutes ◉ Serves 4

There are two kinds of mustard sauce, both are given here. Fresh herrings have one of the most delicate flavours of all fish and mustard sauce is an ideal accompaniment.

Metric Imperial { **Ingredients** } American
4 { **large herrings** } 4
25 g/1 oz { **butter** } 2 tablespoons
to taste { **salt and freshly ground black pepper** } to taste
For the Mustard Sauce:
25 g/1 oz { **butter** } 2 tablespoons
15 g/1/2 oz { **cornflour** } 2 tablespoons
300 ml/1/2 pint { **fish stock** } (see page 88) 11/4 cups
1 tablespoon { **English mustard powder, or to taste** } 11/4 tablespoons
2 to 3 tablespoons { **white malt or wine vinegar** } 2 to 3 tablespoons
To garnish: { **parsley** }

Cut the heads from the herrings, split and bone them (see page 94). Discard all the intestines, except the roes. Fold the fish back into shape with the roes inside. Melt the butter and brush some over the fish; season them lightly. Preheat the grill and cook the herrings for 4 to 5 minutes. Turn them over, brush with the remaining butter and cook for a further 4 to 5 minutes.

To make the sauce, heat the butter in a saucepan, stir in the cornflour, then gradually blend in the fish stock. Bring the sauce to the boil and stir or whisk until thickened. Blend the mustard powder with the vinegar, add to the sauce in the pan and cook for several minutes. Season to taste.

Garnish the fish with parsley and serve with the sauce.

◉ Creamy Mustard Sauce

This more delicate sauce is equally good with herrings.

Heat 25 g/1 oz (2 tablespoons) butter in a saucepan, stir in 25 g/1 oz (1/4 cup) plain flour, then gradually blend in 300 ml/1/2 pint (1 1/4 cups) milk. Stir or whisk as the sauce comes to the boil and thickens, then add 2 to 3 teaspoons French mustard or English mustard, made into a paste with a little milk, and 2 tablespoons double cream. Stir as the sauce cooks gently and becomes the desired consistency, then add seasoning to taste.

◉ Grilled Mackerel

Cooking time: 10 to 12 minutes ◉ Serves 4

Gooseberry Sauce (see page 191), is the classic accompaniment to mackerel as the sharp fruit counteracts the oily flavour of the fish. When gooseberries are out of season use cooking apples or rhubarb instead. Fennel is not an essential ingredient, but it does add interest to the mackerel.

Metric Imperial { **Ingredients** } American
4 { **small to medium mackerel** } 4
4 teaspoons { **chopped fennel leaves, or to taste** } 4 teaspoons
50 g/2 oz { **butter** } 1/4 cup
to taste { **salt and freshly ground black pepper** } to taste
To garnish: { **fennel sprigs** }

Remove the heads then split each fish. Discard the intestines and then bone the fish (see page 94). Sprinkle the cut surfaces of the mackerel with the chopped fennel and add half the butter; season well. Fold the fish back into shape, melt the remaining butter and brush some over the fish.

Preheat the grill and cook the mackerel for 5 to 6 minutes; turn the fish over, brush with the last of the butter and continue cooking for another 5 to 6 minutes.

Garnish with fennel and serve with hot or cold Gooseberry Sauce (see page 191).

◉ Grilled Kippers

Cooking time: 4 to 5 minutes ◉ Serves 4

Both the Isle of Man and Scotland vie for the honour of producing the finest kippers. They are a favourite breakfast dish in both areas.

Metric Imperial { **Ingredients** } American
25 g/1 oz { **butter** } 2 tablespoons
4 { **kippers** } 4

Melt the butter, preheat the grill. Brush the fish with the butter. Cook for 4 to 5 minutes only, without turning, and serve each fish topped with a knob of butter.

Variation:
◉ Kippers can be cooked in several other ways – fried in a very little butter or oil, poached in water or baked. For lightly cooked fish, place them in a dish, add boiling water then cover the dish. Leave the fish standing for several minutes, then drain well and serve.

▣ Poached Fish

Fish should not be cooked in vigorously boiling liquid as this causes the outside flesh to be over-cooked before the centre of the fish is tender. Fish should be poached gently in liquid, with only gentle bubbles forming on the surface.

The liquid can be fish stock, as given below, or water or milk, as used with smoked haddock (see page 90) or Court Bouillon (see pages 98-9).

If the fish is placed in cold liquid, calculate the cooking time from when the liquid reaches simmering point. If it is placed into the hot liquid then increase the cooking times given below by 1 to 2 minutes, for the fish cooks slightly as the cold liquid is brought to the required temperature.

◉ Thin fillets of fish take approximately 5 to 6 minutes total cooking time.
◉ Thick portions of fish take approximately 10 to 12 minutes total cooking time.
◉ For whole fish allow approximately 7 minutes per 450 g/1 lb; a really large fish needs about 6 minutes per 450 g/1 lb.

If possible, place large fish on the rack of a fish kettle, as advised when poaching whole salmon (see page 98).

◉ Fish Stock

Cooking time: 30 to 40 minutes

A good fish stock is essential when making fish soups, sauces to serve with fish or when poaching fish. The heads, skins and bones of fish form the basis of the stock. The shells of shellfish produce an excellent stock, which has a delicate pink colour, (see Lobster Soup, page 47). Fish stock cubes are available when there is no time nor ingredients for which to produce the stock.

Actual quantities of bones and skin are not given as these will vary according to the ingredients available. To produce about 600 ml/1 pint (2½ cups) stock, simmer the head, bones and skins of a large filleted fish in 750 ml/1¼ pints (3¼ cups) water with 1 peeled whole onion, 1 carrot, 2 fresh bay leaves or 1 dried bay leaf, a small sprig of chervil, parsley or thyme or use herbs that are included in the specific recipe. Add 1 or 2 strips of lemon zest and a little seasoning. Simmer for 30 to 40 minutes in a covered pan, then strain the liquid.

Like all stocks this can be cooled and frozen.

Variations:
◉ Use slightly less water and add a little white wine or dry cider.
◉ Instead of white wine or cider add 1 to 2 tablespoons white wine vinegar to the water.

◉ Trout in Cider

Cooking time: 15 to 20 minutes ◉ Serves 4

Trout has always been popular in Britain as it has been plentiful in lakes and rivers throughout the country. Nowadays there are trout farms where the fish is reared commercially, so it is available for everyone. The distinctive and delicate flesh needs very little extra flavouring. Brown (river) trout; rainbow trout (generally from fish farms) and the larger salmon trout are available. The last has the delicate texture of trout with a little of the flavour and colour of salmon. It can be cooked like trout, or like salmon. Cider is an excellent cooking liquid for fish.

Metric Imperial { **Ingredients** } American
4 { **rainbow or brown trout** } 4
250 ml/8 fl oz { **dry cider** } 1 cup
to taste { **salt and freshly ground black pepper** } to taste
15 g/½ oz { **butter** } 1 tablespoon
2 teaspoons { **plain flour** } 2 teaspoons
To garnish: { **lemon, cucumber, tomato slices** }

Take care in cleaning the trout as the skin is easily damaged, so wipe, rather than wash, it. The fish can be cooked by poaching in a pan or baking in the oven.

To poach the fish: lay in a large frying pan, add the cider and a little seasoning. Cover the pan and simmer for 10 minutes, spooning a little of the cider over the fish once or twice during cooking. When cooked, lift the fish out of the pan on to a heated dish and keep hot. Blend the butter and flour together, drop 4 small pieces into the liquid in the pan and whisk briskly until the liquid is thickened slightly. Pour over the fish and garnish.

To bake the fish: preheat the oven to 190°C/375°F, Gas Mark 5. Place the fish in a large ovenproof casserole, add the cider and a little seasoning. Cover the casserole and cook for 20 minutes. Lift the fish out of the casserole, pour the liquid into a saucepan, thicken with the butter and flour as above, then garnish.

◉ Kedgeree

Cooking time: 15 minutes ◉ Serves 4

This is one of the most famous breakfast dishes of the past. It was introduced into Britain by people who had worked in the East India Company in India. Its name is a simplified version of the Indian dish Khichardi. It makes an excellent light luncheon or supper dish. The dish should be soft and creamy, so heat and serve as quickly as possible. The timing is based on using cooked rice and haddock.

Metric Imperial { **Ingredients** } American
2 { **eggs** } 2
1 { **small onion** } 1
50 g/2 oz { **butter** } 1/4 cup
350 g/12 oz { **cooked smoked haddock, weight when bones and skin removed** } 3/4 lb
350 g/12 oz { **cooked long grain rice** } generous 2 cups
to taste { **cayenne pepper and salt, if required** } to taste
little { **single cream or milk, optional** } little
To garnish: { **chopped parsley** }

Hard boil and shell the eggs, then chop the whites and yolks separately.

Peel and chop or thinly slice the onion. Heat half the butter in a small pan and cook the onion until soft. Break the haddock into fairly large flakes.

Heat the remainder of the butter in a large pan, add the haddock and rice and heat together, stirring gently so that flakes of fish are not broken. Add the pepper and salt with enough cream or milk to make a moist texture. Stir in the onion and chopped egg white. Spoon into a neat shape on a hot dish and top with the egg yolks, in the form of a cross, and the parsley.

Variations:
- ◉ Use other fish in the kedgeree instead of smoked haddock. Cooked smoked cod or ready-smoked trout or mackerel are excellent served in this way.
- ◉ Cooked fresh or well-drained canned salmon make a colourful and very pleasing kedgeree. Since the flavour is less strong than when using smoked fish, increase the amount of fish used to 450 g/1 lb instead of the 350 g/12 oz (3/4 lb) given in the recipe above.
- ◉ The recipe using fresh cod in a kedgeree is on page 78.

◉ Finnan Haddie

Cooking time: 10 minutes ◉ Serves 4

Although haddocks are smoked in many parts of Britain the most famous area is Findon, near Aberdeen in Scotland. The name Findon is very often given as Finnan or Finnae. Haddock can be obtained as a large fillet but many people prefer to buy the whole fish.

Metric Imperial { **Ingredients** } American
1 { **really large whole smoked haddock or enough haddock fillet for 4 portions** } 1
450 ml/3/4 pint { **milk, milk and water, or water** } scant 2 cups
2 { **fresh bay leaves or 1 dried bay leaf** } 2
to taste { **freshly ground black or white pepper** } to taste
50 g/2 oz { **butter** } 1/4 cup

If cooking a whole haddock cut away the fins and tail and divide the flesh into 4 portions. Cut the fillet into 4 pieces.

Heat the liquid in a large frying pan or saucepan, add the bay leaves and pepper then put in the haddock and poach steadily until just tender. Remove the fish from the liquid with a fish slice, put on to a heated dish. Top each portion with a knob of the butter. A spoonful of the milk can be poured over the fish.

Variation:
⊙ It is traditional to top each portion of haddock with a poached egg.

⊙ Haddock Toasts

Cook the fish as above, then flake and mix with a little cream in a saucepan. Heat thoroughly then spoon on to hot buttered toast.

⊙ Grilled Finnan Haddock

Poach the portions of smoked haddock in water until just soft; do not over-cook the fish for it must keep its shape when placed under the grill. Drain the fish and dry on absorbent paper. Preheat the grill.

Place a sheet of foil on the grid of the grill pan, add the fish, then top each portion with a little butter. Heat for 3 to 4 minutes, then add a topping of finely grated cheese. Heat for a further 2 to 3 minutes or until the cheese melts.

This makes an excellent light meal served with grilled tomatoes and a green salad.

⊙ Jellied Eels

Cooking time: 45 minutes to 1 hour ⊙ Serves 4 to 6

This dish is considered to be very much a cockney Londoner's choice. You will find these sold when the famous Derby race takes place at Epsom racecourse in Surrey. The eels are usually eaten with a teaspoon.

Metric Imperial { **Ingredients** } American
900 g/2 lb { **fresh eel or eels, weight before skinning** } 2 lb
900 ml/11/2 pints { **water** } 33/4 cups

to taste { **salt and freshly ground black pepper** } to taste
1 teaspoon { **lemon juice** } 1 teaspoon
2 { **fresh bay leaves or 1 dried bay leaf** } 2
1/4 teaspoon { **allspice** } 1/4 teaspoon
7 g/1/4 oz { **gelatine, optional, see method** } 1 envelope

Ask the fishmonger to skin the eel(s). Cut the flesh into 3.5 cm/1½ inch lengths. Put into the water with the seasoning, lemon juice, bay leaves and allspice. Cover the pan and simmer gently until the fish is tender. If using a large eel this will take about 1 hour; smaller and younger eels will be cooked in 45 minutes.

When the fish is cooked remove from the liquid and drain well. Pack into a large container or individual ones. Boil the eel stock until reduced to about 300 ml/½ pint (1¼ cups) – you must have sufficient liquid to cover the fish. This should form a natural jelly but if the weather is very hot use the gelatine. Add this to 2 tablespoons of the water and allow to stand for 2 to 3 minutes, then stir into the very hot eel stock and heat until dissolved. Strain the stock, then pour over the fish.

Leave until the jelly is firm; serve with brown bread and butter.

⊙ Poached Salmon Cutlets

The method of poaching fish is on page 88 and there are special hints on cooking salmon on page 98. This is a very efficient way of cooking salmon cutlets if they are to be served cold. Wrap each cutlet in oiled greaseproof paper and tie with fine string. Put the fish in a pan containing a plentiful amount of cold water.

Gradually bring the water just to boiling point. Remove the pan from the heat immediately then cover it tightly. Leave the fish to become quite cold in the water – it will be tender but not over-cooked.

⊙ Cosseted Herrings

Cooking time: 30 to 40 minutes ⊙ Serves 4

This recipe for stuffed herrings was given to me many years ago by the wife of a Grimsby fisherman, who said it was a traditional dish among their fellow trawlermen. Cosset means to 'pamper' and this is certainly a way of pampering fish.

Metric Imperial { **Ingredients** } American
8 small or 4 large { **herrings with hard roes** } 8 small or 4 large
For the stuffing:
1 { **medium onion** } 1
100 g/4 oz { **button mushrooms** } 1/4 lb
8 small or 4 large { **oysters or scallops** } 8 small or 4 large
50 g/2 oz { **butter** } 1/4 cup

1 teaspoon { **finely grated lemon rind** } 1 teaspoon
2 teaspoons { **lemon juice** } 2 teaspoons
to taste { **salt and freshly ground black pepper** } to taste
To garnish: { **lemon wedges, fried croûtons** } (see page 53)

Split and bone the herrings, as below. Discard the intestines and heads but save the roes. Chop these. Peel and finely chop the onion, wipe and slice the mushrooms, slice the oysters or scallops. Heat the butter and cook the onion for 5 minutes then add the mushrooms and cook for a further 2 to 3 minutes. Put in the remainder of the stuffing ingredients and add the chopped roes. Place inside the herrings and skewer or sew the stuffing in position. Use a large needle and a very fine string; pierce right through the flesh on both sides.

Either poach the herrings in a fish kettle or large saucepan in a little boiling salted water for 15 to 20 minutes or put about 300 ml/1/2 pint (11/4 cups) water into a baking dish with a little seasoning. Add the herrings and cover the dish. Preheat the oven to 180°C/350°F, Gas Mark 4 and bake for 25 to 30 minutes. Lift the herrings out of the container. Drain well, then garnish with lemon and croûtons and serve.

▣ To Bone Herrings

Slit the fish along the stomach. Carefully remove the intestines and discard. Put the roes on one side. Cut off the heads. Turn the fish on to a board, skin side uppermost. Run your forefinger very firmly down the centre of each fish. Turn them over and you will find you can remove the back bones and most of the smaller bones. Take away any remaining bones with tweezers or your fingers.

◎ Fish Pie

Cooking time: 40 minutes ◎ Serves 4

A fish pie can be as simple or as elaborate as you wish. The basic recipe, which consists of cooked white fish in a white sauce topped with creamed potatoes, is highly nutritious but certainly is not exciting. The various additions that most cooks incorporate into the recipe can turn it into an epicure's delight. The simple recipe is given first then suggestions follow for variations.

Metric Imperial { **Ingredients** } American
450 g/1 lb { **white fish, such as cod or fresh haddock, poached (see page 88), weight when skin and bones removed** } 1 lb
For the white sauce:
25 g/1 oz { **butter** } 2 tablespoons
25 g/1 oz { **plain flour** } 1/4 cup
300 ml/1/2 pint { **milk or use half milk and half fish stock** } 11/4 cups
to taste { **salt and freshly ground black pepper** } to taste

For the topping:
550 g/1¼ lb { **creamed potatoes** } (see page 206) 2½ cups
25 g/1 oz { **butter** } 2 tablespoons
To garnish: { **parsley** }

Flake the fish. Heat the butter for the sauce in a pan, stir in the flour, then add the milk, or milk and fish stock, and stir or whisk briskly as the liquid comes to the boil and the sauce thickens. Add the fish and seasoning to taste.

Spoon into a 1.2 litre/2 pint pie dish. Spread the potatoes over the filling and top with small pieces of the butter. Preheat the oven to 200°C/400°F, Gas Mark 6 and bake for 25 minutes. Garnish and serve.

Variations:
- Add peeled prawns, sliced scallops, flaked crabmeat or mussels to the filling.
- Slice several mushrooms, cook gently in a little butter and add to the fish. Make the sauce richer by including a little double cream and add more flavour by infusing strips of lemon zest, sliced onion, chopped celery and a bay leaf in the milk before making the sauce. Warm the milk, allow it to stand for 1 hour, then strain and use. Add a little white wine or sherry to the thickened sauce.
- Substitute the white sauce with a Tomato Sauce (see page 194): this is excellent with most fish.
- Top the filling with puff pastry, made with 175 g/6 oz (1½ cups) flour, etc. (see page 296).

Star-Gazy Pie

Cooking time: 45 minutes ⊙ Serves 4 to 6

This is a most unusual looking fish pie, for the filling is arranged so that the heads of the fish are seen around the edges of the crisp pastry crust. The recipe comes from Cornwall where it was made usually with pilchards, which look like small herrings and have much the same flavour. They are in fact mature sardines. Pilchards used to be very plentiful around the Cornish coasts but during the recent years they have become scarce, so small herrings can be used instead.

Metric Imperial { **Ingredients** } American
For the filling:
8 { **pilchards or small herrings** } 8
2 to 3 { **eggs** } 2 to 3
2 { **medium onions** } 2
100 g/4 oz { **bacon rashers** } ¼ lb
75 g/3 oz { **soft white breadcrumbs** } 1½ cups
3 tablespoons { **milk** } 4 tablespoons
2 tablespoons { **finely chopped parsley or mixed herbs** } 2½ tablespoons
1 teaspoon { **finely grated lemon zest** } 1 teaspoon
1 tablespoon { **lemon juice** } 1¼ tablespoons

to taste { **salt and freshly ground black pepper** } to taste
4 tablespoons { **dry cider** } 5 tablespoons
For the shortcuts pastry:
225 g/8 oz { **flour, etc.**} (see page 295) 2 cups
To glaze: { **1 egg** }

Split and bone the fish (see page 94), but leave the heads on.

Hard boil, then shell and slice the eggs. Peel and finely chop the onions and de-rind and chop the bacon. Put the breadcrumbs into a basin, add the milk, herbs, lemon zest and juice and half the chopped onions. Season lightly and mix together. Use half this mixture as a stuffing for the fish. Arrange the fish on a 23 cm/9 inch deep pie plate, with the tails towards the centre and the heads over the edge of the plate, pointing upwards. Preheat the oven to 200°C/400°F, Gas Mark 6.

Fill the spaces between the fish with the rest of the stuffing, the chopped bacon, remaining onions and the sliced eggs. Spoon the cider over the filling.

Roll out the pastry and cover the filling; take care not to break the fish heads. Beat the egg and brush over the pastry. Bake for 20 minutes then lower the heat to 180°C/350°F, Gas Mark 4 for the remaining 25 minutes. Serve hot.

◉ Crab Patties

Cooking time: 20 minutes ◉ Serves 4

Crab is one of the most plentiful shellfish around Britain's shores. There are particularly good crabs caught on the east coast, in Yorkshire and Cornwall.

These make a very delicious light main dish. Some old recipes suggest frying the patties as Salmon Patties (see page 69), instead of baking them.

Metric Imperial { **Ingredients** } American
1 { **large cooked crab** } 1
2 tablespoons { **double cream** } 3 tablespoons
2 teaspoons { **lemon juice** } 2 teaspoons
to taste { **salt and freshly ground black pepper** } to taste
For the puff pastry:
150 g/5 oz { **flour, etc.** } (see page 296) 1¼ cups
For the topping: { **cream and anchovy essence** }

Prepare the crab (see page 100). Blend the light and dark crabmeat with the cream, lemon juice and seasoning. Divide into 4 portions and chill well.

Make the pastry, roll out very thinly and cut into 4 large rounds. Put the filling in the centre of each round, moisten the edges, gather these together, then turn the patties over and gently roll to make neat rounds. Chill for a short time before baking to help the pastry rise and keep a good shape.

Preheat the oven to 220°C/425°F, Gas Mark 7. Put the patties on to a baking tray and cook for 20 minutes. Lower the heat slightly after 15 minutes if the pastry is browning too quickly. Put on to plates, make a slit in the centre. Blend a little double cream with a few drops of anchovy essence and spoon into the slits.

◘ To Cook Crab

Put the crab(s) into rapidly boiling water and cook for about 20 minutes or until the shells turn bright red. Plunge into cold water to cool.

◉ Cockle Pie

Cockles are plentiful and of excellent quality in both Ireland and Wales, as are clams, whelks and winkles all of which can be used in this recipe either singly or mixed.

Make shortcrust pastry (see page 295) using 300 g/10 oz (2½ cups) flour, etc. Use half to line a 20 cm/8 inch pie plate or flan dish.

In Ireland the pastry is topped with about 1.2 litres (2 pints) cockles (weight when cooked and shelled), a finely chopped onion, a knob of melted butter, a little lemon juice, 3 tablespoons (4½ tablespoons) cream and seasoning. Cover the filling with the rest of the pastry and bake for 35 to 40 minutes in an oven preheated to 200°C/400°F, Gas Mark 6. Lower the heat slightly after 25 minutes.

The Welsh version is similar, except 100 g/4 oz (¼ lb) of chopped bacon is added.

◘ Cold Fish Dishes

The following recipes are some of the most popular classic cold fish dishes. They make ideal summer fare and are perfect for festive occasions. Serve with mayonnaise, or one of the salad dressings on page 212.

◉ Dressed Salmon

Cooking time: see method

A whole salmon is one of the most impressive and delicious of all British classic fish dishes. It must be cooked with care to retain the flavour and appearance.

◉ **To cook a whole salmon:** either bake (see page 72) or poach the fish (see page 88). If cooking a small salmon, follow the cooking times on these pages. If cooking a large salmon then reduce the times by approximately 2 minutes per 450 g/1 lb.

If you have a fish kettle place the fish on the rack. When cooked it can be lifted out of the liquid without fear of it breaking. If poaching without a rack, place a large, thick piece of foil under the fish to support it during cooking.

Information about fish stock is given on page 88 but the fish has more flavour if poached in a Court Bouillon. This is made by simmering 1 or 2 sliced onions, 2 sliced carrots, 1 or 2 slices of lemon rind (without the white pith), 1 or 2 bay leaves and a bunch of parsley in 1.2 litres/2 pints (5 cups) water and 300 ml/1/2 pint (11/4 cups) white wine, with seasoning to taste. The Court Bouillon should be simmered for 25 minutes, then allowed to cool before adding the fish.

To dress the salmon: carefully remove the skin from both sides of the fish; this is easily done when the fish is slightly warm. Leave the head and tail intact.

The simplest way to garnish the fish is with wafer-thin slices of cucumber. These can be arranged in a neat design on and around the fish. Add slices or twists of lemon and small lettuce leaves to the dish.

A more elaborate way to dress salmon is to coat it with a Chaudfroid Sauce. Although not a strictly classic British sauce it has been used in this country for a very long time. It is practical as well as being decorative, for it helps to keep the fish moist. There are many recipes for this sauce but the simplest is as follows. It is sufficient to coat the top of a 3 kg/6 to 7 lb salmon.

Dissolve 15 g/1/2 oz (2 envelopes) gelatine in 450 ml/3/4 pint (2 cups) well-flavoured fish stock. Add 1 tablespoon (11/4 tablespoons) dry sherry. Allow this to become cold, then blend with 450 ml/3/4 pint (2 cups) Mayonnaise (see page 213). Chill until the sauce has become a syrupy consistency and then brush a thin layer over the fish. Allow this to set, then coat again with a slightly thicker layer. Garnishes can be placed on the sauce before it stiffens completely.

◉ Lobster Salad

Cooking time: 20 minutes ⊙ Serves 4

A freshly cooked lobster has a wonderful flavour. Half a lobster makes a perfect start to a meal; if serving as a main course allow a whole lobster per person.

A hen lobster, which contains red coral (roe), has a wider tail than the male. Make sure the lobster feels heavy for its size. If buying a ready-cooked lobster pull out the tail, if the lobster is fresh it should spring back quickly.

Metric Imperial { **Ingredients** } American
2 to 4 { **medium lobsters** } 2 to 4
to taste { **salad ingredients** } to taste
{ **Mayonnaise** } (see page 212)

⊙ **To cook the lobster(s):** wash well, tie the two front claws together if this has not been done by the fishmonger. Fill a large pan with water, bring to the boil. Add the lobster(s) and cook for 20 minutes, or until the shells turn bright red. Place immediately in cold water. If cooking several lobsters, make sure there is plenty of water and it comes back to boiling point quickly after adding the fish.

⊙ **To prepare the lobster(s):** split the fish lengthways, discard the dark intestinal vein and the stomach bag near the head. Remove the claws, discard any grey fingers. Crack the claws and remove the flesh or serve these with lobster picks.

⊙ **For the salad:** serve the lobster body plus the claws with salad or remove the meat from the body and claws and arrange on the salad. Serve with mayonnaise.

◉ Grilled Lobster

Allow half a large or one small lobster per person. The lobsters should be freshly cooked, as above, or buy newly cooked lobsters from the fishmonger. Choose hen lobsters if possible. Split the body of the lobsters, discard any inedible parts, as explained above. Remove the flesh from the claws. Preheat the grill.

Arrange the body of the lobsters, still in their shells, cut sides uppermost and the claws in the grill pan. Cover with a generous amount of melted butter, a good squeeze of lemon juice and a dusting of freshly ground white pepper. Grill steadily until piping hot. Garnish with lemon and Coral Butter, below.

◉ Lobster Coral Butter

Cream together equal amounts of coral and butter, add a squeeze of lemon juice and seasoning. Chill, then form into neat squares or rounds. This is a delicious topping for any white or shellfish.

◘ To prepare Crab

Like all shellfish, crab is highly perishable, so buy a cooked crab from a reliable source. Methods of cooking shellfish are given on page 26.

Always feel a cooked crab before buying it. If it is surprisingly light for its size, that could indicate the fish is watery and could be poor value as you are not getting solid crabmeat. A good crab should be quite heavy.

To prepare the fish:
1. First pull away all the claws from the body of the crab; this is quite easy if you twist them towards you.
2. Next, take the body away from the main shell and remove and discard the stomach bag. Use a teaspoon to remove the dark flesh from the large shell, put this into one basin.
3. Crack the rounded part of the shell and remove the flesh. Keep white and dark crabmeat separately. Discard all grey fingers from the body.
4. Crack the large claws and remove the white crabmeat. Keep small claws for garnishing the dish.

◉ Dressed Crab

This is the term given to the final preparation of the light and dark crabmeat.

It is quite usual to serve the flesh in the large shell, so this should be cleaned and polished with a few drops of olive oil. The crabmeat can be arranged in a dish or on flat plates instead of in the shell.

You can spoon the white and the dark crabmeat in separate halves of the shell or dish and garnish them with chopped parsley, or you may prefer to blend the flesh with a little mayonnaise or salad dressing, recipes on page 212.

If you want to make the flesh go a little further, blend a small amount of soft breadcrumbs with the crabment. Use white crumbs with the white meat and wholemeal crumbs with the dark crabmeat. Lightly season the flesh.

Another addition to the crabmeat is to blend finely chopped hard boiled egg yolk(s) with the white crabmeat and the chopped white(s) with the dark crabmeat, so giving a contrast in colour.

◉ Jellied Fish Cream

Cooking time: 20 minutes ◉ Serves 4 to 6

This is a very light fish mould that is ideal to serve cold. If selecting white fish add a little anchovy essence or tomato purée to give a delicate colour.

In the Victorian and Edwardian era fish creams and moulds formed part of elaborate dinner menus.

Metric Imperial { **Ingredients** } American
450 g/1 lb { **white fish or salmon, weight without skin and bones** } 1 lb
150 ml/¹/₄ pint { **white wine or dry cider** } ²/₃ cup
150 ml/¹/₄ pint { **fish stock** } (see page 88) ²/₃ cup
to taste { **salt and freshly ground black pepper** } to taste
few drops { **anchovy essence or tomato purée** } few drops
11 g/scant ¹/₂ oz { **gelatine** } 2 envelopes
2 tablespoons { **water** } 3 tablespoons
150 ml/¹/₄ pint { **double cream** } ²/₃ cup
2 to 3 tablespoons { **cooked peas, optional** } 2¹/₂ to 3¹/₂ tablespoons

Place the fish in a pan with the wine or cider, stock, a little seasoning and the anchovy essence or tomato purée. Bring to simmering point and cook until just tender. Lift the fish out of the liquid and flake it. Boil the liquid until only 150 ml/¹/₄ pint (²/₃ cup) remains. Sprinkle the gelatine on top of the water, allow to stand for 2 to 3 minutes, then add to the fish stock and heat gently until the gelatine has completely dissolved.

Blend the fish with the warm gelatine mixture and allow to become quite cold, but not stiff. Whip the cream until it holds its shape, fold into the cold fish mixture, then add the cooked peas, if including these. Put into a plain mould and allow to set. Turn out and serve with salad and Cucumber Sauce (see page 106).

◉ Hot Fish Cream

Cook the fish in the seasoned wine and stock, as the recipe above. A few drops of anchovy essence or tomato purée should be added to white fish. Boil the stock until reduced to 150 ml/¼ pint (²/₃ cup).

Flake the fish, blend with the stock, 50 g/2 oz (1 cup) soft breadcrumbs, 4 tablespoons (5 tablespoons) double cream and 2 well beaten eggs. Season to taste and add 1 tablespoon chopped parsley or fennel leaves. Put into a greased 2 pint/1.2 litre (5 cup) basin. Cover with greased foil and steam for 1 hour. Turn out and serve hot with Parsley or Fennel Sauce (see page 103).

◉ Hake with Walnut Sauce

Cooking time: 12 to 15 minutes ◉ Serves 4

Hake is not unlike cod or fresh haddock and either of those fish could be used in this recipe. The flakes of hake are soft and very white with an excellent flavour whether served cold or hot, as in this dish. Pickled walnuts have always been a favourite garnish for foods. Their sharp flavour and dark colour makes an interesting sauce. Hake is particularly popular in the north of England, as are pickles of all kinds.

Metric Imperial { **Ingredients** } American
2 { **eggs** } 2
8 { **pickled walnuts** } 8
4 { **hake cutlets** } 4
to taste { **salt and freshly ground black pepper** } to taste
2 teaspoons { **olive oil or melted butter** } 2 teaspoons
300 ml/½ pint { **double cream, or see below** } 1¼ cups
1 tablespoon { **lemon juice** } 1¼ tablespoons
To garnish: { chopped fennel leaves, lettuce, cucumber slices }

If serving the fish cold, it is important that it is moist but not damp, so steaming is the better method of cooking. If serving hot it can be poached, as the method below. Hard-boil and chop the eggs, chop the pickled walnuts.

To steam the fish: place the cutlets on a large, heat-resistant plate, add a little seasoning. Brush a large piece of foil with the oil or melted butter and place over the fish, tucking in the edges of the foil. Stand the plate over a pan of boiling water and cook for 10 minutes, or until the fish is just cooked. Allow to become quite cold, then arrange on a dish.

Whip the cream until it begins to form soft peaks, add one of the chopped eggs and the chopped walnuts, lemon juice and seasoning to taste. Spoon the sauce over the fish and top with the second chopped egg and the chopped fennel leaves. Garnish the dish with lettuce and sliced cucumber.

If serving the fish hot: poach the fish in about 300 ml/½ pint (1¼ cups) fish stock (see page 88). Lift from the stock and top with the cold sauce, made as above. Garnish and serve at once.

Variations:

- To give a less rich sauce, use low-fat yogurt or fromage frais instead of all, or part of, the cream.
- Halibut or turbot are excellent in this dish; cook for slightly longer than hake.

⊡ Sauces To Serve With Fish

There are many sauces that blend well with fish, some of which are incorporated in the recipes in this chapter. The following are excellent with most cooked fish.

A standard basic sauce in Britain is White Sauce, given below, but the flavour of Béchamel Sauce, also on this page, is better. I have given a slightly more generous amount of milk than you will find in the recipes in cookery books of the past, for today we prefer less thick sauces and, when time permits, you give a better flavour and consistency to the sauce if it is allowed to simmer gently for a short time and so thicken by evaporation.

◎ White Sauce

Cooking time: 10 to 15 minutes ◎ **Serves 4 to 6**

Metric Imperial { **Ingredients** } American
25 g/1 oz { **butter or margarine** } 2 tablespoons
25 g/1 oz { **plain flour** } 1/4 cup
scant 450 ml/3/4 pint { **milk** } scant 2 cups
to taste { **salt and freshly ground white pepper** } to taste

Heat the butter in a saucepan, stir in the flour and continue to stir over a gentle heat for 2 to 3 minutes. Add the milk. This can be incorporated gradually or added all at once. Bring the liquid to the boil, then stir or whisk very briskly to give a perfectly smooth sauce. Simmer gently for a few minutes, add seasoning to taste.

Variations:

- When making this sauce to serve with fish dishes use a little less milk and add some fish stock to the sauce, so the flavour blends well with the fish. Add 1 to 2 tablespoons of cream to the thickened sauce to enrich the flavour.
- **Béchamel Sauce:** put a small piece of carrot, onion and celery into the milk. Heat this, remove from the heat and allow to stand for 1 hour, then strain and use in the sauce above.
- **Fennel Sauce:** make the sauce as above, then add several teaspoons of chopped fennel leaves. Heat gently for 2 to 3 minutes.
- **Parsley Sauce:** make the sauce as above, then add several tablespoons of finely chopped parsley. The sauce can be simmered gently after adding the parsley or this can be added at the last minute to give a fresher taste.

English Butter Sauce

Cooking time: 15 minutes ◉ Serves 4 to 6

This has been a classic sauce for centuries, for butter has always been plentiful in Britain. Serve with fish or vegetables, such as cauliflower or broccoli.

Metric Imperial { **Ingredients** } American
175 g/6 oz { **butter** } 3/4 cup
25 g/1 oz { **plain flour** } 1/4 cup
300 ml/1/2 pint { **water** } 11/4 cups
to taste { **salt and freshly ground white pepper** } to taste
to taste { **grated or ground nutmeg** } to taste
1 to 2 teaspoons { **lemon juice, optional** } 1 to 2 teaspoons

Cut the butter into 1.5 cm/1/2 inch dice; do not allow it to get too soft.

Blend the flour and the water, pour into a saucepan and stir over a moderate heat until thickened. Add a little salt and pepper. Either transfer the mixture to the top of a double saucepan or to a basin over hot, but not boiling, water or turn the heat down very low. It is essential that the mixture does not boil when the butter is added, for this would result in an oily rather than a creamy sauce.

Add the butter gradually to the thickened mixture, whisking vigorously as you do so. When the butter has been incorporated add nutmeg, lemon juice and seasoning.

Egg and Lemon Sauce

Cooking time: 15 minutes ◉ Serves 4 to 6

This is a light textured sauce that is ideal with fish. It can also be served with chicken if the fish stock is replaced by chicken stock.

Metric Imperial { **Ingredients** } American
2 teaspoons { **cornflour** } 2 teaspoons
300 ml/1/2 pint { **fish stock** } 11/4 cups
2 { **eggs** } 2
2 tablespoons { **lemon juice** } 21/2 tablespoons
to taste { **salt and freshly ground white pepper** } to taste

Blend the cornflour with the fish stock. Beat the eggs in a basin, add the fish stock mixture, the lemon juice and a little seasoning. Stand over a saucepan of hot, but not boiling, water and whisk until the sauce thickens.

⊙ Hollandaise Sauce

Cooking time: 10 to 15 minutes ⊚ **Serves 4 to 6**

This is one of the good classic sauces from France that we have adopted. There is a belief that it is very difficult and time-consuming to make, but that is not true today as liquidizers and food processors mean it can be prepared in a very short time.

In old recipes this is sometimes called 'Dutch Sauce'.

Metric Imperial { **Ingredients** } American
175 g/6 oz { **unsalted butter, or see below** } 3/4 cup
3 { **egg yolks** } 3
2 to 3 tablespoons { **lemon juice or white wine vinegar, or as required** } 3 to 4 tablespoons
to taste { **salt and freshly ground white pepper** } to taste
to taste { **cayenne pepper, optional** } to taste

Remove the butter from the refrigerator a short time before making the sauce, so it is not too hard, but do not allow it to become oily; when making the sauce by hand it should be a spreading consistency. Cut the butter into small pieces.

Put the egg yolks with the desired amount of lemon juice or vinegar into the top of a double saucepan or a basin and stand over hot, but not boiling, water. When the water is the correct heat you should just be able to place your finger in it.

Whisk the egg mixture all the time until thick and creamy, then gradually whisk in the butter, never add this too rapidly. Add the salt and peppers to taste and serve hot or cold, as in a Tartare Sauce, below.

Variations:
- ⊚ Reduce the amount of butter to 85 g/3 oz (3/8 cup). This will still produce a good sauce.
- ⊚ **The modern touch:** put the egg yolks and lemon juice or vinegar into a liquidizer or food processor and process until these ingredients are well-blended. Heat the butter to boiling point. Keep the machine running at the lowest speed possible then gradually pour in a slow stream of boiling butter. The sauce will gradually thicken. Season to taste.

⊙ Tartare Sauce

To many people this sauce is an essential accompaniment to fried fish.

Add 2 to 3 teaspoons of finely diced capers, and the same amount of chopped gherkins and finely chopped parsley to the cold Hollandaise Sauce, above, or to approximately 150 ml/1/4 pint (2/3 cup) mayonnaise.

Cucumber Sauce

No cooking ● **Serves 4 to 6**

This cold sauce can be served with hot or cold fish; chill it well before serving.

Metric Imperial { **Ingredients** } American
1/2 { **small cucumber** } 1/2
1 tablespoon { **white wine vinegar or lemon juice** } 1 1/4 tablespoons
150 ml/1/4 pint { **double cream** } 2/3 cup
150 ml/1/4 pint { **Mayonnaise** } (see page 213) 2/3 cup
to taste { **salt and freshly ground white pepper** } to taste

Peel the cucumber and coarsely grate the pulp. Alternatively cut into matchstick pieces instead of grating it. Add the vinegar or lemon juice and leave for about 15 minutes. Whip the cream until it holds its shape, blend with the mayonnaise. Drain away any surplus liquid from the cucumber. Add the dry cucumber to the cream mixture and season to taste.

Variations:
● Add a pinch of sugar to the cucumber.
● Blend in 2 or 3 teaspoons finely chopped chives, fennel or dill leaves. Use thick yogurt in place of the cream.

Sorrel Sauce

Cooking time: 15 to 20 minutes ● **Serves 4 to 6**

Sorrel is a perennial herb that is easily grown. The flavour is very like that of cooked spinach. It makes a wonderful accompaniment to hot fish dishes.

Metric Imperial { **Ingredients** } American
225 g/8 oz { **young tender sorrel leaves** } 1/2 lb
to taste { **salt and freshly ground black pepper** } to taste
300 ml/1/2 pint { **White or Velouté Sauce; amount of sauce when cooked** } 1 1/4 cups
            (see pages 103 and 194)
3 tablespoons { **single cream** } 4 tablespoons

Wash the sorrel leaves in cold water, then place in a very small amount of boiling well-seasoned water. Cook until just tender; this takes about 8 minutes.

Meanwhile make the sauce, cooking it until reduced to 300 ml/1/2 pint (1 1/4 cups). Add the sorrel to the sauce then sieve or liquidize until smooth. Blend in the cream and heat.

Meat Dishes

British meat has always had an enviable reputation for high quality, and it is well-known both for its good flavour and tender texture. This is undoubtedly why prime cuts of meat are cooked and served in simple ways, without elaborate preparations or embellishments. That does not mean the meal is uninteresting – in fact, quite the reverse. When a perfectly roasted joint of sirloin or rib of meat is served with its classic accompaniments of Yorkshire pudding and horseradish you have a well-balanced blend of flavours; roast pork, crowned with crisp, golden crackling and served with traditional sage and onion stuffing and apple sauce offers a blend of tastes and textures that are extremely satisfying.

This chapter begins with information on roasting various kinds of meat, as a joint provides a favourite meal for the family and for special occasions. Cook's hints ensure every type of meat is cooked to perfection, and there are suggestions for adding less familiar accompaniments and flavourings to the joints, for the times you feel you would like a change.

The meat we buy today has changed appreciably over the past 20 or 30 years – joints are better presented by butchers and meat departments in supermarkets, and they contain less fat. This is due to the current recommendations about healthy eating, which urge us to reduce the amount of fat in our diet. Do not let this advice lure you into looking for completely fatless pieces of meat. A certain amount of fat on a joint or cut of meat ensures a good flavour; it also helps to prevent the meat drying out during cooking. If you feel you must reduce the amount of fat you eat, then please do not cut this off the meat before cooking as some health experts recommend, but simply avoid adding too much extra, and sometimes unnecessary, fat in cooking the meat, or cut it of your portion when the meal is served. Properly constructed, covered roasting tins are one way of cooking joints with the minimum of extra fat; do not use one when cooking pork, a rack placed in an open roasting tin gives the best result. A covered roasting tin prevents the crackling from becoming crisp.

Nowadays many people buy frozen joints and, after defrosting, these are better roasted at a relatively low temperature, so look under the LESS FAST timing on pages 109 to 117. One meat that used to be popular and is now missing from butchers shops is mutton. If you are able to obtain young roasting mutton, cook it as lamb on the LESS FAST setting and serve it with creamy Onion Sauce or the strongly flavoured Venison Sauce (see page 194).

Recipes for grilling and frying meats begin on page 118. Some of these would be useful for barbecue cooking too, for the British have taken to outdoor eating in a big way. A special Barbecue Sauce is given for serving with chicken on page 173; this is equally good with meat. You can, of course, cook portions of frozen steak or chops without first defrosting them. Here again our classic accompaniments to grilled steaks, chops and cutlets are simple but on page 118, as well as timings for grilled and fried meats, you will find ideas for giving the food a new taste.

For centuries clever cooks have created good nourishing stews and casseroles which make economical meals from less expensive ingredients. A selection begins on page 126. Busy people often say they have no time to wait for a dish that needs several hours of long slow cooking or the hungry family wants a meal within a short time. Do not forget that most stews and casserole dishes are improved if cooked one day and then reheated the next. They freeze well too, so you could prepare them when time permits, ready to heat and serve at a later date.

It is traditional to have dumplings with many stews, or with boiled beef and boiled bacon. If correctly cooked, these should be as light as a feather and I have included information to ensure this. In the past, when meat was considered an expensive luxury, many families ate dumplings, or Yorkshire pudding, before the main course, the theory being that these foods would blunt the appetite, so less meat would be eaten.

I am sure that even people who have not lived in Britain have heard of our famous steak and kidney pie or pudding. Few meat dishes are more popular than these robust dishes. Watch people in a restaurant when they are on the menu – it is not just the strong men who choose them, for their high reputation is well deserved and the blend of flavours excellent.

There is a recipe for a Pig Pye in Dorothy Hartley's excellent book *Food in England*. It dates back some centuries, but it is very like the classic Melton Mowbray Pork Pie you will find in this book on page 148. Centuries ago we had a reputation for creating pies in wondrous shapes and sizes, known then as 'coffees' or, rather grimly, as 'coffins'. Pies of today are smaller but no less good.

Throughout Britain people still enjoy traditional meat dishes, including Cornish pasties, galantines, brawns and tender bacon joints. If you have never eaten really good home-made faggots you have missed a treat. The recipes for these, plus others, are in this chapter.

◻ To Roast Meat

A meal based on a roasted joint is still considered to be rather special by many people, and with some justification. The full flavour of the meat is retained if it is cooked correctly. It is important to select the right joints for roasting and to treat each type of meat correctly.

Check the weight of the meat to ascertain the total cooking time. If inserting stuffing into the joint then weigh after doing this.

Cooking times are given under FAST and LESS FAST on the pages that follow. If you prefer to use LESS FAST timings for all meat this will give a good result, but FAST cooking is not recommended for less tender joints or defrosted frozen joints. If you use a covered roasting tin or wrap foil loosely around the meat, increase the total cooking time by at least 15 minutes.

◉ Roast Veal

- **Best cuts to choose:** fillet, leg, loin and shoulder. Use FAST timing, unless the meat has been frozen and defrosted, when LESS FAST timing is better.
- **Less expensive cuts:** breast and neck. Use LESS FAST timing.
- **For special occasions:** select rather larger joints of fillet, etc. To choose veal: due to modern opinion about the rearing of veal it is now acceptable that the lean meat should look faintly pink, rather than white. The small amount of fat should be firm and white.

Cooking times

- **Fast:** preheat the oven to 200-220°C/400-425°F, Gas Mark 6-7. Reduce the heat to 190°C/375°F, Gas Mark 5 after 1 hour. Veal must not be served rare.

Well-cooked veal.....................25 minutes per 450 g/1 lb and 25 minutes over.

- **Less fast**: preheat the oven to 180°C/350°F, Gas Mark 4. Reduce the heat to 160°C/325°F, Gas Mark 3 after 1½ hours cooking.

Well-cooked veal.........................40 minutes per 450 g/1 lb and 40 minutes over.

- **Classic accompaniments**: bacon rolls, Parsley and Thyme Stuffing (see page 189) and thickened gravy (see page 159). Bread Sauce (see page 191) and sausages (optional).
- **Newer flavourings**: fruit stuffings blend well with veal, see page 116. Veal can be pot roasted as in the recipe for beef (see page 112).
- **For perfect results**: veal is an exceptionally lean meat so take strips of fat bacon or pork and insert them into the joint before roasting. Use a larding needle and thread the fat through the meat or wrap the joint in very well greased foil or in bacon rashers. A covered roasting tin is ideal for cooking veal.
- **To carve veal**: carve rolled joints across the meat and loin of veal between the bones.

◉ Roast Beef

- **Best cuts to choose**: fillet, rib and sirloin. Use FAST timing.
- **Less expensive cuts**: aitch-bone, fresh brisket, topside. Use LESS FAST timing.
- **For special occasions**: Beef Wellington (see page 114) baron of beef, this is a double sirloin, left uncut along the backbone. Use FAST timing.
- **To choose beef**: make sure there is some cream fat to ensure a good flavour; do not remove this before cooking as it keeps the meat moist. It can be cut away after roasting. The lean should be reddish-brown to bright red.

Cooking times

- **Fast**: preheat the oven to 200-220°C/400-425°F, Gas Mark 6-7. Reduce the heat to 190°C/375°F, Gas Mark 5 after 1 hour.

Rare (under-done) beef.............15 minutes per 450 g/1 lb and 15 minutes over.

Medium-rare beef...................20 minutes per 450 g/1 lb and 20 minutes over.

Well-done beef......................up to 25 minutes per 450 g/1 lb and 25 minutes over.

- **Less fast**: preheat the oven to 180°C/350°F, Gas Mark 4. Reduce the heat to 160°C/325°F, Gas Mark 3 after 1½ hours. Also suitable for defrosted joints.

Rare (under-done) beef.............25 minutes per 450 g/1 lb and 25 minutes over.

Medium-rare beef...................30 minutes per 450 g/ lb and 30 minutes over.

Well-done beef......................35 minutes per 450 g/ lb and 35 minutes over.

- **Classic accompaniments**: Yorkshire Pudding (see page 111), Horseradish Cream or Sauce (see page 111-2), mustard and a thin gravy (see page 159).
- **Newer flavourings**: treat beef as venison and marinate it and cook as the recipe on page 120, see also Pot Roast on page 112.
- **For perfect results**: today an excess of fat is not recommended when roasting meat. You can brown the outside of the joint in a very little hot fat, then pour this away and allow the beef to cook in its own fat. A covered roasting tin or a light covering with foil ensures the beef is kept moist.

⊙ **To carve beef:** the outside of the joint is always a little more cooked than slices towards the centre, so give people who prefer rare or medium-rare beef inner slices.

When carving rib or sirloin that is cooked on the bone, carve from the outside of the joint towards the bone. When carving rolled joints carve across the meat.

⊙ Yorkshire Pudding

Cooking time: see method ⊙ **Serves 4 to 6**

There are two ways of cooking this pudding. In Method 1 the pudding rises and in Method 2 it stays flatter but absorbs the meat juices. Make the batter ahead and chill it.

⊙ **The batter:** Blend 115 g*/4 oz (1 cup) plain flour with a pinch of salt. Add 2 eggs, then gradually beat in 270 ml*/9 fl oz (good 1 cup) milk or milk and water. You can use 1 egg only and 284 ml*/1/2 pint (11/4 cups) milk. (*Use this metric conversion.)

⊙ **Method 1:** ideally the oven heat should be raised to 220-230°C/425-450°F, Gas Mark 7-8 when heating the tin(s). Reduce heat when the puddings have risen.

⊙ **For a large pudding:** heat 25 g/1 oz (2 tablespoons) fat in an oblong Yorkshire pudding tin. Add the batter and bake for 15 minutes or until the pudding has risen. Return the oven to the original heat, bake for a further 10 to 15 minutes.

⊙ **For small puddings:** grease and heat deep patty tins or small Yorkshire pudding tins. Add the batter and cook for 5 to 8 minutes at the high heat then return the oven to the original heat and continue cooking for 5 to 8 minutes.

⊙ **Method 2:** remove the meat from the oven 35 to 45 minutes before it is cooked. Pour out all the fat in the roasting tin except about 2 tablespoons. Pour the batter into this hot fat in the roasting tin then place in the oven. Put the meat on the rack (not in a tin) above the pudding and continue cooking both meat and pudding. The meat juices drop into the pudding as it cooks and give it a wonderful flavour but the pudding does not rise very much. This method is satisfactory on a FAST or LESS FAST oven setting.

⊙ Horseradish Cream

No cooking ⊙ **Serves 4 to 6**

This cream, and the sauce on page 112, are classic accompaniments to roast beef. The cream is excellent with many types of smoked fish too (see page 18). Horseradish grows well in Britain.

Whip 150 ml/1/4 pint (2/3 cup) double cream lightly. Add 2 tablespoons (21/2 tablespoons) finely grated horseradish with 2 teaspoons white malt or wine vinegar or lemon juice. Blend well, then add a little salt, pepper, sugar and dry mustard powder to taste. Chill well before serving.

◉ Horseradish Sauce

Cooking time: 15 minutes ◉ Serves 4 to 6

Make a White Sauce (see page 103). When thickened, add 2 tablespoons (2½ tablespoons) finely grated horseradish with a few drops of vinegar or lemon juice, salt, pepper, sugar and dry mustard powder to taste. Serve hot.

◉ Beef Pot Roast

Cooking time: 2 to 2½ hours ◉ Serves 6 to 8

Although the British Pot Roast has never achieved the fame of the French Pot-au-Feu, it is a splendid way of cooking lean topside of beef. It is not essential to stuff the meat but this does add interest – see page 114.

Metric Imperial { **Ingredients** } American
550 g/1¼ lb { **mixed vegetables, see method** } 1¼ lb
50 g/2 oz { **beef dripping or fat** } ¼ cup
1.5 kg/3 lb { **topside of beef** } 3 lb
a little { **beef stock, water or red wine** } a little
to taste { **salt and freshly ground black pepper** } to taste

Prepare the vegetables. An ideal choice would be small onions or shallots, small carrots (or halved larger ones), sliced red and green peppers, diced celery and button mushrooms.

Heat half the dripping or fat in a large pan, add the meat and cook for several minutes until browned on the bottom side, turn over and repeat this process. Lift out of the pan on to a dish. Add the remaining fat to the pan and put in the vegetables. Cook until lightly browned. Lift out of the pan and pour away any surplus fat. Return the vegetables to the pan, making sure they form a thick flat layer. Add enough stock, water or red wine to cover them. Season lightly.

Place the meat on top of the vegetables and liquid. Cover the pan tightly and cook for approximately 1¾ to 2 hours, or until the meat is cooked to personal taste. The small amount of stock should only simmer gently. Check once or twice to make sure there is adequate liquid in the pan.

Lift the meat on to a dish with most of the vegetables. Sieve or liquidize the remainder of the vegetables with any liquid in the pan to form a sauce. If this is too thick, dilute with more stock, water or red wine.

Joints of lamb, pork or veal or venison could be cooked in the same way.

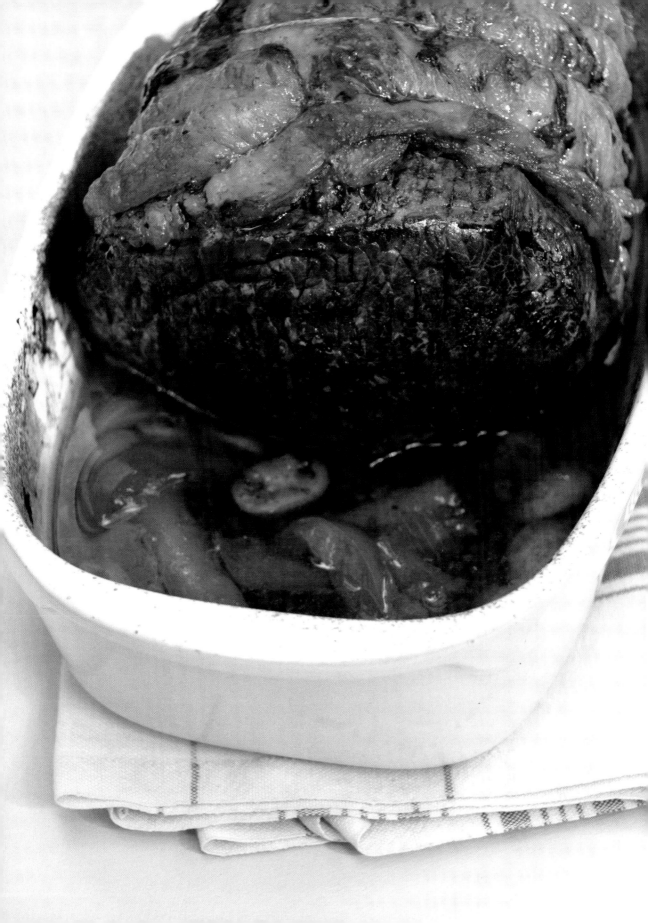

⊙ Beef Wellington

Cooking time: see method ⊙ **Serves 8**

Metric Imperial { **Ingredients** } American
40 g/1½ oz { **butter** } 3 tablespoons
1.3 kg/3 lb { **fillet steak, cut in one piece** } 3 lb
For the filling:
225 g/8 oz { **mushrooms** } ½ lb
3 { **small onions** } 3
50 g/2 oz { **butter** } ¼ cup
1 to 2 tablespoons { **finely chopped parsley** } 1½ to 3 tablespoons
to taste { **salt and freshly ground black pepper** } to taste
1 teaspoon { **made English mustard, optional** } 1 teaspoon
For the puff pastry: 225 g/8 oz { **flour, etc.** } (see page 296) 2 cups
To glaze: { **1 egg** }

Soften the butter and spread over the meat, or spread the butter over a large piece of foil and use to wrap the meat. Preheat the oven, as FAST timing on page 110, and cook the meat to personal taste. The meat continues to cook a little as it cools. Leave to become quite cold.

Wipe and finely chop the mushrooms, peel and finely chop the onions. Heat the butter and cook the onions and mushrooms until soft then add the remainder of the ingredients. Mix thoroughly and cool.

Make the pastry (see page 296) then roll out thinly to make an oblong shape sufficiently large to envelop the meat. Spread with the mushroom mixture, leaving 1.5 cm/½ inch clear at the edges. Place the steak in the centre. Moisten the edges of the pastry and wrap around the meat. Seal all the edges well. Turn over so the join is underneath and make several slits on the top surface. Use any pastry trimmings to make leaf shapes and a rose. Beat the egg, brush over the pastry and decorations, press these on top of the roll. Preheat the oven to 220°C/425°F, Gas Mark 7. Bake for 40 minutes but reduce heat slightly after 20 minutes to 190°C/375°F, Gas Mark 5.

Serve with Port Wine Sauce (see page 160).

⊙ Stuffed Beef Pot Roast

Prepare and brown the vegetables and meat, halve the joint downwards. Sandwich the two halves with a stuffing, as page 115. Tie the joint together firmly and cook as the Beef Pot Roast.

Other joints could be boned, the stuffing inserted, then the meat browned.

◉ Onion and Garlic Stuffing

Peel and chop 2 onions, 2 garlic cloves and 2 tomatoes. Blend with 100 g/4 oz (2 cups) soft breadcrumbs, 4 teaspoons chopped parsley, 1 teaspoon chopped thyme, 25 g/1 oz (2 tablespoons) melted butter, 1 egg, salt and pepper to taste.

◉ Roast Lamb

- ◉ **Best cuts to choose:** leg, loin, rack (best end of neck) and shoulder. Use FAST timing, unless the meat has been frozen and defrosted, when LESS FAST timing is better.
- ◉ **Less expensive cut:** breast of lamb (see page 116). Use LESS FAST timing.
- ◉ **For special occasions:** saddle of lamb (a double loin of lamb), Crown Roast (made with two racks of lamb) see page 116.
- ◉ **To choose lamb:** there is relatively little fat on young lamb, but it should be white and firm. The lean should be pink. When older, the colour deepens.

Cooking times

- ◉ **Fast:** preheat the oven to 200-220°C/400-425°F, Gas Mark 6-7. Reduce the heat to 190°C/375°F, Gas Mark 5 after 1 hour.

Rare (pink) lamb...................15 minutes per 450 g/1 lb and 15 minutes over.
Medium lamb......................18 minutes per 450 g/1 lb and 18 minutes over.
Well-done lamb.....................20 minutes per 450 g/1 lb and 20 minutes over.

- ◉ **Less fast:** preheat the oven to 180°C/350°F, Gas Mark 4. Reduce the heat to 160°C/325°F, Gas Mark 3 after 1½ hours cooking. It is difficult to achieve pink lamb on this lower setting.

Medium lamb......................30 minutes per 450 g/1 lb and 30 minutes over.
Well-done lamb...................35 minutes per 450 g/1 lb and 35 minutes over.

- ◉ **Classic accompaniments:** Mint Sauce or Mint Jelly (see page 159), thickened gravy (see page 159). Lamb blends well with stuffing (see page 116).
- ◉ **Newer flavourings:** insert slivers of peeled garlic into the flesh before roasting or individual rosemary or tarragon leaves. Lamb blends well with most stuffings in this book. A boned and stuffed leg or shoulder of lamb makes an excellent joint. Also see Crown Roast of Lamb (see page 116).
- ◉ **For perfect results:** lamb is an easy meat to roast. Follow the timings carefully.
- ◉ **To carve lamb:** carve boned and rolled joints across the joint. Carve loin between the bones. When carving leg of lamb, cut a fairly thick slice from the centre of the curved part, remove this. Hold the knife at an angle and carve long slices from either side of the initial slice that has been removed.

When carving shoulder of lamb, cut the initial slice in the centre of the rounded side, remove this and then continue carving as for leg. Turn the joint over and carve long horizontal slices from the underside.

Crown Roast of Lamb

Cooking time: as page 115 ⊙ Serves 6 to 7

This is the name given to the joint made from two racks (two best end of necks) of lamb, consisting of 12 to 14 cutlets; these are formed into a round. The centre is filled with a stuffing before cooking, or with cooked seasonal vegetables after cooking.

A butcher will prepare the crown given a reasonable amount of notice. Protect the ends of the cutlets with pieces of foil so they do not burn during cooking. Place the meat in a roasting tin, and fill the centre with the selected stuffing (see below). Calculate the weight of the meat plus that of the stuffing to ascertain the total cooking time. It is a good idea to protect the top of the stuffing with foil to keep it moist, and remove this towards the end of the cooking time.

To serve, remove the foil from the ends of the bones and top these with cutlet frills. Carve between the bones and spoon out the stuffing.

Orange and Walnut Stuffing

Metric Imperial { **Ingredients** } American
3 { **large oranges** } 3
100 g/4 oz { **walnuts** } 1 cup
1 { **medium onion** } 1
50 g/2 oz { **butter** } 1/4 cup
75 g/3 oz { **raisins** } generous 1/2 cup
2 tablespoons { **finely chopped parsley** } 21/2 tablespoons
100 g/4 oz { **soft breadcrumbs** } 2 cups
1 { **egg** } 1
to taste { **salt and freshly ground black pepper** } to taste

This stuffing is excellent with most meats, but particularly good with a Crown Roast. Grate 2 teaspoons orange zest. Cut the peel and pith from the fruit and cut out the segments of fruit, discarding skin and pips. Do this over a basin and save the juice. Halve the segments. Chop the walnuts. Peel and chop the onion, heat the butter and cook the onion for 5 minutes, add to the rest of the ingredients with the orange juice.

Apricot and Walnut Stuffing

Use 225 g/8 oz (1/2 lb) uncooked diced ripe apricots instead of oranges.

⊙ Roast Pork

- ⊙ **Best cuts to choose:** fillet (tenderloin), part of the leg, loin and spare rib. Use FAST timing unless the meat has been frozen and defrosted when LESS FAST timing is better.
- ⊙ **Less expensive cuts:** blade, hand and spring. Use LESS FAST timing.
- ⊙ **For special occasions:** select rather larger joints, such as a whole leg, etc.
- ⊙ **To choose pork:** avoid joints with an excess of fat, although this is rare today as pork is now reared to give the minimum of fat. The lean should be pale pink and the fat white and firm.

Cooking times

- ⊙ **Fast:** preheat the oven to 200-220°C/400-425°F, Gas Mark 6-7. Reduce the heat to 190°C/375°F, Gas Mark 5 after 1 hour. Pork must not be served rare.
Well-cooked pork....................25 minutes per 450 g/1 lb and 25 minutes over.
- ⊙ **Less fast:** preheat the oven to 180°C/350°F, Gas Mark 4. Reduce the heat to 160°C/325°F, Gas Mark 3 after 1½ hours cooking.
Well-cooked pork....................40 minutes per 450 g/1 lb and 40 minutes over.

- ⊙ **Classic accompaniments:** Sage and Onion Stuffing (see page 190), Apple Sauce (see page 191) and thickened gravy (see page 159).
- ⊙ **Newer flavourings:** stuff the joint with prunes and apples as given under goose (see page 166). Follow the recipes for other stuffings and sauces for duck and goose (see pages 189 to 194). Insert a few slivers of peeled garlic or tarragon or rosemary leaves into the joint before roasting. Add chopped garlic to the gravy.
- ⊙ **For perfect results:** no extra fat is required when cooking pork as it has enough natural fat, unless you have bought a tenderloin of pork which is very lean. Wrap in greased foil or wrap de-rinded bacon rashers around the joint. It weighs about 450 g/1 lb.

It is a good idea to stand pork on a rack in the roasting tin. Most people want good crackling with pork. This can be achieved in various ways. Always roast the joint with the rind uppermost (this makes the crackling), make sure the rind is scored (cut) at regular intervals. Brush with olive oil or melted lard and sprinkle lightly with salt.

An even better method is to cut the rind from the joint before roasting and cook in a separate tin or dish with the rind side uppermost.

- ⊙ **To carve pork:** carve rolled joints across the meat. Loin should be cut between the bones.

▣ Grilled and Fried Meats

It is essential when grilling any meats, with the exception of thin bacon rashers, that the grill is preheated before placing the food underneath it. This ensures that the outside of the meat is well sealed and it helps to keep it pleasantly moist inside. Thin bacon rashers curl if placed under a really hot grill and they can burn, so put under the grill and switch on, or ignite, at the same time.

Brush lean meats with melted butter or oil before grilling, then brush again when they are turned over. After sealing both sides of the meat the heat can be reduced and the meat cooked more slowly. Exact cooking times vary according to the thickness and tenderness of the meat, but the times given below are a good guide for grilling or frying. Flavourings can be added to the meat before cooking.

When frying meat, choose a heavy pan so the meat does not burn. For lean meats, heat a little fat (butter or a mixture of butter and oil) or oil in the pan. Fry quickly on either side then reduce the heat to complete the cooking.

Meats to choose and cooking times:
▣ **Beef:** steaks such as entrecote, fillet, minute, porterhouse, rump, sirloin and T-bone. For steaks approximately 2.5 cm/1 inch in thickness allow 6 to 10 minutes cooking time, depending on how well done you like the meat. Minute steaks need a total of 1 minute on either side. Keep steaks well basted with butter or oil during cooking. The steak, or butter used in cooking it, can be flavoured with mustard, mixed herbs or crushed peppercorns or the beef can be marinated (see page 120).
▣ **Lamb:** chops or cutlets from the best end of neck (the rack) or loin or chump chops from the end of the loin. Slices from the top of the leg (fillet). Boned cutlets, can be made into rounds (noisettes). A limited amount of fat only is required in cooking, whether grilling or frying. For fried Reform Lamb Cutlets see page 119.

Allow 10 to 15 minutes cooking time, depending on the thickness of the meat. The lamb can be flavoured with crushed garlic, chopped herbs, finely grated orange or lemon zest, or a very little ground or grated nutmeg before cooking.
▣ **Pork:** chops or cutlets from the loin, spare ribs, chump chops or slices from the leg (fillet). Modern pork is lean, so keep well moistened with butter or oil.

Allow 15 to 20 minutes cooking time for chops and cutlets, a little less time for thin slices of fillet (escalopes). Do not serve pork under-cooked.

The pork can be flavoured by marinating it in red or white wine or cider or apple or orange juice with a little ground ginger; or press sage leaves into the meat.
▣ **Veal:** chops or cutlets from the loin. Slices from the fillet (known as escalopes) which are the most popular way of serving veal. These are generally coated with flour, beaten egg and breadcrumbs and fried.

Cooking times for veal are the same as for pork above. Flavour uncoated veal, or the breadcrumb coating, with chopped herbs or lemon zest.

▣ Fried Meat Dishes

The following three meat dishes are some of the most widely known and popular – and with good reason, for they have an excellent flavour. Each dish serves 4.

◉ Fried Steak and Onions

In this recipe the onions are moist and soft. If you prefer crisp onion rings follow the recipe on page 120.

Peel 4 large onions, slice and separate into rings. Heat 40 g/1½ oz (3 tablespoons) butter and 1 teaspoon olive or sunflower oil in a frying pan. Add the onion rings and fry steadily until soft, this takes 8 to 10 minutes. If the onions are becoming a little brown add a small amount of water to the pan. Season the onions well and lift on to a heated dish. Keep hot while frying the steak.

Choose 4 portions of prime steak (see page 118). Heat 40 g/1½ oz (3 tablespoons) butter and 1 teaspoon of oil in the pan. Add the steaks, cook quickly on either side, then continue cooking for 6 to 10 minutes, according to the thickness of the meat and how well you like the meat cooked. Serve with the onions.

◉ Reform Lamb Cutlets

This dish was created in the nineteenth century by the famous chef, Alexis Soyer, who was the chef at the famous Reform Club in London during the reign of Queen Victoria. He made this dish very popular and it is still enjoyed today. The lamb has interesting additions to the familiar egg and breadcrumbs coating.

◉ **To prepare the coating:** blend 75 g/3 oz (1½ cups) soft fine breadcrumbs with 3 teaspoons finely chopped parsley, 3 teaspoons finely chopped cooked ham, and 3 teaspoons finely chopped cooked tongue.

Coat 8 lamb cutlets in seasoned flour, then dip in a beaten egg and coat with the breadcrumb mixture. Press this firmly into the sides of the cutlets. Chill for a short time before frying as this helps the coating to adhere to the meat.

Heat 40 g/1½ oz (3 tablespoons) butter with 2 teaspoons oil in a frying pan. Add the cutlets and fry quickly on both sides. Lower the heat and cook more slowly for 10 to 12 minutes. Drain on absorbent paper and garnish with cooked ham and tongue.

The classic Reform Sauce is on page 176.

⊙ Beef Collops

Cooking time: 10 to 15 minutes ⊚ **Serves 4**

This is an unusual and very excellent Scottish dish using collops (thin slices) of tender steak. The pickled walnuts are an essential ingredient. The word 'collop' means a small slice or piece of meat.

Metric Imperial { **Ingredients** } American
3 { **medium onions** } 3
550 g/1¼ lb { **fillet or rump steak** } 1¼ lb
4 tablespoons { **Madeira or red wine** } 6 tablespoons
4 { **pickled walnuts** } 4
1 to 2 tablespoons { **liquid from the pickled walnuts** } 1½ to 3 tablespoons
50 g/2 oz { **butter** } ¼ cup
1 tablespoon { **olive or sunflower oil** } 1½ tablespoons
to taste { **salt and freshly ground black pepper** } to taste

Peel and finely chop the onions. Cut the steak into thin slices. Put the meat with just 2 teaspoons of the chopped onions into a dish. Add the wine and leave to marinate for 1 hour. Slice the walnuts thinly and put back into the walnut liquid.

Lift the meat from the wine, drain well and strain the wine. Heat half the butter and half the oil in a frying pan, cook the onions until golden in colour and tender. Lift from the pan on to a heated dish. Add the remainder of the butter and oil to the pan and cook the steaks to personal taste. Place the meat over the onions and keep hot.

Add the wine, walnuts and liquid to the pan, stir well to absorb any meat juices, heat quickly and then spoon over the meat and serve.

▣ Marinated Beef

Leave steaks in a little red wine plus 1 to 2 crushed garlic cloves for 1 hour before grilling or frying. Too long a marinating period makes the meat over-soft.

Mixed Grill

Cooking time: 25 minutes ◦ **Serves 4**

This is one of the most traditional of all English main dishes. It is extremely satisfying and gives a variety of tastes and textures. The selection of foods can be adapted to suit personal taste.

Metric Imperial { **Ingredients** } American
4 small { **lamb or pork chops or cutlets** } 4 small
4 { **lambs' kidneys** } 4
75 g/3 oz { **butter or oil** } 3/8 cup
4 { **sausages** } 4
4 small { **portions of fillet or rump steak** } 4 small
4 small { **portions of calves' or lambs' liver** } 4 small
to taste { **salt and freshly ground black pepper** } to taste
4 { **bacon rashers** } 4
4 { **tomatoes** } 4
8 to 12 { **button mushrooms** } 8 to 12
4 { **eggs** } 4
To garnish: { **Parsley Butter and watercress** }

The list of meats above is given in the order they should be cooked, for the secret of a good mixed grill is to have everything ready to serve at the same time. If the grill is not sufficiently large to accommodate all the ingredients then have a warmed dish in a low oven to keep some foods hot while cooking the remainder.

Preheat the grill. Remove any surplus fat from the chops. Skin and halve the kidneys, cut away any gristle and white fat. If using butter melt about two-thirds of this. Brush a little butter or oil over the kidneys. Place the chops on the rack of the grill pan, cook for 2 to 3 minutes. Add the kidneys and sausages and continue grilling for a few minutes, turning the food over once. Brush a generous amount of butter or oil over the portions of steak and liver, season the meat lightly if desired. De-rind the bacon, halve the tomatoes and prepare the mushrooms. Add these foods to the grill. Always brush lean meats with butter or oil as they are turned over and moisten the tomatoes and mushrooms with butter or oil. Heat the remaining butter or oil in a frying pan, add the eggs and fry. Arrange the foods on plates or a dish, top the steak with the butter and garnish with watercress.

Parsley Butter

Cream 50 g/2 oz (1/4 cup) butter with 3 teaspoons finely chopped parsley, salt and pepper and a good squeeze of lemon juice. Chill well, then cut into 4 portions.

Bacon in Whiskey and Cream

Cooking time: 25 minutes ⦿ Serves 4

This Irish dish combines the bite of Irish whiskey with the tender texture of prime lean bacon. The amount of cream gives a pleasing richness to the dish. Always serve a generous amount of creamed potatoes with the dish – in true Irish fashion.

Metric Imperial { **Ingredients** } American
4 { **lean gammon slices** } 4
25 g/1 oz { **plain flour** } 1/4 cup
to { **taste freshly ground black pepper** } to taste
2 { **medium cooking apples** } 2
1 scant tablespoon { **brown sugar** } 1 tablespoon
50 g/2 oz { **butter** } 1/4 cup
150 ml/1/4 pint { **brown stock** } 2/3 cup
150 ml/1/4 pint { **Irish whiskey, or to taste** } 2/3 cup
4 tablespoons { **double cream** } 5 to 6 tablespoons

Cut away the rind from the gammon slices. Coat the meat with the flour, flavoured with a little pepper. Peel and core the apples and cut into thin slices. Toss in the sugar.

Heat the butter with the gammon rinds in a large pan, add the gammon and cook steadily for 5 to 6 minutes on both sides. Lift on to a heated dish and keep hot. Discard the rinds then add the stock and whiskey to the pan; put in the apples and cook gently for 5 minutes. Stir in the cream then return the gammon to the pan. Heat gently for a few minutes and serve.

Kidneys in Port Wine

Cooking time: 20 minutes ⦿ Serves 4

Skin 8 to 12 lambs' kidneys, halve and remove any excess fat and gristle. Coat the kidneys in 1 tablespoon (1¼ tablespoons) of well-seasoned flour.

Peel and finely chop 2 small onions and wipe 225 g/8 oz (2 cups) of very small button mushrooms, remove the stalks.

Heat 50 g/2 oz (1/4 cup) of butter in a saucepan, add the kidneys and turn in the butter for 4 to 5 minutes. Remove from the pan on to a plate. Add the onions and cook gently for 5 minutes, then return the kidneys to the pan with the mushrooms and 250 ml/8 fl oz (1 cup) of port wine, or use half wine and half water. Simmer for 5 to 10 minutes, stir once or twice. Serve garnished with crisp toast.

Gammon and Fruit

Cooking time: 15 minutes ⊚ Serves 4

This is one of the best ways of cooking gammon. Fruit is an excellent accompaniment to these thick, juicy slices of prime bacon.

Metric Imperial { **Ingredients** } American
40 g/1½ oz { **butter** } 3 tablespoons
4 { **lean gammon slices** } 4
4 { **portions of fruit, see method** } 4
4 teaspoons { **brown sugar** } 4 teaspoons

Melt the butter. Cut the rind off the gammon and slit the fat at regular intervals to stop it curling under the heat of the grill. Preheat the grill. Brush the lean part of the gammon with butter. Place on the rack of the grill pan and cook steadily for 5 minutes, then turn over and brush again with butter. Cook for a further 5 minutes.

Add the fruit to the rack of the grill. This could be rings of cored, but not peeled, dessert apples, skinned and halved peaches, slices of fresh or well-drained canned pineapple, or cooked dried prunes or apricots. Brush the fruit with the last of the butter. Cook both gammon and fruit more slowly for 5 minutes, or until the gammon is tender. Sprinkle sugar over the fruit towards the end of this time to give it a sweet taste and a glaze.

Black Pudding with Apples

Cooking time: 12 minutes ⊚ Serves 4

Many countries produce various forms of blood pudding, also known as black pudding, and Britain is no exception. It has always been a particular favourite in the north of England and is generally served as part of a very satisfying breakfast menu. It is also excellent as a main dish with cooked apples and creamed potatoes. The pudding has already been cooked so only needs heating for a short time.

Metric Imperial { **Ingredients** } American
450 g/1 lb { **black pudding** } 1 lb
4 { **medium cooking apples** } 4
25 g/1 oz { **butter or bacon fat** } 2 tablespoons

Slice the black pudding, there is no need to remove the skin. Core and slice the apples, do not remove the peel. Heat half the butter or fat in a frying pan. Add the apples and cook until tender. Remove from the pan and keep hot. Add the rest of the butter or fat and heat the black pudding for about 3 minutes on either side.

☉ Liver and bacon

Cooking time: 5 to 10 minutes ☉ **Serves 4**

This is the classic way to cook and serve tender calves' or lambs' liver. Do not over-cook this as it makes the liver hard and dry.

Metric Imperial { **Ingredients** } American
4 to 8 { **bacon rashers** } 4 to 8
450 g/1 lb { **calves' or lambs' liver** } 1 lb
1 tablespoon { **plain flour** } 1¼ tablespoons
to taste { **salt and freshly ground black pepper** } to taste
50 g/2 oz { **butter, or to taste, see method** } ¼ cup
150 ml/¼ pint { **beef or lamb stock** } ⅔ cup
To garnish: { **chopped parsley** }

De-rind the bacon and thinly slice the liver. Blend the flour with seasoning and dust over the liver; do not exceed this amount of flour, for too much hardens the outside of the liver. Put the bacon rinds and butter into a large frying pan (use less butter if the bacon is very fat). Heat for 1 to 2 minutes, then add the bacon and liver and cook quickly on both sides. Under-done liver takes only 2 to 3 minutes; well-done liver about 6 minutes. Lift the liver and bacon on to a hot dish, discard the bacon rinds. Add the stock, stir well to absorb the meat juices and heat for 1 to 2 minutes, then pour over the liver. Top with the parsley.

Variations:
- ☉ Use sprigs of sage to garnish the liver and a little chopped sage with the flour.
- ☉ Add 1 to 2 teaspoons finely grated orange zest to the seasoned flour; use orange juice instead of stock as the liquid, add 1 teaspoon brown sugar. Fry peeled and sliced ripe avocados in the pan before cooking the liver. Keep warm while frying the liver.
- ☉ **Liver and onions:** Peel several onions, divide into rings, coat in seasoned flour and fry in hot butter or oil before cooking the liver and bacon. Make gravy (see page 159) in the frying pan, after serving the liver and bacon.

☉ Pig's Fry

This consists of equal amounts of pig's liver, heart, kidney and belly. Cut the various meats into small pieces. Coat in seasoned flour. Either fry steadily in hot fat until tender or brown in a little hot fat, then put into a casserole, cover with pork or beef stock, add a little seasoning and chopped sage. Cover the casserole and bake for 1 hour in an oven preheated to 160°C/325°F, Gas Mark 3.

▣ Stews and Casseroles

There is great diversity in the flavourings of our classic stews, cooked on top of the stoves, and casseroles, which were left to cook in a slow oven. Some of the most interesting versions follow.

The secret of a good flavour is to cook the mixture slowly. It is worthwhile making the dish, allowing it to get cold, then storing it overnight in the refrigerator and reheating it the next day. All cooked dishes must be heated very thoroughly. The stew or casserole develops more flavour by this second heating.

If making a stew it may well be easier to thicken the sauce towards the end of cooking, for the mixture is less likely to stick when cooked in a thinner liquid. There are two ways of doing this. The classic method is given first.

Making a beurre manié: obviously this is not a British term, but it is one known by all good cooks. Simply blend together equal amounts of butter and plain flour. To thicken the liquid, drop a ball of the mixture, the size of a small nut, into the boiling liquid in the saucepan, stir briskly until blended. Continue to add more small balls of beurre manié until the liquid is the desired consistency.

Thickening with flour or cornflour: blend the desired amount of flour or cornflour with a little cold liquid, spoon some of the very hot liquid from the saucepan over this and blend well, then tip into the saucepan and stir until thickened. Cornflour thickens more efficiently than flour so you need only half the amount.

Most casserole dishes are thickened before being cooked. If you use a recipe for a stew and decide to cook it in the oven in a covered casserole instead, you need slightly less liquid, for there is less evaporation than in a saucepan.

▣ Meat, Poultry and Game Stock

Good stock is the secret of many dishes; it is not difficult to make.

▣ **Brown stock**: use beef bones; mutton and lamb bones could be substituted, although the flavour of the stock is not as good. Chop bones into small pieces, if possible. Put the bones, with any small pieces of meat adhering to them, into a saucepan. Add several peeled and sliced onions and carrots, a bunch of mixed herbs with water to cover. Put a lid on the pan and simmer gently for 2 to 3 hours, or use a covered container in a low oven instead or a large bowl in the microwave on LOW setting for 1 hour. Strain, then cool and remove any fat from the surface. Stock is highly perishable so use quickly or store in the refrigerator and bring to boiling point every two days, then cool and replace in the refrigerator.

The best way to store stock is to boil it until reduced in quantity and concentrated in flavour, then cool and freeze it in cubes in ice trays.

- White stock: use veal bones, failing that the carcasses of chicken and turkey.
- Game stock: use the bones of venison or hare or carcasses of game birds.
- Bacon stock: this is from boiling a piece of bacon (see page 138).

Flavoured stock cubes are also readily available.

⊙ Beef Olives

Cooking time: 2¹/4 hours ⊙ Serves 4

This method of cooking beef has always been popular. The stuffing gives it an excellent flavour.

Metric Imperial { **Ingredients** } American
675 g/1¹/4 lb { **good quality chuck steak or topside cut into 4 large thin slices** } 1¹/4 lb
For the filling: { **Parsley and Thyme Stuffing** } (see page 189)
25 g/1 oz { **plain flour** } ¹/4 cup
to taste { **salt and freshly ground black pepper** } to taste
50 g/2 oz { **beef dripping or fat** } ¹/4 cup
450 ml/³/4 pint { **beef stock** } scant 2 cups
To garnish: { **a mixture of diced, cooked vegetables** }

Place each slice of meat between two sheets of greaseproof or waxed paper and flatten gently with a rolling pin, then cut in half. Make the stuffing and divide between the 8 slices of meat. Originally these were gathered up around the stuffing to make an olive shape. Nowadays they are generally formed into a roll. Tie the shapes with cotton or string, so the stuffing does not fall out.

Blend the flour with the seasoning and coat the meat. Heat the dripping or fat and fry the meat until golden brown, then lift into a casserole. Add the stock to the pan in which the olives were browned and stir well to absorb the flour and meat juices. Bring to the boil and cook until slightly thickened. Pour over the meat and cover the casserole. Preheat the oven to 150°C/300°F, Gas Mark 2 and cook for 2 hours. Lift the meat on to a dish, remove the cotton or string. Garnish with the vegetables and spoon a little of the liquid over the meat. Serve the rest separately. Beef Olives can be garnished with a border of piped creamed potatoes if you wish.

⊙ Braised Beef and Vegetables

Dice a selection of vegetables, such as onions, carrots, celery, turnip and celeriac, and toss in the heated fat, as in Braised Beef in Beer (page 128). Place in the casserole. Fry 2 or 3 diced bacon rashers, add to the vegetables. Coat then fry the meat as page 128. Cover the vegetables and bacon with 300 ml/¹/2 pint (1¹/4 cups) red wine or beef stock, add 2 bay leaves, a little chopped parsley and seasoning. Top with the meat. Cover the casserole and cook as page 128. Lamb, pork and veal could be cooked in the same way.

Braised Beef in Beer

Cooking time: 2¼ to 2¾ hours ⊙ Serves 4 to 6

Although braising is not the most typical way of cooking food in Britain, this recipe has always been popular. The use of beer in cooking gives a richness to the mixture. A dark rich stout is ideal. Various cuts of beef are suitable, such as aitchbone, brisket or silverside. More expensive cuts are rib or topside and cheaper cuts are chuck steak or silverside.

Metric Imperial (**Ingredients**) American
175 g/6 oz (**dried prunes**) 3/4 cup
150 ml/1/4 pint (**water**) 2/3 cup
300 ml/1/2 pint (**beer**) 11/4 cups
900 g/2 lb (**beef, see above for choice of cuts**) 2 lb
to taste (**salt and freshly ground black pepper**) to taste
1/2 to 1 teaspoon (**dry mustard powder**) 1/2 to 1 teaspoon
25 g/1 oz (**plain flour**) 1/4 cup
2 (**large onions**) 2
350 g/12 oz (**carrots**) 3/4 lb
50 g/2 oz (**beef dripping or fat**) 1/4 cup
To garnish: (chopped parsley)

Put the prunes in a basin with the water and beer. If using tenderized prunes leave for a few hours, ordinary dried prunes are better left overnight.

Cut the meat into strips 1.5 cm/1/2 inch wide and thick. Blend the seasonings with the flour and coat the meat. Peel the onions and carrots and slice. Heat half the dripping or fat and cook the onions for 5 minutes. Place in a casserole with the carrots, prunes and soaking liquid. Heat the remaining fat, add the meat and cook until golden brown. Meanwhile, preheat the oven to 160°C/325°F, Gas Mark 3. Arrange the meat on top of the vegetables, prunes and liquid. Cover the casserole and cook for 2 hours if using the best cuts of meat; 2¼ hours for the medium tender cuts and 2½ hours for the cheaper cuts. Lift the meat on to a heated serving dish, arrange the vegetables, prunes and liquid around the meat; top with the parsley.

Lancashire Hotpot

Cooking time: 2 hours ⊙ Serves 4 to 6

This dish, as the name suggests, originated in Lancashire and was named after the deep pottery casserole in which it was cooked. Bakers would put these into their bread ovens for families who did not possess good cooking facilities.

By cooking the meat between the layers of vegetables all the good flavour is retained. Be very sparing with the amount of liquid used. (Pictured opposite.)

Metric Imperial { **Ingredients** } American
8 to 12 { **middle neck of lamb chops** } 8 to 12
2 to 3 { **lambs' kidneys** } 2 to 3
675 g/1½ lb { **potatoes** } 1½ lb
350 g/12 oz { **onions, or more if desired** } 3/4 lb
to taste { **salt and freshly ground black pepper** } to taste
250 ml/8 fl oz { **lamb or chicken stock** } 1 cup
For the topping: 25 g/1 oz { **butter** } 2 tablespoons

Divide the meat into neat portions, traditionally the chops are not boned, but this can be done if desired. Cut away any excess fat from the chops. Skin the kidneys, remove any gristle and slice the meat. Peel the potatoes and onions, cut the potatoes into 6 mm/1/4 inch slices but slice the onions more thinly.

Put a layer of potatoes, then onions and then mixed lamb and kidney into a deep casserole. Season lightly, continue like this, ending with a neat layer of potatoes. Add the stock. Melt the butter and brush over the potatoes.

Preheat the oven to 150 or 160°C/300 or 325°F, Gas Mark 2 or 3. Use the lower setting if your oven is inclined to be on the hot side. The casserole can be covered immediately if there is no fear of the lid touching the top potatoes. If the lid fits tightly then bake for 30 minutes, without covering – this makes sure the potatoes stay firm and do not stick to the lid. Cover after this time and bake for a further 1½ hours. The lid may be removed for the last 20 to 30 minutes to encourage the top layer of potatoes to become brown and crisp.

This dish is generally served with pickled red cabbage and/or cooked beetroot.

◉ Irish Hotpot

The Irish recipe substitutes approximately 550 g/1¼ lb diced lean pork for the lamb and adds 2 to 3 peeled and thinly sliced cooking apples to the onions. It uses Guinness instead of stock as the liquid. Cook as the recipe above.

◉ Lamb with Caper Sauce

Cooking time: 1¼ hours ◉ Serves 4

Like so many dishes of the past this was made originally with mutton. It is recorded in *Pickwick Papers* that it was prepared for Mr. Pickwick.

Metric Imperial { **Ingredients** } American
1 kg/2¼ lb { **middle or scrag end of neck of lamb** } 2¼ lb
450 g/1 lb { **mixed root vegetables** } 1 lb
to taste { **salt and freshly ground black pepper** } to taste
25 g/1 oz { **butter** } 2 tablespoons
25 g/1 oz { **plain flour** } 1/4 cup

300 ml/1/2 pint { **milk** } 1 1/4 cups
150 ml/1/4 pint { **lamb stock, see method** } 2/3 cup
3 to 4 teaspoons { **capers** } 3 to 4 teaspoons

Divide the meat into portions. Prepare the root vegetables, leaving whole if small or cutting into neat pieces if large. Put the meat and vegetables into a saucepan, add cold water to cover. Bring the liquid to the boil, add seasoning then cover the pan and simmer gently until the meat is tender.

Heat the butter in a saucepan, stir in the flour, then add the milk and stir or whisk until the sauce thickens. Remove 150 ml/1/4 pint (2/3 cup) of the lamb stock from the saucepan, strain into the sauce, then simmer this for a short time. Dish up the meat and vegetables, add the capers plus a little vinegar from the jar to the sauce. Heat gently, but do not allow to boil. Serve separately.

◉ Irish Stew

Cooking time: 1 1/2 hours ◉ **Serves 4**

Irish Stew is an excellent example of economical Irish dishes – lots of potatoes and root vegetables to eke out the meat. One pot cookery was usual before all homes had an oven.

Metric Imperial { **Ingredients** } American
2 to 3 { **large onions** } 2 to 3
675 g/1 1/2 lb { **old potatoes, weight when peeled** } 1 1/2 lb
8 to 12 { **middle neck of lamb chops** } 8 to 12
450 ml/3/4 pint { **lamb or chicken stock** } (see page 126) 2 cups
1 to 2 teaspoons { **chopped mixed herbs, or to taste** } 1 to 2 teaspoons
to taste { **salt and freshly ground black pepper** } to taste
To garnish: { **chopped parsley** }

Peel and slice the onions. Peel the potatoes and slice about 225 g/8 oz (1/2 lb), leaving the remainder whole. Put the meat, onions and sliced potatoes into a saucepan, add the stock, herbs and seasoning. Cover the pan and cook steadily for 1 hour. Add the whole potatoes.

Cover the pan again and continue cooking for 30 minutes. Lift the meat and whole potatoes on to a warmed dish. Stir the liquid briskly, so the sliced potatoes thicken the liquid. Season to taste and serve around the meat. Top with the parsley.

⊙ Pork Casserole

Cooking time: 1 hour ⊙ Serves 4

This is a favourite Irish dish as pork and bacon are often served in that country.

Metric Imperial { **Ingredients** } American
1/2 to 1 { **small cabbage** } 1/2 to 1
2 { **large onions** } 2
50 g/2 oz { **butter** } 1/4 cup
to taste { **salt and freshly ground black pepper** } to taste
1/2 teaspoon { **chopped fresh sage or pinch dried sage** } 1/2 teaspoon
2 teaspoons { **chopped parsley** } 2 teaspoons
to taste { **grated or ground nutmeg** } to taste
4 { **large pork chops** } 4
150 ml/1/4 pint { **sweet cider or see method** } 2/3 cup
For the topping:
2 to 3 { **apples, see below** } 2 to 3
25 g/1 oz { **butter** } 2 tablespoons
2 tablespoons { **brown sugar** } 21/2 tablespoons

Cut the outer leaves from the cabbage and discard, shred the tender heart finely. Peel and thinly slice the onions, separate into rings. Heat the butter in a saucepan, add the cabbage and onions and stir over a low heat for 5 minutes. Spoon into a large shallow casserole, add a little seasoning, the herbs and nutmeg. Place the pork chops in a single layer over the vegetable base. Pour the cider over the top of the meat to keep it moist; the quantity can be increased to 300 ml/1/2 pint (11/4 cups) if you like a very moist dish.

Preheat the oven to 180°C/350°F, Gas Mark 4, cover the casserole with a lid or with foil and cook for 50 minutes, or until the meat is tender.

While the meat is cooking, peel and core the apples and cut into thin rings. Heat the butter in a frying pan, add the apple rings and cook until tender. Top with the sugar and arrange around the edge of the casserole just before serving.

Variation:
⊙ This dish is traditionally made with cooking apples and a fairly high amount of sugar. If you wish to reduce this quantity, choose a dessert apple that cooks well, like the famous English Cox's Orange Pippin which has a naturally sweet flavour. By doing this, the sugar can be reduced or omitted.

The Miser's Feast

Cooking time: 2 hours ⊙ Serves 4 to 6

This practical Welsh dish, known as Ffest Y Cybydd, provides a satisfying meal for a hungry family with the minimum of expense. It is particularly good when new potatoes are in season. Be sparing with the salt in this recipe, especially if the bacon is smoked and fairly highly salted.

Metric Imperial { **Ingredients** } American
900 g/2 lb { **new or old potatoes** } 2 lb
350 g/12 oz { **onions** } 3/4 lb
225 g/8 oz { **leeks** } 1/2 lb
450 g/1 lb { **thick bacon rashers** } 1 lb
40 g/1½ oz { **butter** } 3 tablespoons
to taste { **salt and freshly ground black pepper** } to taste

Scrape or peel the potatoes and cut into thin slices. Put the potatoes into cold water until ready to use then drain, but do not dry them as the small amount of moisture keeps them more moist. Peel and slice the onions. Wash the leeks very well and cut the white part into thin slices.

De-rind the bacon and heat the rinds for a few minutes in a pan to give some dripping. Discard the rinds. Add the butter and just melt. Use a little of the fat to grease the base and sides of a large casserole.

Put a third of the sliced potatoes and half the onions and leeks into the casserole, season lightly, then top with half the bacon. Add another layer of potatoes with the remaining onions and leeks, season again and cover with the last of the bacon. Arrange the remaining potatoes neatly over the bacon and pour on the melted bacon fat and butter. Cover the casserole.

Preheat the oven to 160°C/325°F, Gas Mark 3 and cook for 1½ hours. Remove the lid of the casserole and cook for a further 30 minutes to allow the potatoes to brown.

Serve with pickled red cabbage and pickled walnuts.

Variation:
⊙   If the bacon is already de-rinded, increase the amount of butter to 50 g/2 oz.

Lamb and Vegetable Hotpot

Use the recipe above but instead of bacon rashers use about 8 small lamb cutlets, from the best end of neck of lamb (rack of lamb). Sprinkle a little finely chopped mint over the lamb.

Mince Collops

Cooking time: 45 minutes ⊙ Serves 4

This basic Scottish recipe for cooking minced beef can be used for cooking venison or other game such as hare or rabbit. The combination of mushroom ketchup and oatmeal gives a good flavour to the dish. The term collops is used, although it really refers to the small pieces of meat, cooked as the recipe on page 120.

Metric Imperial { **Ingredients** } American
2 { **medium onions** } 2
25 g/1 oz { **butter** } 2 tablespoons
2 teaspoons { **oil** } 2 teaspoons
450 g/1 lb { **minced beef** } 1 lb
300 ml/1/2 pint { **beef stock** } 1 1/4 cups
1 tablespoon { **fine oatmeal** } 1 1/2 tablespoons
to taste { **salt and freshly ground black pepper** } to taste
1/4 teaspoon { **grated or ground nutmeg** } 1/4 teaspoon
1 to 2 tablespoons { **mushroom ketchup** } 1 1/2 to 3 tablespoons
To garnish: 2 or 3 { **eggs and toast** }

Peel and finely chop the onions. Heat the butter and oil in a pan, add the onions and cook for 5 minutes. Put in the meat and stir over a low heat until golden brown. Pour in the stock. Bring to the boil, stirring all the time to keep a smooth mixture. Add the remainder of the ingredients and stir briskly until the minced mixture has thickened slightly. Cover the pan and simmer for 30 minutes, or until the meat is tender. Stir once or twice to prevent the meat sticking to the pan.

Hard-boil, shell and quarter the eggs. Arrange the minced meat in the centre of a heated dish with triangles of toast and eggs around the sides.

Devilled Mince

Use the recipe above but omit the nutmeg, mushroom ketchup and the oatmeal.

Cook the onions and meat in the butter and oil as the recipe above. When the beef has turned a golden colour add 1 tablespoon (1 1/4 tablespoons) plain flour and 2 teaspoons curry powder, stir over a low heat for 2 minutes then add the stock, as in the recipe above and stir as the mixture comes to the boil and thickens. Cover the pan and simmer for 30 minutes, stirring from time to time. Add 1 to 2 teaspoons Worcestershire sauce just before serving. Serve with a border of cooked rice.

Devilled Kidneys

Skin and dice 8 to 12 lambs' kidneys and use instead of the minced beef.

⊙ Oxtail Ragout

Cooking time: Start the day before you plan to eat, then 3¼ hours plus 1 hour reheating
⊙ **Serves 4 to 6**

This recipe has been popular for generations. Picked walnuts make an excellent accompaniment.

Metric Imperial { **Ingredients** } American
1.15 kg/2½ lb { **jointed oxtail, see method** } 2½ lb
to taste { **salt and freshly ground black pepper** } to taste
½ to 1 teaspoon { **mustard powder** } ½ to 1 teaspoon
50 g/2 oz { **plain flour** } ½ cup
50 g/2 oz { **fat, dripping or oil** } ¼ cup
4 { **medium onions** } 4
4 { **medium carrots** } 4
4 { **medium tomatoes** } 4
1 to 2 { **garlic cloves** } 1 to 2
900 ml/1½ pints { **beef stock** } 3¾ cups
300 ml/½ pint { **red wine or beef or stout** } 1¼ cups
2 { **fresh bay leaves or 1 dried bay leaf** } 2
little { **lemon juice** } little
1 tablespoon { **chopped parsley** } 1¼ tablespoons

Select rounds of oxtail that are fairly similar in size; small rounds make excellent soup (see page 53). Cut away any large pieces of fat. Blend the seasonings with the flour and coat the oxtail, using all the flour. Heat the fat, dripping or oil in a large saucepan and fry the oxtail steadily until golden brown. Put into a large casserole.

Peel and slice the onions and carrots, skin and slice the tomatoes, peel and crush the garlic. Add all these ingredients to the saucepan. Stir to absorb any fat remaining in the pan. Cook gently for 5 minutes then add all the liquid. Stir as this comes to the boil, so the liquid absorbs the meat juices and any flour left in the pan. Add the bay leaf or leaves with lemon juice to taste, plus any extra seasoning required. Pour over the oxtail, cover the casserole.

Preheat the oven to 150°C/300°F, Gas Mark 2 and cook for 3 hours. Leave until cold then place in the refrigerator. Next day remove the solid fat from the top of the food. If necessary, add a little more stock and thicken this with a beurre manié, (see page 126). Reheat in a saucepan or the covered casserole for 1 hour at 160°C/325°F, Gas Mark 3, then top with the parsley.

Variations:
- ⊙ Add 225 g/8 oz (½ lb) cooked or well-drained canned haricot beans when reheating the casserole. Use 2 to 3 tablespoons tomato purée instead of fresh tomatoes.
- ⊙ Use any left-over oxtail as a basis for soup, (see page 53).

⊙ Creamed Sweetbreads

Cooking time: 40 to 50 minutes ⊙ Serves 4

Calves' sweetbreads are one of the most delicately flavoured of all meats. Lambs' sweetbreads are smaller and have slightly less flavour. Sweetbreads come from the thymus gland which is in the throat and chest of young animals. They also come from the pancreas gland too. Sweetbreads, cooked in either of the methods on this page, have always been regarded as a very special meat dish.

Metric Imperial { **Ingredients** } American
450 g/1 lb { **lambs' or calves' sweetbreads** } 1 lb
1 { **medium onion** } 1
1 { **medium carrot** } 1
to taste { **sprig of parsley and sprig of thyme** } to taste
1 { **strip lemon rind** }1
to taste { **salt and freshly ground white pepper** } to taste
For the sauce:
25 g/1 oz { **butter** } 2 tablespoons
25 g/1 oz { **plain flour** } 1/4 cup
150 ml/1/4 pint { **milk** } 2/3 cup
150 ml/1/4 pint { **stock, see method** } 2/3 cup
150 ml/1/4 pint { **single cream** } 2/3 cup
To garnish: { **lemon slices and fried croûtons** } (see page 53)

Wash the sweetbreads. To blanch them, put into a pan of cold water. Bring the water to the boil, strain this and discard the water. Blanching whitens sweetbreads.

Peel and slice the onion and carrot. Put into a saucepan with the sweetbreads, herbs, lemon rind, water to cover and seasoning. Cover the saucepan and cook lambs' sweetbreads steadily for 20 minutes and calves' sweetbreads for 30 minutes, or until tender. Remove the meat from the pan; strain 150 ml/1/4 pint (2/3 cup) of the stock.

Skin the sweetbreads and remove any gristle. Classic recipes suggest they are put into a container, pressed and then sliced, but this is not essential. Heat the butter in a saucepan, stir in the flour, then add the milk and the stock. Stir as the sauce comes to the boil and thickens, add the cream and sweetbreads and heat for a few minutes. Season to taste and serve garnished with lemon and croûtons.

⊙ Fried Sweetbreads

Blanch the sweetbreads as above, then cook as above. Skin the sweetbreads, then coat in seasoned flour, beaten egg and crisp breadcrumbs. Fry in a pan of hot oil, or in butter with a little oil, until crisp and brown. Drain on absorbent paper and serve with fried bacon, fried mushrooms and lemon slices.

◉ Cream Tripe and Onions

Cooking time: 2¼ hours ◉ **Serves 4**

Tripe is one of the meats about which there is more difference of opinion than any other. Many people, quite rightly, feel that when carefully cooked it makes one of the most delicious and economical dishes; others view it with great distaste as it comes from the stomach lining of cattle. There are three types, known as 'blanket', 'honeycomb' and 'thick seam'. The cooking time and flavour of each is very much the same. The interesting point is that some people who declare they do not like tripe have never eaten it, they look at the white substance and base their opinion on that.

The greatest lovers of tripe come from Lancashire, where it is sold in large quantities. The meat is sold 'dressed', that is partially cooked.

Metric Imperial { **Ingredients** } American
550 g/1¼ lb { **tripe** } 1¼ lb
3 to 4 { **large onions** } 3 to 4
750 ml/1¼ pints { **milk** } generous 3 cups
to taste { **salt and freshly ground white pepper** } to taste
2 { **fresh bay leaves or 1 dried bay leaf** } 2
25 g/1 oz { **plain flour** } ¼ cup
25 g/1 oz { **butter** } 2 tablespoons
to taste { **grated or ground nutmeg** } to taste
To garnish: { **chopped parsley** }

Wash the tripe very thoroughly, then put it into a saucepan with cold water to cover. Bring the water to boiling point, then strain the tripe. Discard the water. This stage is known as 'blanching' and it whitens the tripe.

Cut the meat into neat strips or 7.5 cm/3 inch squares. Peel and neatly chop the onions. Put the tripe, onions and 600 ml/1 pint (2½ cups) of the milk into a saucepan. Bring the milk to simmering point, add a little seasoning and the bay leaf or leaves. Cover the pan and simmer very gently for 1¾ hours, by which time the tripe should be very tender. Remove the bay leaf or leaves.

Blend the flour with the remaining milk, add to the saucepan containing the tripe. Stir carefully as the sauce thickens, then add the butter, any seasoning required and the nutmeg. Heat for 2 to 3 minutes then top with parsley.

This is a well-known dish for invalids as tripe is both nutritious and easily digested. It is served with creamed potatoes or toast.

Variation:
◉   Top the cooked tripe with a layer of crumbled Lancashire cheese. Place under a preheated grill for a few minutes until the cheese melts. Serve with hot toast.

◉ Boiled Beef

Cooking time: 2³/₄ hours ◉ Serves 6 to 8

This is one of the classic and excellent ways of serving salted beef. It is very similar to American corned beef. It is worthwhile buying a good-sized joint as salted meats shrink in cooking and because the meat is equally good served cold for a later meal.

Metric Imperial { **Ingredients** } American
1.8 kg/4 lb { **salted brisket or silverside of beef** } 4 lb
to taste {**few peppercorns or freshly ground black pepper** } to taste
3 teaspoons { **brown sugar, optional** } 3 teaspoons
450 g/1 lb { **small carrots** } 1 lb
450 g/1 lb { **small onions** } 1 lb
3 to 4 { **fresh bay leaves or 2 dried bay leaves** } 3 to 4
4 { **whole cloves, or pinch ground cloves** } 4
For the dumplings: 100 g/4 oz { **flour, etc.** }(see page 187) 1 cup

It is wise to check with the butcher as to the length of time the meat should be soaked. Generally it is advisable to leave in cold water to cover overnight or for a few hours. Discard the soaking water.

Put the meat into a saucepan with the peppercorns or pepper and sugar. Peel the carrots and onions. Slice a carrot and an onion, add to the pan with the bay leaves and cloves. Bring the water to the boil, remove any scum that may float to the top. Cover the pan and simmer gently. The term 'boiled' is wrong – the water must not boil for that will toughen the meat and also over-cook the outside of the joint before the centre is tender. Allow 40 minutes per 450 g/1 lb cooking time. Quality of meat varies, so check carefully to see if tender and increase the cooking time if necessary. Add the rest of the carrots and onions after 2 hours cooking; this means they will still be firm.

Make the dumplings and add to the liquid 15 to 20 minutes before the end of the cooking time. Make sure there is adequate liquid in the pan and allow this to boil briskly for the first 5 to 6 minutes after adding the dumplings (see page 139). Lift the well-drained joint of meat, the whole vegetables and dumplings on to a heated serving dish.

Some of the liquid can be strained and boiled briskly to make a clear sauce to serve with the meat together with English mustard and/or Horseradish Sauce or Cream (see pages 111-2).

◉ Boiled Bacon

A piece of bacon or ham is an ideal joint to cook in liquid. This can be water but it adds interest to the meat if you use part cider and part water. Another interesting flavouring is to add a small quantity of ginger ale or ginger beer to the water. As explained under Boiled Beef, the liquid should simmer and not boil, except for the brief period when dumplings are first put into the liquid.

Various joints of bacon can be used. The prime boiling joint is gammon but less expensive collar and forehock could be used instead.

If the bacon is highly salted then soak for several hours in cold water; a whole ham should be soaked for at least 12 hours. A York ham is considered the finest kind, for it has a very mild flavour. Many bacon joints of today are not smoked and therefore do not need soaking before cooking.

To cook boiled bacon or ham: follow the recipe given for Boiled Beef on page 138 and allow the following times:

Forehock and collar........................40 to 45 minutes per 450 g/1 lb.
Gammon and ham..........................20 minutes per 450 g/1 lb.

Time the cooking from when the liquid reaches simmering point.

Serve hot bacon joints or ham with Parsley Sauce or Madeira Sauce (see pages 103 and 160) or Cumberland Sauce (see page 160) with cold ham.

◉ Good Dumplings

Dumplings are generally served with boiled bacon, as with boiled beef. Make these as instructed on page 187. Make sure the dough is slightly softer than when rolling out pastry and the liquid is boiling when the dumplings are placed into the pan.

The basic suet crust pastry from which British dumplings are made can be varied in a number of different ways. Add made mustard and/or chopped fresh herbs. Add a small amount of crisply fried and finely chopped bacon; bind the dough with a smooth tomato or spinach purée instead of water; add a little finely grated cheese.

◉ Glazed Bacon or Ham

The easiest way to coat cooked bacon or ham is to remove the skin and press fine crisp crumbs against the fat, but sweet glazes add to the flavour and appearance.

Bacon or ham should be a very mild cure in order to roast or bake it in the oven, for this method of cooking retains more of the salt flavour. The timing is as for pork on page 117. A more satisfactory method of dealing with bacon or ham joints is to cook them in liquid until almost tender, drain, remove the fat and score (mark it in a neat design), then top the joint with a glaze and bake it for approximately 30 to 40 minutes in the oven set to 180°C/350°F, Gas Mark 4.

Glazes are varied. Try: brown sugar blended with chopped preserved ginger and moistened with syrup from the ginger, or brown sugar, honey and orange juice; or black treacle blended with a little finely crushed pineapple and brown sugar.

◉ Stuffed Lambs' Hearts

Cooking time: 2¹/₄ hours ◉ Serves 4

Although cooking in foil cannot be described as a traditional method, it is a modern development which makes sure the hearts are kept tender on the outside.

Metric Imperial { **Ingredients** } American
4 { **lambs' hearts** } 4
{ **Sage and Onion Stuffing** } (see page 190)
50 g/2 oz { **butter** } ¹/₄ cup

Wash the hearts in running cold water to remove the blood clots, then drain and dry them well. Cut away the arteries, gristle and excess fat. Prepare the stuffing and insert into the hearts. Soften the butter. Cut 4 squares of foil, spread with half the butter. Place a heart in the centre of each piece of foil.

Spread the top of each heart with the remaining butter. Close the foil parcels and put into an ovenproof dish. Preheat the oven to 160°C/325°F, Gas Mark 3. Cook for 2¹/₄ hours then carefully open the foil; lift out the hearts. Serve with thickened gravy (see page 159).

◉ Cottage Pie

Cooking time: 40 minutes ◉ Serves 4

This is a favourite way of using up cooked meat. Peel and finely chop 2 to 3 medium onions. Skin and dice 3 medium tomatoes. Mince approximately 450 g/1 lb cooked beef, or cut into very small dice.

Heat 25 g/1 oz (2 tablespoons) beef dripping or butter in a pan and cook the onions for 5 to 6 minutes, add the tomatoes and cook for 2 minutes. Pour 150 ml/¹/₄ pint (²/₃ cup) beef stock into the pan and blend with the other ingredients. Add the beef and mix well, season to taste and stir in 1 to 2 teaspoons chopped mixed herbs, or ¹/₂ to 1 teaspoon dried herbs. Spoon into a 1.2 litre/2 pint (5 cup) pie dish or individual white ramekin dishes as shown on the front cover of the book.

Spread approximately 450 g/1 lb creamed potatoes over the top of the meat. Add a few small knobs of butter to encourage the topping to become crisp and brown.

Preheat the oven to 180°C/350°F, Gas Mark 4 and bake the pie for 30 minutes.

Variations:
- ◉ **Shepherd's Pie:** use minced lamb instead of beef. Use uncooked meat and rather more stock. Simmer the meat with the onions and tomatoes and stock until tender, then thicken the stock.
- ◉ Add sliced hard-boiled eggs or small mushrooms to the other ingredients.

Bacon and Egg Pie

Cooking time: 35 minutes ⊚ **Serves 4 to 6**

This simple pie combines two of our favourite foods. It is good hot or cold.

Make shortcrust pastry with 350 g/12 oz (3 cups) of flour as the recipe on page 295. Roll out half the pastry and line a 20 cm/8 inch pie plate.

Grill 350 g/12 oz (3/4 lb) bacon rashers. Drain them well and cut into pieces, cool then place over the pastry. Break 4 to 6 eggs over the bacon. Roll out the remaining pastry and very carefully cover the filling. Seal and flute the edges. Brush the pastry with beaten egg. Preheat the oven to 190°C/375°F, Gas Mark 5 and bake for approximately 35 minutes.

Victorian Mutton Pies

Cooking time: 40 minutes plus time to make pastry ⊚ **Makes 6 to 9**

These small pies were originally made with young prime mutton but are equally good with lamb. They were a favourite picnic dish during Victorian days. Some of the old recipes add a peeled, diced apple.

Metric Imperial { **Ingredients** } American
For the filling:
450 g/1 lb { **mutton or lamb, cut from the leg** } 1 lb
150 g/5 oz { **currants, or as required** } generous 3/4 cup
50 g/2 oz { **soft brown sugar** } 1/4 cup
to taste { **salt and freshly ground black pepper** } to taste
For the hot water crust pastry:
350 g/12 oz { **flour, etc.** } (see page 149) 3 cups
To glaze: { **1 egg** }

Cut the mutton or lamb into very small pieces or put it through a coarse mincer. Pour boiling water over the currants and allow to stand while making the pastry, then drain well. Blend the fruit with the sugar and season the meat.

Make the pastry as on page 149. Roll out just over half and cut rounds to line 6 deep patty tins or 9 shallow ones. Keep the rest of the pastry in a warm place (see page 149). Put a layer of meat into the pies, then a layer of currants and sugar. Fill all the pies. Moisten the edges of the pastry.

Roll out the remaining pastry and cut into rounds to make the lids. Place over the filling. Trim away the surplus pastry then seal the edges around the pies. Make slits in the top of the pastry for the steam to escape. Use any surplus pastry to make leaves and press these on top of the pies. Beat the egg and brush over the pastry. Preheat the oven to 200°C/400°F, Gas Mark 6 and bake the pies for 40 minutes. Serve freshly made.

◉ Cornish Pasties

Cooking time: 45 minutes ◉ Serves 4

Cornish Pasties were first made as a well-flavoured and satisfying packed meal for Cornish tin-miners. The original pasties had a filling at one end of meat, similar to that given below, and one the other end of jam or thick fruit pulp. This meant the men had their main course and pudding in one crisp pastry case. Every enthusiast has their own recipe for these. In Cornwall you may be offered sweet pasties, as well as savoury ones. The most popular filling is given below but you could use diced chicken or rabbit instead.

Metric Imperial { **Ingredients** } American
For the shortcrust pastry: 350 g/12 oz { **flour, etc.** } (see page 295) 3 cups
For the filling:
350 g/12 oz { **rump steak** } 3/4 lb
2 { **medium potatoes** } 2
2 { **medium onions** } 2
1/4 { **medium swede, optional**) 1/4
to taste { **salt and freshly ground black pepper** } to taste
to taste { **few mixed chopped herbs, optional** } to taste
2 to 3 teaspoons { **beef stock** } 2 to 3 teaspoons
To glaze: { **1 egg** }

Preheat the oven to 220°C/425°F, Gas Mark 7. Grease a large baking tray. Make the pastry as on page 295. Roll out and cut into 4 rounds about the size of a tea plate or large saucer.

Cut the meat into 1.5 cm/1/2 inch squares. Peel the vegetables and cut into slightly smaller dice. Blend the meat with the vegetables, seasoning and herbs, if using. Moisten with the stock. Place the filling in the centre of the pastry rounds. Moisten the edges of the pastry with water then bring them together to form the upright pastry shape. Seal firmly and flute the edges. Lift carefully on to the baking tray. Beat the egg and brush over the pastry.

Bake for 15 minutes in the very hot oven to ensure crisp pastry, then lower the heat to 160°C/325°F, Gas Mark 3. Bake for a further 30 minutes. Serve hot or cold.

◉ Forfar Bridies

These pasties are as popular in Scotland as Cornish Pasties are in England.

Cut 450 g/1 lb good quality stewing beef into narrow fingers, 2.5 cm/1 inch long and 6 mm/1/4 inch thick. Dice 2 onions, add to the meat with 75 g/3 oz (generous 1/3 cup) shredded suet and seasoning to taste. Fill the pastry rounds with this mixture. Seal and flute the edges but do not glaze the pastry. Make a small hole in the pastry. Bake as Cornish Pasties but allow 30 minutes longer cooking time at the lower setting to make sure the meat is tender. Serve hot.

◉ Steak and Kidney Pie

Cooking time: 2¹/₂ to 3 hours ◉ **Serves 6**

In order to prevent over-cooking the pastry, it is advisable to simmer the two meats beforehand until almost tender. The choice of pastry is entirely a matter for the cook. The best contrast between the meat filling and the topping is flaky pastry.

Metric Imperial { **Ingredients** } American
For the filling:
675 g/1¹/₂ lb {**stewing beef** }1¹/₂ lb
225 g/8 oz { **ox kidney** } ¹/₂ lb
to taste { **salt and freshly ground black pepper** } to taste
25 g/1 oz { **plain flour** } ¹/₄ cup
50 g/2 oz { **beef dripping or butter** } ¹/₄ cup
600 ml/1 pint { **beef stock** } 2¹/₂ cups
For the flaky pastry: 225 g/8 oz { **flour, etc.** } (see page 296) 2 cups
To glaze: { **1 egg** }

Cut the steak into 2.5 to 4 cm/1 to 1¹/₂ inch dice and the kidney into slightly smaller pieces. Mix the salt, pepper and flour and coat the two meats. Heat the dripping or butter in a saucepan, add the meats and stir over a low heat for 5 to 10 minutes until golden brown. Pour in the stock. Stir as the liquid comes to the boil and thickens slightly.

Cover the saucepan and simmer gently for 1¹/₂ hours, or until both meats are just tender. Do not overcook them. Lift the meat into a 1.2 litre/2 pint (5 cup) pie dish. Cover with gravy, but do not overfill the pie dish – any extra gravy can be served separately. Cover to prevent the meat drying, and cool.

Make the pastry, roll out and cover the pie. Use any trimmings for leaves and a pastry rose to decorate the pie; make a slit in the top of the pastry. Beat the egg and glaze the pastry. Preheat the oven to 220°C/425°F, Gas Mark 7. Bake for 15 to 20 minutes, or until the pastry has risen. Lower the heat to 180°C/350°F, Gas Mark 4 and bake for a further 25 minutes or until the pastry is firm and crisp and the filling heated. If necessary place foil over the pastry and heat the pie for slightly longer to make sure the meat filling is hot.

Variations:
- Use some red wine when cooking the meat instead of all stock.
- Simmer 1 to 2 chopped onions with the meat and add 100 g/4 oz (1 cup) button mushrooms to the cooked meat before covering the pie with pastry.

๏ Fidget Pie

Cooking time: 1¼ hours ๏ **Serves 4 to 6**

This pie is often known as a Fitchett pie, it does not refer to any of the ingredients but it may well have been called after the 'fitched' dish (a five-sided container) in which it was baked. Potatoes are an optional extra in the filling; if omitted increase the amount of onions.

Metric Imperial { **Ingredients** } American
450 g/1 lb { **unsmoked gammon or back bacon** } 1 lb
350 g/12 oz { **potatoes** } ¾ lb
225 g/8 oz { **onions** } ½ lb
350 g/12 oz { **cooking apples** } ¾ lb
25 g/1 oz { **butter** } 2 tablespoons
150 ml/¼ pint { **brown stock** } (see page 126) ⅔ cup
to taste { **salt and freshly ground black pepper** } to taste
2 teaspoons { **brown sugar, or to taste** } 2 teaspoons
1 teaspoon { **chopped thyme or ½ teaspoon dried thyme** } 1 teaspoon
For the shortcrust pastry: 225 g/8 oz { **flour, etc.** }(see page 295) 2 cups
To glaze: { **1 egg** }

Buy the bacon in a single slice if possible so it can be cut into dice. If already cut into rashers, then divide these into smaller pieces. Peel the potatoes, onions and apples, core these too. Cut these ingredients into thin slices. Heat the butter and cook the onions for 5 minutes. Arrange the vegetables and bacon in layers in a 1.2 litre/2 pint (5 cup) pie dish. Blend the stock with seasoning, sugar and thyme. Pour over the ingredients in the dish.

Roll out the pastry and cover the pie. Use any pastry left to make leaves and a rose to decorate the top of the pastry. Make a slit in the pastry.

Beat the egg and brush over the pastry. Preheat the oven to 200°C/400°F, Gas Mark 6. Bake the pie for 25 minutes, then lower the heat to 180°C/350°F, Gas Mark 4 and continue cooking for a further 50 minutes. This long time is necessary as the filling is very substantial and the ingredients are uncooked. If the pie is becoming too brown, cover the top with a sheet of foil.

Serve the pie hot. Although it is not a classic accompaniment, Cumberland Sauce goes well with the bacon filling (see page 160).

Variation:
๏ **Lamb Fidget Pie:** Put 4 to 6 small lamb cutlets in the centre of the other ingredients in the filling and reduce the amount of bacon slightly.

Steak and Kidney Pudding

Cooking time: 4 to 4½ hours ● **Serves 6**

This is one of the most famous of all British meat dishes. Its reputation is well deserved, for it is a delicious combination of light steamed pastry and a rich meat filling.

Metric Imperial { **Ingredients** } American
For the suet crust pastry:
300 g/10 oz { **flour, etc.** }(see page 187) 2½ cups
For the filling:
675 g/1½ lb { **stewing beef** } 1½ lb
225 g/8 oz { **ox kidney** } ½ lb
2 tablespoons { **plain flour** } 2½ tablespoons
to taste { **salt and freshly ground black pepper** } to taste
3 to 4 tablespoons { **beef stock or water** } 4 to 5 tablespoons

Make the suet crust pastry as on page 187. The classic way of blending the meats was to cut long narrow strips of steak and small pieces of kidney, which would be put on each piece of steak and formed into a roll, so distributing the meats evenly. This method takes rather a long time, so instead cut the two meats into 2.5 to 4 cm/1 to 1½ inch cubes and mix together. Blend the flour, salt and pepper and lightly coat the meat.

Roll out the pastry and use just under three-quarters to line the base and sides of a 1.5 litre/2½ pint (6¼ cup) lightly greased basin. Put in the meat and stock or water, this should come three-quarters of the way up the meat filling.

Roll out the remaining pastry into a round to fit the top of the basin. Moisten the edges of the pastry and seal together. Cover with greased greaseproof paper and foil. Put a pleat in these coverings to accommodate the pudding as it rises during cooking. Tie with string around the neck of the basin. Steam over boiling water for 4 to 4¼ hours. The water should boil rapidly for the first 2 hours so the suet crust rises, after which the water can simmer. Keep the saucepan under the steamer well-filled with boiling water.

Traditionally the pudding is served in the basin with a white napkin secured around this. Serve with thickened gravy or Port Wine Sauce (see pages 159-60).

Steak and Game Pudding

Use 550 g/1¼ lb steak and the flesh from a large pheasant or other game birds.

Steak, Kidney and Oyster Pudding

This was the great Victorian favourite. Lift the covers and the top pastry 20 minutes before serving and add 12 small oysters. Replace the covers and continue cooking.

◉ Melton Mowbray Pork Pie

Cooking time: 2¹/2 hours ◉ Serves 6

This is a famous raised pie. It was first made by a baker in Melton Mowbray, Leicestershire, in 1830. The inclusion of salt and anchovy fillets with pork is unusual but very successful.

Metric Imperial { **Ingredients** } American
675 g/1¹/2 lb { **lean boneless pork, from the leg** } 1¹/2 lb
225 g/8 oz { **fat boneless pork, from the belly** } ¹/2 lb
6 to 8 { **anchovy fillets** } 6 to 8
3 tablespoons { **white stock** } (see page 126) 4¹/4 tablespoons
to taste { **salt and freshly ground black pepper** } to taste
For the hot water crust pastry: 350 g/12 oz { **flour, etc.** } (see page 149) 3 cups
To glaze the pastry: { **1 egg** }
For the jelly:
150 ml/¹/4 pint { **white stock** } (see page 127) ²/3 cup
1 teaspoon { **gelatine** } 1 teaspoon

Dice both kinds of pork and blend together. Chop the anchovy fillets and mix with the meat, add the stock. Allow to stand while making the pastry. Season with very little, if any, salt but with pepper. Make the hot water crust pastry as on page 149.

Preheat the oven to 160°C/325°F, Gas Mark 3. Lightly grease an 18 cm/7 inch round tin with a loose base or a proper raised pie spring form tin, which is usually oval. Roll out two-thirds of the dough (keep the rest warm). Cut a shape to fit the base of the tin, and a band the depth and circumference of the sides. Insert the pastry in the tin, moisten and seal the edges. Moisten the top edges of the pastry.

Put in the filling. Roll out the remaining pastry and cut out the lid. Place over the filling and seal the edges. Beat the egg and brush over the pastry.

Traditionally this kind of pie is decorated with pastry leaves and a rose or tassel, so make these from the left-over pastry. Make a slit in the centre of the pastry lid for the steam to escape. Press the leaves and rose or tassel on top of the pie, brush with egg.

Bake for 2¹/2 hours. Lower the heat slightly after 2 hours, if the pastry is becoming too brown. Allow the pie to become quite cold.

Pour the 150 ml/¹/4 pint (²/3 cup) stock into a basin, add the gelatine, stand for 2 to 3 minutes then dissolve over hot water. Cool until like a thick syrup. Insert a small funnel into the slit in the pastry lid and pour the jelly through this. Leave the pie in the refrigerator for several hours for the jelly to set, then serve cold with salad.

⊙ Hot Water Crust Pastry

Cooking time: as specific recipes

This pastry is made by melting the fat in the water, then adding the flour. It is ideal for cold savoury pies. The pastry must be kept warm during rolling and shaping to prevent it breaking. It is also known as raised pie pastry.

Metric Imperial { **Ingredients** } American
350 g/12 oz { **plain flour** } 3 cups
1/4 teaspoon { **salt** } 1/4 teaspoon
100 g/4 oz { **lard or cooking fat** } 1 cup
150 ml/1/4 pint { **milk or water** } 2/3 cup

Sift the flour and salt into a mixing bowl. Put the lard or cooking fat into a saucepan with the milk or water and heat until melted. Remove the pan from the heat then add all the flour to the hot mixture, stir well until blended. Allow the dough to cool slightly, so it can be handled, then knead until smooth. Place the portion required for the base and sides of a pie on a lightly floured board and roll out to desired shape. Keep the rest of the pastry, which may be needed for the lid of a pie, in a warm place. Shape and bake as specific recipes.

Variation:
⊙   You can add an egg yolk for extra flavour without affecting the amount of liquid.

⊙ Veal and Ham Pie

Cooking time: 2 1/2 hours ⊙ Serves 6

To make the Veal and Ham Pie follow the pastry recipe above.

For the filling use a total of 900 g/2 lb veal and ham – this can be equal quantities of each meat or 675 g/1 1/2 lb of veal and 225 g/8 oz (1/2 lb) cooked ham. The meats should be diced and mixed together. The method of filling then baking the pie is as given for the Melton Mowbray Pork Pie (see page 148), but anchovy fillets should be omitted. The stock can be flavoured with a little finely grated lemon zest. It is usual to hard-boil 2 to 4 eggs and put these in the centre of the meat.

When cold the pie is filled with a jellied stock (see page 148).

⊙ Veal, Ham and Chicken Pie

Another less usual version of this pie is made by using approximately 675 g/1 1/2 lb thinly sliced uncooked chicken flesh and layering this with the mixture given for Potted Veal and Ham (see page 13). Bake as the Melton Mowbray Pork Pie (see page 148).

⊙ Toad-in-the-hole

Cooking time: 40 to 45 minutes ⊙ Serves 4

This is a recipe that has changed a great deal over the years. Once it consisted of chops, or a variety of meats, cooked in batter, rather than the sausages of today.

To make sure of a light, crisp and well-cooked dish check that the sausages, or meats, are really hot before adding the batter. You can also cook as individual portions in a four-hole tin.

Metric Imperial { **Ingredients** } American
For the batter:
175 g/6 oz { **plain flour** } 1¹/2 cups
good pinch { **salt** } good pinch
2 { **eggs** } 2
450 ml/³/4 pint { **milk** } 2 cups
For the filling:
2 teaspoons { **oil or a small knob of lard or fat** } 2 teaspoons
450 g/1 lb { **sausages** } 1 lb

Sift the flour and salt into a basin, add the eggs one at a time and beat well, then gradually add the milk. Whisk briskly to give a smooth batter. Allow to stand for a time before cooking. Always whisk the batter before pouring it into the dish, as the flour tends to sink to the bottom of the liquid mixture.

Preheat the oven to 220°C/425°F, Gas Mark 7. Put the oil, lard or fat, into a shallow, oblong 1.2 litre/2 pint (5 cup) casserole or tin and heat for about 3 minutes. Add the sausages and turn in the heated fat. Cook for 5 minutes if small and 10 minutes if large. Add the batter and cook for a further 25 to 30 minutes until well-risen and golden brown. Check after 15 to 20 minutes and lower the heat slightly if the batter is becoming too brown. Lift out of the tin or dish, cut into portions. Serve with gravy or Tomato Sauce (see page 194).

⊙ Luxury-Toad-In-the-Hole

Use 3 lambs' kidneys, 3 rashers of bacon with 3 large sausages and 6 small lamb cutlets instead of the 450 g/1 lb of sausages in the recipe above.

Skin and halve the kidneys, remove all gristle. De-rind the bacon rashers, halve and make into small rolls. Halve the sausages.

Heat the oil or fat, then add the lamb cutlets and sausages. Cook for 5 minutes. Put in the kidneys and bacon rolls and allow a further 5 minutes cooking before adding the batter. Continue as the recipe above. This serves 6 people.

⊙ Cumberland Sausage

Cooking time: 15 minutes ⊙ Serves 4

A Cumberland sausage is only one of the many varieties made in Britain. Most butchers have their own recipes and there is a very large range of flavours available for our traditional 'bangers' as they are affectionately known. Pork has always been the favourite meat; but today you can purchase sausages made with beef, lamb, turkey, venison and other meats. A Cumberland sausage is interesting in that it is wide as well as being about 30 cm/12 inches in length, whereas most sausages are sufficiently small to obtain 6 to 8 to a 450 g/1 lb. With chipolata sausages you have almost double that number. While most sausages are cooked whole, Cumberland sausage is sliced.

There are many ways of cooking sausages – they can be fried, grilled, baked, simmered in water or used instead of meat in casseroles and stews. The method below is one of the quickest and easiest. Sausagemeat forms part of a favourite stuffing for poultry (see page 189) and Sausage Rolls, a favourite savoury (see page 223). It is quite easy to make sausages at home.

Metric Imperial { **Ingredients** } American
1 { **Cumberland sausage** } 1
8 { **bacon rashers** } 8

Cut the sausage into about 8 slices; de-rind the bacon. Heat the bacon rinds for 2 to 3 minutes in a frying pan, then add the sliced sausage and fry steadily for about 5 minutes on both sides. Remove the bacon rinds, add the bacon rashers and continue cooking for 2 to 3 minutes. Serve with mashed potatoes.

Variations:
⊙ **Wiltshire Porkies:** although sliced Cumberland sausage can be used for this dish, it is traditional to make it with sausagemeat. Divide 450 g/1 lb sausagemeat into 8 portions, form these into balls and coat in a little flour.

Blend 175 g/6 oz (1½ cups) plain flour, pinch salt, 1 egg yolk, 1 teaspoon oil and 150 ml/¼ pint (⅔ cup) water together. Heat a deep pan of oil to 175°C/350°F.

Just before cooking the sausage balls, whisk 1 egg white and fold this into the batter. Coat the sausages and fry for 6 to 7 minutes. Meanwhile, coat apple rings in batter and fry for 3 to 4 minutes. Garnish with parsley.

⊙ **Home-made Sausages:** finely mince 450 g/1 lb lean pork, or other lean meat with at least 100 g/4 oz (¼ lb) fat pork or other fat meat – this is necessary to keep the mixture moist. Add finely chopped sage, or other herbs, and a pinch of allspice.

The mixture binds without an egg but this can be added; also a small amount of fine breadcrumbs if desired. Casings are obtainable from butchers and the mixture should be inserted in these or formed into shapes and coated in seasoned flour.

◉ Haggis

Cooking time: 4¹/2 hours ◉ **Serves 6 to 8**

Haggis is famous throughout the world; it is known as the national dish of Scotland. In the commercially made haggis the sheep's lights (part of the pluck) are cooked with the liver and heart.

Haggis has become popular in other parts of Britain as well as in Scotland. Insert a little cooked haggis into the neck cavity of a chicken or turkey to give a flavoursome stuffing. Small portions of haggis make an interesting first course served with Apple and Beetroot Salad (page 211).

Metric Imperial { **Ingredients** } American
450 g/1 lb { **lambs' liver** } 1 lb
350 g/12 oz { **lambs' hearts** } ³/4 lb
350 g/12 oz { **onions** } ³/4 lb
to taste { **salt and freshly ground black pepper** } to taste
450 ml/³/4 pint { **stock, see method** } scant 2 cups
175 g/6 oz { **fine (pinhead) oatmeal** } 1 cup
225 g/8 oz { **suet** } ¹/2 lb
1¹/2 teaspoons { **chopped fresh or ³/4 teaspoon dried sage** } 1¹/2 teaspoons
¹/2 teaspoon { **chopped fresh or ¹/4 teaspoon dried thyme** } ¹/2 teaspoon
to taste { **cayenne pepper** } to taste

Slice the liver. Wash the hearts and remove all the gristle and arteries. Peel the onions. Put these ingredients into a saucepan with enough water to cover them and a generous amount of salt and pepper. Cover the pan and simmer for 1 hour. Strain the liquid and measure out 450 ml/³/4 pint (scant 2 cups). Put the meat and onions through a mincer or chop in a food processor.

Heat the oatmeal in a frying pan until golden brown, stirring well. Mince or finely chop the suet. Blend the ingredients together, season and put into a well-greased 1.8 litre/3 pint (7¹/2 cup) basin. Cover with foil and steam for 3 hours. Turn out and serve with mashed swedes, called 'neeps' in Scotland.

To heat a ready-cooked haggis: prick the coating so the filling does not break through. Put into simmering water and simmer for 45 minutes. Spoon the haggis on to a heated plate.

If the haggis is firm in texture, slice it and fry in a little hot butter.

⊙ Faggots

Cooking time: 13/4 hours ⊙ **Serves 4 to 6**

These small meat cakes have been popular for generations. Sometimes they are known as Savoury Ducks, as their flavour is not unlike that of a duck. Pease Pudding (see page 205) is the usual accompaniment.

The traditional butcher's faggots are wrapped individually in a pig's caul (the thin membrane covering the lower intestines), but the following method of cooking them is satisfactory.

Metric Imperial { **Ingredients** } American
1 { **large onion** } 1
350 g/12 oz { **pig's liver** } 3/4 lb
100 g/4 oz { **pig's heart** } 1/4 lb
100 g/4 oz { **fat belly of pork or fat bacon** } 1/4 lb
450 ml/3/4 pint { **water** } 2 cups
to taste { **salt and freshly ground black pepper** } to taste
good pinch { **ground ginger** } good pinch
1/2 teaspoon { **chopped sage** } 1/2 teaspoon
1/4 teaspoon { **chopped thyme** } 1/4 teaspoon
50 g/2 oz { **soft breadcrumbs** } 1 cup
1 { **egg** } 1

Peel and slice the onion, slice all the meats. Put the onion and meats into a saucepan with the water and a little seasoning. Cover the pan and simmer gently for approximately 45 minutes, or until tender. Strain the liquid, do not discard as a little may be required.

Put the onion and meats through a mincer or chop in a food processor. Add the ginger, herbs, breadcrumbs and beaten egg. If the mixture seems a little dry, moisten with a small amount of the reserved stock. The rest of the stock can be used to make a gravy.

Grease a tin or ovenproof container about 18 to 20 cm/7 to 8 inches square. Preheat the oven to 190°C/375°F, Gas Mark 5. Spread the mixture evenly in the tin, then mark it into about 12 small portions. Cut deeply so these are easily removed when cooked. Cover the tin or dish with a lid or foil and bake for 1 hour.

Carefully lift the faggots from the container and serve hot with gravy and Pease Pudding (see page 205).

Variation:
⊙   Use fine oatmeal or rolled (porridge) oats instead of breadcrumbs. These give a nutty flavour to the mixture.

◉ Rissoles

Cooking time: 20 minutes ◉ **Serves 4**

This is a well-known way of turning a relatively small amount of left-over cooked beef or other meat, poultry or game into an appetizing dish.

Metric Imperial { **Ingredients** } American
450 g/1 lb { **cooked beef or other meat** } 1 lb
1 to 2 { **medium onions** }1 to 2
2 { **medium tomatoes, optional** } 2
25 g/1 oz { **butter or dripping** } 2 tablespoons
25 g/1 oz { **plain flour** } 1/4 cup
150 ml/1/4 pint { **stock, the flavour depends upon the meat used** } 2/3 cup
1 to 2 teaspoons { **chopped parsley, or other herb** } 1 to 2 teaspoons
to taste { **salt and freshly ground black pepper** } to taste
To coat the rissoles:
1 tablespoon { **plain flour** } 11/4 tablespoons
1 { **egg** } 1
50 g/2 oz { **crisp breadcrumbs** } 1 cup
To fry: little { **oil or fat** }

Mince the meat, peel and finely chop the onion(s). Skin, halve and deseed the tomatoes. Heat the butter or dripping in a saucepan and cook the onion and tomatoes until soft. Add the flour and blend well with the ingredients in the pan. Gradually stir in the stock, and continue stirring until the mixture thickens. Remove the pan from the heat, add the meat, herbs and seasoning to taste.

Divide the mixture into 8 portions, chill for a short time. Form into neat round cakes and coat in the flour, then the beaten egg and crumbs. Chill again if possible. Heat the oil or fat in a frying pan; cook the rissoles quickly until crisp and brown on both sides; lower the heat and cook for a few minutes. Drain on absorbent paper and serve.

Variations:
- ◉   Use a little less meat and add 50 g/2 oz (1 cup) soft breadcrumbs to the mixture.
- ◉   Omit the tomatoes and use milk when making the sauce instead of stock. This is particularly suitable with cooked chicken or turkey instead of meat.
- ◉   Form the mixture into finger-shapes (known as croquettes), coat as above and deep fry in hot oil.

⊚ Pressed Ox Tongue

Cooking time: approximately 3 hours plus soaking time ⊚ **Serves 8 to 10**
A whole ox tongue, pressed and glazed with jelly makes an excellent dish for a cold buffet. Lambs' tongues have a very good flavour and can be served hot or cold.

Metric Imperial { **Ingredients** } American
1 { **salted ox tongue** } 1
2 { **medium onions** } 2
2 to 3 { **medium carrots** } 2 to 3
2 { **fresh bay leaves or 1 dried bay leaf** } 2
1 { **strip of lemon rind, optional** } 1
1 teaspoon { **black peppercorns** } 1 teaspoon
1 teaspoon { **gelatine** } 1 teaspoon

Put the tongue in cold water to cover and soak for 12 hours. Discard the water and put the tongue into a saucepan with fresh cold water to cover. Peel the onions and carrots, add to the water with the bay leaves, lemon rind and peppercorns.

Bring the water in the saucepan to the boil, remove any scum, cover the pan and allow the liquid to simmer gently for 3 hours, or until the tongue is tender when tested with the tip of a knife. Make sure the tongue is covered with water throughout the cooking period.

Lift the tongue from the liquid, cool sufficiently to handle then remove all the skin and the small bones at the root of the tongue. Roll the tongue round to fit tightly into a cake tin or saucepan. Boil the stock until just 150 ml/1/4 pint (2/3 cup) remains, then strain. Soften the gelatine in 4 tablespoons (5 tablespoons) cold water, add to the very hot stock, and stir until dissolved. Pour over the tongue. Put a small plate on top of the tongue to help it to form a good shape. Leave until cold then invert on to a serving dish. Serve with mixed salads.

⊚ Tongue in Madeira Sauce

Make the sauce as on page 160, but use a little extra stock and Madeira wine, for the liquid evaporates during the heating process. Add slices of cooked tongue and simmer in the sauce for 5 to 10 minutes. Serve with pickled walnuts.

⊙ Galantine of Beef

Cooking time: 2 hours ⊙ Serves 6 to 8

A Galantine is defined as a dish of boned meat, jellied and served cold. That rather soulless description does not do justice to the many recipes that have been made in Britain for generations. This is an ideal dish for a buffet or picnic meal.

Metric Imperial { **Ingredients** } American
225 g/8 oz { **lean bacon rashers, without rinds** } 1/2 lb
450 g/1 lb { **topside of beef or fresh brisket** } 1 lb
225 g/8 oz { **pork or beef sausage meat** } 1/2 lb
50 g/2 oz { **soft breadcrumbs** } 1 cup
1 teaspoon { **chopped fresh sage** } 1 teaspoon
2 { **eggs** } 2
little { **beef stock, see method** } little
to taste { **salt and freshly ground black pepper** } to taste

Dice the rashers. Cut the meat into small pieces and put through a mincer with the bacon or chop in a food processor. Blend with the sausagemeat, breadcrumbs and sage. Beat the eggs, mix with the other ingredients then add enough stock to make a soft mixture, but one that can be moulded if desired. Add seasoning to taste.

Traditionally the meat mixture was formed into a neat roll and covered in a buttered cloth. It is easier to place it into a greased 1.2 litre/2 pint (5 cup) mould and cover this with greased greaseproof paper and foil. Either place in a steamer over boiling water or on an upturned saucer in a large saucepan, partially filled with boiling water. Make sure this only comes halfway up the mould. Steam for 2 hours. Add more water as required. Remove from the pan and allow to become quite cold. Unwrap or unmould. To give a more professional appearance, and to keep the meat moist, coat in aspic jelly as described below.

⊙ Galantine of Chicken

Substitute 450 g/1 lb chicken meat (weight without skin and bones) for the beef. Choose pork sausagemeat. Substitute chopped parsley or chervil for the sage. Bind the mixture with the beaten eggs, then with a mixture of equal amounts of chicken stock and double cream. Cook as above.

⊙ To coat in Aspic Jelly

Use about 450 ml/3/4 pint (2 cups) of aspic jelly. Allow this to cool until it is the consistency of a thick syrup. Place the mould on a wire cooling tray with a large dish underneath to catch any drips. Brush enough jelly over the meat mixture to give a thin coating. Allow to set in the refrigerator. Repeat this process with a second layer of jelly.

⊙ Veal Brawn

Cooking time: 3 hours plus soaking time ⊙ Serves 8

In Dorothy Hartley's book, *Food in England* she quotes the *Boke of Nurture*, dated 1460. The author Russell says 'Set forth mustard and brawne'. Brawns made from veal, pig's or lamb's head have always been a favourite recipe for farmer's wives to make. The men took slices of brawn into the fields to eat with bread or potatoes and plenty of mustard sauce. It is an ideal summer dish.

Metric Imperial { **Ingredients** } American
1 { **calf's head** } 1
to taste { **salt** } to taste
2 { **small onions** } 2
2 { **medium carrots** } 2
1 to 2 teaspoons { **black peppercorns** } 1 to 2 teaspoons
to taste { **mixed herbs, see method** } to taste
1 { **lemon** } 1
225 g/8 oz { **stewing steak, optional** } 1/2 lb

Split the head down the centre. Wash in cold water then soak for 1 hour in lightly salted cold water. Remove the white brains, these can be cooked separately if desired.

Peel the onions and carrots, but leave them whole. Lift the head from the water in which it was soaked, put into a large saucepan with the vegetables and fresh cold water to cover. Add the peppercorns and a good pinch of salt, together with a mixture of herbs. Veal has a delicate flavour so do not overwhelm this with too many herbs. Choose a small bunch of parsley, 1 to 2 sprigs of thyme and 2 fresh or 1 dried bay leaf. Pare 2 to 3 strips of zest, without any bitter pith, from the lemon, add to the herbs and tie in a muslin bag. Cover the pan.

Simmer gently for 1 1/2 hours. Dice the steak, if using this, add to the pan and continue cooking for a further 1 1/2 hours. Allow the meat to cool sufficiently to handle, lift from the liquid. Boil this briskly while preparing the meat from the head, so it is reduced to about 450 ml/3/4 pint (2 cups). Strain this and then halve the lemon, squeeze out the juice and add a little to the stock.

Take away all the meat from the bones, skin the tongue. Cut the veal and steak into neat dice. Pack into a basin, add sufficient stock to cover and allow to set.

⊙ Lamb's Brawn

Use a lamb's head. Omit the steak from the recipe above. Add a sprig of mint to the other herbs. There is a smaller amount of meat, so the brawn serves 4 to 6 people.

⊙ Pork Brawn

Use a pig's head. Omit the steak from the recipe on page 158. Add 2 sprigs of sage to the other herbs and a little chopped celery to the vegetables. Omit the lemon and flavour the stock with a good pinch of grated nutmeg and a blade of mace.

◎ Onion Gravy

This adds flavour to many dishes. Chop one or more onions finely and cook slowly in a little fat from the meat or in oil. When soft, continue as Good Gravy below. Chopped garlic can be added or use shallots for a milder flavour.

◎ Good Gravy

Cooking time: 15 minutes ◎ Serves 6

Many a splendid roast meal is spoiled by a poor gravy. This should be perfectly smooth, very hot and not over-thickened. Modern tastes are for less thickened sauces, which includes gravy. Always taste the gravy, for often a little extra flavouring will improve it.

The stock should complement the meat, i.e. beef stock with beef, etc., but if no stock is available use the liquid from cooking vegetables, to make sure that this nutritionally valuable liquid is not wasted.

◎ **To make gravy:** pour away all the dripping from the meat tin, except 1½ tablespoons (2 tablespoons) but retain all the residue from the meat.

◎ **For a thin gravy:** blend 1½ level tablespoons (2 tablespoons) plain flour into the dripping and cook gently, stirring all the time, until it turns brown. Gradually blend in 600 ml/1 pint (2½ cups) stock and stir until thickened then strain the gravy. Reheat with seasoning and any extra flavourings needed.

◎ **For a thicker gravy:** follow the directions for a thin gravy but increase the amount of flour to 2 to 3 tablespoons (2½ to 3½ tablespoons).

◎ **To add extra flavour:** there are many gravy flavourings and meat stock cubes on the market that help to add flavour, but so do the following:

◎ **Beef:** add a little red wine and made mustard.

◎ **Lamb and pork:** a slightly sweet flavour blends with these meats, add a little redcurrant jelly and/or sweet sherry.

◎ **Veal, chicken and turkey:** add a little dry sherry or dash of white vermouth.

◎ **Duck and goose:** add a little red or port wine and apple or redcurrant jelly.

◎ **Game birds:** as for chicken or turkey, or one of the sauces on pages 191 to 194.

◎ **Venison:** as for beef, or use the special sauce on page 193.

◎ Mint Sauce

No cooking ◎ Serves 4 to 6

Finely chop a good handful of young mint leaves. Add 1 tablespoon (1¼ tablespoons) caster sugar and white malt vinegar to cover. Leave standing for a short time, so the sugar dissolves. The sauce can be made in a liquidizer.

⊙ Cumberland Sauce

Cooking time: 25 minutes ⊙ Serves 4 to 6

Pare the rind from 2 medium oranges and 1 lemon (a potato peeler is ideal for this). Discard any white pith, use just the top zest. Cut this into narrow matchstick pieces. Soak in 225 ml/8 fl oz (1 cup) water for 15 minutes then tip into a saucepan and simmer for 15 minutes. Halve the fruit, squeeze out the juice and blend with 1 teaspoon English mustard powder and 1 teaspoon arrowroot. Add to the ingredients in the pan with 4 tablespoons (5 tablespoons) port wine and 4 tablespoons (5 tablespoons) redcurrant jelly (or to taste). Stir over a low heat as the sauce thickens and becomes clear. Serve cold. This is excellent with hot or cold ham, game, other meats and pâtés.

⊙ Oxford Sauce

This is a similar basic mixture. Add a good shake of cayenne pepper, 2 tablespoons (3 tablespoons) quartered glacé cherries and 1/2 to 1 teaspoon Worcestershire sauce. This is excellent with cold game.

⊙ Madeira Sauce

Cooking time: 20 minutes ⊙ Serves 4 to 6

Heat 25 g/1 oz (2 tablespoons) butter or meat dripping in a saucepan, stir in 25 g/1 oz (1/4 cup) flour and cook gently for 2 to 3 minutes. Gradually blend in 225 ml/7 1/2 fl oz (scant 1 cup) ham, beef or game stock and 225 ml/7 1/2 fl oz (scant 1 cup) sweet or dry Madeira. Stir or whisk as the sauce comes to the boil and thickens. Add seasoning to taste and simmer gently for 10 minutes.

⊙ Port Wine Sauce

Cooking time: 15 minutes ⊙ Serves 4 to 6

Put 100 g/4 oz (3/4 cup) sultanas or raisins into a basin, add 150 ml/1/4 pint (2/3 cup) port wine and allow to stand for 15 minutes. Meanwhile, put 1 tablespoon (1 1/4 tablespoons) dripping from the meat tin, 300 ml/1/2 pint (1 1/4 cups) brown stock (see page 126) and 25 g/1 oz (1/2 cup) breadcrumbs into a saucepan. Bring to the boil, allow to stand for 10 minutes. Add the port wine and fruit, then stir briskly as the sauce heats and the breadcrumbs thicken the sauce. Season to taste. This is excellent with most meats.

Poultry and Game Dishes

The kind of chickens we can buy today are very different from those of the past. Although there were plump young chickens suitable for roasting, many of the birds available were elderly, contained a great deal of fat and were sold primarily for boiling. Their great virtue was that they had real flavour. Nowadays it is virtually impossible to obtain these fat birds unless you rear them yourself. The birds of today are all young, so suitable for roasting and other means of cooking. If they are 'boiled', as on page 176, they should be cooked gently for a limited time only, otherwise the flesh breaks.

After years of having chickens reared intensively, there is now a great demand by the public to return to the flavour of the birds of the past and many poulterers and supermarkets specialize in offering 'free-range' birds. These are bred under more natural conditions and have free movement rather than being restrained in cages. Frozen chickens and frozen turkeys are always available and, although they lack some of the taste and texture of fresh birds, they are a means of producing economical and nutritious meals throughout the year. That is one of the great changes in the way we regard chickens and turkeys. Once these were a special treat for the average family; today they are cheaper than meat. Roast turkey is still the favourite dish for Christmas and at that time of the year there is a wide choice; turkey farmers produce magnificent fresh birds.

The availability of a range of chicken and turkey portions, such as breast slices which can be cooked like escalopes, or chicken legs that are ideal for grilling or barbecueing, has created a whole range of new dishes, such as those on page 171. The classic stuffings and sauces for chicken and turkey are on pages 188 to 194, and these enhance the flavour of the birds. Guinea fowl is a bird that can be served with the same accompaniments as chicken but it is equally good when treated like a game bird. Either method is appropriate for the flavour of a guinea fowl, which is really a combination of chicken and a game bird. Take particular care when cooking to keep it moist – be generous with the butter or fat bacon used to cover the bird in cooking.

Ducks have become very much more popular during the last few years, chiefly because they are bred to produce 'meaty' birds with a far smaller proportion of fat. Like geese, they must be cooked carefully, so that any excess fat runs out of the bird. The fat from goose should be cherished as a valuable commodity. Unlike the fat from other poultry it becomes firm when cold and it is ideal for general cooking purposes, including roasting potatoes. Geese were once the favourite bird for Christmas, as well as for Michaelmas celebrations. They have now been surpassed by turkey, but good geese are still available and they are becoming popular once more. The interesting recipe for Duckling with Green Pea Sauce on page 167, which originated many years ago, was passed on to me by Cherry Valley Farms who have done so much to popularize ducks in Britain and overseas.

Country people can still obtain a good range of game birds but town-dwellers found this quite difficult until recently. There is so much interest in cooking game that first-class poulterers and supermarkets are now stocking some of the less well-known varieties, as well as the more plentiful pheasant and quail. The season for game birds is short and it is well worth obtaining and cooking these during the winter months. The classic fried Game Chips and Fried Crumbs are ideal to complement the lean flesh of the birds and other winter commodities, such as Brussels sprouts, chestnuts and celeriac which also make excellent accompaniments.

Jugged Hare is one of the oldest classical dishes, for until recent years hares abounded in the countryside. The method of 'jugging' is not confined to hare; other game can be cooked in the same way, as can beef, venison and rabbits with slight adjustments to the flavourings (see page 180). The title refers to the large stone jug, which was a familiar utensil in kitchens of the past. It was sufficiently deep to hold the large portions of hare and other foods. A hare provides a number of portions so it is possible to use just the legs of the hare for jugging (casseroling) and the back, known as the saddle, for roasting.

Rabbits have always been appreciated by country people, for their economy and flavour. There are several recipes using rabbit in this chapter.

Venison has become very plentiful during the last few years, so the classic recipes of the past can be revived. Both wild and farmed venison are sold. Undoubtedly the farmed variety has a more consistent flavour and it is more tender. This is why marinating the flesh before cooking is not essential but it should be done with the wild type. A marinade has more than one advantage though; the primary purpose is to tenderize meat but the oil in the classic type of mixture also keeps the lean meat beautifully moist. Suitable cuts of venison can be roasted, grilled, fried or put into a casserole, just like other meats. The flavour is not unlike that of beef. Treat tender fillets of farmed venison like fillet steak.

◙ To Roast Poultry

All types of poultry are suitable for roasting and, while cooking times are similar, chicken, turkey and guinea fowl need completely different treatment from duck and goose. The first three kinds of birds contain relatively little fat and it is important to roast them in such a way that they do not become dry during cooking. Although the ducks and geese one buys today are carefully reared so they contain less fat than those of years ago, they still have a fairly high proportion of natural fat and could be greasy after cooking, if the right technique is not followed. Information on achieving perfect results is given on page 166.

If you have purchased frozen birds it is essential that they are completely defrosted before cooking. To roast a partially defrosted bird could be a dangerous health hazard, as harmful bacteria might not be destroyed in cooking.

Recently it has been found that it is unwise to place stuffing inside the body of the bird, whether fresh or defrosted after freezing, because the stuffing often prevents the correct heat reaching the centre of the bird. Put stuffing into the skin of neck end only and bake other stuffings in a separate container. An interesting way to stuff the bird before cooking is to spread it under the skin of the breast. Gently loosen the skin with the tip of your finger, taking care not to break it, and then spread the stuffing over the flesh and under the skin.

Weigh the bird after inserting stuffing to calculate the cooking time. This is given under two headings: FAST – which is a relatively high temperature, suitable for fresh poultry and LESS FAST – which is better for defrosted frozen birds. It must be stressed that any timings must be approximate. Birds vary in their tenderness and plumpness and it is wise to test the flesh before deciding the bird is cooked. Insert the tip of a knife where the leg joins the body and check the colour of the juice that runs out. If pink the bird is not quite cooked.

If you use a covered roasting tin or wrap foil loosely over the bird, increase the total cooking time by at least 15 minutes. A duck or goose should be placed on a rack on the roasting tin and the tin should not be covered.

◘ To Roast Game

Game birds should be treated like chicken, for they must not be allowed to become dry in cooking. Specific timings for the various birds are on page 168.

There is a choice between wild venison, which is better cooked at the LESS FAST timing and the farmed variety, which tends to be more tender and therefore needs less marinating before cooking (see page 170). This could be roasted on the LESS FAST or the FAST timing, according to the particular joint. Young hare (leveret) and young rabbit are excellent roasted (see page 170).

◉ Roast Chicken and Turkey

◉ **Chickens:** small spring chickens (poussin) provide one large or two small portions. With larger birds allow approximately 350 g/12 oz (3/4 lb) per person. When buying an oven-ready frozen bird allow at least 450 g/1 lb per person.

◉ **Guinea Fowl and Turkey:** amount as for chicken; with small turkeys there tends to be a high proportion of bone so 450 g/1 lb per person would be a wiser amount. When buying an oven-ready bird allow this amount or even 550 g/1¼ lb per person.

◉ **To choose the poultry:** the beak on fresh birds should be bright red and the flesh firm, white and plump. A little fat is an asset. Choose a plump frozen bird.

Cooking times

Simmer the giblets of the bird in water to give stock to make gravy.

◉ **Fast:** suitable for fresh poultry. Preheat the oven to 200-220°C/400-425°F, Gas Mark 6-7. Reduce heat to 190°C/375°F, Gas Mark 5 after 1 hour.

Allow 15 minutes per 450 g/1 lb and 15 minutes over for birds up to 5.4 kg/12 lb. After this allow an extra 12 minutes for each additional 450 g/1 lb up to 9 kg/20 lb, then allow an extra 10 minutes for each additional 450 g/1 lb.

◉ **Less fast:** for defrosted frozen birds but quite suitable for fresh birds too. Preheat the oven to 180°C/350°F, Gas Mark 4. Reduce the heat to 160°C/325°F, Gas Mark 3 after 1½ hours.

Allow 22 to 25 minutes per 450 g/1 lb (lesser time for larger birds) and 22 to 25 minutes over for birds up to 5.4 kg/12 lb. After this allow an extra 20 minutes for each additional 450 g/1 lb up to 9 kg/20 lb, then allow an extra 15 minutes for each additional 450 g/1 lb.

◉ **Classic accompaniments:** Parsley and Thyme Stuffing, Chestnut Stuffing (see pages 188-9), Bread Sauce (see page 191) and Cranberry Sauce (see page 192) with sausages, bacon rolls (see page 187) and thickened gravy (see page 159).

◉ **Newer accompaniments:** Fruit, Rice or Liver Stuffings (see page 189).

◉ **For perfect results:** cover the breasts of birds with butter or fat bacon. Turkeys and large chickens should be roasted with the breast side downwards for the first half of the cooking time. A covered roasting tin helps to keep the bird moist or place foil like a tent over the bird until the last 30 minutes of the cooking time.

- To carve chickens and turkeys: small chickens and guinea fowl can be jointed. With large chickens and turkeys cut away the legs, thus allowing long slices to be carved from the breast and then slices carved from the legs.

⊙ Lemon Chicken

Cooking time: see method ⊙ Serves 4

This is a very simple and interesting way to add flavour to a chicken before roasting. Remove the pips from the lemon before inserting it inside the bird as these give a bitter taste to the flesh.

Metric Imperial (**Ingredients**) American
2 kg/4¹/2 lb (**chicken, weight when trussed**) 4¹/2 lb
2 (**lemons**) 2
75 g/3 oz (**butter**) 3/8 cup

Wash and dry the chicken. The giblets can be simmered to make stock; do not use the liver if making Velouté Sauce as it gives too dark a colour. Halve the lemons, remove any pips. Rub the cut sides of the lemons all over the outside flesh of the bird. Put one of the halved lemons inside the bird for a mild flavour or use both lemons to give a strong taste. Place half the butter inside the bird and soften the remainder and spread over the breast. Preheat the oven at either the FAST or LESS FAST setting on page 164 and cook the bird as the timings given.

Use some of the lemon-flavoured drippings to make the Velouté Sauce, page 194.

Variations:
- Omit the lemon inside the bird but blend 3 teaspoons finely chopped lemon balm with the butter placed inside the body of the bird.
- **Prune Stuffed Chicken:** use only a little lemon juice and butter on the outside of the bird and place about 16 soaked, but not cooked, prunes inside the body. Do not exceed this number for there must be space inside the bird when roasting.
- **Lemon Rabbit:** flavour the outside of the rabbit with lemon juice before roasting.

⊙ Glazed Turkey

Cooking time: see method ⊙ Serves 8

Roast a 4 kg/9 lb turkey as the timing on page 164. For this dish it should be stuffed with Chestnut Stuffing (see page 188) at the neck end. Bring the bird out of the oven 30 minutes before the end of the cooking time. Pour out the dripping from the pan. Blend 2 tablespoons (2¹/2 tablespoons) of the strained dripping with 4 tablespoons (5 tablespoons) thin honey, the finely grated zest of 1 lemon plus 1 tablespoon (1¹/4 tablespoons) lemon juice. Spread this mixture over the breast of the turkey and return it to the oven to complete the cooking.

⊙ Roast Duck and Goose

⊙ **Duck:** ducks have large bones, so be generous with the amount allowed. A small duck can be halved; with larger ducks allow at least 350 g/12 oz (3/4 lb) per person.

⊙ **Goose:** this has a high percentage of bone to flesh so allow at least 450 g/1 lb per person. With frozen birds allow at least 550 g/11/4 lb.

⊙ **To choose the poultry:** avoid fresh ducks or geese that have an excessive amount of fat in the body cavity. Choose fresh or frozen birds with the maximum amount of flesh on the breast and plump legs.

Cooking times

Simmer the giblets of the bird to give stock to make gravy. Save the lightly cooked goose liver for pâté, see below.

⊙ Follow the fast and less fast temperatures and timings as page 164.

⊙ **Classic accompaniments:** Sage and Onion Stuffing (see page 190) and Apple Sauce (see page 191).

⊙ **Newer accompaniments:** Gooseberry or Orange Sauce (see pages 191 and 192), Port Wine Sauce (see page 160), Green Pea Sauce (see page 167), Sorrel Sauce (see page 106), Honey-Orange Glaze (below).

⊙ **For perfect results:** by placing the bird on the rack of a roasting tin you allow surplus fat to run into the tin during cooking. If you have no rack, use an upturned ovenproof dish or tin. Lightly prick the skin at the end of 30 minutes cooking and at 30 minute intervals throughout the cooking time. Do not allow the fine skewer to pierce deeply into the flesh, otherwise the fat runs inwards, rather than spurting out.

⊙ **To carve duck and goose:** the British generally joint a duck but it could be carved instead. Remove the legs from a goose so you can carve the breast and then the legs.

⊙ Goose Pâté

Pound or liquidize the lightly cooked goose liver with 50 g/2 oz (1/4 cup) softened butter, 1 to 2 peeled and crushed garlic cloves, a little brandy or port wine to moisten and seasoning. Allow to become cold. This makes an excellent garnish for roast goose if served on rounds or crescents of toast or fried bread.

⊙ Honey-Orange Glaze

This helps to make the skin of duck or goose very crisp with a delicious taste. Blend 2 teaspoons finely grated orange zest with 2 tablespoons (21/2 tablespoons) clear honey. Spread over the breast of a duck 30 to 40 minutes before the end of the cooking time. Use twice as much for a large goose and add as timing for duck.

Duckling with Green Pea Sauce

Cooking time: approximately 2½ hours, but see method ⊙ Serves 4

This is based on traditional seventeenth and eighteenth century recipes for cooking duck. In those days duck was a seasonal bird and only available in the early summer, the time of green peas.

Metric Imperial { **Ingredients** } American
1 { **large duckling with giblets** } 1
to taste { **salt and freshly ground black pepper** } to taste
For the sauce:
2 tablespoons { **duck dripping and juices** } 2½ tablespoons
5 to 6 { **outer lettuce leaves** } 5 to 6
to taste { **sprigs of mint, sage and parsley** } to taste
25 g/1 oz { **flour** } 2 tablespoons
450 ml/¾ pint { **duck stock, from cooking giblets** } 2 cups
175 g/6 oz { **peas, weight when shelled** } 1 cup
1 to 2 tablespoons { **double cream** } 1½ to 2 tablespoons
1 to 2 teaspoons { **lemon juice** } 1 to 2 teaspoons
good pinch { **grated or ground nutmeg** } good pinch

Put the giblets into a saucepan with plenty of water to cover. Season lightly and simmer for about 1 hour, then measure out 450 ml/¾ pint (2 cups) of the stock. Weigh the duck to ascertain the cooking time. Allow 30 minutes per 450 g/1 lb.

Preheat the oven to 180°C/350°F, Gas Mark 4. Prick the duck skin gently with a fork and sprinkle with salt. This is one way of making sure the skin is crisp. Roast the duck for two-thirds of the cooking time, then lift out of the oven.

To make the sauce: remove 2 tablespoons (2½ tablespoons) dripping and juices from the roasting tin and pour these into a saucepan. Replace the duck in the oven to continue cooking.

Shred the lettuce finely, tie the herbs together with cotton or put into a muslin bag. Stir the flour into the dripping, cook over a gentle heat for 1 minute, then gradually blend in the giblet stock. Bring to the boil and cook until thickened. Add the peas, lettuce and herbs. Cover the pan and simmer gently for 15 to 20 minutes. Sieve or liquidize the sauce, with or without the herbs. Return to the saucepan, add the cream, lemon juice, seasoning and nutmeg to taste. Heat gently. Joint or carve the duckling and serve with the sauce.

Variation:
⊙ This dish can now be made throughout the year with defrosted frozen, or fresh, duck and frozen peas. A slightly different timing for cooking modern tender duck is on page 164.

⊙ Roast Game Birds

The birds should be plump and have a pleasant smell, although when well-hung this can be fairly strong. The legs should be pliable, indicating the bird is young. A small grouse or similar sized bird serves one person; a large grouse can be halved to serve two. A large pheasant can serve three to four people. The classic accompaniments to game are on page 190.

Before cooking: always cover the outside of the birds with softened butter or fat bacon. A generous knob of butter placed inside the bird helps to keep it moist, with a fresh or ½ dried bay leaf or a small onion to impart flavour.

Cooking times

If giblets are available simmer these to make stock for the sauce or gravy. When young and tender any of the birds listed below can be roasted, as the timings given. If frozen, defrost completely before roasting and use the LESS FAST oven temperature. Details of this and the FAST temperature are on page 164.

Place a slice of toast under each small bird in the roasting tin to absorb the meat juices as the bird cooks; serve this with the bird.

- ⊙ **Capercailzie** (this is a large grouse; also known as capercaillie or wild turkey): use LESS FAST setting and timing as turkey on page 164. Serve as roast turkey.
- ⊙ **Golden Plover, Plover, Ptarmigan (all kinds of grouse) and Grouse:** use the FAST setting and 35 minutes roasting time if small, 45 minutes for larger birds. Golden Plover is often cooked with the intestines left inside. A sprig of heather can be placed inside grouse before roasting.
- ⊙ **Mallard (wild duck):** use LESS FAST setting and timing as poultry on page 164. Serve with Orange Sauce (see page 192) and classic accompaniments or as duck.
- ⊙ **Partridge:** an excellent small bird. Use FAST setting and allow 30 minutes cooking time. Serve with classic accompaniments (see page 190) and Velouté Sauce (see page 194).
- ⊙ **Pheasant:** the most plentiful game bird. Use FAST setting on page 164. An average sized bird takes about 1 hour. Serve with classic accompaniments (see page 194) or with accompaniments to roast chicken (see pages 187 to 190).
- ⊙ **Pigeon:** young birds suitable for roasting are known as squabs. Use LESS FAST setting and allow about 50 minutes cooking. These are excellent served with red cabbage and Port Wine Sauce (see page 160).
- ⊙ **Quail:** best when cooked wrapped in paper or vine leaves. Available throughout the year (see page 169).
- ⊙ **Snipe:** use the FAST setting and allow 25 minutes. Serve with cooked mushrooms.
- ⊙ **Teal and Widgeon:** both are kinds of small wild duck. Use the FAST setting and allow 25 minutes cooking. Serve with same accompaniments as duck (see pages 190 and 191).
- ⊙ **Woodcock:** do not take out the intestines for this bird. Always place on toast when cooking. Use the FAST setting and allow 25 to 30 minutes cooking time. Serve with classic accompaniments and a purée of chestnuts.

⊙ Quail in a Parcel

Cooking time: 25 minutes ⊙ **Serves 4**

Many of the quails on sale are now imported but these tiny birds have been known in Britain for centuries and although the fame of English wines means more vine leaves (the classic wrapping) are available, you can substitute tender cabbage leaves for those from a vine. The leaves add an interesting flavour and keep the birds moist. Boned quail are available.

Other small birds, such as partridge or woodcock, could be cooked in the same way.

Metric Imperial { **Ingredients** } American
40 g/1½ oz { **butter** } 3 tablespoons
8 { **quail** } 8
16 to 24 { **young vine leaves or about 8 cabbage leaves** } 16 to 24
4 { **long rashers of fat bacon** } 4

Preheat the oven to 200°C/400°F, Gas Mark 6. Soften the butter and spread over each bird. Wrap the vine or cabbage leaves around the birds. How many you use will depend on the size of the leaves. De-rind, stretch, then halve the rashers, twist around the cabbage leaves. Place the birds into a roasting tin and cook for 25 minutes or until tender.

Serve with Port Wine Sauce (see page 160).

Variations:

⊙ Use young spinach leaves instead of cabbage leaves or omit the leaves and simply wrap the quail, or other small birds, well in the bacon.

⊙ **Quail in Paper:** blend a little chopped thyme with 50 g/2 oz (¼ cup) butter, spread over the birds. Place each bird in a greaseproof paper bag, seal and roast as above.

⊙ **Stuffed Quail:** fill boned quail with finely chopped cooked apricots and walnuts. Cover the birds with butter; put in greaseproof paper bags and roast as above.

⊙ Pheasant with Grapes

Cooking time: 1 hour ⊙ **Serves 3 to 4**

Preheat the oven to 200°C/400°F, Gas Mark 6. Put about 12 deseeded grapes inside the body of a young large pheasant. Cover the breast with butter and roast for 1 hour. Serve with Velouté Sauce (see page 194), to which are added skinned and deseeded grapes.

Variation:

⊙ **Herb-stuffed Pheasant:** blend finely chopped tarragon and chopped chives with 75 g/3 oz (⅜ cup) butter. Put half inside the bird and spread half over the breast. Roast as above.

⊚ Roast Venison

Best cuts to choose: saddle and haunch. Use FAST roasting temperature as page 164 for farmed venison but LESS FAST for wild venison.

Less tender joint: shoulder. Use LESS FAST temperature as page 164 for both farmed and wild venison. This temperature is suitable for all joints if preferred.

To choose venison: the meat should be dark and close-grained; any fat on the meat should be white and firm. Generally there is more fat on wild venison than on farmed.

Before cooking: marinate the meat in a mixture of ingredients as below. As stressed on page 164, this is not essential for prime farmed venison, but it does keep it moist during cooking. The quantity of marinade is sufficient for a 2 kg/4^{1}/2 lb joint.

For the marinade: blend 3 tablespoons (4 tablespoons) olive oil with 1 peeled and chopped onion, 1 to 2 peeled and crushed garlic cloves, 6 to 8 juniper berries (optional) and 300 ml/^{1}/2 pint (1^{1}/4 cups) red wine or stock. Leave farmed venison for 1 hour only but wild venison for several hours. Lift from the marinade.

Cover the joint with a generous amount of butter or fat before roasting, or lard the meat, i.e. insert strips of fat bacon or fat pork through the joint with a larding needle. You can heat fat in a pan and brown the outside on all sides then roast as timing below, but that is not essential.

Cooking times

⊚ **Fast:** preheat the oven as page 164 and allow 15 minutes per 450 g/1 lb for under-done (pink) meat and up to 22 minutes per 450 g/1 lb for well-done meat.

⊚ **Less fast:** preheat the oven as page 164 and allow 25 minutes per 450 g/1 lb for under-done (pink) meat and up to 35 minutes per 450 g/1 lb for well-done meat.

⊚ **Classic accompaniments:** Game Chips, Bread Sauce (see page 191), Fried Crumbs (see page 190) and Venison Sauce (see page 193), but excellent with Fruit Sauces (see pages 191 to 192).

⊚ Roast Hare

Marinate the saddle of hare as above and roast on FAST setting if young (a leveret) and the LESS FAST setting if a large and older hare. Hare is not pleasant when pink, so should be cooked thoroughly. It improves the flavour to roast it on a bed of thickly sliced onions; these can be sieved or liquidized and added to the gravy. Serve with classic accompaniments, as above. Venison Sauce is excellent with hare.

⊚ Roast Rabbit

Marinating rabbit is not essential; cover with fat bacon and roast as either of the timings above, dependent upon age. Rabbit must be completely cooked – not under-done. Serve with the classic game accompaniments or with Sage and Onion Stuffing and Apple or Gooseberry Sauce, and thickened gravy (see pages 190, 191 and 159).

◉ Quick Poultry and Game Recipes

Cooking time: as individual recipes ◉ Each dish serves 4

The young tender portions of poultry and game that are available today enable dishes to be prepared within a very short time. The following recipes may not be exactly as they were made years ago, for at that time people did not have such young birds or farmed venison. These dishes, which are based upon old recipes, are establishing a new type of British cuisine.

◉ Duck with Fruit Sauce

Use 4 portions of young duckling. Heat 25 g/1 oz (2 tablespoons) butter and 2 teaspoons oil in a large frying pan, add the duck and brown quickly all over. Pour in 150 ml/1/4 pint (2/3 cup) red wine or dry cider with a little seasoning. Lower the heat and cook gently for about 15 minutes, or until tender. Fruit has always been an accompaniment for duck as it blends well with the flesh. Some old recipes mention serving cooked plums or apricots with the duck. Apple and Gooseberry Sauces (see page 191) are other alternatives but the duck is nicer with a clear thin sauce, which today is known as a 'coulis'. Cook and sieve sweetened blackcurrants, cherries or cranberries and serve the purée with the duck.

◉ Fried Squabs

Halve 4 young pigeons (squabs). Take 450 g/1 lb sausagemeat or use the same amount of Chestnut and Sausage Stuffing (see page 188-9). Press this against the 8 cut sides of the squabs. Coat the birds in seasoned flour, then a beaten egg and finally soft fine breadcrumbs.

Fry the birds for 10 minutes in a little hot oil (it would have been dripping in days past) then place in a roasting tin. Cook in an oven preheated to 200°C/400°F, Gas Mark 6 for 25 minutes. Serve with Venison Sauce (see page 193).

◉ Mustard Rabbit

The rabbit must be very young for this dish. Just use the legs.

Make deep cuts in the flesh and spread made English mustard into these. Coat the flesh with seasoned flour, then a beaten egg and fine crumbs. Fry the joints, then complete the cooking in the oven, as Fried Squabs, above. Some recipes add a little cider to the dish while the rabbit is in the oven.

◉ Venison with Apples

Cut thin slices of prime fillet of venison into neat rounds. Heat a generous amount of butter in a large pan and cook the venison for 5 to 8 minutes, or to personal taste. Remove from the pan and keep hot, then fry rings of dessert apple in the pan until tender. Serve the venison on the apple rings.

☉ Spatchcock of Chicken

Cooking time: 15 minutes ☉ Serves 4

This is a classic way of cooking small spring chickens, now often known as broilers or poussins. In the past the birds would be cooked over an open fire. A grill or a barbecue are both ideal. The term spatchcock means the small bird is cut right down the centre of the back before being grilled. The flesh is flattened and kept in place with small fine skewers.

Metric Imperial { **Ingredients** } American
4 { **spring chickens** } 4
75 g/3 oz { **butter** } 3/8 cup
2 teaspoons { **finely grated lemon zest** } 2 teaspoons
3 teaspoons { **lemon juice** } 3 teaspoons
1 teaspoon { **chopped parsley** } 1 teaspoon
1/2 teaspoon { **chopped thyme or lemon thyme** } 1/2 teaspoon
1/2 teaspoon { **chopped rosemary or tarragon** } 1/2 teaspoon
to taste { **salt and freshly ground black pepper** } to taste

Preheat the grill or barbecue fire thoroughly before cooking. Slit each chicken down the back so it can be opened out flat. Blend the butter with the rest of the ingredients. Spread a little over the cut side of the birds, which should be uppermost. Cook for 5 minutes, then turn the birds and spread the rest of the butter mixture over the skin side of the birds and complete the cooking until when pricked with the tip of a knife by the thigh, any juice runs clear. Spoon any of the buttery mixture which drops into the grill pan over the birds before serving.

☉ Devilled Chicken

Cooking time: 15 to 20 minutes ☉ Serves 4

Metric Imperial { **Ingredients** } American
4 { **spring chickens or young chicken legs** } 4
75 g/3 oz { **butter** } 3/8 cup
1 to 2 teaspoons { **curry paste or powder** } 1 to 2 teaspoons
few drops { **Worcestershire sauce** } few drops
to taste { **salt and cayenne pepper** } to taste

Slit spring chickens, as in the recipe above, remove the skin from these or from the chicken legs. Make shallow slits in the flesh, so the butter mixture will penetrate. Blend the butter with the flavourings, spread half over one side of the chickens. Cook as above, turn over, add the rest of the butter mixture and continue cooking. The legs of chickens need a little longer cooking than spring chickens.

⊙ Grilled Chicken

Cooking time: 15 to 20 minutes ⊙ Serves 4 to 6

Portions of chicken are equally good for cooking under the grill indoors or over a barbecue. Preheat the grill before cooking the chicken; make sure a barbecue is glowing red before putting food over the fire. A whole chicken can be barbecued.

Melt 75 g/3 oz (3/8 cup) butter, add a little freshly ground black pepper. Brush over 4 to 6 chicken joints, cook steadily on one side for 5 minutes, turn over and brush the second side with butter and cook quickly, then lower the heat and complete the cooking, brushing the joints with butter throughout the cooking period. Breast joints take approximately 15 minutes, leg joints 20 minutes.

Variations:

- ⊙ **Herbed chicken:** add 2 teaspoons chopped rosemary leaves and 2 teaspoons chopped chives to the melted butter, with 1 peeled and crushed garlic clove.
- ⊙ **Mustard chicken:** blend 1 to 2 tablespoons made English or French mustard with the butter. Mustard has been a traditional accompaniment to foods in Britain since the eighteenth century.

⊙ Barbecue Sauce

Cooking time: see method ⊙ Serves 4 to 6

Metric Imperial { **Ingredients** } American
6 to 8 { **spring onions or shallots** } 6 to 8
1 to 2 { **garlic cloves** } 1 to 2
2 tablespoons { **mustard pickle** } 2 1/2 tablespoons
2 tablespoons { **tomato ketchup** } 2 1/2 tablespoons
3 tablespoons { **white wine** } 4 tablespoons
1 tablespoon { **white wine vinegar** } 1 1/4 tablespoons
150 ml/1/4 pint { **olive oil** } 2/3 cup
to taste { **salt and freshly ground black pepper** } to taste

Peel and chop the onions or shallots, garlic and the pickle. Mix with the remaining ingredients and heat gently in a saucepan. Brush the chicken or chicken joints with the sauce before and during cooking. The cooking time for a whole chicken is as given on page 164 for roast chicken. For chicken portions as above.

◘ Stews and Casseroles

Salmis of Pheasant (see page 175) is a very old and traditional British dish and, although it shares the advantages of a casserole in that the food can be prepared ahead and placed in the oven when required, it is not a typical casserole. You must use prime game birds or poultry and these have to be lightly roasted first, then jointed and reheated in a rich sauce.

◎ Braised Grouse

Cooking time: 1³/4 to 2 hours ◎ Serves 4

Braising is a classic cookery technique that was brought to Britain from France. It is often described as a combination of roasting and casseroling, and by changing the cooking times you can braise tender, or less tender, meats or birds.

Cut 2 or 3 young grouse into neat portions, do not bone them. Heat a little butter in a pan and brown the birds. Remove from the pan. Peel and slice 6 shallots or small onions and 2 medium carrots, skin and slice 4 medium tomatoes; wipe and slice 100 g/4 oz (1/4 lb) mushrooms.

Heat 1 tablespoon (1¹/4 tablespoons) oil in a pan and cook the vegetables for 5 minutes, add a little seasoning and 1 to 2 tablespoons finely chopped mixed herbs. Place in a flat layer in a casserole. Top with just enough game stock, or a mixture of stock and red wine, to cover the vegetables.

Arrange the grouse on top of this layer. Do not add extra liquid. Cover the casserole very tightly. Preheat the oven to 180°C/350°F, Gas Mark 4. Cook young birds for 1 hour but allow 1³/4 to 2 hours for older birds. Sieve or liquidize the vegetables and liquid from the casserole, add a little more stock or wine if necessary. Serve as the sauce with the grouse.

Use exactly the same method for beef, venison, poultry and other game birds. You can alter the selection of vegetables and the liquid to suit the basic food. Beer or light ale are ideal liquids when braising venison and beef.

◎ Turkey with Chestnuts

Follow the recipe for Salmis of Pheasant (see page 175). Cut the lightly roasted turkey into neat joints (do not bone these unless it is difficult to fit them into the casserole). Add 225 g/8 oz (1/2 lb) skinned and lightly cooked chestnuts to the other ingredients. Cook as the Salmis of Pheasants. Serves 4 to 6.

Hints on skinning and cooking chestnuts are on pages 188-89.

Salmis of Pheasant

Cooking time: 45 minutes ⊚ Serves 4 to 6

This is one of the great classic dishes with game. The birds must be lightly roasted first and the sauce should contain alcohol. The cooking time refers only to the reheating of the roasted pheasants. The timing for roasting birds is given on page 164.

Metric Imperial { **Ingredients** } American
2 { **young lightly roasted pheasants** } 2
2 to 3 { **shallots** } 2 to 3
3 { **medium carrots** } 3
100 g/4 oz { **button mushrooms** } 1/4 lb
75 g/3 oz { **dripping from roasting birds** } 3/8 cup
50 g/2 oz { **plain flour** } 1/2 cup
600 ml/1 pint { **game stock** } 2 1/2 cups
150 ml/1/4 pint { **sweet sherry or sweet Madeira wine** } 2/3 cup
2 teaspoons { **chopped chervil or parsley** } 2 teaspoons
1 { **fresh bay leaf or 1/2 dried bay leaf** } 1
1/2 teaspoon { **ground mace** } 1/2 teaspoon
to taste { **salt and freshly ground black pepper** } to taste
100 g/4 oz { **cooked ham, cut in one slice** } 1/4 lb
50 to 75 g/2 to 3 oz { **glacé cherries** } 1/4 to 1/3 cup
To garnish: { **fried croûtons** } (see page 53)

Skin and joint the roasted birds. Peel the shallots and carrots and wipe the mushrooms. Chop the shallots and slice the carrots. Heat the dripping in a saucepan, stir in the flour and cook gently for 2 to 3 minutes. Gradually blend in the stock and the sherry or Madeira wine. Stir as the sauce comes to the boil and thickens. Add the herbs, mace and seasoning. Simmer for 20 minutes then remove the bay leaf and sieve or liquidize the mixture.

Return the sauce to a large saucepan, add the jointed pheasants. Cover the pan and simmer for 15 minutes or until the birds are thoroughly heated and tender, do not over-cook. Dice the ham and stir into the sauce with the cherries. Continue cooking slowly for another 10 minutes. Garnish with the croûtons.

Variation:
⊚ Prepare the sauce as above. Put the jointed pheasants and sauce into a casserole. Cover and cook in a preheated oven set to 180°C/350°F, Gas Mark 4 for 45 minutes to 1 hour. Add the ham and cherries towards the end of the cooking time.

Chicken and Bacon Hotpot

Follow the recipe for Hotpot (see page 128), using raw chicken joints for the lamb. Add chopped bacon rashers and a generous amount of chopped parsley, thyme and chives to the layers.

⊙ Boiled Chicken

Cooking time: 1¹/4 to 1¹/2 hours ⊙ **Serves 4 to 6**

Metric Imperial { **Ingredients** } American
25 g/1 oz { **butter** } 2 tablespoons
1 x 2 kg/4¹/2 lb { **chicken with giblets** } 4¹/2 lb
{ **water, see method** }
2 { **large onions** } 2
1 { **small bunch parsley** } 1
to taste { **salt and freshly ground black pepper** } to taste
For the dumplings:
100 g/4 oz { **flour, etc.** } (see page 187) 1 cup
2 tablespoons { **chopped herbs: chives, parsley and thyme** } 2¹/2 tablespoons

Spread the butter over the breast of the chicken, put the bird, breast uppermost, and giblets, except the liver (which makes the liquid bitter), into a large saucepan. Add water to come just to the breast.

Peel the onions, leave whole. Add the onions to the pan with the parsley and seasoning. Cover the saucepan, bring the liquid to simmering point, then simmer gently for 1 hour, or until the chicken is tender. The term 'boiled' is a misnomer. Remove the chicken from the liquid, put on a heated dish and keep hot while cooking the dumplings.

Make the dumplings, but add the herbs to the flour mixture before blending in the water. Roll into 8 to 12 small balls with floured fingers. Drop into the boiling liquid. Cook briskly for 10 minutes then lower the heat and cook steadily for 10 minutes. Lift the dumplings on to the dish with the chicken.

Serve with Velouté or Parsley or Onion Sauce (see pages 194, 103 and 193). Reform Sauce, below, is an unusual accompaniment but it adds additional flavour and colour to the chicken.

⊙ Reform Sauce

This is based on a sauce created by Alexis Soyer, a French chef of Victorian days, for the Reform Club, London, to serve with Reform Cutlets (see page 119). It is excellent with chicken too.

Peel and finely chop 2 small onions, wipe and slice 100 g/4 oz (¹/4 lb) button mushrooms. Heat 25 g/1 oz (2 tablespoons) butter and cook the onions for 5 minutes, add the mushrooms and cook for 3 minutes. Pour in 300 ml/¹/2 pint (1¹/4 cups) Brown Sauce (see page 194), then add 2 to 3 tablespoons finely diced cooked ham, 2 to 3 tablespoons finely diced cooked tongue, 1 diced hard-boiled egg white and 4 teaspoons redcurrant jelly. Heat gently then add a little sherry, salt, pepper and 2 tablespoons diced pickled gherkins. Heat for 2 to 3 minutes only.

⊙ Hindle Wakes

Cooking time: approximately 1 3/4 hours ⊙ Serves 6 to 8

This is one of the oldest recorded recipes based upon chicken. The name comes from 'Hen of the Wake', wake being the old name for fairs held in the north of England which meant a holiday for workers. Originally it would have been an elderly boiling fowl that was cooked for some hours. Chopped prune stones were traditionally used instead of almonds. You have to disregard the warning on page 163 about not stuffing the body of a bird for this particular recipe but pack this in loosely.

Metric Imperial { **Ingredients** } American
For the stuffing:
450 g/1 lb { **prunes** } 1 lb
50 g/2 oz { **almonds** } scant 1/2 cup
50 g/2 oz { **butter or suet** } 1/4 cup
3 teaspoons { **finely chopped parsley** } 3 teaspoons
1 teaspoon { **finely chopped thyme** } 1 teaspoon
1 tablespoon { **lemon juice** } 1 1/4 tablespoons
to taste { **salt and freshly ground black pepper** } to taste
To cook the chicken:
1 x 2.5 kg/6 lb { **chicken** } 6 lb
150 ml/1/4 pint { **red wine vinegar** } 2/3 cup
1 { **large onion** } 1
2 tablespoons { **brown sugar** } 2 1/2 tablespoons
1 tablespoon { **lemon juice** } 1 1/4 tablespoons
For the sauce:
450 ml/3/4 pint { **chicken stock** } 2 cups
1 1/2 tablespoons { **cornflour** } 2 tablespoons
3 { **lemons (save one for garnish)** } 3
150 ml/1/4 pint { **double cream** } 2/3 cup

Soak the prunes for several hours in cold tea, rather than water, to impart flavour. Strain and then stone the prunes. Blanch and chop the almonds. Melt the butter or grate the suet. Mix with three-quarters of the prunes, all the nuts and the other stuffing ingredients. Stuff the neck end and body of the chicken. Place in a pan of water with the vinegar, whole peeled onion and other ingredients. Season well. Cover the pan and simmer until the chicken is tender; leave in the liquid until cold. Measure out the stock for the sauce.

Blend the cornflour with the stock, cook until thickened. Grate the rind from 2 lemons, halve the fruit, squeeze out the juice and add this to the sauce to give a strongly lemon taste. Cool, then add the cream. Season well. Coat the chicken with the sauce, top with the grated rind. Garnish with the reserved prunes and lemon.

◉ Rabbit Stew

Cooking time: 1¹/₂ to 2 hours ◉ Serves 4 to 6

Both wild and tame rabbits were staple diet for people living in the country and very popular with town people too. The very lean flesh is improved with the addition of fat bacon, as in the recipe below.

Metric Imperial { **Ingredients** } American
3 { **medium onions** } 3
3 { **medium carrots** } 3
1 { **small dessert apple** } 1
225 g/8 oz { **thick fat bacon rasher** } ¹/₂ lb
50 g/2 oz { **butter or lard** } ¹/₄ cup
25 g/1 oz { **plain flour** } ¹/₄ cup
to taste { **salt and freshly ground black pepper** } to taste
1 { **jointed rabbit** } 1
750 ml/1¹/₄ pints { **chicken stock, cider or water** } 3 cups
1 { **small bunch mixed herbs** } 1
For the dumplings:
100 g/4 oz { **flour, etc.** } (see page 187) 1 cup

Peel and slice the onions, carrots and apple. De-rind the bacon and dice the rasher. Heat the butter or lard and bacon rind, add the vegetables and apple and cook gently for 5 minutes. Remove from the pan with a perforated spoon.

Blend the flour and seasoning, coat the rabbit, add to the pan with the bacon and cook gently for 10 minutes, stirring once or twice. Remove the bacon rind, add the liquid and stir as this comes to the boil. Replace the vegetables and apple, add the herbs and seasoning to taste. Cover the pan and simmer gently for 1¹/₄ to 1¹/₂ hours, or until the rabbit is almost tender. Remove the bunch of herbs.

To make the dumplings, first check there is an adequate amount of liquid in the saucepan. Make the Suet Crust Pastry (see page 187). This should be sufficiently soft that you need floured fingers to roll it into 8 to 12 balls. Allow the liquid to boil briskly, add the dumplings and cook rapidly for 10 minutes, then lower the heat and cook more slowly for a further 10 minutes.

Serve the rabbit with the dumplings, bacon, vegetables and sauce.

Variations:
- ◉ **Rabbit Casserole:** when the liquid is thickened place the rabbit, other ingredients and sauce in a casserole. Preheat the oven to 160°C/325°F, Gas Mark 3. Cover the dish and cook for 1³/₄ to 2 hours. Omit the dumplings.
- ◉ **Chicken Stew:** use a jointed chicken instead of the rabbit. Omit the apple, add 100 g/4 oz (¹/₄ lb) button mushrooms instead. Cook as above but for only 1 hour.
- ◉ **Chicken Casserole:** prepare the mixture as for Chicken Stew. Transfer to a casserole, cover and cook for 1¹/₄ hours at 160°C/325°F, Gas Mark 3.

◉ Civet of Venison

Cooking time: 2 to 2½ hours ◉ **Serves 4 to 6**

The term 'civet' is French but, like so many French culinary terms, it has been used in Britain for a long time. It means a stew or casserole in which wine is an integral part. The timing for this dish is for tender venison. If stewing meat, allow 3 hours in the oven at 150°C/300°F, Gas Mark 2.

Metric Imperial 〔 **Ingredients** 〕 American
900 g/2 lb 〔 **venison** 〕 2 lb
1 tablespoon 〔 **olive oil** 〕 1½ tablespoons
2 tablespoons 〔 **brandy or red wine vinegar** 〕 3 tablespoons
to taste 〔 **salt and freshly ground black pepper** 〕 to taste
225 g/8 oz 〔 **fat pork** 〕 ½ lb
24 〔 **small pickling onions** 〕 24
225 g/8 oz 〔 **small button mushrooms** 〕 ½ lb
50 g/2 oz 〔 **butter or game dripping** 〕 ¼ cup
25 g/1 oz 〔 **plain flour** 〕 ¼ cup
300 ml/½ pint 〔 **game or beef stock** 〕 1¼ cups
150 ml/¼ pint 〔 **red wine** 〕 ⅔ cup
2 teaspoons 〔 **chopped mixed herbs** 〕 2 teaspoons
4 tablespoons 〔 **double cream** 〕 5 tablespoons

Cut the venison into narrow fingers about 2.5 cm/1 inch in thickness. Marinate in the oil, brandy or vinegar and a little seasoning for several hours. Cut the pork into narrow strips, peel the onions and wipe the mushrooms.

Heat the pork in a large pan for 5 to 10 minutes until the fat flows, then add the onions. Fry for 8 minutes until golden in colour. Lift the pork and onions into a casserole with a perforated spoon, so any fat is left behind. Add the butter or dripping to the pan. Lift the venison from the marinade, drain well. Cook in the pan for 10 minutes, stirring and turning over once. Transfer to the casserole with the mushrooms. Blend the flour with the fat in the pan, heat for 2 to 3 minutes then stir in the stock, wine and herbs. Bring to the boil and cook until slightly thickened. Season to taste. Pour over the venison and other ingredients. Cover the casserole and cook for 1½ to 1¾ hours in a preheated oven set to 160°C/325°F, Gas Mark 3. Add the cream 10 minutes before the end of the cooking time.

◉ Civet of Hare

Use a young jointed hare (leveret) instead of venison. Stir 1 to 2 tablespoons rowan jelly into the stock to add a sweeter taste. Allow 2¼ hours in the oven.

⊙ Jugged Hare

Cooking time: 4½ hours ⊙ **Serves 6 to 8**

Many British dishes of the past were described as 'jugged' because the containers used were like large jugs. The food would be cooked in the fireside oven.

Metric Imperial (**Ingredients**) American
1 (**jointed hare with liver and blood**) 1
2 tablespoons (**vinegar**) 2½ tablespoons
1 litre/1¾ pints (**water**) 4¼ cups
to taste (**salt and freshly ground black pepper**) to taste
2 to 3 (**medium onions**) 2 to 3
2 to 3 (**medium carrots**) 2 to 3
75 g/3 oz (**butter or lard**) ⅜ cup
50 g/2 oz (**plain flour**) ½ cup
150 ml/¼ pint (**port wine**) ⅔ cup
3 tablespoons (**redcurrant jelly**) 4 tablespoons

Put the blood of the hare on one side. Place the hare in cold water to cover plus the vinegar and soak for 1 hour. Put the liver with the 1 litre/1¾ pints (4¼ cups) water in a saucepan, add a little seasoning. Cover the pan; simmer for 40 minutes. Lift the liver from the stock, strain this and retain 900 ml/1½ pints (3¾ cups).

Peel and slice the onions and carrots. Lift the hare from the liquid and dry well. Heat half the butter or lard in a large pan and fry the hare gently for 10 minutes then remove. Add the rest of the butter or lard and cook the vegetables for 5 minutes. Stir in the flour, then add the liver stock and blood and stir briskly as the sauce comes to the boil and thickens slightly. Dice the cooked liver, add to the sauce with the port wine and redcurrant jelly. Simmer for 15 minutes then sieve or liquidize and season to taste. The liver thickens the sauce as well as flavouring it. Put the hare and sauce into a large casserole.

Preheat the oven to 150°C/300°F, Gas Mark 2. Cover the casserole and cook for 3 hours. Serve with Forcemeat Balls (see page 189), redcurrant jelly and fried croûtons (see page 53).

Variation:
- ⊙ **Jugged beef, venison, game birds or rabbit:** dice 1.1 kg/2½ lb stewing beef or venison. Joint 2 older pheasants (or equivalent in smaller birds); joint 1 large or 2 small rabbits. These foods are not soaked, so omit that stage, as well as simmering the liver. Brown the meat or game, then the vegetables, as above, add the flour then make the sauce with 900 ml/1½ pints (3¾ cups) beef or game stock, port wine and redcurrant jelly. Simmer as before then sieve or liquidize the mixture. Season and add to the flesh in the casserole. Cover and cook for 2½ to 3 hours as above.

◘ Pies – Hot and Cold

Pies have enjoyed a reputation in Britain for centuries and various districts produced pies of different shapes. As explained on page 109 the term used for most pies in the past was a 'coffin'. In Lancashire they called a pie a 'foot', further south we knew it as a 'turnover', both had pastry below and above the filling. There is a selection of pies made with meat, poultry and game birds in this book. They can be used as 'blue-prints' for other fillings. To make a successful pie, the cooking temperature and time must be calculated to make sure both pastry and filling are cooked, but not over-cooked. Ovens vary so check when making the pie for the first time and lower the heat a little earlier than suggested if your oven is hotter than average.

Make sure the pie dish is adequately filled, so the pastry will be supported during baking. The pie dish for the Chicken Charter Pie (see page 182) is large but this is because there is generous amount of liquid and one does not want this to boil out in cooking. If the filling does not fill the dish completely place an unturned egg cup or pie support under the crust. Below are suggestions for varying the pies in this book.

◉ Partridge and Ham Pie

To make a hot pie: follow the recipe for Pigeon Pie (see page 183) but omit the mushrooms. Use 4 birds and about 225 g/8 oz (1/2 lb) sliced ham or boiled gammon. Flavour the stock with a little ground mace and add 1 teaspoon finely chopped tarragon.
To make a cold pie: follow the recipe for Veal and Ham Pie (see page 149) but substitute the flesh from partridge for the veal.

Grouse or pheasant, or other game birds, can also be used instead.

◉ Rabbit Pie

Use young rabbit in place of chicken in the pies on pages 182 and 184.

To give a rabbit a more delicate taste, soak it for 1 to 2 hours in cold water to cover with 2 tablespoons lemon juice, before cooking.

◉ Turkey Pies

Use turkey flesh instead of chicken in the pie on page 182, also instead of the veal in the Veal and Ham Pie on page 149.

◉ Venison Pie

To make a hot pie: follow the recipe for Steak and Kidney Pie (see page 144). Instead of the gravy given in the recipe, Game or Venison Sauce (see pages 193-4) could be substituted.

To make a cold pie: follow the recipe for Melton Mowbray Pie (see page 148) and substitute tender venison for the lean pork. Retain the fat pork in the recipe. The anchovies are a pleasant flavouring with venison.

This pie is excellent with Cranberry Sauce (see page 192).

⊙ Chicken Charter Pie

Cooking time: 2 hours ⊚ Serves 4 to 6

This is a traditional recipe from south-west England, where cream has always been an important part of family catering. It gives a wonderful flavour to the pie.

Metric Imperial { **Ingredients** } American
1.3 kg/3 lb { **chicken** } 3 lb
1 { **small onion** } 1
75 g/3 oz { **chicken fat or butter** } 6 tablespoons
For the sauce:
25 g/1 oz { **flour** } 1/4 cup
150 ml/1/4 pint { **milk** } 2/3 cup
300 ml/1/2 pint { **double cream**} 11/4 cups
to taste { **salt and freshly ground white pepper** } to taste
2 tablespoons { **chopped parsley** } 3 tablespoons
For the shortcrust pastry:
225 g/8 oz { **flour , etc.** } (see page 295) 2 cups
To glaze: 1 { **egg** }

Joint the chicken; peel and finely chop the onion. Heat 50 g/2 oz (1/4 cup) chicken fat or butter in a large frying pan. Add the chicken and onion and fry until just golden in colour. Put into a 1.8 litre/3 pint (71/2 cup) pie dish. Melt the remaining fat or butter in the frying pan, add the flour and stir over a gentle heat. Blend in all the milk and half the cream. Stir briskly until thickened, then add the seasoning and parsley, Spoon over the chicken and onion in the dish then allow to cool.

This gives time to make the pastry and allow it to stand in a cool place (see page 295). Make the pastry, roll it out and cover the pie. Decorate with pastry leaves and flute the edges of the pastry. Make a hole in the centre of the pastry and put a small funnel of foil in this so that the hole does not close during cooking. Beat the egg, brush over the pastry. Preheat the oven to 200°C/400°F, Gas Mark 6.

Bake the pie for 20 minutes then reduce the heat to 160°C/325°F, Gas Mark 3 and bake for a further 11/2 hours. Cover the pie with foil or greaseproof paper towards the end of the cooking time so the pastry does not become too dark.

Remove the foil from the centre hole and pour the remaining cream into the hole just before serving. There is no need to warm the cream but, if you do, make sure it does not boil.

⊙ Pigeon Pie

Cooking time: 1½ hours, plus time to make stock ⊚ Serves 4 to 6

This hot pie can be made with any game birds. The timing depends upon their being young and tender, but if using older birds, cook them first by boiling, as chicken (see page 176) and reduce the baking time for the pie to 1 hour.

Metric Imperial { **Ingredients** } American
For the puff pastry:
175 g/6 oz { **flour etc.** } (see page 196) 1½ cups
For the filling:
4 { **pigeons** } 4
300 ml/½ pint { **game stock, see method** } 1¼ cups
2 { **eggs** } 2
25 g/1 oz { **plain flour** } ¼ cup
to taste { **salt and freshly ground black pepper** } to taste
3 { **shallots or small onions** } 3
3 { **bacon rashers** } 3
50 g/2 oz { **butter** } ¼ cup
100 g/4 oz { **button mushrooms, optional** } ¼ lb
To glaze: 1 { **egg** }

Make the pastry (see page 296), wrap and leave in the refrigerator to relax while preparing the filling.

Bone the pigeons, put the bones in a pan with water to cover and simmer for an hour to make the stock, strain and cool.

Hard-boil, shell and slice the eggs. Coat the pigeon flesh with the flour and a little seasoning. Peel and chop the shallots or onions, de-rind the bacon and cut the rashers into small pieces. Heat the butter and bacon rinds in a pan, add the shallots or onions and cook gently for 5 minutes, remove from the pan. Discard the bacon rinds. Add the pigeon and turn in the fat for 5 minutes then lift out of the pan. Put half the pigeon flesh into a 1.5 litre/2½ pint (6¼ cup) pie dish; add the sliced eggs, shallots or onions and mushrooms, if using these. Top with the rest of the pigeon flesh. Add sufficient stock to cover the filling.

Preheat the oven to 220°C/425°F, Gas Mark 7. Roll out the pastry and cover the pie, making a slit in the top for the steam to escape. Beat the egg and brush over the pastry. Bake for 20 minutes at the temperature above, then lower the heat to 180°C/350°F, Gas Mark 4 and bake for a further 1 hour. Cover the pastry with foil or greaseproof paper if it is becoming too dark.

Welsh Chicken and Leek Pie

Cooking time: 45 minutes, plus time to cook the filling ⊙ Serves 6 to 8

This Welsh pie, known as Pastai Ffowlyn Cymreig, has a certain similarity to the West Country Chicken Charter Pie (see page 182) as it has cream as one of the ingredients too. This recipe has the advantage of being equally good served hot or cold. The chicken must be cooked first, preferably boiled (see page 176). The ingredients can be varied, some people use parsley instead of leeks and add cooked tongue to the ham and chicken.

Metric Imperial { **Ingredients** } American
For the filling:
1.3 kg/3 lb { **chicken, boiled and allowed to become cold** } (see page 176) 3 lb
300 ml/1/2 pint { **chicken stock, see method** } 11/4 cups
2 to 3 { **shallots or small onions** } 2 to 3
6 { **medium leeks** } 6
25 g/1 oz { **butter** } 2 tablespoons
to taste { **salt and freshly ground black pepper** } to taste
225 g/8 oz { **cooked ham** } 1/2 lb
150 ml/1/4 pint { **double cream, or to taste** } 2/3 cup
For the shortcrust pastry:
225 g/8 oz { **flour, etc.** } (see page 295) 2 cups
To glaze: 1 { **egg** }

Cut the chicken into neat slices. The stock from boiling the chicken should be simmered until reduced in volume then allowed to become cold. Remove all the fat from the top of the stock.

Peel and finely chop the shallots or onions, cut the leeks into 2.5 cm/1 inch pieces. Heat the butter, cook the shallots or onions for 5 minutes. Simmer the leeks in a very little well-seasoned water for 5 minutes, until slightly softened then drain well and cool. Put the leeks at the bottom of a 1.2 litre/21/2 pint (61/4 cup) pie dish, top with a layer of chicken and shallots or onions and ham, fill like this in layers and add enough of the stock to cover the filling.

Make and roll out the pastry, cover the pie and make a very distinct slit in the top. Beat the egg and brush over the pastry. Preheat the oven to 200°C/400°F, Gas mark 6 and bake the pie for 25 minutes then reduce the heat to 180°C/350°F, Gas Mark 4 for a further 20 minutes to make sure the filling is heated.

If serving the pie hot, warm the cream and pour it through the slit in the centre. The cold cream should be added when the pie has cooled if you intend serving it cold.

Kentish Chicken Pudding

Cooking time: stock 1 hour; pudding 3 hours ⊙ Serves 6

Metric Imperial { **Ingredients** } American
2 kg/4¹/₂ lb { **chicken with giblets** } 4¹/₂ lb
900 ml/1¹/₂ pints { **water** } 3³/₄ cups
to taste { **salt and freshly ground black pepper** } to taste
2 { **large onions** } 2
2 { **large carrots** } 2
For suet crust pastry: 300 g/10 oz { **flour, etc.** } (see page 187) 2¹/₂ cups

Cut away all the flesh from the chicken, dice this neatly and discard the skin. Put the chicken giblets and carcass into a saucepan with the water and a little seasoning. Cover the pan and simmer steadily for 30 minutes. Remove the liver and heart of the chicken if you want to add these to the filling in the pudding. Continue simmering the bones and remainder of the ingredients for at least another hour to make good stock then strain the liquid.

Peel and slice the onions and carrots, dice the liver and heart of the chicken, if using these. Blend all the ingredients for the filling together.

Make the suet crust pastry (see page 187). Roll out and use part of this to line a lightly greased 1.5 litre/2¹/₂ pint (6¹/₄ cup) basin (see page 147). Put in the filling with enough stock to come half way up the basin. Moisten the edges of the pastry. Roll out the remaining dough to form a lid. Place this over the filling and seal the edges of the pastry. Cover with greased greaseproof paper and steam in a large saucepan for 3 hours. Make sure the pan does not boil dry – add more boiling water if necessary. Make gravy with the remaining stock.

Rabbit and Bacon Pudding

Use a jointed rabbit in place of the chicken in the recipe above together with 225 g/8 oz (¹/₂ lb) diced bacon (buy as one thick rasher if possible so it can be cut into neat cubes). Use chicken stock in the pudding. Cook as the Chicken Pudding above.

Game Pudding

Use 1 large or 2 smaller pheasants, or equivalent in smaller birds, instead of the chicken in the recipe above. Omit the carrots and add 100 to 225 g/4 to 8 oz (¹/₄ to ¹/₂ lb) small button mushrooms. Use 8 to 12 small shallots instead of large onions. Use game stock instead of chicken stock and add the liver and heart of the birds. The recipe is ideal for older and less tender birds.

There is a Steak and Game Pudding on page 147.

◘ Accompaniments to Poultry

The following pages give the classic sauces and stuffings that are served with poultry dishes. Bacon is an excellent accompaniment to game and veal, as well as to chicken and turkey.

The suet crust pastry is used in making dumplings and pudding crust for poultry and meat dishes as well as sweet puddings.

◘ Bacon Rolls

Cooking time: about 10 minutes, depending upon oven heat. Choose streaky bacon rashers with an even distribution of fat and lean. Cut off the rinds, stretch the bacon rashers with the back of a knife, so they become pliable. Halve them if long and roll lightly. Secure with wooden cocktail sticks. Put in a metal or ovenproof dish and bake. They can be twisted around small sausages so the sausages and bacon cook together.

◉ Suet Crust Pastry

Cooking time: as specific recipes

Metric Imperial { **Ingredients** } American
225 g/8 oz { **plain or self-raising flour, see method** } 2 cups
good pinch { **salt** } good pinch
110 g/4 oz { **suet or vegetarian suet** } 1/4 lb
To bind: { cold water or as recipe }

The choice of whether to use plain or self-raising flour in a steamed sweet or savoury pudding is a matter of taste. Plain flour gives a thin delicate crust, whereas self-raising flour gives a thicker but very light pastry. When making dumplings use self-raising flour, or plain flour sifted with 2 teaspoons baking powder.

Sift the flour, or flour and baking powder, and salt. Grate fresh suet or use the ready-grated suet, add to the flour. Gradually add enough water to give a soft rolling consistency, softer than shortcrust pastry. Roll out on a floured board and use as the recipe. Dough for dumplings should be even softer (see page 139).

Variation:
◉ Use butter, margarine or polyunsaturated fat instead of suet.

◘ Boning poultry and game birds

Most poulterers and good butchers will bone the birds for you if you give sufficient notice. However, it is useful to know how to do this, for a boned bird is easier to carve and has the advantage that the stuffing can be spread over the flesh. When cooked, simply slice the flesh with the stuffing inside.

- ◉ Cut the skin at the neck by the wishbone and carefully cut away this bone. Turn the bird with the back uppermost and make a deep cut along the bone, then gently ease the flesh away from rib bones on both sides of the back.
- ◉ Carefully work around the bird cutting away the flesh from the bones; do not waste any flesh, scrape each bone clean. Save the drumsticks of larger birds, such as chicken, turkey, duck or goose, as these help to make a more interesting looking joint.
- ◉ Open out the flesh. You can cover this with greaseproof paper then pass a rolling pin over it to give a more even thickness. Spread the stuffing over the flesh, then roll firmly and sew securely.
- ◉ Turn so the breast side is uppermost. Insert the drumsticks through slits in the skin.

◘ Making stuffings

The following recipes include some of the best known stuffings, which are rightly regarded as classic accompaniments.

Cooking time: often the stuffing is inserted into the joint or poultry, but if you are baking it separately use a tightly covered container. The cooking time will vary according to the heat being used in the oven but approximately 35 to 40 minutes at 190°C/375°F, Gas Mark 5 or a little longer at a lower setting will cook the stuffing adequately. A microwave cooks most stuffings well, consult your manufacturers' manual for timings.

Many stuffings, such as the Parsley and Thyme recipe (see page 189), can be prepared entirely in a food processor. This blends all the ingredients together, as well as chopping the parsley and bread.

◉ Chestnut stuffing

Cooking time: 30 minutes ◉ Serves 6

Chestnuts are one of the favourite nuts in Britain; they are not as large as those grown in warmer climates but their flavour is excellent.

Serve with turkey and chicken, but extremely good with game birds too. Wash 450 g/1 lb chestnuts and slit the flat side of the nuts in the form of a cross. This makes it easy to remove the shells and brown skin. Place into boiling water and cook for 8 to 10 minutes, strain and shell while warm.

Add the nuts to 300 ml/1/2 pint (11/4 cups) bacon, poultry, vegetable, or any white stock. Simmer for 20 minutes, strain and sieve or liquidize. Melt 50 g/2 oz (1/4 cup) butter, add to the purée with seasoning. Blend in a little stock to give a softer mixture.

- **Chestnut Purée:** heat the mixture and serve as an accompaniment.
- **Chestnut and Ham Stuffing:** dice 100 to 225 g/4 to 8 oz (1/4 to 1/2 lb) cooked ham, add to the chestnut mixture.
- **Chestnut and Herb Stuffing:** add 3 tablespoons (4 tablespoons) finely chopped parsley, 1 teaspoon chopped thyme and 1/2 teaspoon chopped rosemary.
- **Chestnut and Sausagemeat Stuffing:** prepare the chestnut stuffing then blend with an equal amount of pork sausagemeat.

⦾ Sausagemeat Stuffing

To each 450 g/1 lb sausagemeat add 2 tablespoons (21/2 tablespoons) chopped parsley, 1 teaspoon chopped sage, 1 egg and 3 tablespoons (4 tablespoons) poultry or bacon stock. Cooking time for stuffings baked separately is given on page 188.

⦾ Glazed Chestnuts

Cooking time: 30 minutes ⦾ Serves 4 to 6

These make an excellent alternative to any of the stuffings above. Make sure the chestnuts are really tender before coating them with the glaze.

Slit 450 g/1 lb of chestnuts as described above. Put into boiling water and cook for 8 to 10 minutes then skin them. Place in 300 ml/1/2 pint (11/4 cups) chicken or bacon stock, with a peeled onion and 1 garlic clove to give flavour and simmer for 20 minutes, then strain. To glaze, turn the chestnuts in a little hot butter until golden in colour.

⦾ Parsley and Thyme Stuffing

Cooking time: see page 188 ⦾ Serves 4 to 6

This is one of the classic stuffings for chicken, turkey and veal. It is extremely good in breast of lamb too.

Melt 50 g/2 oz (1/4 cup) butter and blend with 100 g/4 oz (2 cups) soft breadcrumbs, 11/2 tablespoons (2 tablespoons) chopped parsley, 1 teaspoon chopped thyme or 1/2 teaspoon dried thyme, 1 teaspoon finely grated lemon zest, 2 teaspoons lemon juice, 1 egg and seasoning to taste.

Variations:
- Use shredded suet instead of butter.
- **Forcemeat Balls:** follow the recipe above but use a small egg or egg yolk only so the mixture can be rolled into 12 to 16 balls. Place in an ovenproof dish. Bake in an oven preheated to 180°C/350°F, Gas Mark 4 for 20 to 25 minutes until firm.

- **Liver Stuffing**: add the lightly cooked, finely chopped chicken or turkey liver to the ingredients above. To counteract the slightly bitter taste, add 2 to 3 tablespoons of raisins.

◉ Sage and Onion Stuffing

Cooking time: see page 188 ◉ **Serves 4 to 6**

This stuffing blends well with goose, duck or pork; some people like it with chicken.
Peel and finely chop 2 large onions. Put into 150 ml/¼ pint (⅔ cup) water and cook gently for 10 minutes, or until the onions are slightly softenened and much of the liquid has evaporated. Strain the onions, but see 'Variations'. Blend with 50 g/2 oz (1 cup) soft breadcrumbs, 2 teaspoons chopped sage or 1 teaspoon dried sage, 50 g/2 oz (scant ½ cup) shredded suet and 1 egg. Season to taste.

Variations:
- Use 50 g/2 oz (¼ cup) butter instead of suet. Omit the egg and use the onion stock to bind, this makes a lighter textured and more crumbly stuffing.
- **Onion and Apple Stuffing**: add 225 g/8 oz (½ lb) diced cooking apples.
- **Onion and Prune Stuffing (1)**: add about 100 g/4 oz (¾ cup) chopped cooked prunes.
- **Onion and Prune Stuffing (2)**: another way of stuffing poultry (generally goose) is to put equal quantities of lightly cooked whole onions and soaked, but not cooked, prunes into the bird.

▣ Accompaniments to Roast Game

Although the following are the classic accompaniments for roast game they are quite suitable to serve with other game dishes, such as the Salmis (see page 175).
Redcurrant or rowan jelly is often offered instead of bread sauce. Port Wine Sauce (see page 160) is another alternative to gravy. Add a few raisins to the sauce when serving it with game. Garnish roast birds with watercress.

◉ Fried Crumbs

Cooking time: few minutes ◉ **Serves 4**

Most recipes suggest using fine crisp crumbs but when made with coarse fresh crumbs the texture and flavour and appearance are better.
- **With crisp breadcrumbs**: heat 50 g/2 oz (¼ cup) butter in a frying pan. Add 100 g/4 oz (1 cup) breadcrumbs and heat in the butter. Drain on absorbent paper.
- **If using soft breadcrumbs**: take about 100 g/4 oz (¼ lb) soft bread (weight without crusts), pull into fairly coarse crumbs with your fingers. Heat 50 g/2 oz (¼ cup) butter in a frying pan and turn the crumbs in this until golden brown and crisp. Drain on absorbent paper. Either kind of crumbs can be fried ahead, placed on a flat ovenproof plate and reheated in the oven for 2 minutes before serving.

Game Chips

Cooking time: few minutes ⊙ Serves 4

Cut about 350 g/12 oz (3/4 lb) peeled potatoes into wafer-thin slices. Heat a deep pan of oil to 190°C/375°F. Fry the potatoes in batches for 2 to 3 minutes. Drain and place on a flat dish. When all the potatoes are cooked, reheat the oil to the original temperature and fry the potatoes for 1 minute. Drain on absorbent paper.

These could be fried ahead, placed on a flat tin and reheated for 2 minutes in the oven.

Bread Sauce

Cooking time: 10 minutes ⊙ Serves 4

Make 50 g/2 oz (1 cup) soft white breadcrumbs. Heat a peeled onion with 300 ml/1/2 pint (11/4 cups) milk. Insert 2 to 3 cloves into the onion (optional).

Remove the pan from the heat, add a little seasoning to the milk. Cover and leave for 1 hour. Add the crumbs with 25 g/1 oz (2 tablespoons) butter and heat gently until the sauce is smooth and has thickened. Add 1 to 2 tablespoons cream if desired. Remove the onion and serve the sauce. A double saucepan or a microwave is ideal for making this. Reduce the amount of milk slightly if using a microwave.

Apple Sauce

Cooking time: 10 minutes ⊙ Serves 4 to 6

Peel and slice 450 g/1 lb cooking apples, put into a pan with 2 to 3 tablespoons (3 to 4 tablespoons) water and simmer to a soft purée. Add 1 to 2 tablespoons (2 to 3 tablespoons) sugar and 25 g/1 oz (2 tablespoons) butter and blend with the fruit.

A good cooking apple becomes smooth with brisk stirring but the sauce can be sieved or liquidized. Serve hot or cold with roast pork or duck.

Variations:
- ⊙ Use cider instead of water. Add 1/2 teaspoon ground ginger or a pinch of ground cloves.
- ⊙ Add several tablespoons sultanas or raisins to the smooth sauce.

Gooseberry Sauce

This is not only excellent with mackerel but an ideal sauce with rich meats, cheese and other foods. Follow the same proportions as for Apple Sauce if the gooseberries are ripe, but increase the water to 150 ml/1/4 pint (2/3 cup) and the sugar to 50 to 75 g/2 to 3 oz (1/4 to scant 1/3 cup) if the fruit is very firm. Top and tail the gooseberries and cook with the water and sugar to a smooth purée. Serve with cooked mackerel.

To have whole berries in the sauce, heat the water and sugar until the sugar has dissolved. Add the berries and cook gently until tender.

◉ Cranberry Sauce

Cooking time: 12 to 15 minutes ◉ **Serves 6 to 8**

Put 150 to 175 g/5 to 6 oz (3/8 to 3/4 cup) caster sugar, or to taste, and 4 tablespoons (5 tablespoons) water into a saucepan, stir until the sugar has dissolved. Add 4 tablespoons (5 tablespoons) port wine or extra water and 450 g/1 lb cranberries. Bring the liquid to simmering. Cover the pan tightly and cook for 10 minutes. If there is a little too much liquid, remove the berries with a perforated spoon then let the liquid boil rapidly until reduced. Pour over the fruit. Serve cold.

Variation:
◉   **Orange and Cranberry Sauce:** use orange juice in place of the water and port wine and add 1 teaspoon finely grated orange zest. Serve cold with roast turkey.

◉ Orange Sauce

Cooking time: 25 minutes ◉ **Serves 4 to 6**

There are many recipes for Orange Sauce: this one is particularly good with duck or goose. When bitter Seville oranges are in season they make a wonderful sauce.

Metric Imperial { **Ingredients** } American
2 { **oranges, bitter or sweet** } 2
150 ml/1/4 pint { **water** } 2/3 cup
2 tablespoons { **dripping from meat tin or butter** } 21/2 tablespoons
2 teaspoons { **arrowroot or cornflour** } 2 teaspoons
300 ml/1/2 pint { **duck, goose or chicken or game stock** } 11/4 cups
1 teaspoon { **lemon juice** } 1 teaspoon
3 tablespoons { **red or white wine** } 4 tablespoons
1 tablespoon { **redcurrant jelly, or to taste** } 11/4 tablespoons
to taste { **sugar** } to taste
to taste { **salt and freshly ground black pepper** } to taste

Cut away the top peel (zest) from the oranges, then cut this into matchstick pieces. Put into a saucepan with the water, soak for 1 hour, then cover the pan and simmer gently for 10 minutes. Halve the oranges, squeeze out the juice and reserve. Leave the peel in the liquid until ready to add to the sauce.

Heat the dripping or butter in saucepan; blend the arrowroot or cornflour with the stock, pour into the pan. Bring to the boil and cook until thickened. Add the lemon juice, wine, jelly and orange juice. Heat gently, stirring from time to time, until the jelly has melted and the sauce is clear. Strain the orange peel, add to the sauce with sugar and seasoning to taste just before it is required. The peel is nicer if not over-cooked. If the sauce is too thick, add a little of the liquid in which the peel was softened to give the desired consistency.

⊙ Onion Sauce

Cooking time: 20 minutes plus time for making the sauce ⊙ **Serves 4 to 6**

Peel and coarsely chop 2 medium onions, put into a saucepan with 300 ml/¹/₂ pint (1¹/₄ cups) water or chicken stock. Cook for 20 minutes or until the onions are tender. Sieve or liquidize the onions with a little of the liquid or chop finely.

Make either Velouté Sauce (see page 194) or White Sauce (see page 103), or English Butter Sauce (see page 104). Add the onion purée or onions and heat for a few minutes.

Variation:
- ⊙ **Creamy Onion Sauce:** add a little double cream to the sauce with the onions.

⊙ Venison Sauce

Cooking time: 30 minutes ⊙ **Serves 4 to 6**

Although particularly good with venison, this can be served with game birds, roast hare and rabbit too.

Metric Imperial { **Ingredients** } American
1 { **medium onion** } 1
1 { **large tomato** } 1
2 { **large mushrooms** } 2
50 g/2 oz { **butter or game dripping** } ¹/₄ cup
25 g/1 oz { **flour** } ¹/₄ cup
300 ml/¹/₂ pint { **brown stock** } 1¹/₄ cups
150 ml/¹/₄ pint { **red wine** } ²/₃ cup
2 tablespoons { **dry sherry** } 3 tablespoons
4 tablespoons { **redcurrant or rowan jelly** } 5 tablespoons
2 teaspoons { **sugar** } 2 teaspoons
2 teaspoons { **brown malt or red wine vinegar** } 2 teaspoons
to taste { **salt and freshly ground black pepper** } to taste

Peel and chop the onion, skin and halve the tomato, remove the seeds and dice the pulp. Wipe and slice the mushrooms. Heat the butter or dripping and cook the vegetables for 5 minutes. Stir in the flour and cook gently for 2 or 3 minutes then blend in the stock. Stir as the sauce comes to the boil and thickens. Simmer for 10 minutes then sieve or liquidize the mixture. Return to a clean pan.

Bring the smooth sauce to the boil, then blend in the wine and sherry, half the jelly and half the sugar together with all the vinegar and seasoning. Stir until the jelly has dissolved, then taste the sauce. You may want to add the rest of the jelly and sugar but this depends on personal taste. A sweet sauce blends well with venison and hare but a less sweet sauce is better with other game.

Variations:

- **Brown Sauce:** add a small peeled onion, carrot and a little diced celery to 450 ml/3/4 pint (2 cups) brown stock (see page 126). Heat for 5 minutes, then allow to stand for an hour. Heat 25 g/1 oz (2 tablespoons) butter or dripping in a pan, add 25 g/1 oz (1/4 cup) flour, stir over a low heat until golden-brown, then strain the stock into the pan. Stir as it comes to the boil and thickens, season to taste. Serve with meat or game.
- **Game Sauce:** make the Brown Sauce above, add 2 teaspoons sugar plus a little red wine, redcurrant jelly and vinegar to taste. Heat gently for 2 to 3 minutes.

◉ Velouté Sauce

Cooking time: 15 minutes ◉ Serves 3 to 4

A creamy white sauce but without milk. Heat 25 g/1 oz (2 tablespoons) butter in a saucepan. Stir in 25 g/1 oz (1/4 cup) plain flour, then add 300 ml/1/2 pint (11/4 cups) well-strained chicken stock. Stir as the sauce comes to the boil and thickens, then season to taste.

Variations:

- **A modern touch:** to produce a less thick sauce, increase the amount of stock to a scant 450 ml/3/4 pint (2 cups).
- **To serve with game:** use stock made from the carcass of game birds.
- **Sour Cream Sauce:** make the sauce as above with 300 ml/1/2 pint (11/4 cups) stock. When thickened, add 150 ml/1/4 pint (2/3 cup) soured cream and heat without boiling. This is excellent with game.

◉ Tomato Sauce

Cooking time: 25 minutes ◉ Serves 4

Tomato sauce could be described as a modern classic recipe, for tomatoes have not been part of British fare for as long as one might imagine. For information about tomatoes, see page 199. This sauce is a favourite of today; it blends well with most foods.

Slice 450 g/1 lb tomatoes, choose the plum-type if possible for they have more flavour in cooking. Peel and chop 1 medium onion and 1 or 2 garlic cloves. Heat 1 tablespoon (11/4 tablespoons) olive or sunflower oil in a saucepan, add the onions and garlic and cook for 5 minutes, then add the tomatoes and cook for a further 5 minutes. Take care the foods do not brown. Add 150 ml/1/4 pint (2/3 cup) chicken or vegetable stock or water, together with 1 teaspoon light brown sugar and a little salt and freshly ground black pepper. Cover the pan and simmer for 15 minutes. Sieve or liquidize the mixture and return to the pan and heat.

Variations:

- For a thicker sauce blend 1 teaspoon cornflour with the tomato mixture after sieving or liquidizing, stir as the mixture comes to the boil and thickens.
- For a stronger flavour, add 1 to 2 tablespoons concentrated tomato purée.

Vegetables and salads

It would be gratifying, but not strictly true, to say the British have always been expert at cooking and serving vegetables. In the past we were inclined to regard most vegetables as mere accompaniments to the meat, fish or poultry and we devoted little imagination or skill to cooking them.

On country estates, where gardeners tended large kitchen gardens, you would find a variety of produce but in towns the choice of vegetables was limited. When they reached the kitchen they were frequently drowned in an excess of water and badly over-cooked.

How that situation has changed! Good greengrocers and supermarkets offer a wide range of vegetables, not all of course home-grown. Cooks, both in the home and in restaurants, have learned to cook them so they retain the maximum flavour, texture and nutritional value. They are now a pleasure to behold.

The improved methods of cooking vegetables undoubtedly began during the Second World War, when rationing of basic foods made unrationed vegetables important. The absence of imported citrus fruits meant the population would be dangerously short of essential vitamins unless they learned to eat and enjoy both raw vegetables and correctly cooked ones and the Ministry of Food devoted much publicity and education to this matter. There were no exciting vegetables during those days; we relied upon the humble potato, carrot and other root vegetables plus the homely cabbage. We did, however, come to appreciate the fact that even these had a good flavour if they were correctly cooked.

What is the golden rule about cooking vegetables? They must not be over-cooked, whichever method is used.

In boiling, which is the basic way we cook vegetables in this country, one should use the minimum amount of water. Green vegetables should be cooked quickly, root vegetables steadily. Do not add water to spinach, let it cook in the water adhering to the leaves. Peas, beans and sweetcorn are so easily over-cooked, check carefully and salt towards the end of the cooking period. There is an old adage 'a potato boiled is a potato spoiled'. If the water boils too rapidly the potatoes break on the outside before they are cooked in the centre.

Potatoes have been known in Britain for centuries. It is recorded that Sir Francis Drake first saw potatoes in South America, in the year 1577. They were the staple diet of Indians in Southern Chile. The first potatoes were not grown here but were brought into this country by Sir Walter Raleigh. They were sweet potatoes, not the type we know. Interestingly enough, Britain's large ethnic population from the West Indies have been responsible for the popularity of sweet potatoes once again.

Baked jacket potatoes have increased in popularity due to the speed with which they can be cooked in a microwave and their suitability for cooking over a barbecue. Onions and sweet potatoes can be baked in the same way.

Braised vegetables take a little more time and trouble to cook, there is a recipe for Braised Celery (see page 199), but you are making a delicious vegetable sauce at the same time as cooking the basic vegetable.

Fried vegetables have been much criticized of late, the good old chip in particular, due to its great popularity and the fact that nutritionists are anxious that the British should reduce their total fat intake. Like any food, an excess of chips is not ideal but from time to time who can resist their delicious crispness?

Grilling is ideal for cooking mushrooms and tomatoes (not a vegetable, but always regarded as one). This technique can be used for red and green peppers (happily grown by many British people today) and portions of cucumber too.

One can reduce the fat considerably when roasting vegetables. Do not cook them in fat. Simply heat a little fat, or oil if preferred, and just brush the outside of the vegetables with this. They will become beautifully brown and crisp. Carrots, onions, parsnips, swedes, young turnips and sweet potatoes can be roasted just as satisfactorily as potatoes. Boil the root vegetables for 5 to 10 minutes before roasting, unless they are very young. Cooked beetroot is delicious if skinned and roasted for about 15 minutes.

▣ Salads

It may come as a surprise to many people to learn that salads, or sallets as they were known, were made as far back as the Tudor period. They were much more imaginative than post-war salads. Happily once again creativity has returned to British salads and they are no longer a stereotyped arrangement of lettuce, tomato, cucumber, radish and boiled egg. Various green leaves are used and fresh herbs, fruit and even edible flowers have their place.

Whatever may have been the British shortcomings during the nineteenth and early twentieth century regarding vegetable cookery and the preparation of salads (so often called 'rabbit food'), today we can surpass the cooks of most other countries in the way we present these.

◉ Fried Vegetables

Cooking time: 6 to 8 minutes

Always dry the vegetables thoroughly before cooking. Make sure the oil or fat is the correct temperature (see page 62) and drain the vegetables on absorbent paper after frying. Never fill the pan with too much oil or too much food.

◉ **Chipped Potatoes:** peel about 450 g/1 lb old potatoes and cut into fingers, the thinner they are the more delicious. Dry the potatoes well.

Heat the oil to 170°C/340°F. Heat the frying basket in the oil so the potatoes will not stick to it. Half fill the frying basket with potatoes, lower into the hot oil and cook for 5 to 6 minutes, depending on the thickness. The chips should be cooked but still pale. Lift out of the pan, hold the basket over the pan so any surplus oil drains out. Keep the chips warm. Continue like this until all the potatoes are cooked.

Just before serving, heat the oil to 190°C/375°F and cook the chips for 1 to 2 minutes, or until crisp and brown. Drain and serve at once. The potatoes can be lightly salted before serving. Sliced raw potatoes are cooked in the same way.

Variations:
◉ Fry very small new potatoes in their skins as above.
◉ **Carrots and parsnips:** peel and slice or cook baby carrots whole. Fry as above.
◉ **Celeriac:** peel, slice and fry as above.
◉ **Jerusalem artichokes:** peel and slice, or if small fry whole, method as above.

◉ Coated Vegetables

Cooking time: 3 to 4 minutes ◉ Serves 4

Some vegetables are better if coated before frying. Toss in seasoned flour, then coat with beaten egg and fine crisp breadcrumbs or the light batter given overleaf.

- **Crisp Onion Rings:** peel and cut 4 medium onions into 6 mm/1/4 inch slices, then separate into rings. Coat in seasoned flour then in this batter.

Blend 50 g/2 oz (1/2 cup) plain flour, a pinch of salt, 1 egg, 6 tablespoons (7 1/2 tablespoons) water and 1 tablespoon (1 1/4 tablespoons) corn or sunflower oil.

Heat the oil to 190°C/375°F and fry the onions until crisp and golden brown then drain on absorbent paper and serve at once. Double frying is not necessary.

Variation:
- Coat and fry courgette, young marrow, cucumber slices or whole small mushrooms or lightly cooked florets of cauliflower or broccoli in the same way.

Globe Artichokes

Cooking time: 5 minutes ⊙ Serves 4

Details of cooking this vegetable are given in the Starters section (see page 30). If you have sufficient vegetables, the bottoms (often called the hearts) can be fried as below.

Fried Artichoke Hearts: cook the artichokes as page 30, pull off the leaves and serve these separately. Coat about 12 to 16 hearts with seasoned flour and fry in a little hot butter. Serve with lemon or with Hollandaise Sauce (see page 105).

Jerusalem Artichokes

Cooking times: see recipes ⊙ Serves 4

These were very much more popular in the past than they are today. Like globe artichokes these are being grown in Britain and are now available in farmers' markets when in season. They are easily grown and have a slightly earthy taste. The vegetables should be washed well, then scraped, rather than peeled which is wasteful. To keep them white, place in 600 ml/1 pint (2 1/2 cups) cold water with 1 1/2 teaspoons lemon juice or white malt vinegar while waiting to cook them. Allow 450 g/1 lb for 4 people.

The vegetables can be topped with butter and chopped herbs, or with English Butter, or White, Cheese or Tomato Sauces (see pages 104, 103, 200 and 194).

- **Boiled:** put into boiling salted water to which a few drops of lemon juice is added, then cook steadily for 10 to 15 minutes. Strain and serve.

They are excellent mashed with a pinch of ground or grated nutmeg or with a little chopped fresh savory or rosemary.

- **Fried:** coat in a batter (see above) and fry in shallow or deep oil for 5 to 7 minutes, depending on the size. Drain on absorbent paper. Serve with lemon.
- **Roasted:** roll in the fat around the joint or in a little hot oil and roast for 45 minutes at 190°C/375°F, Gas Mark 5. Particularly good with beef or pork.

⊚ Asparagus

Cooking time: 12 to 20 minutes plus time to brown topping ⊚ Serves 4

Details of cooking asparagus are given in the Starters section (see page 28).

To make this into a more complete meal serve with Cheese Sauce (see page 200) or **au gratin:** put the cooked asparagus into a flameproof dish, top with Cheese Sauce, then with grated cheese and fine breadcrumbs. Brown under the grill. **With bacon:** country people used to serve cooked asparagus (generally picked straight from the garden) with rashers of crisp bacon. The two flavours blend well together. A fried egg was often added and the yolk formed a good sauce for the asparagus.

⊚ Braised Celery

Cooking time: 45 minutes ⊚ Serves 4 to 8

This method of cooking celery makes it an excellent hot dish, ideal to serve with various kinds of meat or poultry or as a vegetarian dish.

Wash 2 heads of celery well, remove the outer sticks and chop these very finely. Divide the heart into 8 portions. Heat 50 g/2 oz (1/4 cup) of butter, or use vegetarian fat if preferred, in a large saucepan. Add the celery and cook gently until golden in colour, remove from the pan.

Peel 2 medium onions, 2 medium carrots, place in the saucepan, wash and halve 2 medium leeks and add to the pan with 2 medium tomatoes, 2 teaspoons finely chopped chives and the chopped celery. Season the mixture and just cover with water.

Place the celery on top of the mixed vegetables. Cover the pan very tightly and cook slowly for 45 minutes, or until the celery is tender. Lift this out of the pan. Sieve or liquidize all the vegetables in the pan, adding a little extra water if necessary and serve as the sauce with the meal.

Variation:
⊚ Whole leeks, whole onions or heads of chicory can be cooked in the same way.

⊚ Stuffed Tomatoes

Cooking time: 10 minutes ⊚ Serves 4

Tomatoes are such an essential ingredient, and used in a wide variety of dishes today, that it seems strange that they were not as popular in the past. They were described as 'love-apples', especially when they were not quite ripe. In Eliza Acton's book of 1845 they are called tomatas. She recommends roasting them around a joint. This is her recipe for 'Forced Tomatas' which is very similar to the way we stuff tomatoes today.

Slice off the tops from 8 fine tomatoes and scoop out the insides; press the pulp through a sieve and mix with it 25 g/1 oz (1/2 cup) of fine breadcrumbs, 25 g/1 oz (2 tablespoons) of butter, broken very small, some pepper or cayenne and salt. Fill the tomatoes with this mixture and bake them for 10 minutes in a moderate oven (180°C/350°F, Gas Mark 4). Serve them with brown gravy in the dish. A few small mushrooms stewed tender in a little butter, then minced and added to the tomato pulp will very much improve this recipe.

Variation:
- Add a little grated cheese and chopped chives to the breadcrumbs.

◉ Cauliflower Cheese

Cooking time: 20 minutes ◉ Serves 4

In the days before we all worried about retaining vitamins in vegetables the cauliflower would be cooked whole. This certainly looked impressive but, by breaking the flower into florets, the cooking time is reduced, and more vitamins retained.

Metric Imperial { **Ingredients** } American
1 { **medium cauliflower** } 1
to taste { **salt and freshly ground black pepper** } to taste
For the Cheese Sauce:
225 g/8 oz { **Cheddar, Cheshire or Lancashire cheese** } 1/2 lb
40 g/1½ oz { **butter** } 3 tablespoons
40 g/1½ oz { **plain flour** } 3/8 cup
450 ml/ 3/4 pint { **milk** } 2 cups
1 to 2 teaspoons { **made English mustard** } 1 to 2 teaspoons
little { **cauliflower stock, optional** } little

Trim the cauliflower and divide into florets for speedy cooking. Put into a small quantity of boiling salted water and cook until just tender. Make the sauce while the cauliflower is cooking.

Grate the cheese (Lancashire is a crumbly cheese so cut this into small pieces). Heat the butter in a saucepan, stir in the flour and cook for 2 to 3 minutes then add all the milk. Stir or whisk as the liquid comes to the boil and the sauce thickens. Add most of the cheese, seasoning and the mustard. Heat gently to melt the cheese, but do not cook for long, otherwise the cheese becomes tough.

Strain the cauliflower. You can add a little of the vegetable stock for a less thick sauce, and one that has some of the cauliflower flavour. Arrange the cauliflower in a heated dish, top with the sauce and the last of the cheese. You can sprinkle on some smoked paprika or a little cayenne pepper too if you like.

Variations:
- **Cauliflower au Gratin:** put the cauliflower into a flameproof dish, top with sauce, grated cheese and fine breadcrumbs. Brown under the grill.
- **Vegetable Pie:** cook a good selection of vegetables, put into a pie dish, cover with the Cheese Sauce, made as above, then with creamy mashed potatoes. Put into a preheated oven, set to 200°C/400°F, Gas Mark 6 and heat for 25 to 30 minutes.

⊙ Leek Pie

Cooking time: 45 minutes ⊙ Serves 4 to 6

This pie is interesting for it is made with Suet Crust Pastry, as the recipe on page 187. That pastry is excellent for baking, as well as being used in steamed puddings. Shortcrust pastry could be substituted and is used in the flan.

Metric Imperial { **Ingredients** } American
For the suet crust pastry:
225 g/8 oz { **flour, etc.** } (see page 187) 2 cups
For the filling:
900 g/2 lb { **young leeks** } 2 lb
to taste { **salt and freshly ground black pepper** } to taste
225 g/8 oz { **streaky bacon rashers** } 1/2 lb
25 g/1 oz { **butter, but see method** } 2 tablespoons
2 { **eggs** } 2
300 ml/1/2 pint { **single cream or milk** } 1 1/4 cups

Make the pastry (see page 187) and put on one side while preparing the filling.

Wash and trim the leeks, use just a little of the tender part of the green stems as well as the white part. Cut into 2.5 cm/1 inch pieces. Put into a little well seasoned boiling water and cook for 5 minutes only, then strain and discard the liquid.

De-rind and chop the bacon rashers, add the rind to the pan in which the leeks were cooked and heat for about 5 minutes. Remove the rind. Add the butter to the bacon fat, heat for 1 minute then put in the leeks and cook gently until golden brown. If there are no bacon rinds use double the amount of butter. Remove the leeks from the pan with a slotted spoon. Add the bacon and fry for 5 minutes.

Put the bacon and leeks into a 1.5 litre/2 1/2 pint (6 1/4 cup) pie dish. Beat the eggs, add the cream or milk and strain over the leeks and bacon.

Roll out the pastry and cover the filling. This type of pastry is rarely glazed. Preheat the oven to 200°C/400°F, Gas Mark 6 and bake the pie for 30 minutes. Serve hot.

Variations:
⊙ **Onion Pie:** use sliced and lightly cooked onion rings instead of leeks.
⊙ **Leek Flan:** make and lightly bake a flan case (see page 220). Prepare and cook just 450 g/1 lb leeks, as directed above, and cook the same amount of bacon. Put the leeks and bacon into the lightly cooked pastry case. Strain the egg and cream mixture over the top. Bake for about 30 minutes in an oven preheated to 160°C/325°F, Gas Mark 3.

◉ Stuffed Mushrooms

Cooking time: 14 minutes ◉ **Serves 4**

During the past few years there has been enormous interest in the various kinds of mushrooms available. Town folk have been rushing to the country to hunt for wild mushrooms. The generous amount of filling in these mushrooms means you need the large flat type.

Metric Imperial { **Ingredients** } American
12 { **large flat mushrooms** } 12
150 ml/¼ pint { **milk** } ⅔ cup
to taste { **salt and freshly ground black pepper** } to taste
1 { **medium onion** } 1
4 { **rashers of streaky bacon** } 4
100 g/4 oz { **Cheddar cheese** } ¼ lb
25 g/1 oz { **butter** } 2 tablespoons
50 g/2 oz { **soft breadcrumbs** } 1 cup
1 teaspoon { **chopped marjoram or oregano** } 1 teaspoon

Remove the stalks from the mushrooms and chop these finely. Wipe the caps then put into the milk with a little seasoning and simmer gently for 5 minutes in the milk. Remove and drain.

Meanwhile, peel and finely chop the onion, de-rind and chop the bacon very finely. Grate the cheese. Heat the bacon rinds and butter in a pan, add the onion and mushroom stalks, cook for 3 minutes. Remove the rinds, put in the bacon and cook for another 3 minutes. Blend the breadcrumbs, herbs and cheese with the bacon mixture. Spoon over the mushroom caps. Preheat the grill and cook the mushrooms for 2 or 3 minutes until very hot. Serve with grilled tomatoes or sliced raw tomatoes.

Variation:

◉ **Stuffed Marrow:** a very small young marrow can be stuffed with the same mixture as the mushrooms. A larger marrow would need exactly twice as much filling. Halve the marrow lengthways. Scoop out and discard the seeds. Peel the marrow and cut into 4 portions. Put in a steamer, add a little seasoning and steam over boiling water for 10 minutes. Remove and fill the cavity in each section with the bacon and onion mixture. Put into a baking dish. Preheat the oven to 190°C/375°F, Gas Mark 5. Bake the marrow for 20 to 25 minutes. Serve with baked tomatoes.

◘ Peas and Beans

Both peas and beans are important vegetables that grow particularly well in Britain. They are part of a group known as pulses, which are rich in protein and therefore excellent as the basis for main meals as well as accompaniments to meat.

◎ Fresh Peas

Remove the peas from the pods, put into a small amount of boiling water, with a sprig of mint and cook steadily for 8 to 10 minutes or until tender. Add a little salt towards the end of the cooking time. As the peas get older, add 1 to 2 teaspoons caster sugar to give them the sweet taste of young peas. Strain and blend with a little melted butter. To make a more interesting dish you can toss the peas in diced crisp bacon and chopped chives or with lightly fried small spring onions.

Variation:
- ◎ **Fresh Pease Pudding:** instead of dried peas as page 205, cook 450 g/1 lb fresh or frozen peas with 2 finely chopped onions and a little chopped parsley and mint. Strain the peas, then liquidize them and blend with the butter and egg as in the recipe on page 205. Steam for 30 minutes only, serve with Faggots (see page 154) or with other meats.

◎ Runner Beans

The scarlet flowers make an attractive sight in gardens and the plants produce an excellent crop if there is sufficient rain during the summer. Top and tail and string (slice) the beans. Cook in a little boiling water, adding a little salt towards the end of the cooking time. Keep a fairly firm texture to the beans. Strain and blend with melted butter and chopped savory.

They are excellent topped with a little soured cream, chopped parsley and ham.

◎ Broad Beans

When really young, shell the broad beans. Cook the tender beans in one pan. Top and tail, then slice the pods and cook these in a separate pan, like runner beans above. The beans and pods should then be mixed together with chopped chives, chopped parsley and a little melted butter or topped with Parsley Sauce (see page 103).

◎ Bean Salad

Either cooked runner or French beans or broad beans make excellent salads. Strain and toss in a little olive oil and lemon juice while hot. Cool and add chopped spring onions, chopped parsley, savory (a perfect herb with beans) and garlic.

◉ Pease Pudding

Cooking time: 3½ hours plus soaking time ◉ Serves 4 to 6

This pudding freezes well, so it is worthwhile cooking a larger amount and freezing the surplus in small containers. It is the perfect accompaniment to Faggots (see page 154).

Metric Imperial { **Ingredients** } American
225 g/8 oz { **dried split peas** } ½ lb
2 { **small onions** } 2
to taste { **sprigs of parsley and thyme** } to taste
1 teaspoon { **chopped mint** } 1 teaspoon
to taste { **salt and freshly ground black pepper** } to taste
25 g/1 oz { **butter** } 2 tablespoons
1 { **egg** } 1

Put the peas to soak in water to cover and leave overnight or for several hours. Strain and discard this water. Peel and roughly chop the onions. Put the split peas, onions and herbs into a saucepan. Cover with a generous amount of cold water. Bring the water to the boil, add a little seasoning then cover the pan tightly and simmer gently for 2 to 2½ hours, or until the peas are tender. Remove the lid towards the end of the cooking period so any excess liquid evaporates. The peas should be pleasantly moist. Do not remove the herbs.

Either sieve the mixture or put it into a food processor. Blend the butter and egg with the pea purée, season to taste and spoon into a greased basin. Cover tightly with greased greaseproof paper or foil and steam for 1 hour. Turn out and serve hot.

◉ Green Peas and Carrots

These are a pleasant combination of colour and flavour. Dice or slice young carrots and cook with shelled peas until tender, add very little seasoning, but a good pinch of sugar, during cooking. Strain and toss in melted butter.

Variation:
◉ **Carrot Cakes:** cook and mash carrots until smooth, adding just a little ground or grated nutmeg and a few caraway seeds. Form into flat cakes with floured hands. Either fry in a little hot butter or bake on a well-greased dish in an oven preheated to 200°C/400°F, Gas Mark 6. The cakes should not brown, but just be hot. They look very attractive topped with spoonfuls of cooked peas.

◘ Root Vegetables

In the past, before the days of freezers, these would be the standby when the weather was too severe to pick green vegetables.

◉ Glazed Carrots

These are usually cooked in a little boiling salted water, but they are particularly good cooked in chicken stock, especially when they are getting older and losing their sweet flavour. The cooked carrots have a pleasant flavour and a shiny glazed appearance. Finely chopped onions, seasoning and a little sugar can be added to improve the taste. When the carrots are nearly tender any excess liquid should be boiled rapidly until it has evaporated.

◉ Carrots and Potatoes

Cook equal amounts of carrots and potatoes together, strain and mash with butter. The colour is most inviting and this dish is an excellent way to tempt children.

You can also cook turnips with carrots. Use twice as many carrots as turnips, so their milder flavour is not overwhelmed. When cooked, strain and mash with a little grated nutmeg and butter.

◉ Parsnip Cakes

Peel and dice parsnips. Cook in boiling salted water until tender then strain and mash them. To each 450 g/1 lb cooked parsnips, add 50 g/2 oz (1/2 cup) of flour, a good pinch of ground cinnamon, salt or celery salt, and freshly ground black pepper. Form into 8 to 10 round flat cakes. Coat with a little seasoned flour, beaten egg and breadcrumbs and fry. In the old days these would be cooked in beef dripping; nowadays they can be cooked in a mixture of butter and corn or sunflower oil.

◉ Creamy Mashed Potatoes

It was Sir Francis Drake who said in Elizabethan times: 'These potatoes be the most delicate rootes that may be eaten, and do farre exceed our passeneps and carets'.

He was of course referring to the first potatoes to arrive here – sweet potatoes – but since that time most potatoes have justified this high praise.

When cooking potatoes to mash do not cut them in too small pieces, otherwise they absorb too much water. Cook steadily in salted water until soft, then strain and heat in the saucepan for 1 minute to make sure there is no excess moisture. Mash the potatoes with a fork or a potato masher. To each 450 g/1 lb of potatoes allow at least 25 g/1 oz (2 tablespoons) butter and a little milk. Warm the milk and butter. Add to the potatoes and beat very hard until fluffy and white.

Potato Nests

Sieve the cooked potatoes. To each 450 g/1 lb add 25 to 50 g/1 to 2 oz (2 to 4 tablespoons) butter plus 1 or 2 egg yolks. Blend well and season to taste. Pipe the potatoes into nest shapes. Bake for 15 to 20 minutes at 190°C/375°F, Gas Mark 5. Fill with vegetables or crisp bacon and peas.

Pan Haggerty

Cooking time: 20 minutes ◉ Serves 4 to 6

This is a very popular dish in Northumberland. Haggerty is an old English word meaning to chop or mince. The vegetable dish can be served as an accompaniment to meat, such as ham or sausages, or as a light supper dish by itself.

Metric Imperial { **Ingredients** } American
3 { **large old potatoes** } 3
2 { **large onions** } 2
175 g/6 oz { **Cheddar cheese** } 1½ cups when grated
75 g/3 oz { **dripping or lard or butter** } 3/8 cup
to taste { **salt and freshly ground black pepper** } to taste

Peel and thinly slice the potatoes and onions. Dry the vegetables well on absorbent paper. Grate the cheese. Heat 50 g/2 oz (¼ cup) of the fat in a large and very strong frying pan. Arrange alternate layers of well-seasoned potatoes, onions and cheese in the pan, finishing with potatoes. Cover the pan very tightly and cook slowly for approximately 15 minutes, or until the vegetables are tender.

Preheat the grill and melt the remaining fat. Brush this over the potatoes and place the pan under the grill. Leave until the potatoes are very brown. Cut into wedges to serve.

Clapshot

When in Scotland you may be offered 'neeps'. This can be turnips or swedes, for both are given this title. In this dish either are blended with potatoes.

Cook approximately 450 g/1 lb potatoes and the same amount of turnips or swedes in salted water until soft. Strain and mash together. Add a good knob of butter and 2 to 3 tablespoons finely chopped chives. When these are not available use the tender part of spring onions instead. Season well.

Partie Oatie

Add 50 g/2 oz (¼ cup) melted butter plus 75 g/3 oz (½ cup) fine oatmeal to 450 g/1 lb cooked and mashed potatoes. Blend thoroughly, season to taste and allow to cool. Flatten or roll out on a surface coated with oatmeal, until 2.5 cm/1 inch in thickness. Cut into small rounds and fry in a pan in a little hot dripping or butter, or cook on a greased and heated griddle, until golden brown on both sides. Serve with cooked meats or fish.

◉ Boxty (Potato) Pancakes

Cooking time: see method ◉ Makes 8 to 10

There are many variations on this famous Irish recipe. The pancakes are frequently served at Hallowe'en.

Metric Imperial { **Ingredients** } American
450 g/1 lb { **old potatoes** } 1 lb
50 g/2 oz { **plain flour** } 1/2 cup
1 teaspoon { **baking powder** } 1 teaspoon
1/4 teaspoon { **salt** } 1/4 teaspoon
a little { **milk** } a little
To fry: 75 g/3 oz { **lard or cooking fat** } 3/8 cup

Peel the potatoes and grate them fairly coarsely. Squeeze them between your hands to extract any liquid. Do this over a basin so you retain the liquid. Sift the flour with the baking powder and salt, add to the potatoes. Strain the liquid in the basin after it has been standing a short time and add any deposit to the potato mixture, then discard the liquid. Gradually beat in enough milk to make the consistency of a thick batter. Heat a little of the lard or fat in a frying pan.

Drop in one or two large spoonfuls of the potato mixture. Fry steadily for 2 to 3 minutes, or until golden brown on the under-side then turn over and cook for the same time on the second side. Lift the pancakes from the pan on to a heated dish and keep hot in the oven while frying the remainder.

Serve topped with butter and a sprinkling of sugar. Brandy Butter (see page 315) gives an excellent topping.

Variations:
◉ Cook the pancakes on a greased griddle instead of in fat in the frying pan.
◉ Add 1 teaspoon caraway seeds to the potato mixture.
◉ Use 225 g/8 oz (1/2 lb) grated raw potatoes and 225 g/8 oz (1 cup) mashed potatoes.

◉ Boxty (Potato) Bread

Preheat the oven to 180°C/350°F, Gas Mark 4 and grease a 900 g/2 lb loaf tin. Blend 225 g/8 oz (1/2 lb) grated raw potatoes, 225 g/8 oz (2 cups) plain flour sifted with 4 level teaspoons baking powder, and 225 g/8 oz (1 cup) mashed potatoes together, add 1/4 teaspoon salt, 50 g/2 oz (1/4 cup) melted butter and the residue from the potato liquid. Do not add milk. Put into the tin and bake for 35 minutes.

◉ Bubble and Squeak

Cooking time: 15 minutes ◉ Serves 4

It is interesting how this dish has changed over the years. Although it contains meat the cabbage is so important that it justifies being among vegetable dishes.

Classic Bubble and Squeak: chop and cook a large cabbage, strain and chop it again until very fine. Reheat with plenty of butter. Slice cooked beef and heat the slices in a generous amount of beef dripping or butter. Arrange the meat in the centre of a dish in a border of cabbage. Serve with Brown Sauce (See page 194).

Today's Bubble and Squeak is a mixture of cooked mashed potatoes and cooked cabbage, fried as below. It is excellent with cold meat.

Mash 350 g/12 oz (3/4 lb) cooked potatoes with 25 g/1 oz (2 tablespoons) butter and a very little milk. Mix this with an equal amount of lightly cooked and finely chopped cabbage, or other green vegetable. Season well.

Heat 40 g/1½ oz (3 tablespoons) butter or good dripping in a large frying pan. Add the vegetable mixture and spread evenly over the pan. Cook slowly for about 6 to 7 minutes, or until the bottom of the vegetable mixture has formed a crisp brown crust. Tip on to a plate, so the brown side is uppermost. Heat another 25 g/1 oz (2 tablespoons) butter in the pan and slide the vegetable mixture back into the pan and cook on the second side until this is also brown. Cut into wedges to serve.

◉ Champ

Cooking time: 30 minutes ◉ Serves 4

Although there is a generous amount of leeks in this dish it is Irish, not Welsh.

Peel a generous 450 g/1 lb potatoes and prepare up to 350 g/12 oz (3/4 lb) leeks, cutting these into 5 cm/2 inch pieces. The vegetables can be cooked together or in separate pans in slightly salted water. Strain and mash together, season well and add 1 to 2 tablespoons of chopped parsley.

Spoon the vegetables into a very hot dish and make a well in the centre of the mixture. Melt at least 50 g/2 oz (1/4 cup) butter and pour it into the well. Each person helps themselves to the vegetables plus butter.

Variations:
◉ Use onions instead of leeks in the recipe above.

Interesting Sallets

The sallet or sallat on this page is of Tudor origin and a well-documented dish, although the name is given in several different ways.

Salad ingredients had been grown and served far earlier than the Tudor era, documented by Alexis Soyer, who was not only an outstanding chef but an enthusiastic historian as well. I find his book *The Pantropheon* a most intriguing record of the past. He details the various salad ingredients, such as lettuce, which the Greeks enjoyed at the end of the meal. The Romans served it at the start of the repast. In the book we read that Virgil thought endive bitter 'but he did not speak ill of it'. Watercresses were not particularly popular with the Persians but accepted by the Greeks and Romans. There are many references to salad ingredients being dressed with oil and vinegar.

Salamagundy

Cooking time: 10 minutes, meats etc. already cooked ⊙ Serves 6 to 8

This unusual name was well known some centuries ago, for a Salamagundy was a recognized form of a main dish salad. The decorations around the dish of flowers makes it a delight to the eye as well as the palate. Approximate quantities are given but the final choice of ingredients is a matter of personal choice.

Metric Imperial { **Ingredients** } American
4 to 8 { **eggs** } 4 to 8
450 g/1 lb { **cooked chicken** } 1 lb
350 g/12 oz { **cooked beef** } 3/4 lb
to taste { **salad dressing** } (see page 212) to taste
few { **anchovy fillets** } few
2 to 3 teaspoons { **capers** } 2 to 3 teaspoons
to taste { **cooked vegetables, see method** } to taste
to taste { **fruit, see method** } to taste
To decorate: { various flowers, see method }

Hard-boil, shell and halve the eggs. Slice the chicken and beef and arrange on a large dish with the eggs. Top with a little salad dressing, anchovy fillets and capers.

Dice cooked beetroot, carrots and green beans and add a few cooked peas. Spoon around the edge of the dish with neat piles of pickled red cabbage and pickled onions. Add slices of orange and lemon. Finally, decorate the food with marigolds, violets, and nasturtium flowers and leaves.

Apple and Beetroot Salad

Dice peeled dessert apples, mix with diced cooked beetroot, chopped hazelnuts or walnuts and finely chopped marjoram. Serve on a bed of young spinach leaves. This is particularly good with wild or ordinary duck or pork.

Curried Egg Salad

Hard-boil eggs, halve and carefully remove the yolks. Blend these with a little curry paste, smooth chutney and either soft butter or mayonnaise. Spoon back into the whites of the eggs. Arrange on a bed of lettuce and endive, slices of dessert apple, dipped in lemon juice, and orange segments. Serve with mayonnaise. This is excellent with cold chicken and ham.

Potato Salad

With our liking for potatoes this must be one of Britain's favourite salads. There is a saying 'Mix a potato salad when the potatoes are hot and eat it when they are cold'. That is true, the potatoes absorb the flavourings so much better when they are hot. You will find the salad improves with being kept in the refrigerator for some hours before serving. Cover it tightly.

Carefully cook 450 g/1 lb old or new potatoes until just soft. Slice or dice them and blend with the required amount of mayonnaise, plenty of finely chopped parsley and chopped spring onions or chives. Add a very little oil and vinegar dressing so the salad is not too cloying and stiff. Just before serving top with more chopped parsley and chives. Sliced raw young leeks are excellent in this salad.

Russian Salad

This is a salad from overseas that we have adopted. To most British people it is a selection of diced cooked vegetables in mayonnaise. The real Russian salad is much more interesting as it includes diced cooked tongue and chopped hard-boiled eggs. Top with chopped parsley.

Yorkshire Ploughman's Salad

The version I was given in Yorkshire was to mix together 1 tablespoon (1¼ tablespoons) black treacle and 2 tablespoons (2½ tablespoons) of vinegar. Add a little black pepper and spoon this over shredded lettuce and sliced spring onions.

In her book *Food from England*, Dorothy Hartley gives much the same recipe except it is with shredded red cabbage, which is much more robust than lettuce.

If you add to this finely diced cucumber, watercress sprigs and diced cooked ham, you have an excellent main dish.

◘ Salad Dressings

As explained on page 210, an oil and vinegar dressing dates back through the centuries and is still the favourite dressing today. The diversity of oils, including nut oils, and the quality of vinegar, especially the balsamic kind, means you can make a dressing that enhances most salads. Use at least twice as much oil as vinegar or lemon juice.

◉ Mayonnaise

This is not a truly British recipe, but one that has been used in this country for a very long time. Admirers of Eliza Acton's book, dated 1845, must have found her description of salad dressings and mayonnaise of various kinds interesting. These were certainly in vogue in Britain at that time.

Put the yolks of 2 fresh eggs into a bowl, add a little salt, pepper, mustard and sugar (if desired) then gradually whisk in up to 300 ml/1/2 pint (11/4 cups) of the finest virgin olive oil, or the oil you prefer. When thick and creamy, whisk in up to 2 tablespoons (21/2 tablespoons) lemon juice or wine vinegar. I often add a tablespoon of boiling water to give a lighter texture. It is important that eggs and oil are at room temperature.

Variations:
- ◉ **Red Mayonnaise:** blend in a little lobster coral. This is ideal with fish salads.
- ◉ **Green Mayonnaise:** either blend in a little spinach juice or a good quantity of chopped fresh mixed herbs. Choose those that blend with the salad.
- ◉ **Tartare Sauce:** add finely chopped parsley, capers and gherkins to the mayonnaise.
- ◉ **The modern touch:** use whole eggs in a liquidizer or food processor. Put the eggs or yolks into the goblet or bowl, add the seasonings and sugar. Switch on for a few seconds, then add the oil slowly with the machine running at low speed. Add the lemon juice and boiling water, if desired, when the mayonnaise has thickened.

◉ Hard-Boiled Egg Dressing

Hard-boil and shell 2 eggs. Rub the yolks through a sieve or put into a liquidizer, blend with 1 to 2 teaspoons mustard powder, 2 tablespoons (21/2 tablespoons) virgin olive oil, 1 tablespoon (11/4 tablespoons) lemon juice or vinegar, 5 tablespoons (61/2 tablespoons) double cream and a little salt and freshly ground white pepper.

◉ Potato Salad Dressing

Follow the Hard-Boiled Egg Dressing above, but add 4 tablespoons (5 tablespoons) absolutely smooth mashed potatoes to the sieved or liquidized egg yolks before the other ingredients. The potatoes should be floury, not creamed with butter and milk.

Savoury Dishes

This is accepted as a general title for the kind of foods that make excellent light meals and snacks. Savouries, on the whole, do not require a great deal of time or effort to prepare. They have a special appeal, since often they are served on informal, light-hearted occasions.

It is true to say that one of the most important, and popular, group of savouries are sandwiches. These were a genuine British invention and, as so often happens, they came about by accident, or the circumstances of the moment.

The fourth Earl of Sandwich was a well-known eighteenth century figure and during his lifetime he filled a number of important Government posts, including that of First Lord to the Admiralty. Sadly it is recorded that the corruption and incapacity of the administration during his tenure was unique in the history of the navy. He was a great gambler and on one particular occasion he sat at the gaming tables for 24 hours, without stopping for a meal. Someone prepared two slices of bread with a filling of sliced beef – and there was the first sandwich.

What are the secrets of good sandwiches? Fresh bread, a reasonable amount of butter, or other spread, and an interesting filling. This should be chosen to be full of flavour, pleasantly moist, but not so soft that it will make the bread soggy. The variety of breads available today, plus imaginative fillings, mean that sandwiches do not become monotonous.

The thickness of the bread for sandwiches depends upon the appetite of the diners and the occasion for which they are prepared. Hungry people on an outdoor expedition would undoubtedly be appreciative of fairly substantial sandwiches. Teatime sandwiches should look elegant, with the crusts removed. The menu for formal tea parties in both the Victorian and Edwardian eras generally included sandwiches. To be correct these had to be made with paper-thin bread, they were so fragile and small that they could be consumed in a single mouthful.

Surely one of the most tempting combinations of savoury foods is to be found in the traditional British breakfast. This is known throughout the world. Sadly it is far less popular today than it was forty or fifty years ago. With people's busy lifestyles, and the emphasis on not eating too much fat, breakfasts often consist of cereals with or without toast to follow. Try to give yourself a treat and serve a true British breakfast from time to time – if not early in the morning, then later in the day. It is one of the meals that is appetizing at any time.

Just what does constitute a British breakfast? If one goes back a hundred years or more you will find that wealthy households had sideboards groaning with various meats and other foods, and alcohol at breakfast time was quite normal. That is not the breakfast menu served in some homes and in good hotels today. Most menus would look something like this:

Orange Juice or Grapefruit
or Compôte of Fruit
Cereal or Porridge
Bacon, Eggs and Sausages
with Black Pudding, Mushrooms and Tomatoes
Toast or Rolls
Butter, Marmalade or Honey

Of course orange juice, grapefruit and cereals have no savoury flavour but porridge can have. Many Scots disdain sugar on porridge, serving it with salt instead.

Assembling a perfect breakfast is not unlike preparing a mixed grill (see page 121). One needs to plan the order of cooking, so everything comes to the table cooked to perfection.

Both eggs and cheese are excellent ingredients for quick dishes, and there is a good selection of egg dishes on pages 218 to 222. The golden rule when cooking any egg or cheese dish is to time the cooking carefully so they are not over-cooked. A guide to British cheeses can be found on pages 344-346.

The savoury dishes that follow are ideal for light and speedy meals.

⊙ Cheese soufflé

Cooking time: 40 minutes ⊙ Serves 4

This is not one of our classic dishes but it has been served as a dinner party savoury or light luncheon dish for such a long time that perhaps we may regard it as British.

Put 25 g/1 oz (2 tablespoons) butter into a saucepan, add 25 g/1 oz (1/4 cup) plain flour, cook for 2 to 3 minutes, then add 175 ml/6 fl oz (3/4 cup) of milk. Bring to the boil and stir over a low heat until a thick sauce forms. Remove from the heat. Stir in 100 g/4 oz (1 cup) finely grated Parmesan or mature Cheddar cheese and 3 egg yolks. Season to taste. Preheat the oven to 190°C/375°F, Gas Mark 5.

Whisk 4 egg whites until they form soft peaks. Fold into the mixture then spoon it into a buttered 15 cm/6 inch soufflé dish. Bake for 40 minutes, or until well-risen but slightly soft inside. Serve immediately.

⊙ Cheese straws

Cooking time: 7 to 12 minutes ⊙ Makes about 48

These are probably Britain's favourite cheese savoury and are served with drinks. There are many more economical recipes but the ingredients given below produce the classic crisp rich biscuits. Although Parmesan is not a British cheese, it has been appreciated and used in this country for many years.

Metric Imperial { **Ingredients** } American
75 g/3 oz { **Parmesan cheese** } 3/4 cup when grated
110 g/4 oz { **plain flour** } 1 cup
to taste { **salt and cayenne pepper** } to taste
1 teaspoon { **mustard powder, or to taste** } 1 teaspoon
110 g/4 oz { **butter** } 1/2 cup
1 { **egg yolk** } 1
To glaze: 1 { **egg yolk** } or 1 { **egg white** }

Preheat the oven to 220°C/425°F, Gas Mark 7. Grease several baking trays or line these with baking parchment. Finely grate the cheese.

Sift the flour with the seasonings. Rub in the butter, add the cheese and then the egg yolk. Mix thoroughly then gather the mixture together with your fingers. If the cheese is fairly dry and the yolk small you may need a few drops of water to bind the mixture. If slightly sticky, chill for a time.

Roll out on a lightly floured surface until 6 mm/1/4 inch in thickness and cut into fingers 6 mm/1/4 inch in width and 7.5 cm/3 inches in length. Place on the baking trays. Beat the egg yolk with a few drops of water and brush over the straws or use an unwhisked white.

Bake for 7 to 10 minutes until firm and golden in colour. Cool for a few minutes before removing from the trays. When cold, store in airtight tins until ready to serve.

⊙ Cheese Pudding

Cooking time: 30 minutes ⊙ Serves 4

This could be described as a homely version of a soufflé, for the mixture rises well and is light in texture. Choose a mature cheese to give the maximum flavour. Do not over-cook the pudding, it should be pleasantly soft and moist.

Metric Imperial { **Ingredients** } American
300 ml/1/2 pint { **milk** } 1 1/4 cups
40 g/1 1/2 oz { **butter** } 3 tablespoons
75 g/3 oz { **fine soft white breadcrumbs** } 1 1/2 cups
to taste { **salt and freshly ground black pepper** } to taste
1 teaspoon { **made English mustard** } 1 teaspoon
175 g/6 oz { **Cheddar, Cheshire or Lancashire cheese** } generous 1/3 lb
150 ml/1/4 pint { **single cream** } 2/3 cup
3 { **eggs** } 3

Heat the milk in a saucepan with the butter. Remove from the heat, add the breadcrumbs, salt, pepper and mustard. Cover and allow to stand for 30 minutes.

Finely grate the cheese. Preheat the oven to 190°C/375°F, Gas Mark 5. Grease a 1.2 litre/2 pint (5 cup) soufflé or pie dish.

Beat the cream with the eggs and strain into the breadcrumb mixture. Add the cheese. Spoon the mixture into the dish and bake for 30 minutes or until well risen and golden brown. Serve at once.

⊙ Cheese Butterflies

These attractive biscuits are made with the same rich cheese pastry as the Cheese Straws on page 215. As they have a filling, a less strongly tasting dough could be made by using very finely grated Cheddar cheese in place of Parmesan.

Roll out the dough until just over 6 mm/1/4 inch in thickness. Cut into rounds about 2.5 to 4 cm/1 to 1 1/2 inches in diameter. Cut half the rounds through the centre (these are the 'wings'). Bake as the Cheese Straws.

Make Cheese Cream by blending 50 g/2 oz (1/4 cup) butter with the same amount of finely grated Cheddar cheese (or use a cream cheese and no butter). Season well. Pipe a narrow line of the soft creamy mixture down the centre of the round biscuits and press the 'wings' in position. Top with paprika or parsley.

◨ Egg Dishes

Apparently the Romans considered eggs boiled in their shells the most wholesome way to eat them. In Britain they rarely were boiled before the sixteenth century; instead they were baked in the soft ash of a wood fire. In the past eggs were not eaten during Lent, which is why pancakes were made on Shrove Tuesday to use up the eggs in the house before Lent began.

Boiled eggs, as well as chocolate ones, are a part of the Easter Sunday tradition. Often the breakfast boiled eggs are decorated or coloured. Onion skins can be put into the saucepan of water to tint the shells instead of using a culinary colouring.

The following are some of the classic ways in which eggs are cooked in Britain.

◉ Baked Eggs

These are generally baked in small individual dishes or ramekins and served with a teaspoon. Preheat the oven to 200°C/400°F, Gas Mark 6. Coat the dishes with a generous amount of butter. Break an egg into each container, top with a spoonful of cream and a little seasoning. Bake for 6 to 10 minutes, depending upon how firm you like eggs.

Variations:
- ◉ **Asparagus Eggs:** place a few cooked asparagus tips into the dishes before adding the eggs and cream. Allow an extra 1 to 2 minutes cooking time.
- ◉ **Cheesey Baked Eggs:** put a little grated cheese into the dishes before adding the eggs and sprinkle a layer of cheese over the cream before cooking.
- ◉ **Ham Eggs:** place finely diced or minced cooked ham at the bottom of the dishes before adding the eggs and cream. Allow an extra 1 to 2 minutes cooking time.
- ◉ **Boiled Eggs:** Eggs should be stored in the refrigerator to keep them fresh but, if time permits, bring them out for a short time before boiling and there is less possibility of the shells cracking. Allow enough water to cover the egg(s); if you do not the egg will be cooked unevenly. Either place the egg(s) in boiling water and boil for 3^1/$_2$ to 4 minutes for a soft-boiled egg or put in cold water and bring this steadily to the boil, then time the cooking. A soft-boiled egg cooked this way takes 3 minutes. Hard-boiled eggs take 10 minutes by either method. Crack the shells of hard-boiled eggs and plunge them into cold water if you are having them cold as this prevents them over-cooking and developing a dark line around the yolk.
- ◉ **Coddled Eggs:** Put the egg(s) into boiling water, cover the pan and allow this to stand in a warm place, but one where there is no possibility of the water beginning to boil again, for 7 to 8 minutes. The eggs should be lightly cooked at the end of that time and less solid than when boiled in the usual way.
- ◉ **Eggy Bread:** This was popular during the Second World War when eggs were rationed. Cut a fairly thick slice of bread into several fingers. Beat an egg, season this and coat the fingers of bread in the egg. Fry in a little hot fat.

- **Fried Eggs:** make sure the butter or bacon fat is really hot before adding the eggs. Break the first egg into the pan, or on to a saucer first and then slide it into the pan. Allow the white of the first egg to begin to set around the edges before adding the second egg. If you dislike the uncovered yolk spoon a little of the fat from the pan over this and it will be covered with a white film. Modern non-stick (silicone) pans mean only a very small amount of fat, or few drops of oil, are needed to cook the eggs.
- **Bacon and Eggs:** cut the rinds from the rashers and use this to give the extra fat in the pan. Add the bacon, fry to personal taste then either remove to a heated dish and keep hot while frying the eggs or pull the rasher(s) to one side of the pan and fry the egg(s).
- **Eggs in Brown Butter:** use a generous amount of butter. Fry the eggs then lift on to a heated dish. Heat the butter until dark brown. Spoon over the eggs.
- **Poached Eggs:** While these can be cooked in hot butter in cups over water in a poacher, they are much lighter if cooked in water. Use a frying pan or wide saucepan. Add a pinch of salt to the water; a few drops of vinegar can be added too to help prevent the white from spreading. Slide the egg into the water that is just boiling, then boil gently until the eggs are set.
- **Scrambled Eggs:** Heat a small knob of butter in a pan. Beat and season the eggs, a little milk or cream can be added. Pour the eggs into the pan and cook very slowly, stirring from time to time. Do not stir too much. Add flavouring in the form of chopped chives, or other herbs.
- **English Monkey:** add several tablespoons of grated cheese, plus the same amount of fine soft breadcrumbs to the eggs as they cook, plus mustard to flavour the mixture.
- **Mumbled Eggs:** allow at least 1½ tablespoons (2 tablespoons) double cream to each egg and scramble lightly.

◉ Anglesey Eggs

Cooking time: 45 minutes ◉ Serves 4 to 6

This simple, but satisfying, savoury dish is an interesting way of using leeks. Do not over-cook the leeks, let them retain a fairly firm texture.

Metric Imperial { **Ingredients** } American
450 g/1 lb { **old potatoes, weight when peeled** } 1 lb
450 g/l lb { **young leeks** } 1 lb
6 to 8 { **eggs** } 6 to 8
100 g/4 oz { **Cheddar or other good cooking cheese** } ¼ lb
to taste { **salt and freshly ground black pepper** } to taste
50 g/2 oz { **butter** } ¼ cup
25 g/1 oz { **plain flour** } ¼ cup
300 ml/½ pint { **milk** } 1¼ cups
To garnish: { **chopped parsley** }

Peel the potatoes, wash and slice the leeks. Use some of the tender green stalks as well as the white part. Hard-boil and shell the eggs. Grate the cheese.

Put the potatoes into boiling salted water and cook until soft. The leeks can be added towards the end of the cooking period or they can be cooked in another pan of boiling well-seasoned water for about 10 minutes. Strain the vegetables. Either mash the potatoes and leeks together or mash the potatoes and then add the leeks. Stir in 25 g/1 oz (2 tablespoons) of the butter and season the mixture.

Preheat the oven to 200°C/400°F, Gas Mark 6. Melt the remaining butter in a saucepan, stir in the flour and cook over a gentle heat for a few minutes then blend in the milk. Stir or whisk as the sauce comes to the boil and thickens. Add three-quarters of the cheese and seasoning to taste.

Arrange the mixture of potatoes and leeks on the bottom and sides of a shallow ovenproof casserole. Slice the eggs and blend with the sauce and spoon in the centre of the vegetables. Top with the remaining cheese and heat in the oven for 20 minutes. Garnish with the parsley.

Variation:
⊚   If the vegetables and sauce are hot they can be put into a flameproof dish, then heated and browned under the grill for approximately 5 minutes.

◉ Bacon and Egg Flan

Cooking time: 45 minutes ⊚ **Serves 4 to 6**

This is a British version of a French quiche. It has a slightly firmer filling.

Metric Imperial { **Ingredients** } American
For the shortcrust pastry: 175 g/6 oz { **flour, etc.** } (see page 295) 1½ cups
For the filling:
225 g/8 oz { **bacon rashers** } ½ lb
3 { **eggs** } 3
250 ml/8 fl oz { **milk** } 1 cup
to taste { **salt and freshly ground black pepper** } to taste

Make the pastry (see page 295); roll out and line a 20 cm/8 inch flan tin or dish. Preheat the oven to 190°C/375°F, Gas Mark 5 and bake the flan 'blind' (see page 240) for just 15 minutes or until firm but still pale in colour. Reduce the oven setting to 160°C/325°F, Gas Mark 3.

Meanwhile, de-rind and grill or fry the bacon until just crisp. Cut into small pieces and put into the pastry case.

Beat the eggs, add the milk and a little seasoning. Strain over the bacon and cook for 25 minutes or until just firm. Serve hot or cold.

Scotch Eggs

Cooking time: see method ◉ Serves 4

This is the version of the recipe that has been made for a long time. In the past however, before sausagemeat was available, the classic Scottish recipes were based on a forcemeat made from minced or finely chopped cooked ham, anchovy fillets, breadcrumbs, herbs and spices.

Metric Imperial { **Ingredients** } American
4 { **eggs** } 4
350 g/12 oz { **sausagemeat** } 3/4 lb
For the coating:
25 g/1 oz { **plain flour** } 1/4 cup
to taste { **salt and pepper** } to taste
1 { **egg** } 1
50 g/2 oz { **crisp breadcrumbs** } 1 cup

Hard-boil and shell the eggs. Divide the sausagemeat into 4 portions. Blend the flour with a little seasoning and lightly coat the egg whites.

Press out the first portion of sausagemeat until it is large enough to wrap around an egg. Seal the joins firmly and mould into a good shape. Continue like this with the remaining eggs. Coat in a little seasoned flour. Beat the egg and brush over the sausagemeat, then roll in the crisp breadcrumbs.

◉ **To deep fry:** heat oil or fat to 170°C/340°F (a cube of day-old bread should turn golden in 1 minute – no shorter time). Fry the Scotch Eggs steadily for 10 minutes, then drain on absorbent paper.
◉ **To shallow fry:** heat 2 tablespoons (3 tablespoons) oil in a frying pan. Add the Scotch Eggs and fry steadily for 15 minutes. Turn over frequently. Drain as above.
◉ **To bake:** preheat the oven to 200°C/400°F, Gas Mark 6. Grease and heat a baking sheet. Add the Scotch Eggs and bake for 25 minutes. Turn over once during cooking.

Halve the Scotch Eggs lengthways and serve with salad.

Buck Rarebit

Cooking time: 5 to 6 minutes ◉ Serves 2

This makes a Welsh Rarebit twice as sustaining. Prepare the Welsh Rarebit and toast (see page 226). The quantities given in the recipe are for 4 small portions, but it will serve 2 people for a more sustaining savoury dish. Poach 2 eggs (see page 219), place on top of the piping hot golden-brown cheese and serve.

Variation:
◉ York Rarebit: put slices of lean ham on the hot buttered toast, top with the Welsh Rarebit mixture and brown under the grill.

⊙ Aberdeen Toasties

Cooking time: 15 minutes, plus time to cook haddock ⊚ Serves 4

This is a delicious way of using up a small amount of cooked smoked haddock. Undoubtedly the dish got its name from the sensible Scottish habit of using up all small quantities of good food and Finnan, where the finest haddocks are smoked, is only six miles from Aberdeen.

Put 50 g/2 oz (1/4 cup) butter into a pan, add 1 oz/25 g (1/4 cup) plain flour, then 150 ml/1/4 pint (2/3 cup) milk, stir or whisk as the sauce comes to the boil and thickens. It will look very 'buttery' at this stage.

Flake 225 g/8 oz (1/2 lb) cooked smoked haddock. Grate 50 g/2 oz (good 1/2 cup) Arran or Cheddar cheese. Add the haddock to the sauce, blend thoroughly and cook for 1 minute. Beat 2 eggs, add to the haddock mixture with the grated cheese and a little salt and pepper to taste. Scramble lightly and serve on hot toast.

▣ Sausages as a Savoury

Sausages have many different roles – small cooked sausages can be served on sticks as a cocktail savoury; larger sausages are served at various times of the day, for breakfast, for a main meal with creamed potatoes (bangers and mash), as a snack with crusty bread or toast or in the dishes that follow.

⊙ Sausage Rolls

Cooking time: see method ⊚ makes about 36 tiny rolls or 12 larger ones

These are probably one of Britain's favourite savouries; they can be bite-sized for parties or large and sustaining for picnics or buffets.

Make flaky pastry (see page 296) with 225 g/8 oz (2 cups) flour, roll out thinly and cut into long strips. Roll about 450 g/1 lb sausagemeat in a roll just under half the width of the pastry, lay the lengths of sausagemeat down the centre of the pastry strips. Damp the edges of the pastry, fold over to enclose the sausagemeat. Seal and flake the edges; cut the rolls into the required lengths.

Make 2 slits on top of each sausage roll, brush the pastry with beaten egg. Preheat the oven to 220°C/425°F, Gas Mark 7. Put the rolls on baking sheets or trays. Bake small sausage rolls for about 15 minutes, larger ones for 25 to 30 minutes. Reduce the heat slightly after 15 to 20 minutes, to about 190°C/375°F, Gas Mark 5 when the pastry has risen. Serve hot or cold.

Variations:
⊙ Use 350 g/12 oz (3/4 lb) frozen puff pastry instead of flaky pastry.

⊙ Pig in a Hole

Cooking time: 1¼ hours ⊙ **Serves 4**

This rather odd title is the name by which I was introduced to this dish. It is made with large onions and pork sausages. It was stressed to me that you need the spiciest pork sausages possible. British onions, with their strong taste, are ideal.

Peel 4 large onions and put them into a saucepan of boiling water, add salt and pepper to taste. Cover the pan and simmer for 40 minutes. Lift the onions out of the pan, save a little liquid to make a gravy (see page 159). Pull the centres out of the onions, these can be chopped and simmered in the gravy. Preheat the oven to 180°C/350°F, Gas Mark 4. Melt 25 g/1 oz (2 tablespoons) of butter.

Push a large pork sausage into the centre of each onion. Place in an ovenproof dish. Brush the outside of the onions with the butter. Bake for 35 minutes.

▣ Savouries on Toast

Quick snacks on toast, such as baked beans, cheese, eggs in various forms, or sardines have always been part of family fare. The following savouries serve two for a light meal or four as a classic savoury; cut the crusts off the toast and halve large slices of toast if serving as an after-dinner savoury.

⊙ Classic Savouries

Cooking times: 5 to 10 minutes ⊙ **Serves 4**

Savouries at the end of a meal have long been a feature of British dinner menus. They are served instead of a dessert or after this course. The portions are small, but they are quite adequate for the end of a meal. More generous amounts make an excellent light lunch or supper dish.

⊙ **Angels on Horseback:** de-rind 4 long rashers of streaky bacon. Stretch the bacon with the back of a knife by stroking it very firmly. The bacon rashers become longer and more pliable. Halve each bacon rasher. Squeeze a little lemon juice over 8 small or 4 halved large oysters, and wrap the bacon around them. Secure with wooden cocktail sticks. Place under a preheated grill and cook for about 5 minutes, or until the bacon is very crisp. Serve on small slices of hot buttered toast and dust with paprika pepper. (Pictured opposite.)

⊙ **Devils on Horseback:** follow the recipe above but use large cooked and stoned prunes instead of the oysters. The prunes can be filled with potted ham or game. (Pictured opposite.)

⊙ **Bengal Toasts:** heat 25 g/1 oz (2 tablespoons) butter in a pan, stir in 25 g/1 oz (1¼ cup) flour, then add 150 ml/¼ pint (⅔ cup) milk. Bring to the boil and stir as the mixture forms a very thick sauce. Chop 100 g/4 oz (¾ lb) lean ham, add to the sauce with 2 tablespoons (3 tablespoons) double cream, a pinch of curry powder and seasoning. Spread on small slices of hot buttered toast. Top with chutney.

⊚ **Scotch Woodcock:** heat 1 oz/25 g (2 tablespoons) butter in a saucepan. Beat 4 eggs with 2 tablespoons (3 tablespoons) single cream or milk and a little seasoning. Pour the eggs into the pan and cook gently, stirring from time to time, until they are lightly scrambled. Spoon on to small slices of hot buttered toast and top with a lattice of well-drained strips of canned anchovy fillets.

⊚ **Welsh Rarebit:** this is the classic cheese on toast. There are many different opinions as to which cheese to use, each one gives a different flavour. Double Gloucester is considered one of the best. (Pictured page 225.)

Heat 20 g/3/4 oz (1½ tablespoons) butter in a saucepan. Add 20 g/3/4 oz (scant ¼ cup) flour, blend well then add 2 tablespoons (3 tablespoons) milk and 2 tablespoons (3 tablespoons) beer or ale. Stir well until the mixture forms a very thick sauce. Add 1 teaspoon made English mustard, a good shake of black or cayenne pepper and a little salt. Finally stir in 175 to 225 g/6 to 8 oz (1½ to 2 cups) finely grated cheese. Spoon the mixture on to 4 small slices of hot buttered toast. Put under a preheated grill until golden brown and bubbling.

⊚ Herring Roes on Toast

Cooking time: 10 minutes ⊚ **Serves 2 to 4**

Poach 450 g/1 lb of soft herring roes in well-seasoned milk, or steam them between two plates over hot water. In this case top the fish with a generous knob of butter and a little seasoning. Either of these methods keep the herring roes in a good shape. They can be fried in hot butter instead, but stirring, so they do not burn, is inclined to break the roes, so they do not look quite as appetising. Serve on 2 to 4 slices of buttered toast and top with cayenne pepper.

Hard herring roes could be fried in butter and served in the same way.

Puddings and Desserts

The old title for these was 'Conceited Dishes' and I think anyone who produces a featherlight steamed pudding or a perfect home-made ice cream has every right to be conceited about his or her achievements.

This section starts with hot puddings and the very first recipe is for a Jam Roly Poly. If your only recollection of this is eating it at school and having suffered a rather heavy dough with a scarcity of jam, then please do make it at home. Whether it is the version that is baked and beautifully crisp, or the one that is steamed with a moist light result, you should be very happy to serve it to even the most pernickety family. The recipes are on page 229.

When steaming most puddings, it is advisable to allow the water to boil briskly for the first half of the cooking period to make sure the pudding mixture rises quickly and well. There are exceptions to this rule – a Christmas Pudding (see page 311) can be cooked steadily throughout the cooking period, for it does not contain any form of raising agent. The Chocolate Pudding mentioned below and the other recipes on that page are steamed slowly. Gentle simmering in the water below the steamer is required because of the high egg content and small amount of flour.

One of my favourite chocolate puddings with a chocolate sauce is on page 234. The recipe was given me by my grandmother who told me it had been handed down from her grandmother.

A crumble has become one of the most popular of puddings. The crispy top is a lovely contrast to the soft fruit below. If anyone asks me the origin of this pudding, I must confess I do not know. Some years ago the late Michael Smith, who was an admirer of British food and a great expert on the subject, asked me if I had any information about how this pudding began. I promised to look through all the records I had, for he had made me extremely interested in the subject. I could find nothing and we both came to the conclusion that it owed its origin to the Second World War. The fat was scarce, the flour was heavy, so made poor pastry, but it produced a perfectly good crumble. You will find the recipe on page 242.

I was very intrigued some years ago to find English Pudding on a menu in Portugal. My husband and I ordered it, curious to know what would appear. We made various guesses – all of which turned out to be wrong. When our dessert arrived it was a bread and butter pudding – and a very good one too. This dish has certainly journeyed from the nursery these days, for many famous chefs are proud to serve it in their restaurants.

It is strange how many cooks make pancakes on Shrove Tuesday and after that day forget about them for the rest of the year. What a pity! Pancakes filled with fruits of various kinds are a splendid pudding throughout the year. You can even have the dramatic contrast of piping hot pancakes filled with ice cream.

What makes a good rice pudding? I would say a lovely creamy texture with the rice just firm and of the right consistency, achieved by long slow cooking. I find a little knob of butter or suet added to the other ingredients helps to give just the right result. If you are anxious to avoid too much fat, you can use half the amount I suggest in the recipe (see page 250), which is only 25 g/1 oz (2 American tablespoons).

Many people imagine that all British desserts are fairly heavy and substantial. Not at all! There are beautifully light fruit fools, snows, flummery or syllabub, the rich trifles and tipsy cake which were known to our ancestors, and enjoyed by them. All of these are in this section.

There is no recipe for the classic junkets, for sadly rennet and our modern pasteurised milk are not good partners. If you have milk that is not pasteurised, buy rennet and follow the instructions on the bottle.

Several of our most famous British tarts are included, including a Bakewell tart (called a pudding in the old days). There is such a diversity of recipes for this dish, each one claiming to be the original one. I have included two, as I make both of them. Although very different from each other, they are both excellent. The Highland Tart from Scotland is another of my favourites.

A Sherry Trifle was always considered the cold dessert for special occasions. It seemed to go out of favour for a long time, possibly because the classic version was rarely made. Do produce one with all the extras and a velvety smooth egg custard. If you are not a sherry lover then make a Scottish trifle. There are several versions of this, but in the one I like best the sponge cakes are moistened with a mixture of whisky and white wine.

Our ancestors of the Edwardian era were great lovers of jellies, the port wine-flavoured one on page 256 was a great favourite. They had far more trouble dealing with the gelatine of the era than we have with the modern product.

⊙ Baked Jam Roly Poly

Cooking time: 50 minutes ⊙ Serves 4 to 6

This is one of the traditional puddings, associated with boarding school fare. When made well though, it is most appetizing.

Metric Imperial ⦃ **Ingredients** ⦄ American
For the suet crust pastry:
225 g/8 oz ⦃ **self-raising flour** ⦄ 2 cups (see page 187)
       ⦃ **or plain flour sifted with 2 teaspoons baking powder etc.**⦄
For the filling: 225 g/8 oz ⦃ **jam of any flavour** ⦄ 1/2 lb

Preheat the oven to 200°C/400°F, Gas Mark 6. Make the pastry (see page 187). Roll out on a lightly floured board to make a neat oblong shape, the pastry should be about 8 mm/1/3 inch thick. Spread with jam, keeping well away from the edges of the pastry. Fold in the ends of the pastry to enclose the jam.

Roll as though making a Swiss roll. Place on a lightly greased baking tray and cook for 25 minutes, then reduce the oven setting to 180°C/350°F, Gas Mark 4 and cook for a further 25 minutes. Slice and serve with custard and Jam Sauce, see page 230.

⊙ Steamed Jam Roly Poly

Cooking time: 2 hours ⊙ Serves 4 to 6

Prepare the roll exactly as the recipe above. In the past this would have been wrapped in a floured cloth but today it is easier to enclose it in greased greaseproof paper and foil. Wrap these loosely, but securely, around the pastry for it must have room to rise in cooking.

Place in a covered steamer over a saucepan of boiling water. Allow the water to boil rapidly for the first hour as this makes sure the pastry will be light, then lower the heat and cook more gently for the second hour. Make sure the pan does not boil dry. Unwrap the roll, top with a generous amount of caster sugar and serve with custard and Jam Sauce, see page 230.

⊙ Jam Sauce

Put 225 g/8 oz (1/2 lb) jam into a saucepan. Blend 1 teaspoon arrowroot or cornflour with 150 ml/1/4 pint (2/3 cup) water and 1 tablespoon (11/4 tablespoons) lemon juice. Add to the jam, and stir over a moderate heat until the jam has melted and the sauce has become thickened and clear. Serve hot.

⊙ Cumberland Pudding

Cooking time: 21/4 to 21/2 hours ⊙ Serves 4 to 6

This is sometimes known as The Duke of Cumberland's Pudding. Some recipes include a tablespoon of black treacle in the ingredients.

Metric Imperial { **Ingredients** } American
100 g/4 oz { **cooking apples, weight when peeled** } 1/4 lb
100 g/4 oz { **currants** } 2/3 cup
100 g/4 oz { **caster sugar** } 1/2 cup
75 g/3 oz { **shredded suet** } generous 1/2 cup
100 g/4 oz { **self-raising flour or plain flour sifted with 1 teaspoon baking powder** } 1 cup
75 g/3 oz soft { **breadcrumbs** } 11/2 cups
1 teaspoon { **grated lemon rind** } 1 teaspoon
2 tablespoons { **chopped mixed crystallized peel** } 3 tablespoons
2 { **eggs** } 2

Cut the apples into 1.5 cm/1/2 inch dice. Mix with all the other ingredients. Put into a well-greased 1.2 litre/2 pint (5 cup) basin and cover with greased greaseproof paper and/or foil. Steam for 21/4 to 21/2 hours, making sure the pan does not boil dry. Serve with Lemon Sauce (see page 231). The sauce for this particular dish should be allowed to become well thickened by simmering for some minutes.

Variation:
- ⊙   Use butter or margarine instead of suet. Cream the fat with the sugar, then add all the other ingredients. Steam for only 13/4 to 2 hours.

⊙ Bread Pudding

Cooking time: 21/4 hours ⊙ Serves up to 8

This is not only a splendid way of using stale bread but makes a fine dish for hungry people. There has always been great competition as to who has the best recipe.

Slice 450 g/1 lb stale bread. Put into a mixing bowl, add 300 ml/1/2 pint (11/4 cups) warm milk. Leave for 30 minutes, beat briskly until smooth. Add 100 g/4 oz (1/2 cup) melted butter or grated suet, 150 ml/1/4 pint (2/3 cup) milk, 175 g/6 oz (1 cup) mixed dried fruit, 100 g/4 oz (good

½ cup) moist brown sugar, 50 g/2 oz (⅓ cup) chopped crystallized peel, 2 to 3 tablespoons of marmalade, 1 to 2 teaspoons ground allspice, ½ teaspoon grated or ground nutmeg and 2 beaten eggs. Mix well.

Put the ingredients into a well greased 23 cm/9 inch square tin. Melt 25 g/1 oz (2 tablespoons) butter, brush over the top of the pudding. Preheat the oven to 180°C/350°F, Gas Mark 4. Bake for 2¼ hours, reducing the heat to 160°C/325°F, Gas Mark 3 after the first hour. Top with brown sugar and serve hot or cold.

⊙ Snowdon Pudding

Cooking time: 1¾ to 2 hours ⊚ Serves 4 to 6

This is one of the most interesting light steamed puddings. As the name suggests, it is particularly popular in Wales, where it is known as Pwdin Eryri.

Metric Imperial { **Ingredients** } American
40 g/1½ oz { **butter** } 3 tablespoons
175 g/6 oz { **raisins** } 1 cup
175 g/6 oz { **fine soft breadcrumbs** } 3 cups
25 g/1 oz { **cornflour** } ¼ cup
100 g/4 oz { **shredded suet** } ⅘ cup
50 g/2 oz { **caster sugar** } ¼ cup
1 teaspoon { **grated lemon rind** } 1 teaspoon
1 teaspoon { **grated orange rind** } 1 teaspoon
4 tablespoons { **orange marmalade** } 5 tablespoons
1 { **egg** } 1
For the Lemon Sauce:
1 { **large lemon** } 1
150 ml/¼ pint { **water** } ⅔ cup
75 g/3 oz { **caster sugar** } scant ⅓ cup
25 g/1 oz { **cornflour** } ¼ cup
300 ml/½ pint { **white wine or water** } 1¼ cups

Use most of the butter to grease the base and sides of a 1.2 litre/2 pint (5 cup) basin. Press half the raisins against the butter. Mix all the remaining ingredients for the pudding together, except the remaining butter. Spoon into the basin.

Spread the butter over greaseproof paper and cover the pudding with this and with foil. Steam over boiling water for 1¾ hours, making sure the pan does not boil dry. Turn out and serve with the sauce.

To make the sauce: pare the rind from the lemon, take care to use only the top rind (zest) and none of the bitter white pith. Squeeze out the juice. Put the rind into a saucepan with the water, cover the pan and simmer gently for 10 minutes. Strain the liquid and return to the pan with the lemon juice and sugar. Blend the cornflour with the wine or water, add to the pan and stir over a low heat until the mixture has thickened to the desired consistency.

Turn the pudding out on to a heated dish, top with a little of the sauce and serve the rest separately. In this particular recipe the sauce is quite thin.

Variations:
- Substitute melted butter or margarine for the suet in the pudding.
- Use lemon marmalade instead of orange marmalade in the pudding.

◉ Fruit Pudding

Cooking time: 2 hours ◉ Serves 4 to 6

One of the nicest of our traditional steamed puddings is the one made with light suet crust pastry and filled with fruit. By cooking the fruit in the pastry no flavour is lost. This can be made throughout the year, using fruits in season.

Metric Imperial { **Ingredients** } American
For the suet crust pastry: 225 g/8 oz { **flour etc.** } (see page 187) 2 cups
For the filling:
675 g/1½ lb { **seasonal fruit, weight when prepared** } 1½ lb
little { **water or orange or other fruit juice** } little
to taste { **sugar** } to taste

Make the pastry (see page 187) and roll out thinly. If you would like a fairly substantial amount of pastry, increase the amount of flour to 300 g/10 oz (2½ cups) and the fat proportionately. Grease a 1.5 litre/2½ pint (6¼ cup) basin and use three-quarters of the pastry to line the basin. Prepare the fruit – slice apples, halve and stone plums, dice rhubarb. Put the fruit into the pastry, add water or fruit juice to come halfway up the filling, then add sugar to taste. Roll out the remaining pastry for the lid. Moisten the edges then place the pastry lid over the fruit and press the edges together. Cover the pudding with greased greaseproof paper and foil. Put a pleat in both layers to allow for the pudding to rise in cooking. Steam over rapidly boiling water for 1 hour, then simmer gently for another hour. Make sure the pan does not boil dry.

Turn the pudding out of the basin, sprinkle with sugar and serve with cream.

◉ Sussex Pond Pudding

Make the pastry and line the basin, as in the recipe above. Prick a large ripe lemon with a thick needle or fine skewer and place in the basin. Cut 100 g/4 oz (½ cup) unsalted butter in small pieces, place around the lemon with 100 g/4 oz (½ cup) sugar. Cover the pudding and steam as above.

When the pudding is cut, a rich lemon curd flows out. About 150 g/5 oz (scant 1 cup) of dried fruit can be packed around the lemon to make a more solid filling.

⊙ Toffee Apple Pudding

There are many recipes called 'Toffee Apple Pudding'. One of the nicest is to spread a pudding basin with a thick layer of butter and brown sugar before lining it with suet crust pastry. Continue as the Fruit Pudding on page 232. While apples blend particularly well with this sweet coating other fruits can be used.

⊙ Sponge Pudding

Cooking time: 1¼ to 1½ hours ⊙ Serves 4

The technique of making the sponge is exactly as described for Victoria Sandwich (see page 285). This is an infinitely adaptable pudding and, because it is so light, it can be served throughout the year. The flavourings for Victoria Sandwich are equally suitable for this pudding.

Cream 110 g/4 oz (½ cup) butter with 110 g/4 oz (½ cup) caster sugar until soft and light. Beat 2 large eggs and gradually add them to the creamed mixture.

Sift 110 g/4 oz (1 cup) self-raising flour, or plain flour with 1 teaspoon baking powder. Fold into the other ingredients. Grease a 1.2 litre/2 pint (5 cup) basin and spoon in the mixture. Cover with greased greaseproof paper and/or foil. Place in the steamer over a saucepan of boiling water. Cook quickly for at least 40 minutes then lower the heat and cook more gently for a further 25 to 40 minutes, making sure the pan does not boil dry. Turn out and serve with Jam Sauce (see page 230), hot cooked fruit or Fruit Sauce (see page 191-2).

⊙ **The modern touch:** Either soften the butter at room temperature or use one of the quick creaming soft margarines. Put all the ingredients into a bowl together and cream.

Variations:

⊙ **Apricot Pudding:** put well drained, cooked fresh or dried apricots into the basin before adding the sponge. Serve with Lemon Sauce (see page 231).

⊙ **Blackcap Pudding:** put several tablespoons of blackcurrant jam or cooked blackcurrants into the basin before adding the sponge.

⊙ **Castle Puddings:** grease 8 to 10 small castle pudding tins (often called dariole moulds). Half-fill with the sponge mixture, cover and steam for 20 to 25 minutes. Turn out and serve with Jam Sauce (see page 230). A little jam or golden syrup can be put into the moulds before adding the sponge mixture.

⊙ **Chocolate Pudding:** omit 25 g/1 oz (¼ cup) of flour and substitute the same weight of chocolate powder (type used for making chocolate drinks). Serve with Chocolate Sauce (see page 234).

⊙ **Date Pudding:** add 75 g/3 oz (good ½ cup) finely chopped dates to the sponge mixture. Other dried fruit can be substituted. Do not exceed this weight.

⊙ **Ginger Pudding:** add 1 teaspoon ground ginger to the flour. 2 to 3 tablespoons of finely diced crystallized ginger can be added to the creamed mixture. Put a layer of golden syrup at the bottom of the basin.

- **Golden Cap Pudding:** put 2 to 3 tablespoons of golden syrup into the basin before adding the sponge. Serve with hot golden syrup to which you can add a little lemon juice to give a sharper taste.

Light Chocolate Pudding

Cooking time: 1 hour plus standing time ⊙ Serves 4

This recipe may appear unusual, since there is only 25 g/1 oz (1/4 cup) of flour in the ingredients, but that is why it is so light. The breadcrumbs should be white, as wholemeal bread makes a heavier mixture. The water under the steamer should boil so gently that you could just bear the tip of your finger in it. Good quality plain chocolate is best for the pudding, bitter chocolate has too pronounced a flavour.

Break 150 g/5 oz (5 squares) of chocolate into small pieces. Pour 300 ml/1/2 pint (11/4 cups) milk into a saucepan, add the chocolate with 50 g/2 oz (1/4 cup) unsalted butter and 50 g/2 oz (1/4 cup) caster sugar. Heat gently until the chocolate and butter have melted. Stir in 100 g/4 oz (2 cups) fine white breadcrumbs and simmer the ingredients for 5 minutes, by which time the excess milk should be absorbed and you have a thick creamy consistency. Allow the mixture to stand for at least 40 minutes.

Separate 2 eggs. Beat the yolks then add the mixture from the saucepan and 25 g/1 oz (1/4 cup) plain flour. Finally, whisk the 2 egg whites and fold these into the other ingredients.

Grease a 1.2 litre/2 pint (5 cup) basin. Spoon in the mixture, cover with greased greaseproof paper. Steam gently for 1 hour. Turn out and serve with the Chocolate Sauce on this page.

Variations:
- **Macaroon Pudding:** use macaroon biscuit crumbs instead of breadcrumbs and reduce the sugar by half. This is delicious with heated apricot conserve or cooked apricots.
- **Mocha Pudding:** use half milk and half strong coffee instead of all milk.
- **Orange Chocolate Pudding:** the flavour of oranges and chocolate blend well together. Use orange juice, instead of milk, in which to melt the chocolate. When the pudding is cooked, serve hot with raw orange segments.

Chocolate Sauce

Put 150 ml/1/4 pint (2/3 cup) milk into a saucepan. Break 100 g/4 oz (4 squares) plain chocolate into pieces, add to the milk together with a few drops of vanilla essence, 25 g/1 oz (2 tablespoons) butter and 1 tablespoon (11/4 tablespoons) caster sugar. Melt the ingredients slowly. Serve the sauce freshly made and piping hot.

If serving cold, add 3 extra tablespoons (4 tablespoons) of milk, to prevent the chocolate setting when cold. To give the sauce a nice shine when cold, add 1 tablespoon (11/4 tablespoons) golden syrup to the milk and other ingredients.

Highland Tart

Cooking time: 30 to 40 minutes ● Serves 4

Both the recipes on this page were given to me many years ago when I was in Scotland by an enthusiastic cook who said they had been known for generations. I have no record that the Balmoral Tartlets have any connection with the royal residence of that name.

Metric Imperial { **Ingredients** } American
For classic or sweet shortcrust pastry: 175 g/6 oz { **flour etc.** } (see page 295) 1½ cups
For the filling:
50 g/2 oz { **butter** } ¼ cup
50 g/2 oz { **soft brown sugar** } ¼ cup
1 { **egg** } 1
50 g/2 oz { **rolled oats** } generous ½ cup
2 tablespoons { **sultanas** } 3 tablespoons
2 tablespoons { **currants** } 3 tablespoons
2 tablespoons { **finely chopped mixed crystallized peel** } 3 tablespoons
2 tablespoons { **diced glacé cherries** } 3 tablespoons

Make the pastry (see page 295). Roll out and line an 18 to 20 cm/7 to 8 inch flan tin or dish. Chill for a short time. Preheat the oven to 190°C/375°F, Gas Mark 5.

Cream the butter and sugar until soft and light. Beat the egg and add to the creamed mixture with all the other ingredients. Spoon into the pastry case. Bake for 15 to 20 minutes, then lower the heat to 160°C/325°F, Gas Mark 3 for a further 15 to 20 minutes, or until the pastry is cooked. Serve hot as a pudding.

Balmoral Tartlets

Make shortcrust pastry with 175 g/6 oz (1½ cups) flour etc. (see page 295). Roll out and line 12 patty tins. Preheat the oven to 190°C/375°F, Gas Mark 5.

Cream 75 g/3 oz (⅜ cup) butter with 100 g/4 oz (½ cup) caster sugar. Beat in 2 eggs, then add 25 g/1 oz (½ cup) soft fine cake crumbs, 2 teaspoons rice flour or flour, 2 tablespoons (3 tablespoons) finely chopped glacé cherries, 2 tablespoons (3 tablespoons) finely chopped mixed peel and 2 teaspoons whisky or brandy. Finally, whisk 1 egg white until stiff and blend with all the other ingredients. Spoon into the tartlet cases and bake for 20 minutes. Serve cold.

Welsh Cheesecakes

Line 12 patty tins with pastry, as above. Put a teaspoon of raspberry jam in each pastry case. Preheat the oven to 190°C/375°F, Gas Mark 5. Beat 2 eggs with 50 g/2 oz (¼ cup) caster sugar until thick and creamy. Fold in 50 g/2 oz (½ cup) self-raising flour, or plain flour sifted with ½ teaspoon baking powder. Spoon into the tartlet cases, bake for 15 to 20 minutes. Dust with sifted icing sugar. Serve cold.

⊙ Bakewell Tart

Cooking time: 45 minutes ⊙ Serves 4 to 6

This very well-known Derbyshire dish is often referred to as Bakewell Pudding. Recipes for the dish vary a great deal. The first recipe is the better known, the second one produces a more luxurious and interesting pudding.

Metric Imperial { **Ingredients** } American
For shortcrust pastry: 175 g/6 oz { **flour, etc.**} (see page 295) 1½ cups
For the filling:
3 tablespoons { **raspberry jam** } scant ¼ cup
75 g/3 oz { **butter** } ³/8 cup
75 g/3 oz { **caster sugar** } ³/8 cup
1 { **egg** } 1
25 g/1 oz { **plain flour** } ¼ cup
75 g/3 oz { **ground almonds** } ¾ cup
40 g/1½ oz { **fine plain sponge cake crumbs** } generous ½ cup
2 tablespoons { **milk** } 3 tablespoons
For the topping: a little { **icing sugar** }

Make the pastry as page 295. Roll out and line an 18 to 20 cm/7 to 8 inch flan tin or dish. Chill for a short time. Preheat the oven to 190°C/375°F, Gas Mark 5.

Spread the base of the pastry case with the jam. Cream the butter and sugar until soft and light, add the egg and beat well, then stir in the remainder of the ingredients. Spoon into the pastry case and bake for 45 minutes, or until firm. Cool slightly then top with sifted icing sugar. Serve when cold.

⊙ Rich Bakewell Pudding

Make flaky pastry with 175 g/6 oz (1½ cups) flour etc., as the recipe on page 296. Line a 20 to 23 cm/8 to 9 inch flan tin or dish. Chill well before filling. Preheat the oven to 220°C/425°F, Gas Mark 7.

Melt 100 g/4 oz butter, allow to cool, but not set again. Place 4 large eggs with 100 g/4 oz (½ cup) caster sugar into a bowl, whisk until thick and creamy. Gradually whisk in the butter then add 100 g/4 oz (1 cup) ground almonds. Spread raspberry jam into the pastry base, as in the recipe above, then cover with the filling. Bake for 15 minutes then reduce the oven heat to 160°C/325°F, Gas Mark 3 and cook for a further 30 minutes or until the pastry is well risen and firm and the filling set.

◉ Tafferty Tart

Cooking time: 40 to 45 minutes ◉ **Serves 4 to 6**

This old name describes an apple tart. This is still a favourite dessert in Britain, for our apples have such a fine flavour. Many people serve cheese with apple tarts and pies for 'An apple pie without cheese, is as a kiss without a squeeze'. Old recipes always used the butter in the filling, for this adds richness to the taste.

Metric Imperial { **Ingredients** } American
For the shortcrust pastry: 300 g/10 oz { **flour, etc.**} (see page 295) 2½ cups
For the filling:
675 g/1½ lb { **cooking apples** } 1½ lb
1 { **lemon** } 1
pinch { **grated or ground nutmeg** } pinch
75 g/3 oz { **sugar, preferably light brown** } ⅜ cup
a little { **semolina** } a little
25 g/1 oz { **butter, optional** } 2 tablespoons

Make the pastry (see page 295). Roll out and use just over half to line a 20 cm/8 inch pie plate or flan dish. Peel, core and slice the apples fairly thinly. Grate the rind from the lemon and squeeze out 1 to 2 tablespoons juice (amount depends upon personal taste). Mix with the apples, nutmeg and nearly all the sugar.

To prevent the bottom layer of pastry becoming too soft from the apple juice, sprinkle with a little semolina and the rest of the sugar. Arrange the apples over the pastry. Add the butter in small pieces over the fruit. Dampen the edges of the pastry.

Preheat the oven to 200°C/400°F, Gas Mark 6. To encourage the bottom pastry to become crisp, heat a strong baking sheet in the oven during this time.

Roll out the remaining pastry to a round sufficiently large to cover the filling. Place over the fruit and cut away any surplus pastry. Seal and flute the edges. Make a slit in the top of the pie for steam, to escape. Place the tart on the heated baking sheet. Cook for 20 to 25 minutes, or until the pastry is becoming golden. Lower the heat to 180°C/350°F, Gas Mark 4. Cook for 15 to 20 minutes to make sure the fruit is tender. Serve hot or cold.

Variation:
◉ The pie can be topped with caster or sifted icing sugar before serving. Old recipes coated the pie with a thin layer of icing. To make this, blend 100 g/4 oz (1 cup) sifted icing sugar with a little lemon juice. Spread the icing over the hot pie immediately before serving or allow the pie to become cold then add the icing.

⊙ Fruit Pie

Cooking time: 30 to 35 minutes, but see method ⊙ Serves 4 to 6

There are certain traditions about pies in Britain. A savoury pie can be adorned on top with pastry leaves, a rose or tassel before baking but a sweet pie should be left plain. Shortcrust pastry is generally chosen for sweet pies. (See also recipe for Fruit Tart on page 293.)

Metric Imperial { **Ingredients** } American
For the shortcrust pastry: 175 g/6 oz { **flour, etc.** } (see page 295 and below) 1½ cups
For the filling:
675 g/1½ lb { **fruit, see method** } 1½ lb
little { **water if necessary, see method** } little
to taste { **sugar** } to taste

Make the pastry (see page 295). The amount given above is sufficient for a thin crust but increase this to 225 g/8 oz (2 cups) of flour, etc. for a thicker crust.

Prepare the fruit, apples should be sliced thinly, apricots and plums halved if large and the stones removed, soft fruit washed in cold water.

Put the fruit into a 1.2 litre/2 pint (5 cup) pie dish. If likely to shrink during cooking put a pie support, or upturned egg cup, in the dish. Add a little water with hard fruit, soft fruit can be cooked without liquid. Add sugar to taste.

Roll out the pastry, cut a long narrow strip to go around the rim of the pie dish. Moisten the rim with water, press the strip in position and moisten this. Cover with the pastry. Seal the edges and flute by pressing between your forefinger and thumb at regular intervals to give a decorative effect. Preheat the oven to 200°C/400°F, Gas Mark 6 and bake for 15 minutes then reduce the heat to 190°C/375°F, Gas Mark 5 and cook for a further 15 minutes or a little longer if using very firm plums or other fruit. In this case, reduce the heat further for the last few minutes. Dust the pie with sugar and serve hot or cold.

⊙ Fruit Tarts

Crisp tartlet cases, filled with summer fruits, always look inviting. Use shortcrust or sweet shortcrust pastry (see page 295). (Pictured opposite.)

Pastry made with 225 g/8 oz (2 cups) of flour will give approximately 18 small cases. Roll out the pastry and line the patty tins. Chill for a time as this helps the pastry to keep a good shape. Prick the bottom of the pastry to prevent it rising.

Preheat the oven to 200 to 220°C/400 to 425°F, Gas Mark 6 to 7. Use the lower setting for sweet shortcrust. Bake for 12 minutes, or until pale golden and crisp. Allow to cool. Fill the tarts with stoned cherries, strawberries or raspberries.

Heat 4 tablespoons (5 tablespoons) redcurrant jelly with 2 teaspoons of lemon juice, cool slightly and brush over the fruit.

⊙ Custard Tart

Cooking time: 1 to 1¹/4 hours ⊙ **Serves 4**

This tart is as traditional in Britain as roast beef and has always been a great favourite in the north of England. The only problem when making this is to ensure the pastry remains in place and the custard becomes beautifully firm and set.

Metric Imperial { **Ingredients** } American
For the shortcrust pastry: 175 g/6 oz { **flour, etc.**} (see page 295) 1¹/2 cups
For the filling:
1 { **egg** } 1
2 to 3 { **egg yolks** } 2 to 3
1 to 2 tablespoons { **caster sugar, or to taste** } 1¹/2 to 3 tablespoons
300 ml/¹/2 pint { **milk** } 1¹/4 cups
To decorate: { **grated or ground nutmeg** }

Make the pastry (see page 295). Roll out and line an 18 to 20 cm/7 to 8 inch flan dish or tin. Chill the pastry for a short time. Preheat the oven to 200°C/400°F, Gas Mark 6 and bake the pastry blind (explained below) for 15 minutes only or until just set and still pale. Reduce the oven setting to 150°C/300°F, Gas Mark 2.

Meanwhile, beat the egg and egg yolks with the sugar. Save a little egg white in the shells. You have a firmer and richer custard with 3 egg yolks. Warm the milk and pour over the beaten eggs and sugar. Brush the pastry base with the egg white. Strain the custard into the pastry case and top with the nutmeg. Bake for 45 minutes to 1 hour until the custard has set. Serve hot or cold.

⊙ Treacle Tart

Make the pastry flan and bake it blind, as in the previous recipe.

Blend 4 to 5 tablespoons (5 to 6 tablespoons) golden syrup with 3 teaspoons lemon juice and 50 g/2 oz (1 cup) soft breadcrumbs. Put into the partly cooked pastry, lower the heat and bake for 20 to 25 minutes at 160°C/325°F, Gas Mark 3. (Pictured opposite.)

⊙ Norfolk Treacle Tart

Omit the breadcrumbs in the Treacle Tart, but blend 2 egg yolks and 1 tablespoon (1¹/4 tablespoons) cream or milk with the golden syrup and lemon juice. Bake as before.

To bake pastry blind: insert lightly greased greaseproof paper (greased side next to the pastry) or foil in the uncooked pastry, top with crusts of bread, or dried or plastic baking beans. Bake as the recipe, then remove the filling.

⊙ Fruit Crumbles

Cooking time: 35 minutes plus time to cook the fruit ⊙ Serves 4

The crisp crumble topping on fruit makes a change from a pastry crust. Crumble mixtures are quickly and easily prepared. You could prepare a large batch and keep the mixture in the freezer then remove the quantity required.

It is important that the fruit under the crumble is not too moist otherwise it spoils the texture of the topping. As mentioned on page 227, it seems fairly certain that crumbles became popular during the Second World War. That popularity has certainly remained.

Choosing the fruit: all fruits are suitable. If selecting soft fruits, such as raspberries and loganberries, do not pre-cook them, simply put them into a 1.2 litre/2 pint (6 cup) pie or other ovenproof dish with a little sugar. The fruit will be adequately cooked in the time taken to crisp the crumble.

If cooking firm fruits prepare these, put in the dish with a very little liquid and sugar, to taste. Cover the dish and cook for 10 to 15 minutes, or until the fruit is beginning to soften, in a preheated oven, set to 180°C/350°F, Gas Mark 4.

To make a Fruit Crumble for 4 to 6 people you need 450 to 675 g/1 to 1½ lb fruit, depending on the wastage when the peel and any stones are removed. Slice hard fruit like apples and pears, halve plums, if ripe. Make sure you have a flat layer on which to sprinkle the crumble mixture.

⊙ **To add flavour to the fruit:** use apple, or orange or pineapple juice with hard fruits instead of water. Add a few sultanas or other dried fruit.

⊙ **For the crumble:** rub 85 g/3 oz (3/8 cup) butter into 175 g/6 oz (1½ cups) flour. This should be plain flour but you will not spoil the crumble if self-raising is used. Add approximately 100 g/4 oz (1/2 cup) caster or Demerara sugar. Sprinkle the mixture evenly over the fruit and bake for 35 minutes or until golden coloured and crisp.

Variations:

⊙ **Coconut Crumble:** add 50 g/2 oz (2/3 cup) desiccated coconut to the basic mixture.

⊙ **Oaty Crumble:** omit 50 g/2 oz (1/2 cup) flour and substitute the same amount of oatmeal. This is particularly good if a little mixed spice is blended with the flour and 1 to 2 tablespoons of chopped nuts too.

⊙ **Flapjack Crumble:** put 85 g/3 oz (3/8 cup) butter into a saucepan with 50 g/2 oz (1/4 cup) sugar and 2 level tablespoons (2½ tablespoons) golden syrup. Stir over the heat until melted. Remove from the heat and add 175 g/6 oz (1¾ cups) rolled oats. Mix thoroughly, then sprinkle over the fruit and smooth evenly with a knife. Bake for approximately 25 minutes in an oven preheated to 160°C/325°F, Gas Mark 3.

Cherry Cobbler

Cooking time: 30 to 35 minutes ⊙ Serves 4 to 6

Magnificent black and red dessert cherries are grown in Kent, Buckinghamshire and other fruit growing areas of Britain. This topping has retained its popularity. The name probably originated because of the similarity in shape of the roughly formed scone topping to a cobbler's tool. Nowadays the dough is cut into neat rounds.

Metric Imperial { **Ingredients** } American
450 to 675 g/1 to 1½ lb { **ripe cherries** } 1 to 1½ lb
2 to 3 tablespoons { **water** } 3 to 4 tablespoons
50 g/2 oz { **sugar** } ¼ cup
For the cobbler:
175 g/6 oz { **self-raising or plain flour sifted with 1½ teaspoons baking powder** } 1¼ cups
50 g/2 oz { **butter** } ¼ cup
50 g/2 oz { **caster sugar** } ¼ cup
a little { **milk** } a little
For the glaze: { **milk and sugar** }

Preheat the oven to 180°C/350°F, Gas Mark 4. Stone the cherries if possible, put into a 1.2 litre/2 pint (5 cup) pie dish or casserole. Add any juice left from stoning the fruit plus the water and sugar. Cover the dish and cook for 10 to 15 minutes. Raise the oven setting to 200°C/400°F, Gas Mark 6.

Sift the flour, or flour and baking powder, into a bowl. Rub in the butter, add the sugar and enough milk to make a soft rolling consistency. Either pat into rounds with your hands or roll out until 1.5 cm/½ inch thick and cut into rounds.

Brush the top of the rounds with milk and sprinkle with a little sugar. Arrange over the fruit and cook for 20 minutes until well risen and firm. Serve hot.

Pwdin Efa

Cooking time: 50 minutes ⊙ Serves 5 to 6

This Welsh version of Eve's Pudding has a soufflé topping over apple purée.

Use the same amount of apples, sugar and lemon juice as in Eve's Pudding (see page 244), but increase the water to 150 ml/¼ pint (⅔ cup). Simmer the apples in the water, sugar and lemon juice until a purée forms. Put into a dish, as on page 244. Preheat the oven to 160°C/325°F, Gas Mark 3. Heat 50 g/2 oz (¼ cup) butter in a pan, add 50 g/2 oz (½ cup) plain flour, blend with the butter and cook gently for 2 minutes. Pour 300 ml/½ pint (1¼ cups) milk into the saucepan, stir as the liquid comes to the boil and thickens. Add a few drops of vanilla essence and 50 g/2 oz (¼ cup) caster sugar. Remove the pan from the heat. Separate 2 eggs, beat the yolks into the sauce. Whisk the egg whites, fold into the mixture and blend with the other ingredients. Spoon over the apples and bake for 40 minutes. Top with sifted icing sugar.

⊙ Cranachan

Toasted oatmeal is delicious with fruit. Although raspberries are the usual fruit in this Scottish recipe, other fruits can be used. Ripe, juicy cherries are particularly good and sliced strawberries. You need 225 to 350 g/8 to 12 oz (1/2 to 3/4 lb) for 4 to 6 people. (Pictured opposite.)

Spread 50 g/2 oz (1/3 cup) oatmeal or rolled oats (good 1/2 cup) on to a flat tin and toast under the grill until golden in colour. Allow to cool.

Whip 300 ml/1/2 pint (11/4 cups) double cream until it just stands in peaks. Add the oatmeal, or rolled oats, with sugar to taste. Arrange layers of raspberries, or other fruit, and the oatmeal cream in glasses and chill well.

⊙ Eve's Pudding

Cooking time: 1 hour ⊙ Serves 4 to 6

As the name suggests this dish must be made with apples. The English and Welsh versions of the pudding are quite different.

Metric Imperial { **Ingredients** } American
675 g/11/2 lb { **cooking apples** } 11/2 lb
2 tablespoons { **water** } 3 tablespoons
50 g/2 oz { **caster or light brown sugar** } 1/4 cup
2 to 3 teaspoons { **lemon juice** } 2 to 3 teaspoons
For the topping:
110 g/4 oz { **butter or margarine** } 1/2 cup
110 g/4 oz { **caster sugar** } 1/2 cup
2 { **eggs** } 2
110 g/4 oz { **self-raising flour or plain flour sifted with 1 teaspoon baking powder** } 1 cup
To decorate: { **caster sugar** }

Preheat the oven to 160°C/325°F, Gas Mark 3. Peel, core and thinly slice the apples. Put into a 1.2 litre/2 pint (5 cup) pie dish with the water, sugar and lemon juice. Cover and heat for 10 minutes.

Make the topping as the Victoria Sandwich (see page 285). Spoon evenly over the fruit and bake for 50 minutes, or until firm and golden in colour. Top with caster sugar and serve hot or cold.

⊙ Apple Charlotte

Cooking time: 1 hour ⊙ **Serves 4**

This mixture of fruit and bread has always been a great favourite. The recipe can be used with other fruits throughout the year.

Metric Imperial { **Ingredients** } American
450 g/1 lb { **cooking apples, weight after peeling** } 1 lb
75 g/3 oz { **granulated or caster sugar** } 3/8 cup
a little { **water** } a little
4 to 5 { **large slices of bread, crusts removed** } 4 to 5
75 g/3 oz { **butter** } 3/8 cup

Peel and slice the apples very thinly. Put into a saucepan with half the sugar and just a very little water. Cook steadily, adding only enough water as needed until a thick smooth pulp forms. Cut the bread into neat fingers.

Melt the butter and dip the bread in this until coated on both sides. Fit about a third of the slices into a 900 ml to 1.2 litre/1½ to 2 pint (3¾ to 5 cup) pie dish. Add a light sprinkling of the remaining sugar then half the apple pulp. Put another layer of buttered fingers of bread and a sprinkling of sugar over the apples, then add the rest of the apple pulp. Top the fruit with a neat layer of bread and the last of the sugar.

Preheat the oven to 180°C/350°F, Gas Mark 4 and bake for 45 minutes. Serve hot.

Variations:
- ⊙ Flavour the apples with lemon zest or add a little mixed spice or ground ginger.
- ⊙ Heat the butter in a frying pan instead of melting it. Fry the fingers of bread in the butter until pale golden. This gives a crisper result to the pudding.
- ⊙ Use about 150 g/5 oz (3 cups) coarse breadcrumbs instead of slices of bread. Either blend these with 60 g/2½ oz (½ cup) shredded suet or toss in 75 g/3 oz (3/8 cup) melted butter until coated. Fill the dish as above and bake as before.

⊙ Baked Apples

The high quality of British cooking apples makes this simple dish into a special dessert. Today the apples can be cooked by microwave within a few minutes. (Pictured opposite.)

Core large apples, slit the skins around the middle. Place the apples in a dish and fill the centres with your selected mixture, such as butter and brown sugar; dried fruit and golden syrup; bramble (blackberry) jelly or mincemeat.

Preheat the oven to 180°C/350°F, Gas Mark 4. Bake for approximately 45 minutes.

⊙ Bread and Butter Pudding

Cooking time: 1½ hours, but see method ⊙ **Serves 4**

This pudding has suddenly become popular in many restaurants. Caterers have discovered what most home cooks have known for years, that although it is often described as 'nursery food', a good Bread and Butter Pudding is one of the most appetizing desserts.

Cut 2 to 4 thin slices of bread. The number depends upon how substantial you like the pudding. Spread these with a generous amount of butter, then cut them into squares or triangles. Fit them neatly into a 1.2 litre/2 pint (5 cup) pie dish.

Add 75 g/3 oz (good ½ cup) sultanas or other dried fruit. Beat 3 large eggs, or use 2 eggs and 2 egg yolks, with 50 g/2 oz (¼ cup) caster sugar. Warm 600 ml/1 pint (2½ cups) milk and pour over the eggs and sugar. Strain the custard into the dish and allow to stand for at least 30 minutes.

Top with a little grated nutmeg or ground cinnamon and a sprinkling of sugar.

Preheat the oven to 150°C/300°F, Gas Mark 2 and bake for 1½ hours. The pudding can be baked at a slightly hotter temperature, i.e. 160°C/325°F, Gas Mark 3, for just over an hour but check carefully that the custard is not beginning to boil.

Variations:
- ⊙ Add diced macaroon biscuits and strips of tenderized dried apricots to the bread and butter or add a mixture of chopped candied peel.
- ⊙ Spread the bread and butter with a little marmalade.

⊙ Osborne Pudding

This is a very special Bread and Butter Pudding, spread the slices of bread with butter and marmalade, as suggested above. Flavour the milk with finely grated orange zest and with 1 to 2 tablespoons brandy, sherry or rum. When the pudding is nearly cooked, top with a layer of brown sugar. Return to the oven for 10 minutes.

⊙ Queen of Puddings

Make 50 g/2 oz (1 cup) of fine breadcrumbs (plain cake could be used instead). Spread the bottom of a 1.2 litre/2 pint (5 cup) pie dish with jam. Add the crumbs.

Separate 2 eggs, beat the yolks with 1 tablespoon (1¼ tablespoons) sugar. Heat 300 ml/½ pint (1¼ cups) milk, pour it on to the egg yolks and sugar and then strain this over the crumbs in the dish. Allow to stand for 30 minutes.

Preheat the oven to 160°C/325°F, Gas Mark 3 and bake for approximately 45 minutes, until just firm. Spread with jam. Whisk the egg whites until stiff, fold 50 g/2 oz (¼ cup) sugar into these, spoon over the top of the pudding. Decorate with small pieces of glacé cherries and angelica. Return to the oven, lowering the heat to 150°C/300°F Gas Mark 2, and bake for 30 minutes. Serve hot.

◉ Shrove Tuesday Pancakes

Cooking time: 2 to 3 minutes each pancake ◉ Makes 12 to 18

The following recipe is the one used today but older recipes for the batter were considerably richer. The rich mixture is so delicious I have given it as a choice for special occasions. These pancakes were made for Shrove Tuesday to use up eggs and flour in the home before fasting during Lent.

Metric Imperial (**Ingredients**) American
110 g/4 oz (**plain flour**) 1 cup
pinch (**salt**) pinch
2 (**eggs**) 2
275 ml/scant 1/2 pint (**milk or milk and water**) scant 11/4 cups
To cook: little (**oil**)
To serve: (**caster sugar, lemon wedges**)

Blend the flour and salt. Add the eggs and enough liquid to make a stiff batter. Mix until smooth then gradually beat in the remaining liquid and whisk well.

Heat 1 to 2 teaspoons oil in a pancake pan. Pour in enough batter to give a wafer thin covering. Cook for 1 to 11/2 minutes on the underside until golden in colour. You can tell if the bottom is cooked when the pancake moves freely in the pan. Turn or toss and cook for the same time on the second side. Roll the pancake, dredge with sugar and serve with lemon. Continue like this. You should find that no oil is required after cooking the first pancake.

To keep pancakes hot: place on a heated dish in the oven, set to 140 to 150°C/275 to 300°F, Gas Mark 1 to 2 or stand the dish over a pan of boiling water.

Notes:
◉   To prevent pancakes sticking to the pan, add 1 tablespoon (11/4 tablespoons) melted butter or oil to the batter immediately before cooking and mix thoroughly.
◉   This is a great asset if freezing the pancakes as it stops them becoming leathery.
◉   The more economical batter using 1 egg is under Yorkshire Pudding (see page 111).

◉ Luxury Pancakes

Use 1 egg and 3 egg yolks and single cream instead of milk in the batter. Layer the cooked pancakes with poached apricots or apricot conserve. Serve with cream.

◉ Norfolk Batter Pudding

Preheat the oven to 220°C/425°F, Gas Mark 7. Heat 25 g/1 oz (2 tablespoons) butter in a pie dish or casserole. Add 450 g/1 lb prepared fruit plus 2 to 3 tablespoons dried fruit, cover the dish and heat for 10 minutes. Pour the pancake batter over the fruit and cook for 25 to 30 minutes. Reduce the heat slightly after 15 minutes.

◉ Rice Pudding

Cooking time: 2 to 3 hours if possible ◉ **Serves 4**

A really creamy rice pudding depends upon long slow cooking, that little knob of butter (suet was used in the past) and full cream milk. Stir the pudding once or twice during cooking – this releases the starch grains and helps to thicken the pudding.

Metric Imperial { **Ingredients** } American
50 g/2 oz { **short grain (pudding) rice** } good 1/3 cup
600 ml/1 pint { **milk** } 2 1/2 cups
2 tablespoons { **sugar** } 2 1/2 tablespoons
25 g/1 oz { **butter** } 2 tablespoons
For the topping: { **grated nutmeg** }

Preheat the oven to 150°C/300°F, Gas Mark 2. Put the rice into a 1.2 litre/2 pint (5 cup) pie dish, add the milk, sugar and the butter, cut into small pieces about the size of a pea. Add the nutmeg and bake for 2 to 3 hours. Stir during this time, see above. Serve with cooked fruit or Jam Sauce (see page 230).

◉ Rice Soufflé Pudding

Use the ingredients as above but omit the nutmeg.

Cook the rice with the milk, sugar and butter in the top of a double saucepan, or basin over hot water, until the mixture has thickened and the rice is soft. Flavour the pudding with several leaves of lemon balm. Take off the heat and remove the herbs. Separate 2 eggs, beat the yolks and blend with the rice pudding. Whisk the egg whites, fold into the rice pudding. Spoon the mixture into a 18 cm/7 inch buttered soufflé dish. Preheat the oven to 160°C/325°F, Gas Mark 3 and bake for 25 to 30 minutes. Serve with a hot fruit purée or with one of the wine sauces below and on page 252.

◉ Sweet Wine Sauce

This is excellent with a milk pudding or a plain steamed sponge.

Heat 300 ml/1/2 pint (1 1/4 cups) good red wine with 75 g/3 oz (3/8 cup) sugar and a little finely grated lemon or orange zest.

⊙ Sherry Sauce

This is not only good with poached pears or a plain steamed sponge, but it is an excellent sauce to serve with the Christmas Pudding (see page 311).

Make the egg custard, as given in the Sherry Trifle (see page 258). Meanwhile, simmer the pared rind of 1 orange in 150 ml/¼ pint (⅔ cup) water for 10 minutes, until there is only 2 tablespoons (2½ tablespoons) left. Add 150 ml/¼ pint (⅔ cup) sweet sherry, warm, then strain into the custard. Whisk to blend.

⊙ Baked Custard

Cooking time: 1¼ hours ⊙ Serves 4

The secret of any good egg custard is to use rather more egg yolks than whites, if this is possible. This gives a richer taste. Check the baking time carefully, see below.

Warm 600 ml/1 pint (2½ cups) milk with a little vanilla essence. Better still, put a vanilla pod into the milk. When the milk is warmed remove the pod, rinse it in cold water and allow it to dry so it can be used again. Preheat the oven to 150°C/300°F, Gas Mark 2.

Beat 2 large eggs and 3 egg yolks (or use 4 eggs) with 50 g/2 oz (¼ cup) caster sugar (you can use a little less). Add the warm milk and mix well. Strain into a 900 ml to 1.2 litre/1½ to 2 pint (3¾ to 5 cup) pie dish. Top with a little grated nutmeg. Stand the dish in a tin of warm water and bake until just firm, check after 1 hour. Prolonged cooking, as well as too great a heat, makes a custard curdle. Serve hot or cold.

⊙ Caramel Custard

Cooking time: 1½ hours ⊙ Serves 4

To make the caramel: put 75 g/3 oz (⅜ cup) sugar and 3 tablespoons (4 tablespoons) water into a strong saucepan. Stir over a low heat until the sugar has melted. Allow the mixture to boil, without stirring, until the mixture turns a golden brown. Take off the heat. Either add another 2 to 3 tablespoons cold water to cool down the caramel or plunge the saucepan into a metal container of cold water. If you add cold water you make a thinner caramel which does not coat the mould as well and you must continue to stir over a low heat until the extra water and caramel have blended together. Pour the caramel into a 900 ml/1½ pint (3¾ cup) soufflé dish or ovenproof mould (a pie dish is not sufficiently deep for this dessert). When the caramel has cooled slightly turn the mould around until coated inside with the caramel.

Make the egg custard as above, strain into the mould and proceed as above. Because of the greater depth of mixture you need a slightly longer cooking time.

Note:
⊙ If your oven is inclined to be fierce, use 140°C/275°F, Gas Mark 1. You may need to cook the custard for a slightly longer time. Cool then turn out.

Variations:
- ◉ **Caramel Cream:** use half single cream and half milk in the recipe on page 252.
- ◉ **Coffee Custard:** flavour the baked custard with 2 to 3 teaspoons instant coffee dissolved in the warm milk.

◉ Summer Fruit Compote

Cooking time: 5 to 10 minutes ◉ Serves 4 to 6

This is a most colourful and delicious mixture of summer fruits. People who grow fruit in the garden can adjust the quantities according to what is available.

Metric Imperial { **Ingredients** } American
250 ml/8 fl oz { **water** } 1 cup
1 tablespoon { **lemon juice** } 1¼ tablespoons
675 g/1½ lb { **mixed summer fruits, see method** }1½ lb
50 g/2 oz { **sugar** } ¼ cup

Put the water and lemon juice into a wide saucepan, or use a frying pan. Add prepared firm fruits, such as blackcurrants, cherries, ripe gooseberries and loganberries to the hot liquid and poach until just softened. Cool slightly then lift out with a perforated spoon and place into the serving bowl. Add the sugar to the syrup and stir until dissolved. This makes sure the blackcurrant skins are not toughened. Allow to cool.

Add the prepared soft fruits, raspberries, strawberries, white and red currants to the serving bowl and pour over the syrup.

◉ Summer Pudding

Cooking time: as required by the fruits used ◉ Serves 4 to 6

This has always been a favourite pudding in private homes but during the past years it has moved into good restaurants, so it has been promoted to 'haute cuisine'.

The secret of success is to use fruit with plenty of flavour and colour; to cut really thin slices of bread (or plain cake for a luxurious version) and to allow adequate time for the pudding to stand.

Cut 350 g/12 oz (¾ lb) bread or cake into thin slices (the weight of bread is without crusts). Line the base and sides of a 1.2 litre/2 pint (5 cup) basin or mould or use 4 to 6 individual small containers. Leave sufficient bread or cake for the topping.

You need 900 g/2 lb mixed fruit. An ideal blend would be raspberries, redcurrants and blackcurrants. Cook the fruit with a very little water and sugar to taste, do not over-cook it. If you dislike pips, sieve the fruit. Pour the warm fruit into the lined container(s). Any surplus juice can be served as a sauce. Cover with the rest of the bread or cake, then with greaseproof paper. Put a plate, or plates, on top with a light weight(s). Leave overnight in a cool place. Turn out and decorate with fruit and leaves if available. Serve with cream.

Fruit Fool

Cooking time: as individual fruit ⊚ Serves 4

This simple dessert is a great favourite, especially when gooseberries are in season. The correct name is Fruit Foule, the word means the fruit is in small pieces. (Blackberry Fool pictured opposite.)

Metric Imperial { **Ingredients** } American
450 g/1 lb { **gooseberries, or other fruit** } 1 lb
very little { **water** } very little
to taste { **sugar** } to taste
450 ml/3/4 pint { **thick custard, as Cup Custards** } (see page 257) 2 cups
         or { **half custard and half double cream, or all double cream** }
To decorate: { **whipped cream and crystallized rose or violet petals or whole fruit** }

Prepare and cook the fruit with the minimum of water and sugar to taste until it is soft. Sieve or liquidize or mash into small pieces. Allow to become quite cold. Make the custard and allow this to cool. Blend with the fruit. If using cream, whip this until it stands in peaks and fold into the fruit, or fruit and custard. Chill well, then spoon into glasses and decorate. Chill well before serving.

Variation:
⊚ The custard can be made with custard powder instead of eggs.

Fruit Snow

This is excellent made with any fruit purée, but it is particularly good with those with a sharp flavour, such as gooseberries.

    Cook the fruit, as above, then sieve or liquidize. To each 300 ml/1/2 pint (11/4 cups) of fruit purée allow 1 egg white plus 1 tablespoon (11/4 tablespoons) sugar. Whisk the egg white until very stiff, fold in the sugar then fold this into the fruit. Spoon into glasses and chill for a short time. This must be made fairly soon before serving the dessert.

Variation:
⊚ **Frosted Fruit Snow:** put the mixture into a tray in the freezer and leave until lightly frosted, then spoon into glasses and serve with lightly whipped cream.

Irish Coffee Pudding

Cooking time: 10 minutes ⊙ Serves 6

The recipe for this light dessert was given to me years ago by a student when I was lecturing at a college she attended. She explained that it had been handed down in her family. Although not a well known Irish recipe, I think it deserves to be included as 'a classic' because of its similarity to the famous Irish (Gaelic) Coffee. It is fairly sweet so the amount of sugar can be reduced.

Metric Imperial { **Ingredients** } American
4 { **eggs** } 4
100 g/4 oz { **caster sugar** } 1/2 cup
300 ml/1/2 pint { **very strong cold coffee** } 11/4 cups
3 tablespoons { **Irish whiskey** } 4 tablespoons
11 g/scant 1/2 oz { **gelatine** } 2 envelopes
300 ml/1/2 pint { **double or whipping cream** } 11/4 cups
To decorate: little extra { **whipped cream and chopped walnuts** }

Separate the eggs, put the yolks and half the sugar into a basin, whisk until smooth then add three-quarters of the coffee. Stand the basin over a saucepan of hot, but not boiling, water and whisk or stir briskly until a thickened custard. Blend the whiskey into the mixture. Sprinkle the gelatine into the remaining coffee, allow to stand for 2 to 3 minutes then dissolve over hot water. Blend with the coffee mixture then allow to stiffen slightly.

Whip the cream until it stands in peaks. Whisk the egg whites in a separate bowl until stiff, blend the remaining sugar with these. Fold the cream and then the egg whites into the jellied mixture. Spoon into a large serving dish or individual glasses and allow to set. Top with cream and walnuts.

Port Wine Jelly

Cooking time: 10 minutes ⊙ Serves 4

Pare the zest from a lemon. Put 450 ml/3/4 pint (2 cups) water into a saucepan, add the lemon zest and 50 g/2 oz (1/4 cup) sugar. Stir until the sugar dissolves. Simmer for 10 minutes and strain. Measure out 300 ml/1/2 pint (11/4 cups).

Measure out 300 ml/1/2 pint (11/4 cups) port wine. Put 3 tablespoons (4 tablespoons) of this in a basin, add 11 g/scant 1/2 oz (2 envelopes) gelatine, allow to stand for 2 to 3 minutes then dissolve over hot water, add to the lemon-flavoured syrup and the rest of the port wine. Put into a mould, rinsed out in cold water, allow to set. Serve decorated with whipped cream.

⊙ Burnt Cream

Cooking time: 1¹/₂ hours ⊙ **Serves 4**

Scottish Burnt Cream is very similar to the French Crème Brûlée.

Metric Imperial { **Ingredients** } American
300 ml/¹/₂ pint { **double cream** } 1¹/₄ cups
300 ml/¹/₂ pint { **milk** } 1¹/₄ cups
2 { **large eggs** } 2
3 { **egg yolks** } 3
50 g/2 oz { **caster sugar** } ¹/₄ cup
¹/₄ teaspoon { **vanilla essence** } ¹/₄ teaspoon
For the topping: 50 g/2 oz **caster sugar** ¹/₄ cup

Preheat the oven to 140°C/275°F, Gas Mark 1. Warm the cream and milk together. Beat the eggs and egg yolks with the sugar. Add the cream and milk and essence and blend thoroughly. Strain into a 900 ml/1¹/₂ pint (3³/₄ cup) flameproof deep dish. Stand this in a tin containing hot water. Bake until the custard is set. Allow to cool. Top with the caster sugar. Place under a preheated hot grill and leave until the top is brown. Chill well before serving.

Variations:

⊙ Use 4 large eggs instead of the 2 eggs and 3 egg yolks.
⊙ Make Cup Custards (see below), put into flameproof dishes. When cold top with the sugar and grill as the recipe above.

⊙ Cup Custards

Cooking time: 15 to 20 minutes ⊙ **Serves 4**

Metric Imperial { **Ingredients** } American
4 { **egg yolks** } 4
25 g/1 oz { **caster sugar** } 2 tablespoons
600 ml/1 pint { **single cream or milk** } 2¹/₂ cups
¹/₄ teaspoon { **vanilla essence or other flavouring** } ¹/₄ teaspoon

Whisk the egg yolks with the sugar. Heat the cream or milk with the essence. Pour over the egg yolks and mix thoroughly. Strain into the top of a double saucepan, or use a basin. Place over hot, but not boiling, water and stir until the mixture coats a wooden spoon. Pour into 4 cup-shaped dishes and allow to cool.

⊙ Sherry Trifle

Cooking time: 15 minutes ⊙ Serves 6 to 8

Metric Imperial { **Ingredients** } American

For the custard:
2 { **eggs** } 2
3 to 4 { **egg yolks** } 3 to 4
50 g/2 oz { **caster sugar** } 1/4 cup
1 teaspoon { **cornflour, optional** } 1 teaspoon
600 ml/1 pint { **milk or half milk and half single cream** } 2 1/2 cups
1 { **vanilla pod or a little vanilla essence** } 1

For the base:
6 to 8 { **small trifle sponge cakes** } 6 to 8
3 to 4 tablespoons { **raspberry jam** } 4 to 5 tablespoons
150 ml/1/4 pint { **sweet sherry** } 2/3 cup
small amount { **canned apricots in syrup, optional** } small amount
18 { **ratafias** } 18

To decorate:
300 ml/1/2 pint { **double or whipping cream** } 1 1/4 cups
2 to 3 teaspoons { **caster sugar, optional** } 2 to 3 teaspoons
{ **Maraschino or glacé cherries** }
{ **angelica leaves, ratafias, browned almonds** }

Blend the eggs and egg yolks with the sugar in a good sized basin. Add the cornflour, if using this. The small amount does not affect the texture of the custard but it helps to prevent it curdling. Warm the milk, or milk and cream, pour over the egg mixture then add the vanilla pod or essence. Stand over a saucepan of hot, but not boiling, water. Whisk or stir briskly until the custard forms a fairly thick coating over a wooden spoon. Remove the vanilla pod.

Split the sponge cakes, then sandwich the halves together with the jam. Put into a large serving dish or individual dishes. Soak with the sherry or add the sherry to a few tablespoons of the syrup from the canned fruit and pour this over the sponges. Dice the apricots, if using these, and add to the dish with the ratafias then pour the warm custard over the ingredients. Cover the dish(es) to prevent a skin forming and leave until absolutely cold.

Whip and sweeten the cream. Pipe or spread some over the custard, then pipe a design around the edge of the trifle(s). Decorate with halved cherries, angelica, ratafias and browned almonds.

The flavour is better if the trifle is made a day ahead of being served.

⊙ Flummery

Cooking time: 5 to 6 minutes ⊙ Serves 6

A flummery is another of the very light desserts that have been popular for a long time. It is a little firmer in texture than a syllabub, also on this page. Most chemists, as well as good grocers, sell orange flower water.

The original old recipe for a syllabub suggested you pour wine into a large bowl, then carry this to the cowshed and milk the cow, allowing the required amount of milk to blend with the wine. You then drank this concoction.

Metric Imperial { **Ingredients** } American
100 g/4 oz { **almonds** } 1 cup
300 ml/½ pint { **single cream** } 1¼ cups
1 x 5 cm/2 inch { **portion of cinnamon stick** } 1 x 5 cm/2 inch
2 teaspoons { **finely grated orange zest** } 2 teaspoons
    or 1 teaspoon { **orange flower water** } 1 teaspoon
50 g/2 oz { **caster sugar, or to taste** } ¼ cup
150 ml/¼ pint { **sweet white wine** } ⅔ cup
2 level teaspoons { **gelatine** } 2 level teaspoons
2 tablespoons { **brandy** } 3 tablespoons
150 ml/¼ pint { **double cream** } ⅔ cup

Blanch the almonds by putting them into boiling water for a few seconds, then removing the skins. Dry and chop finely. Put the single cream into a saucepan with the cinnamon stick and the orange zest or orange flower water. Bring just to boiling point then remove from the heat. Remove the cinnamon stick; add half the almonds and all the sugar.

Pour half the wine into a basin, add the gelatine and allow to stand for 2 to 3 minutes. Place over a pan of very hot water or in a bowl in the microwave and leave until dissolved. Whisk into the hot cream, then add the rest of the wine and the brandy. Leave until the mixture sets very lightly.

Whip the double cream until it stands in soft peaks. Beat a tablespoon into the jellied mixture, then fold in the remainder. Spoon into individual glasses and allow to become firm. Place the rest of the almonds on a baking tray and heat under the grill until golden brown. Cool and sprinkle over the top of the dessert.

⊙ Lemon Syllabub

Whip 450 ml/¾ pint (2 cups) double cream until it just holds its shape, then blend in 150 ml/¼ pint (⅔ cup) single cream. Add 3 to 4 teaspoons lemon juice, 150 ml/¼ pint (⅔ cup) white wine and a little brandy. Blend in sugar to taste. Spoon into glasses and top with crystallized flowers.

Sieved raspberries or other fruit can be used instead of lemon juice.

⊙ Sweet Fantasy

Cooking time: 10 minutes ⊙ **Serves 6 to 8**

The term 'Sweet Fantasy' is used in a number of traditional British desserts. This is the most interesting, for it combines a light sponge, for which we are famous, with a very unusual topping. It makes a good alternative to the well-known trifle.

Metric Imperial { **Ingredients** } American
1 x 23 cm/9 inch { **sponge sandwich** (see page 285) } 1
For the filling:
150 ml/1/4 pint { **double cream** } 2/3 cup
150 ml/1/4 pint { **sweet white wine** } 2/3 cup
2 tablespoons { **raspberry jam** } 3 tablespoons
For the topping and decoration:
2 { **eggs** } 2
150 ml/1/4 pint { **double cream** } 2/3 cup
25 g/1 oz { **butter** } 2 tablespoons
75 g/3 oz { **icing sugar** } 2/3 cup
2 teaspoons { **sweet white wine** } 2 teaspoons

Place one half of the sponge on a serving dish. Whip the cream until it stands in soft peaks. Moisten the sponge with half the wine, spread with the jam and then the cream. Add the second half of the sponge. Moisten with the remainder of the wine.

Hard-boil the eggs for the decoration, shell these and remove the yolks. The whites are not needed for this recipe but make a good garnish on salads. Whip the cream for the topping until it forms firm peaks, spread over the top of the sponge.

Cream the butter and sugar until soft and light, then add the wine and the egg yolks. Rub this egg yolk mixture through a coarse sieve so that it falls over the top of the cake in small balls. Chill well before serving.

⊙ Tipsy Cake

This is another of the classic British desserts. It is based on the Victoria (Butter) Sponge Cake (see pages 285 and 286).

Cut the sponge into 3 horizontal layers. Put the first layer on to the serving plate. Spread this with raspberry jam and moisten with sweet sherry. Add the second layer of sponge and spread this with apricot jam and moisten with sweet sherry. Put on the third layer of sponge and spread this with damson or greengage jam and once again moisten with sweet sherry.

Whip sufficient cream to cover the entire sponge. Coat the top and sides with cream and decorate with ratafias, glacé cherries, angelica leaves and blanched almonds. Chill well before serving.

◉ Old-Fashioned Ice Cream

Cooking time: 10 minutes ◉ **Serves 6**

This is a rich ice cream with the true custard flavour of the ices of the past.

Metric Imperial { **Ingredients** } American
2 { **egg yolks** } 2
1 { **egg** } 1
300 ml/1/2 pint { **single cream or full cream milk** } 11/4 cups
50 g/2 oz { **caster sugar** } 1/4 cup
1 { **vanilla pod, or use vanilla essence to taste** } 1
300 ml/1/2 pint { **double or whipping cream** } 11/4 cups

Put the egg yolks and egg into a heatproof bowl, add the single cream or milk with the sugar and vanilla pod or essence. Whisk the ingredients together. Stand over a saucepan of hot, but not boiling, water and stir briskly or whisk until the custard thickens sufficiently to just coat the back of a wooden spoon. Remove the vanilla pod, rinse this in cold water, dry and store. Cover the custard so a skin does not form and allow to cool.

Whip the cream until it stands in soft peaks, fold into the custard and freeze. It makes a lighter ice cream if this is beaten once during freezing.

◉ Chocolate Ice Cream

Dissolve 100 g/4 oz (4 squares) of plain chocolate in the hot custard. This is better made with milk than single cream. Sifted cocoa or chocolate powder to taste could be used instead. Proceed as the recipe above, reducing the sugar to 25 g/l oz (2 tablespoons), if you wish.

◉ Coffee Ice Cream

Use 300 ml/1/2 pint (11/4 cups) milk with the egg yolks and egg. Heat the milk with 3 teaspoons finely ground coffee (strain if necessary), coffee essence or instant coffee. Blend over the egg yolks and eggs, then add the sugar and proceed as the recipe above.

The modern touch: If using an ice cream maker which freezes and aerates the mixture, you can replace the single cream in the custard with milk and the double or whipping cream with single cream. This will still produce a rich and creamy mixture.

Variation:
◉ For a change of flavour replace the cream with full fat yogurt.

Brown Bread Ice Cream

Cooking time: 10 to 15 minutes plus time for making ice cream ◎ Serves 6

This is one of the most unexpected recipes, for its flavour is exceptionally good. It is difficult to realize that it is bread that produces the special taste and texture. It was a feature of Edwardian dinner parties.

Metric Imperial { **Ingredients** } American
Ingredients as: { **Ice Cream** (see page 262) }
100 g/4 oz fine { **brown or wholemeal breadcrumbs** } 2 cups
to taste { **brandy or rum** } to taste

Prepare the ingredients for the ice cream (see page 262). Freeze very lightly while crisping the bread. This makes it easier to distribute the crumbs evenly.

Preheat the oven to 150°C/300°F, Gas Mark 2. Put the crumbs in a single layer on baking trays and crisp for 10 to 15 minutes then allow to become quite cold. Blend evenly with the lightly frozen ice cream and add brandy or rum to taste.

Crème de Menthe Ice Cream

Use the Old-Fashioned Ice Cream recipe on page 262 and flavour it with a small glass of crème de menthe. Be sparing with sugar, for liqueurs are very sweet.

Fruit Ice Creams

The Old-Fashioned Ice Cream on page 262 is a good basis for fruit ices. Add 300 ml/1/2 pint (1 1/4 cups) of a really thick smooth fruit purée to the quantity in the recipe and sweeten to taste.

Gooseberry Ice Cream

Follow the Fruit Fool recipe (see page 254), using gooseberries and half cream and half custard. Blend the ingredients together and freeze.

Ginger Ice Cream

If you are a lover of preserved ginger then you will approve of this ice cream. I have adapted a recipe from the book *The Complete Confectioner* of 1789 by Frederick Nutt. This clearly proves that ice creams have been a favourite for a long time in this country.

Use the Old-Fashioned Ice Cream recipe on page 262. Add approximately 100 g/4 oz (1/4 lb) finely diced preserved ginger to the milk in the recipe. I also add a little of the syrup from the jar. When frozen this is delicious.

◉ Sorbets

Cooking time: see method ◉ Serves 6

These were first made popular during the days of very heavy meals in the Victorian and Edwardian eras. They were served in the middle of a seven or eight course meal to refresh the palate. Sorbets are popular today and they can be served during a meal or for a dessert. Lemon sorbet is still the most popular.

The modern ice cream makers are excellent for sorbets, they aerate the mixture.

◉ Lemon Sorbet

Pare the top zest from 2 large lemons, put into a saucepan with 450 ml/³/4 pint (2 cups) water and 100 g/4 oz (1¹/2 cups) sugar. Stir until the sugar has dissolved, then simmer for 5 minutes, press the zest in the pan while simmering to extract the maximum flavour. Cool then strain, mix with the juice of 2 lemons. Freeze very lightly. Whisk 2 egg whites until stiff and blend these with the frosted lemon ice. Continue to freeze the mixture but bring out of the freezer well before required. The sorbet mixture can be put into lemon cases and frozen like that.

Variations:
- **Melon Sorbet:** sieve or liquidize the pulp from the melon. Simmer the zest from 1 lemon with 300 ml/¹/2 pint (¹/4 cups) water and 50 g/2 oz (¹/4 cup) sugar. Strain and mix with the melon pulp and lemon juice to flavour. Freeze and blend with the 2 whisked egg whites as above. The melon can be flavoured with a little ground ginger or add 1 to 2 mint leaves to the water, sugar and lemon zest.
- **Orange Sorbet:** use the zest and juice from 3 large oranges in place of lemons, but use only 300 ml/¹/2 pint (1¹/4 cups) water. Continue as for the Lemon Sorbet above. 1 or 2 tablespoons of lemon juice adds a pleasing sharpness to the flavour.
- **Raspberry Sorbet:** sieve 450 g/1 lb raspberries then proceed as for the Melon Sorbet above. The lemon is not essential, you could just make a syrup of 300 ml/¹/2 pint (1¹/4 cups) water and the sugar and blend this with the raspberry pulp.
- Other soft fruits, black and redcurrants and loganberries in particular, make excellent sorbets, follow the method above, adding the desired amount of sugar.

◉ English Cream

If serving the sorbet as a dessert it can be combined with an ice cream or a little of this sauce. Strangely enough, one rarely sees this sauce on a British menu, but I have seen it in France a number of times.

Make an egg custard sauce with 2 eggs, or 3 egg yolks, and 300 ml/¹/2 pint (1¹/4 cups) milk and sugar to taste. It should be thick enough to give a good coating on a wooden spoon. The method is given in Sherry Trifle (see page 258). Allow it to cool, stirring from time to time. Blend in at least 150 ml/¹/4 pint (²/3 cup) double cream.

Baking

Good baking can be described as an art; to bring a cake or loaf of bread out of the oven that looks perfect, and proves to be equally so when cut, requires know-how and skill. Few forms of cookery are as rewarding, and as much appreciated, by friends and family. A typical afternoon tea, like the menu on page 307, is seen all too rarely today, although its success in hotels means people enjoy it thoroughly.

There are various things that are essential in making successful breads, cakes, pastries and biscuits. Firstly, it is important to follow recipes carefully, especially the first time you make the dish. That extra tablespoon or two of liquid or golden syrup that people sometimes add, because they feel it would improve the texture or taste, could upset the balance of ingredients, and it could result in failure. You can certainly alter flavourings, using a little less, or more, spice or lemon rind, but the basic proportions should be left. When you have made the recipe once you are in a better position to judge if you could make it a little softer with a little extra liquid. Always beware of increasing the amount of treacle or syrup, they are very heavy products.

The choice of ingredients is important. If a recipe specifies plain flour, it is best to use it. All spoon measures are level, so be particularly accurate when measuring baking powder or bicarbonate of soda – too much tastes horrible. Butter is used in recipes but margarine can be substituted.

The way one handles the ingredients for the various dishes is important. The easiest way to incorporate fat into flour is by the 'rubbing-in' method. This must be done lightly for pastry (see page 295), but that is far less important in biscuit-making. Creaming and beating are brisk actions, but folding a gentle one.

When using equipment like an electric mixer or food processor, try to adjust and time these in such a way that they emulate hand actions. The appliances are excellent if used correctly but over-beating or over-processing can spoil the texture. Too vigorous beating will certainly mar the light cakes and sponges on pages 285 and 286, whether done by hand or with an electrical appliance.

People often despair of their skill in pastry-making or – as they say – lack of skill. Often they have persuaded themselves they will never be successful. That is not true. It is good to have cool hands for handling pastry: if yours are inclined to be hot then run ice cold water over them and your wrists before beginning. Keep utensils and the kitchen cool, give yourself adequate time to prepare the pastry but, at the same time, handle it as quickly and lightly as possible. Follow the proportions given in classic recipes and you will soon notice an improvement in your pastry making.

The section begins with a recipe for home-made bread, which includes information on using the modern easy-type of dried yeast that is mixed with the flour. The wonderful smell of bread cooking rewards you for any effort made. If you have never made bread before do not think it is very time-consuming. You certainly must wait for it to rise (or prove) but you can plan to do other things while this is happening. If you have a microwave you could hasten this process. You do, however, have to use the microwave with enormous care to make sure the dough does not become too hot – if it does you destroy the ability of the yeast to make the dough rise. Do check most carefully with your manufacturer's handbook about the timing and setting for your microwave.

Light scones are always a delight. Years ago there was a music hall song which had a line 'and don't dilly dally on the way'. That should be the motto of scone makers. Mix them quickly (make sure the dough is sufficiently soft), handle them quickly and bake for a short time in a hot oven. When cold, serve them with whipped or clotted, cream and jam to give friends and family a real West Country Cream Tea. If you enjoy yeast cookery, then you will find a recipe for real Cornish Splits on page 270.

Oven temperatures are very important in baking. It must be remembered that ovens do vary quite a lot. The Victoria Sandwich recipe (see page 285) is a very good one by which you can judge your oven. If the cake is cooked in the time and at the temperature given, then your oven is average. If it takes quite a little longer to cook you may get better results if you raise the temperature slightly.

Users of fan ovens must reduce heat for most baking and other forms of cookery by 10°C/25°F.

If you have a solid range, always consult the manufacturer's handbook to ascertain which oven to use. There are differences between various models so general advice is not particularly helpful.

Yes, baking does take time and trouble but it is infinitely rewarding.

⊙ Home-Made Bread

Cooking time: 45 minutes ⊙ Makes 1 loaf

If you have never cooked with yeast before, it is a good idea to make a small amount of bread first. The following method is the classic one, using fresh yeast, which you can obtain from health food shops. The method using the easy type, which is added to flour, is explained afterwards. Choose strong (hard wheat) flour, which gives a better rise and texture to bread. Plain flour could be substituted.

Proportions to use: 15 g/1/2 oz (1/2 cake) fresh yeast; approximately 300 ml/1/2 pint (11/4 cups) water; 450 g/1 lb (4 cups) flour and 1 level teaspoon salt. If you add 25 g/1 oz (2 tablespoons) of butter, you have a more moist loaf.

Adding the yeast: put the yeast into a basin. Warm the water until it is just blood heat, i.e. 37 to 43°C/98 to 108°F. Blend with the yeast. Sift the flour and salt into a bowl, rub in the fat if using. Make a well in the centre of the flour and add the yeast and water. Blend well with a knife and then with your fingers. If the dough seems dry add a little more water; if too sticky to handle add a little more flour. Different makes of flour absorb different amounts of water. The dough should be soft but leave the mixing bowl clean.

⊙ **Kneading:** turn the ball of soft dough on to a floured surface; knead until smooth. This means stretching the dough by pushing and then folding with the base of the hand (known as the heel). This is very important as it distributes the yeast evenly. To test if sufficiently kneaded, press with the tip of a floured finger. If the impression stays then knead a little more. When sufficiently kneaded the impression comes out. Return the dough to the bowl and cover with a cloth or put it into a very large, lightly oiled polythene bag. It must have room to double in size.

⊙ **Proving:** leave in a warm place until just double the size, this takes about 11/2 to 2 hours at room temperature but less in a warm airing cupboard or similar place.

Do not over-knead the dough or let it rise any more than described.

⊙ **Knocking back:** turn the dough on to the floured surface again and knead as before.

⊙ **Preparing for baking:** grease a 900 g/2 lb loaf tin. Shape the dough to fit the tin. Cover the tin and prove again until the dough has almost doubled in size.

⊙ **Baking:** preheat the oven to 220°C/425°F, Gas Mark 7. Bake the loaf for 45 minutes.

⊙ **Testing:** take the loaf out of the tin and knock the base. If cooked the bread sounds hollow. Place on a wire cooling tray. Using dried yeast: modern dried yeast can be added to the flour. Follow the instructions, which may suggest slightly warmer water is used than given above. When the water is added, knead as above and then follow the packet directions.

⊙ Different Types of Bread

Cooking time: 45 minutes ⊙ Makes 1 loaf

All these breads are based on the recipe on page 267. The baking time is very similar.

⊙ Apple Bread

Follow the proportions in the recipe on page 267 but substitute either apple juice or a thin apple purée for the water. The purée can be sweetened with a little sugar or honey. About 50 g/2 oz (1/3 cup) sultanas can be added to the flour.

⊙ Brown Bread

Follow the recipe on page 267 but use half white and half wholemeal strong (hard wheat) flours. You will find the wholemeal flour absorbs a little more liquid than all white flour.

⊙ Cheese Bread

Follow the recipe on page 267 and allow the dough to prove. Add 100 g/4 oz (1 cup) of grated Cheddar or Cheshire cheese to the dough. Mix well, then knock back as the recipe. 1 tablespoon (1 1/4 tablespoons) chopped parsley or mixed herbs can be added to the flour and salt, with freshly ground black pepper and a little mustard.

⊙ Fruit Bread

Follow the recipe on page 267 but add up to 100 g/4 oz (2/3 cup) mixed dried fruit to the flour. Do not exceed this amount as the proportion of yeast in the recipe would be inadequate to make the dough rise.

⊙ Milk Bread

Use warm milk in the bread recipe on page 267 instead of water. This is very pleasant for a Fruit Bread, as above. To make a sweet bread, add up to 50 g/2 oz (1/4 cup) caster sugar to the flour.

⊙ Oatmeal Bread

Omit 50 g/2 oz (1/2 cup) of flour in the bread recipe on page 267 and add the same amount of oatmeal. When the dough is in the tin waiting to prove, brush the top with milk and sprinkle rolled oats on this.

⊙ Wholemeal Bread

Use strong (hard wheat) wholemeal flour instead of white flour in the recipe on page 267. This flour absorbs slightly more liquid and takes a little longer to cook. The bread looks attractive if brushed with milk before baking.

Aberdeen Softies

Cooking time: 12 to 15 minutes ◉ makes 12

Metric Imperial { **Ingredients** } American
450 g/1 lb { **flour, etc.** } (as page 267) 4 cups
75 g/3 oz { **butter** } 3/8 cup
25 g/1 oz { **caster sugar** } 2 tablespoons

Make the basic bread dough as the recipe on page 267. Allow this to prove and then knead until smooth again. Melt the butter. Return the dough to a bowl and work in the butter and sugar. When thoroughly mixed tip on to a floured board and knead again. Form into 12 round portions. Put on to a lightly greased baking tray. Allow to prove once more until nearly double in size (this takes about 25 minutes). Meanwhile, preheat the oven to 220°C/425°F, Gas Mark 7. Bake for 12 to 15 minutes, or until well risen and firm.

Lardy Cake

Cooking time: 35 to 40 minutes ◉ Makes 1 cake

This is an 'old-fashioned' cake with a flaky texture, made by incorporating lard into the dough in the same way as one does in flaky pastry. Prepare the bread dough (see page 267), knead it until smooth, let it prove, then knock it back as described. This cake is not traditional to any one part of Britain; when country cooks made bread many used part of the dough for the cake. As a child I was shown how to make it by an aunt who lived in the Forest of Dean. You can add 75 g/3 oz (1/2 cup) currants with the lard and sugar. Butter can be substituted for lard; this does not give the traditional flavour but it makes a very good yeast cake.

◉ **To make the cake:** you need the bread dough made as page 267 and 100 g/4 oz (1/2 cup) of lard, 50 g/2 oz (1/4 cup) caster sugar and 1 teaspoon mixed spice.

Roll out the bread dough to a neat oblong. Divide the lard into small portions and add half the lard, half the sugar and half the spice to the top half of the oblong of dough. Bring the part of the dough without lard up to cover the top half. Seal the edges of the dough turn at right angles and roll out to an oblong again. Repeat the process with the rest of the lard, sugar and spice.

Fold and roll twice more, without adding lard, etc., then form into a neat round. Place on a baking sheet or tray. Mark the top in a criss-cross pattern with a knife and allow to prove until well risen. Preheat the oven to 220°C/425°F, Gas Mark 7 and bake for 25 minutes, then lower the heat to 190°C/375°F, Gas Mark 5 and cook for a further 10 to 15 minutes. Serve when freshly made.

⊙ Cornish Splits

Cooking time: 12 to 15 minutes ⊙ Makes 12 to 16

One of the pleasures of visiting Devon and Cornwall are the delicious cream teas which provide an opportunity to taste the famous clotted cream of the West Country. These yeast-based soft sweet rolls are the genuine splits but nowadays you may find you are served light scones, such as those on page 278, instead. Similar rolls are a feature of Devon teas, often known as Chudleighs. These tend to be slightly smaller than the Cornish version.

Metric Imperial { **Ingredients** } American
20 g/3/4 oz { **fresh yeast** } 3/4 cake
300 ml/1/2 pint { **milk or half milk and half water** } 1 1/4 cups
450 g/1 lb { **strong flour** } 4 cups
1 teaspoon { **salt, or to taste** } 1 teaspoon
50 g/2 oz { **butter** } 1/4 cup
50 g/2 oz { **caster sugar, or to taste** } 1/4 cup

Cream the yeast. Warm the liquid until tepid then pour over the yeast. Add a sprinkling of flour and leave in a warm place until the surface is covered with bubbles. Meanwhile, sift the flour and salt into a large bowl. Rub in the butter and add the sugar and then the yeast liquid. Knead until smooth then return to the bowl, cover and allow to prove until double in size. Turn out on to a lightly floured board, knead again until smooth (known as 'knocking back' the dough).

Either divide into 12 to 16 portions and form these into round balls or roll out the dough until approximately 2.5 cm/1 inch in thickness and cut into rounds. Place on 1 to 2 lightly greased baking trays and allow to prove once more.

Meanwhile preheat the oven to 220°C/425°F, Gas Mark 7. Bake the splits for 12 to 15 minutes until well risen and pale golden in colour. Serve cold with clotted cream and jam.

▣ Using Dried Yeasts

There is more than one form of dried yeast. The most popular is the type which is not creamed or mixed with liquid but added to the flour. Follow the direction for quantity given on the packet.

A second type of dried yeast is one in which you do need to blend it with liquid and it is generally recommended that a little sugar is added to the mixture.

To each 25 g/1 oz (1 cake) fresh yeast allow just 15 g/1/2 oz (1 level tablespoon) dried yeast. Blend 1 teaspoon sugar with the tepid liquid, add the dried yeast. You can add a sprinkling of flour. Allow to stand until the surface is covered in bubbles It takes a little longer for this to happen than when using fresh yeast.

Singing Hinnies

Cooking time: 8 to 10 minutes ⊙ Makes 10 to 12

This is a Northumberland scone, the word 'hinnie' is a term of affection in that part of England. The reason given for the strange name is because the teacakes give a definite singing sound as they cook.

Metric Imperial { **Ingredients** } American
450 g/1 lb { **plain flour** } 4 cups
pinch { **salt** } pinch
scant 3/4 teaspoon { **bicarbonate of soda** } scant 3/4 teaspoon
scant 11/2 teaspoons { **cream of tartar** } scant 11/2 teaspoons
100 g/4 oz { **lard or butter** } 1/2 cup
175 g/6 oz { **currants** } 1 cup
300 ml/1/2 pint { **milk** } 11/4 cups

Sift the flour, salt, bicarbonate of soda and cream of tartar once or twice. Rub in nearly all the lard or butter; save a little to grease the griddle. Add the currants and then the milk to make a fairly firm rolling consistency. Roll out the dough on a floured surface until 8 mm and 1.5 cm/1/3 to 1/2 inch thick.

Cut into large rounds. Preheat and lightly grease the griddle. Test by shaking on a little flour, it should turn golden within 1 minute. Cook the cakes for 4 to 5 minutes or until golden on the under side, then turn and cook for the same time on the second side. Wrap in a clean cloth, to keep the scones soft, and place on a wire cooling tray. Split and serve with butter.

Crumpets

Cooking time: 6 minutes ⊙ Makes about 8

These are made with a yeast batter using plain, rather than strong, flour.

Heat 150 ml/1/4 pint (2/3 cup) milk with 15 g/1/2 oz (1 tablespoon) butter. Allow to cool until just blood heat, i.e. 37-43°C/98-108°F, then blend with 7 g/1/4 oz (1/4 cake) fresh yeast.

Sift 100 g/4 oz (1 cup) plain flour with a pinch of salt into a bowl. Add the yeast liquid and beat well until a very smooth mixture. Allow to prove for about 45 minutes, or until the batter has doubled in bulk.

Grease and heat a griddle. To test if it is the right heat shake on a little flour. This should turn golden in 1 minute. You can drop spoonfuls of the batter on to the griddle but to make well-shaped crumpets you need proper crumpet rings (pastry cutters could be used). Spoon the batter into the rings, cook for 3 minutes, turn over and cook for the same time on the second side.

⊙ Soda Bread

Cooking time: 14 to 30 minutes, see method ⊙ Makes 1 loaf

There is a wealth of excellent breads made in Ireland, but soda bread is the best known and unequalled for its light texture. Buttermilk is an asset but not essential, see under variations.

Metric Imperial { **Ingredients** } American
450 g/1 lb { **plain white flour** } 4 cups
          { **or half white and half wholemeal flour for brown soda bread** }
1/2 to 1 teaspoon { **salt, or to taste** } 1/2 to 1 teaspoon
1/2 teaspoon { **bicarbonate of soda** } 1/2 teaspoon
1/2 teaspoon { **cream of tartar** } 1/2 teaspoon
300 ml/1/2 pint { **butter milk, or as much as required** } 1 1/4 cups

Sift the dry ingredients together. Add sufficient buttermilk to make a soft dough, but one that can be kneaded. Flours vary slightly in the amount of liquid they absorb. Turn on to a lightly floured board and knead until smooth.

⊙   **To cook on a griddle:** form into a round 6 to 8 mm/1/4 to 1/3 inch in thickness. Mark into quarters (known as 'farls'). Do not cut right through the bread. Heat a griddle but do not grease this. To test shake on a little flour, it should turn golden in 1 1/2 to 2 minutes. Cook the bread for 6 to 7 minutes, or until firm on the under side, turn and cook on the second side for the same time.

⊙   **To bake in the oven:** preheat the oven to 220°C/425°F, Gas Mark 7. Form the dough into a round 2.5 to 3.5 cm/1 to 1 1/2 inches in thickness. Mark into 'farls'. Place on an ungreased baking sheet and cook for 30 minutes; reduce the heat slightly towards the end of the cooking time if the bread is becoming too brown. Soda bread should be pale in colour. Wrap in a cloth after baking to keep the bread soft.

Variations:
⊙   Rub 25 g/1 oz (2 tablespoons) lard or butter into the flour.
⊙   If buttermilk is unavailable use skimmed milk and 1 teaspoon cream of tartar.
⊙   Bake the bread the traditional way. Press the dough into a well greased, very strong cake tin. Cover and bake as above but allow a little longer.

⊙ Fruit Soda bread

Add 75 g/3 oz (1/2 cup) mixed dried fruit or sultanas with 50 g/2 oz (1/4 cup) sugar to the dry ingredients before mixing with the buttermilk.

⊙ Treacle Soda Bread

Blend 1 1/2 tablespoons (2 tablespoons) black treacle with the buttermilk. Add 25 g/1 oz (2 tablespoons) sugar to the flour. Dried fruit could be added to this bread.

◉ Barm Brack

Cooking time: 1¼ hours ◉ Makes 1 loaf

This famous Irish speckled bread is generally eaten at Hallowe'en. Often a wedding ring, wrapped in paper, was baked in the bread. The legend stated that whoever had the slice containing the ring would be engaged by the end of the year. Barm is the froth that forms on the top of fermenting malt liquors and was used instead of yeast in the past. Today yeast is the ingredient used to raise the dough.

Metric Imperial { **Ingredients** } American
20 g/¾ oz { **fresh yeast** } ¾ cake
250 ml/8 fl oz { **milk** } 1 cup
450 g/1 lb { **plain flour** } 4 cups
1 teaspoon { **grated or ground nutmeg** } 1 teaspoon
100 g/4 oz { **caster sugar** } ½ cup
2 teaspoons { **caraway seeds** } 2 teaspoons
175 g/6 oz { **butter** } ¾ cup
100 g/4 oz { **mixed crystallized peel** } ¼ lb
225 g/8 oz { **currants** } 1¼ cups
225 g/8 oz { **raisins** } 1¼ cups
3 { **eggs** } 3

Cream the yeast. Warm the milk until just tepid then pour over the yeast. Add a sprinkling of flour and leave in a warm place until the surface is covered with bubbles.

Sift the rest of the flour with the nutmeg, add the sugar and caraway seeds. Melt the butter and chop the peel. Blend the yeast liquid with the flour, add the butter and the rest of the ingredients. Beat the mixture for a short time then turn out on to a lightly floured board and knead until smooth.

Return the dough to the bowl, cover with a cloth and level to prove for approximately 1½ hours or until just double in size. Knock back the dough and knead again.

Grease a 23 cm/9 inch round cake tin. Press the dough into the tin, cover the top of the tin with a cloth to prevent a hard skin forming on the cake and allow to prove for approximately 50 minutes or until the dough has risen well in the tin.

Preheat the oven to 190 to 200°C/375 to 400°F, Gas Mark 5 to 6 and bake for 30 minutes, then reduce the heat to 160°C/325°F, Gas Mark 3 and bake for a further 45 minutes or until firm to the touch. Turn out of the tin on to a wire cooling tray.

Note: details of using dried yeast instead of fresh yeast are on page 270.

⊙ Little Puddings

Cooking time: 12 to 15 minutes ⊙ **Makes 12 to 15**

These may be said to be the British equivalent of French brioche. Although they can be served hot as a pudding with jam or fruit, they are almost nicer as a sweet bread or cake.

Metric Imperial { **Ingredients** } American
15 g/½ oz { **fresh yeast** } ½ cake
2 tablespoons { **water** } 2½ cakes
225 g/8 oz { **strong or plain flour** } 2 cups
pinch { **salt** } pinch
50 g/2 oz { **caster sugar** } ¼ cup
5 tablespoons { **double cream** } ½ cup
2 { **large eggs** } 2
1 teaspoon { **finely grated lemon zest** } 1 teaspoon

Cream the yeast. Heat the water to blood heat, i.e. 37 to 43°C/98 to 108°F, blend with the yeast. Sift the flour and salt into a bowl; add the sugar, the yeast liquid and the cream. Whisk the eggs and grated lemon zest. Add to the other ingredients and beat well until a smooth batter-like consistency forms. Cover the bowl and leave in a warm place for approximately 1 hour or until the dough is light and has risen to almost double the original size. Beat the mixture until it once again becomes like a batter.

Grease 12 to 15 dariole moulds (often called castle pudding tins) with a generous amount of butter. Half-fill these with the soft dough, do not over-fill for the mixture rises well. Place the tins on a baking tray so they are easy to handle in the oven. Put a sheet of oiled clingfilm or greaseproof paper over the tins and leave for approximately 20 to 30 minutes or until the dough has risen to the top of the tins. Remove the clingfilm.

Preheat the oven to 200°C/400°F, Gas Mark 6 and bake for 12 to 15 minutes or until well risen and firm. Allow to cool in the tins for 2 to 3 minutes, then turn out on to a wire cooling tray. Serve freshly baked as a bread or cake.

Variations:
- ⊙ Use grated orange zest instead of the lemon zest.
- ⊙ Omit the lemon zest and sift a little grated or ground nutmeg or ground ginger with the flour. These flavourings are particularly good when the puddings are served with hot apple purée.
- ⊙ Use 1½ level teaspoons dried yeast instead of the fresh yeast. Details of using dried yeast are on page 270.

⊙ Sally Lunns

Cooking time: 25 minutes ⊙ Makes 2 to 3 teacakes

These are very famous teacakes, named after the lady who lived in Bath during the eighteenth century.

Metric Imperial { **Ingredients** } American
15 g/1/2 oz { **fresh yeast** } 1/2 cake
150 ml/1/4 pint { **milk, or milk and water** } 2/3 cup
350 g/12 oz { **strong (hard wheat) or plain flour** } 3 cups
pinch { **salt** } pinch
50 g/2 oz { **butter** } 1/4 cup
1 { **egg** } 1

Cream the yeast. Warm the milk, or milk and water, to blood heat, i.e. 37 to 43°C/98 to 108°F and blend with the yeast. Blend the flour and salt, rub in the butter then add the yeast liquid and the egg. Mix well, then turn on to a floured board and knead (see page 267). Allow to prove until double in size then knock back and divide into 2 or 3 rounds. Put these into 2 x 15 cm/6 inch greased sandwich tins or 3 x 12.5 cm/5 inch tins. Allow to prove again.

Preheat the oven to 220°C/425°F, Gas Mark 7 and bake for 25 minutes. Split while warm and serve with butter.

⊙ Chelsea Buns

Cooking time: 15 to 20 minutes ⊙ Makes 9 to 12

Make the enriched dough as above, allow it to prove, then roll out to a large oblong shape on a floured surface about 1.5 to 2 cm/1/2 to 3/4 inch in thickness.

Soften 50 g/2 oz (1/4 cup) butter and spread evenly over the dough. Sprinkle 50 g/2 oz (1/4 cup) caster sugar over the butter then add 100 g/4 oz (2/3 cup) mixed dried fruit with a pinch of ground cinnamon and a little grated nutmeg. Roll up the dough, like a Swiss roll; do this lightly for the dough will rise during the next proving. Cut into 9 to 12 portions.

Arrange these with the cut side uppermost in a lightly greased 23 to 25 cm/9 to 10 inch square tin, they should fit the tin tightly, so they keep a good shape in baking. Preheat the oven to 220°C/425°F, Gas Mark 7.

Bake for 15 to 20 minutes. Blend 2 tablespoons (21/2 tablespoons) sugar with 2 tablespoons (21/2 tablespoons) boiling water. Brush this glaze over the buns when they come from the oven.

◉ Scones

Cooking time: 10 minutes ◉ Makes 12 to 18

Scones are made very quickly and they are excellent when fresh. They freeze well, so it is worthwhile making quite a large batch. Do not exceed the quantity of fat given in the recipe, for that does not improve the scone dough. Make sure the oven is preheated thoroughly before baking the scones.

Metric Imperial { **Ingredients** } American
225 g/8 oz { **self-raising flour, but see method** } 2 cups
pinch { **salt** } pinch
50 g/2 oz { **butter** } 1/4 cup
50 g/2 oz { **caster sugar** } 1/4 cup
150 ml/1/4 pint { **milk** } 2/3 cup

Sift the flour and salt. If using plain flour, sift with 2 1/2 teaspoons baking powder or with 1/2 teaspoon of bicarbonate of soda and 1 teaspoon of cream of tartar. Make sure the spoons are absolutely level; do not exceed these amounts.

Rub the butter into the flour, add the sugar and milk to make a soft rolling consistency. Roll out until approximately 2 cm/3/4 inch in thickness and cut into rounds. For an afternoon tea make about 18 very small ones. Put on to an ungreased baking tray. Preheat the oven to 220°C/425°F, Gas Mark 7. Bake the scones for 10 minutes or until they feel firm when gently pressed at the sides.

Lift on to a cooling tray. Serve freshly baked with butter.

Variations:

- ◉ **Almond Scones:** add 1 to 2 spoonfuls of finely chopped blanched almonds to the flour. Brush the scones with a little butter and top with nuts.
- ◉ **Cheese Scones:** omit the sugar in the recipe above, sift a little mustard powder and a shake of freshly ground black pepper with the flour. Add 50 g/2 oz (1/2 cup) finely grated Cheddar or other cheese. Bind with an egg and a little less milk.
- ◉ **Cream Scones:** mix the scones with single cream instead of milk, these do not rise quite as much but they are delicious.
- ◉ **Fruit Scones:** add 50 g/2 oz (1/3 cup) currants, sultanas or chopped dates.
- ◉ **Treacle Scones:** these are a great speciality in Scotland. Sift 1/4 teaspoon ground cinnamon and/or the same amount of mixed spice with the flour. Use only 25 g/1 oz (2 tablespoons) sugar and add 1 to 2 tablespoons black treacle before adding the milk. You will need less milk than in the basic recipe. Bake as above but time the cooking carefully for these are inclined to scorch.

⊙ Jersey Wonders

Cooking time: 5 to 6 minutes ⊙ Makes 12 to 15

These are one of the many traditional recipes in the Channel Islands. These fried cakes are light and crisp and not unlike European Crullers.

Metric Imperial { **Ingredients** } American
225 g/8 oz { **self-raising flour or plain flour sifted with 2 teaspoons baking powder** } 2 cups
1/2 teaspoon { **ground ginger** } 1/2 teaspoon
1/2 teaspoon { **grated or ground nutmeg** } 1/2 teaspoon
50 g/2 oz { **butter** } 1/4 cup
50 g/2 oz { **caster sugar** } 1/4 cup
2 { **small eggs – size 3 or 4** } 2
a little { **milk** } a little
To fry: { **oil or fat** }
To coat: { **caster sugar** }

Sift the flour and spices, rub in the butter, add the sugar. Beat the eggs, stir into the flour mixture, then add just sufficient milk to make a soft rolling consistency. Roll out to approximately 6 mm/1/4 inch in thickness and cut into the desired shapes. These can be circles, fingers, or bows.

Heat the oil or fat to 175°C/350°F and drop the cakes into this gently, so their shapes are not impaired. Fry for 5 to 6 minutes, or until crisp and golden brown. Remove from the pan and drain on absorbent paper. Roll in caster sugar. Eat warm or when freshly made.

⊙ Doughnuts

Cooking time: 5 to 6 minutes ⊙ Makes 12 to 15

Doughnuts have been made in England for centuries. The round shape is the most traditional.

Follow the recipe for enriched dough (see page 277) or plain bread dough (see page 267). Allow the dough to prove in bulk, then knock back as described in the recipes.

Knead well and form into small balls. Make a hole in the centre of each ball, fill with a little jam, then knead again to cover the jam with the dough. Place on lightly greased baking trays and allow to prove once more until nearly double in size.

Heat the oil or fat to 175°C/350°F and fry the balls until crisp and golden brown. Drain on absorbent paper and roll in sugar until evenly coated.

⊙ Gingerbread

Cooking time: 1¹/4 hours ⊙ **Makes 1 cake**

Ginger in various forms was brought into this country by the East India Company. Preserved ginger has been appreciated since the eighteenth century and ground ginger has always been a favourite spice in Britain. Originally gingerbreads were, as the name suggests, breads that were sliced and spread with butter. Often the mixture would be baked in ornate moulds and, for special occasions, they were covered in gilt – hence the expression 'the gilt on the gingerbread' to denote a special advantage. Today a gingerbread is served as a cake, rather than a bread.

Metric Imperial { **Ingredients** } American
175 g/6 oz { **butter, lard or cooking fat** } ³/4 cup
110 g/4 oz { **moist brown sugar** } ²/3 cup
225 g/8 oz { **black treacle** } ²/3 cup
110 g/4 oz { **golden syrup** } ¹/3 cup
350 g/12 oz { **plain flour** } 3 cups
1 teaspoon { **bicarbonate of soda** } 1 teaspoon
¹/2 to 1 teaspoon { **allspice, or to taste** } ¹/2 to 1 teaspoon
2 teaspoons { **ground ginger, or to taste** } 2 teaspoons
2 { **large eggs** } 2
2 tablespoons { **milk** } 3 tablespoons
150 ml/¹/4 pint { **water** } ²/3 cup

Preheat the oven to 150°C/300°F, Gas Mark 2. Line a 20 cm/8 inch square or 23 cm/9 inch round cake tin with greased greaseproof paper or baking parchment.

Put the fat, sugar, treacle and syrup into a large saucepan, stir over a moderate heat until melted. Sift the flour with the bicarbonate of soda, allspice and ginger. Pour the melted ingredients over the flour then stir in the beaten eggs and milk and mix together.

Heat the water in the saucepan in which the fat was melted, stir to absorb any of the mixture left in the pan, then add to the other ingredients. Beat briskly to a smooth soft consistency. Spoon into the cake tin and bake for 1¹/4 hours or until firm to the touch. A fine wooden skewer inserted into the cake should come away quite clean. Cool in the tin; remove the paper or parchment. Store for several days before cutting.

⊙ Fruit and Almond Gingerbread

Use only 2 tablespoons (3 tablespoons) water in the recipe above and add 75 g/3 oz (³/4 cup) blanched and chopped almonds and 75 g/3 oz (¹/2 cup) raisins. Bake as the timing given above.

▣ Choosing Apples

Although cooking apples, like a Bramley Seedling, are best in this particular apple cake, you have an interesting texture if you select an apple that is both good for dessert and for cooking as the pieces of apple are cooked but stay fairly firm.

◉ Apple Cake

Cooking time: 1¼ hours ⊚ Makes 1 cake

Every fruit-growing area in Britain boasts that their apple cake is best. This is an excellent cake from the West Country. It is good with Cheddar or other cheese.

Metric Imperial { **Ingredients** } American
350 g/12 oz { **self-raising flour, or plain flour sifted with 3 teaspoons baking powder** } 3 cups
150 g/5 oz { **butter** } ⅝ cup
175 g/6 oz { **caster or light brown sugar** } ¾ cup
2 { **medium cooking apples** } 2
25 g/1 oz { **Demerara sugar** } 2 tablespoons
½ to 1 teaspoon { **ground cinnamon** } ½ to 1 teaspoon
1 { **egg** } 1
1 tablespoon { **milk** } 1¼ tablespoons
For the topping:
2 tablespoons { **caster sugar** } 3 tablespoons
¼ teaspoon { **ground cinnamon** } ¼ teaspoon

Preheat the oven to 180°C/350°F, Gas Mark 4. Grease and flour or line a 20 cm/8 inch cake tin. Sift the flour, or flour and baking powder, into a bowl, rub in the butter, add the caster or light brown sugar.

Peel and core the apples, cut the flesh into 2 cm/¾ inch dice. Blend the Demerara sugar with the cinnamon and roll the apples in this mixture. Add to the flour and other ingredients. Blend with the egg and milk. Do not exceed the amount of liquid as the juice from the apples flows during baking. Spoon into the cake tin and top with the caster sugar and cinnamon.

Bake for 1¼ hours, or until firm. Check the oven after 50 minutes to 1 hour and if the cake is becoming too brown lower the heat to 150°C/300°F, Gas Mark 2.

Eat this cake when warm or on the day of baking. It is often served with butter and a sprinkling of sugar.

◉ Potato Apple Cake

Cooking time: 30 minutes ◉ **Makes 1 cake**

The Irish love of potatoes is reflected in this cake. In the past it was cooked in a large, strong frying pan over a slow burning fire but it is easier to bake in the oven. The combination of apples and the light potato mixture is a very pleasing one.

Metric Imperial { **Ingredients** } American
450 g/1 lb { **old potatoes, weight when peeled** } 1 lb
to taste { **salt** } to taste
100 g/4 oz { **self-raising flour, or plain flour sifted with 1 teaspoon baking powder** } 1 cup
50 g/2 oz { **butter** } 1/4 cup
50 g/2 oz { **caster or granulated sugar** } 1/4 cup
1 { **egg** } 1
For the topping:
2 { **large cooking apples** } 2
25 g/1 oz { **butter** } 2 tablespoons
4 to 6 { **cloves** } 4 to 6
1/2 to 1 teaspoon { **ground cinnamon** } 1/2 to 1 teaspoon
2 tablespoons { **brown sugar** } 3 tablespoons

Cook the potatoes in salted boiling water until just soft. Strain and replace in the pan and dry for 1 or 2 minutes to make sure the potatoes are floury and not too moist. Mash them until quite smooth. Sift the flour, or flour and baking powder, into a large bowl, rub in the butter then add the sugar and the mashed potatoes. Mix thoroughly. Beat the egg and add this gradually to make a soft pliable dough. Grease a flat baking tray, or cover this with baking parchment, or grease a 20 cm/ 8 inch round cake tin; preferably with a loose base. Preheat the oven to 190°C/375°F, Gas Mark 5. Either form the potato mixture into a neat round and place on the baking tray or press it into the cake tin.

Peel and core the apples and cut into slices of an even thickness. Arrange on top of the cake. Melt the butter, brush over the apples, then arrange the cloves at intervals on the apples. Blend the cinnamon and sugar and sprinkle evenly over the apples. Bake for approximately 30 minutes, or until golden brown with a topping of soft apples. This cake should be eaten when freshly cooked.

Variation:
◉ Bake the potatoes in their jackets or cook in the microwave. Split and scoop out the pulp. Weigh and mash this. This method of cooking the potatoes is a good one.

Ginger Meringue Cake

Cooking time: 1 hour 25 minutes ⊚ Makes 1 cake

This is a very unusual ginger cake, the base has a shortbread consistency and it is topped with meringue. It was a feature of harvest time on Welsh farms.

Metric Imperial { **Ingredients** } American
225 g/8 oz { **plain flour** } 2 cups
1 teaspoon { **baking powder** } 1 teaspoon
1 teaspoon { **ground ginger** } 1 teaspoon
110 g/4 oz { **butter** } 1/2 cup
2 { **egg yolks** } 2
For the topping:
3 tablespoons { **apricot jam** } 4 tablespoons
2 { **egg whites** } 2
110 g/4 oz { **caster sugar** } 1/2 cup

Preheat the oven to 190-200°C/375-400°F, Gas Mark 5-6. Use the lower setting if the oven is on the hot side. Grease a 20 cm/8 inch cake tin, preferably one with a loose base.

Sift the flour, baking powder and ginger, rub in the butter. Add the egg yolks and blend thoroughly. Press the dough into the tin and bake for 20 to 25 minutes until golden in colour. Reduce the heat to 120°C/250°F, Gas Mark 1/2. Allow the cake to cool for 15 minutes. Sieve the jam and spread over the top of the cake. Whisk the egg whites until very stiff, whisk in half the sugar and fold in the remainder. Pipe or spread over the top of the cake and bake for 1 hour. Cool and carefully remove from the tin. Serve when fresh.

Drop Scones

Cooking time: 4 minutes ⊚ Makes 12

These scones are given this name as you drop the batter on to the griddle. In a tribute to their origin they are also known as Scotch Pancakes, for they are made with a thick batter.

Sift 100 g/4 oz (1 cup) self-raising flour and a pinch of salt into a bowl. Add 1 egg and 150 ml/1/4 pint (2/3 cup) milk. Beat well until a smooth mixture. Melt 25 g/1 oz (2 tablespoons) butter and add this to the batter.

Grease and preheat the griddle. To test the heat, drop a small spoonful of the batter on to the preheated and greased griddle – this should form bubbles within 2 minutes if the heat is correct. Drop spoonfuls of the batter onto the surface. Cook for 2 minutes, then turn over and cook for the same time on the second side. Lay on a clean cloth over the wire cooling tray. Serve with butter.

◉ Victoria Sandwich

Cooking time: 20 to 25 minutes ◉ Makes 1 cake

This light cake, described in America as a 'Butter Sponge' is really an adaptation of the older, true sponge cake (see page 292). These light cakes prove the skill in baking, which has been a British tradition for centuries. The Victoria Sponge, as its name suggests, came into real prominence during the Victorian era, when elegant afternoon teas, such as described on page 307, became the vogue.

The old way of weighing the ingredients for this cake was to place the eggs on the scales, instead of a weight, then balance them against the butter, the sugar and then the flour. The average weight of an egg is 55 to 60 g/2 oz. Weights are given in the recipe below. The technique of making this cake is given in detail in the method because, if you appreciate the importance of the stages, you can then achieve perfect results when making other cakes by the same creaming method. (Pictured on page 287.)

Metric Imperial { **Ingredients** } American
3 { **eggs – size 1 or 2** } 3
175 g/6 oz { **butter** } 3/4 cup
175 g/6 oz { **caster sugar** } 3/4 cup
175 g/6 oz { **self-raising flour** } 1 1/2 cups
                 { **or plain flour sifted with 1 1/2 teaspoons baking powder** }
To fill and top: see method

Preheat the oven to 180-190°C/350-375°F, Gas Mark 4-5. Use the lower setting if your oven is inclined to be on the hot side. Grease and flour two 19 to 20 cm/7 1/2 to 8 inch sandwich tins or line the base with greased greaseproof paper or baking parchment.

Put the butter and sugar into a mixing bowl – it is important to use caster sugar in this light type of mixture. Cream together with a wooden spoon until soft and light, or use an electric mixer. This stage is very important to dissolve the grains of sugar and to introduce air into the mixture.

Beat the eggs, then gradually add a little egg to the creamed mixture and beat again. Continue like this until all the eggs are incorporated but, if you see any signs of the mixture curdling (separating), beat in a little of the sifted flour.

Sift the flour, or flour and baking powder. Gently fold the flour into the mixture with a metal spoon. You may find that you prefer to do this stage by hand, even when using an electric mixer. If you use the mixer then turn to the slowest speed. Over-beating of the flour gives the sponge an uneven texture.

Spoon the mixture into the tins, making sure you have divided it equally, then bake for approximately 20 to 25 minutes, or until firm to a gentle touch. Allow to cool in the tins for a few minutes. Turn out and place onto a wire cooling tray.

When cold, sandwich together with jam or lemon curd or another filling and top with caster or sifted icing sugar. The sponge can be topped and coated with icing.

⊡ Based on a Victoria Sandwich

The following recipes are various forms of the Victoria Sandwich (see page 285). The mixture can be flavoured with various essences or with finely grated lemon or orange zest.

◉ Victoria Sponge Cake

Use the same proportions as in the Victoria Sandwich, but put the mixture into a well greased and floured, or lined, 19 to 20 cm/7¹/₂ to 8 inch cake tin. Preheat the oven to 160°C/325°F, Gas Mark 3 and bake the cake for 45 to 50 minutes.

Variation:
- **One-stage Victoria Sandwich or Sponge Cake:** use the same proportions as the Victoria Sandwich but substitute soft margarine for the butter. You could use butter if this is softened by standing it in a warm place for a time. As less air is introduced into the mixture by prolonged creaming, it is advisable to add 1 teaspoon baking powder to the 175 g/6 oz (1¹/₂ cups) self-raising flour or 2¹/₂ teaspoons baking powder to the same quantity of plain flour. This is not essential but it does produce a lighter sponge.

  Put all the ingredients together into a bowl and beat by hand for approximately 2 minutes, 1 minute in an electric mixer or 30 to 45 seconds in a food processor. Bake as the timing for the Victoria Sandwich or the Sponge Cake above.

◉ Light Chocolate Sandwich

Follow the proportions for the Victoria Sandwich but omit 25 g/1 oz (¹/₄ cup) flour and substitute the same weight of cocoa powder; sift this with the flour. Bake as the Victoria Sandwich. When cold fill and top with this icing.
- **Chocolate Butter Icing:** melt 75 g/3 oz (3 squares) plain chocolate, allow to cool. Cream 100 g/4 oz (¹/₂ cup) butter with 150 g/5 oz (1¹/₄ cups) sifted icing sugar, add the softened chocolate. Sifted cocoa or chocolate powder to taste can be used instead of melted chocolate. If using cocoa, increase the icing sugar to 175 g/6 oz (1¹/₂ cups).

◉ Light Coffee Sandwich

Follow the recipe for Victoria Sandwich but choose small eggs and beat these with 1 tablespoon (1¹/₂ tablespoons) very strong coffee or coffee essence. Bake as the Victoria Sandwich. When cold fill and top with this icing.
- **Coffee Butter Icing:** cream 100 g/4 oz (¹/₂ cup) butter with 175 g/6 oz (1 cup) sifted icing sugar. Add very strong coffee or coffee essence to taste. Chopped walnuts are often added to the filling and halved walnuts used to decorate the top of the cake.

Rich Madeira Cake

Cooking time: 1¾ hours ⊚ Makes 1 cake

This is undoubtedly one of the most important British cakes. The name is somewhat confusing – there is no Madeira wine in the cake, but it was usual to serve it with a glass of Madeira, a favourite wine in the late eighteenth and early nineteenth century. The ingredients produce a rich cake with a smooth texture.

Metric Imperial { **Ingredients** } American
225 g/8 oz { **butter** } 1 cup
225 g/8 oz { **caster sugar** } 1 cup
1 to 2 teaspoons { **finely grated lemon zest** } 1 to 2 teaspoons
½ teaspoon { **vanilla essence** } ½ teaspoon
225 g/8 oz { **plain flour** } 2 cups
1 level teaspoon { **baking powder** } 1 level teaspoon
pinch { **salt** } pinch
4 { **large eggs** } 4
To decorate: 3 teaspoons { **caster sugar, large, thin slice crystallized lemon peel** }

Preheat the oven to 160°C/325°F, Gas Mark 3. Grease and flour an 18 cm/7 inch cake tin or line this with greased greaseproof paper or baking parchment.

Cream the butter, sugar, lemon zest and vanilla essence until soft and light. Sift the flour with the baking powder (do not exceed this amount) and the salt. Whisk the eggs well. Beat the eggs gradually into the creamed mixture; add a little of the flour if the mixture shows any signs of curdling (separating). Fold in the flour. Spoon the mixture into the prepared cake tin. Sprinkle the sugar evenly over the mixture and place the peel in the centre.

Bake for 1¾ hours or until firm and golden in colour. Cover the peel with a small piece of foil after 1¼ hours if it is becoming too dark in colour. Cool the cake in the tin for 10 minutes then turnout onto a wire cooling tray.

Variations:
- ⊚ Bake in a 20 cm/8 inch cake tin for just about 1½ hours.
- ⊚ Add the crystallized peel topping to the cake after baking for 1¼ hours.

Economical Madeira Cake

Reduce the amounts of butter and sugar to 175 g/6 oz (¾ cup). Use plain flour sifted with 1½ teaspoons baking powder. Add 3 eggs and 2 tablespoons (3 tablespoons) milk. Bake for approximately 1½ hours at 160°C/325°F, Gas Mark 3.

◘ Based on Madeira Cake

◉ Almond Cake

Cream 175 g/6 oz (3/4 cup) butter and 175 g/6 oz (3/4 cup) caster sugar with a few drops of almond essence. Beat in 3 large eggs. Sift 175 g/6 oz (1½ cups) plain flour with 1½ teaspoons baking powder and blend with 75 g/3 oz (3/4 cup) ground almonds. Do not add any milk. Bake as the Economical Madeira Cake (see page 288). If desired, top the cake mixture with blanched and flaked almonds before baking.

◉ Coconut Cake

Follow either of the recipes for Madeira Cake (see page 288) but use only 175 g/6 oz (1½ cups) flour and add 75 g/3 oz (1 cup) desiccated coconut. The quantity of baking powder is the same as given in the Madeira Cake recipes. Top the cake mixture with caster sugar and a light dusting of desiccated coconut before baking. Bake as the timings given on page 288.

◉ Cornflour Cake

The use of cornflour gives a very light texture to the cake.

Follow the directions for either of the Madeira Cakes on page 288 but use only 175 g/6 oz (1½ cups) flour and 50 g/2 oz (½ cup) cornflour. The proportion of baking powder is the same. Bake as the timings given on page 288.

◉ Genoa Cake

In spite of the Italian name, this has been a classic favourite cake in Britain for many years. Do not exceed the amount of dried fruit and peel given below.

Use the Economical Madeira Cake recipe (288) and add 175 g/6 oz (1 cup) mixed dried fruit and 50 g/2 oz (1/3 cup) finely chopped mixed crystallized peel. Bake as the Economical Madeira Cake (see page 288).

◉ Seed Cake

This has been a favourite cake in Britain for a long time. The seeds in the cake and the topping give a very interesting taste.

Follow the proportions for either of the Madeira Cakes (see page 288) and add 2 to 3 teaspoons caraway seeds to the cake mixture. Top the cake with a generous sprinkling of caster sugar and ½ to 1 teaspoon caraway seeds before baking. Bake as the timings given on page 288.

Rich Cherry Cake

Cooking time: 1½ hours ◎ Makes 1 cake

The small amount of baking powder used and the slow cooking help to prevent the cherries dropping in the cake. If they are excessively sticky rinse in cold water and dry them.

Metric Imperial { **Ingredients** } American
175 g/6 oz { **butter sugar** } ¾ cup
175 g/6 oz { **caster sugar** } ¾ cup
3 { **large eggs** } 3
225 g/8 oz { **plain flour, see method** } 2 cups
1 teaspoon { **baking powder** } 1 teaspoon
200 g/7 oz { **glacé cherries** } scant cup

Preheat the oven to 150°C/300°F, Gas Mark 2. Grease and flour a 20 cm/8 inch cake tin, or line this with baking parchment or greased greaseproof paper.

Cream together the butter and sugar until soft and light. Beat the eggs and add these gradually to the creamed mixture. Sift the flour and baking powder. If preferred you could use half plain and half self-raising flour.

Halve the cherries and mix with the flour. Fold the flour and cherries into the other ingredients. Do not add any liquid. Spoon into the prepared tin. Bake for 1½ hours or until the cake is firm. Cool for 3 to 4 minutes then turn out.

Variation:
◎ **Cherry Almond Cake:** omit 50 g/2 oz (½ cup) of the flour and use 75 g/3 oz (¾ cup) of ground almonds. Use the same amount of baking powder as given above.

Rich Genoa Cake

Preheat the oven to 160°C/325°F, Gas Mark 3. Grease and flour a 20 cm/8 inch cake tin or line it as suggested above.

Cream 175 g/6 oz (¾ cup) butter, 175 g/6 oz (¾ cup) caster sugar and 1 teaspoon finely grated lemon zest until soft and light. Beat 4 eggs and add these gradually to the creamed mixture. Add a little of the flour if the mixture shows signs of curdling.

Sift 225 g/8 oz (2 cups) plain flour with 1 teaspoon baking powder, fold into the other ingredients then add 225 g/8 oz (1¼ cups) mixed dried fruit and 50 g/2 oz (⅓ cup) chopped mixed crystallized peel. Spoon into the tin. Sprinkle a little sugar over the top of the cake. Bake for 1 hour at 160°C/325°F, Gas Mark 3, then reduce the heat to 150°C/300°F, Gas Mark 2 and continue cooking for 30 minutes.

◉ Dundee Cake

Cooking time: 2 hours ◉ Makes 1 cake

This fruit cake is justly famous. Dundee Cakes are exported worldwide by Scottish firms to many people who cherish the flavour. This cake without the almond topping is a good basis for a Simnel Cake (see page 309).

Metric Imperial { **Ingredients** } American
175 g/6 oz { **butter** } 3/4 cup
175 g/6 oz { **caster sugar** } 3/4 cup
3 { **large eggs** } 3
225 g/8 oz { **plain flour** } 2 cups
1 teaspoon { **baking powder** } 1 teaspoon
25 g/1 oz { **ground almonds** } 1/4 cup
2 tablespoons { **sherry or milk** } 2 1/2 tablespoons
50 g/2 oz { **glacé cherries** } 1/4 cup
50 g/2 oz { **chopped mixed crystallized peel** } 1/3 cup
450 g/1 lb { **mixed dried fruit** } 1 lb
For the topping: { **almonds** }

Preheat the oven to 160°C/325°F, Gas Mark 3. Grease and flour or line a 20 cm/8 inch cake tin. Cream the butter and sugar until soft and light. Beat the eggs and add to the creamed mixture. Save a little egg white to glaze the topping of almonds. Sift the flour, baking powder and ground almonds together. Fold into the creamed ingredients with the sherry or milk.

Chop the glacé cherries into small pieces. Mix with the peel and dried fruit, then stir into the cake mixture. Spoon into the prepared tin. Arrange about 50 g/2 oz (scant 1/2 cup) blanched almonds over the top of the cake and brush with egg white.

Bake the cake for 30 minutes then reduce the heat to 150°C/300°F, Gas Mark 2 and continue baking for a further 1 1/2 hours, or until firm to the touch.

▣ Testing Cakes

The first test is always by pressing the top of the cake to see if it is firm. Next, see if the cake has shrunk away from the sides of the tin. Insert a fine wooden, not metal, skewer into the cake – if it comes out clean the cake is cooked.

With a very rich cake, such as the Christmas cake, listen carefully. If cooked there is no noise; if not completely cooked there is a humming noise, which indicates it needs longer in the oven.

⊙ Sponge Cake

Cooking time: 30 minutes ⊙ Makes 1 cake

This is the very light delicate sponge that has been made for a very long time in Britain. In Dorothy Hartley's book *Food in England*, there are sketches of towering sponges made in elaborate moulds.

Metric Imperial { **Ingredients** } American
85 g/3 oz { **plain or self-raising flour, see method** } 3/4 cup
3 { **large eggs** } 3
100 g/4 oz { **caster sugar** } 1/2 cup

Sift the flour twice to lighten it and leave it on a plate in the warm kitchen for a short time. As so much air is beaten into the eggs and sugar you can use plain flour and no raising agent, but self-raising flour can also be used.

Preheat the oven to 160°C/325°F, Gas Mark 3. Line an 18 to 19 cm/7 to 7 1/2 inch cake tin with baking parchment or greaseproof paper; both of these should be lightly greased.

Whisk the eggs and sugar until thick and creamy, you should see the trail of the whisk. Fold the flour in gently and carefully. Pour into the tin and bake for approximately 30 minutes but test a little earlier than that. Use a gentle pressure with one finger to see if the sponge is firm. Cool for a few minutes then carefully turn out.

The sponge can be split and filled with jam or whipped cream and jam and it can be iced on top, see below.

⊙ Glacé Icing

This is the icing suitable for a delicate sponge. It is often known as water icing.

To make a thin coating on the sponge above, sift 175 g/6 oz (1 1/3 cups) icing sugar into a bowl, add sufficient water to bind. Instead of water, you could use lemon or orange juice.

⊙ Swiss Roll

Line a Swiss roll tin measuring 30.5 x 23 cm/12 x 9 inches with greased baking parchment or greaseproof paper. Preheat the oven to 190°C/375°F, Gas Mark 5.

Make the sponge as above. Pour into the tin and bake for 8 to 10 minutes, or until firm to the touch. Turn out on greaseproof paper sprinkled with a generous layer of caster sugar. Remove the cooking paper from the sponge. Spread with warm jam and roll up.

Berffro Cakes

Cooking time: 12 to 15 minutes ⊚ Makes 10 to 12

These Welsh shortcakes should be baked in scallop shells – these can be the genuine ones from the fishmonger or ovenproof moulds or tins of that shape.

Metric Imperial { **Ingredients** } American
150 g/5 oz { **butter, preferably unsalted** } 5/8 cup
50 g/2 oz { **caster sugar** } 1/4 cup
175 g/6 oz { **plain flour** } 11/2 cups
To decorate: { **caster sugar** }

Preheat the oven to 160°C/325°F, Gas Mark 3. Wash and dry then lightly grease the inside of the scallop shells or moulds.

Cream the butter and sugar until soft and light, add the flour and knead together. Chill for a short time then place on to a lightly floured board and roll out very firmly until a thin dough. Cut into large rounds and press these into the shells. Trim the edges; knead this surplus and roll out again to make more rounds.

Stand the scallop shells on baking sheets and cook for 12 to 15 minutes, or until firm around the edges. Cool in the shells, remove and dust with caster sugar.

Variations:

⊚ The dough can be cut into small rounds and baked on greased trays as ordinary biscuits. In this case the butter can be reduced to 110 g/4 oz (1/2 cup).

⊚ The authentic scallop-shaped shortcakes are an excellent basis for desserts if filled with fruit and cream or ice cream just before serving.

⊚ The creamed butter and sugar can be flavoured with vanilla or other essences, mixed spice or finely grated lemon zest.

Fruit Tart

You need shortcrust pastry made with 350 g/12 oz (2 cups) of flour, etc (see page 295 for shortcrust pastry and page 238 to follow recipe for Fruit Pie). Line a 23 cm/9 inch shallow pie plate or a 20 cm/8 inch deeper flan dish or tin with just over half the pastry. Sprinkle with a little flour, semolina or cornflour and sugar. This helps to thicken any juice that flows from the fruit and prevents the bottom pastry becoming soggy. Add the fruit and sugar; add only a few drops of water, even with hard fruit, and cover with the pastry. Seal and flute the edges.

Always heat a flat baking sheet or tray when preheating the oven and place the tin or dish on this. It is particularly important if using a ceramic dish. It encourages the bottom pastry to become crisp. Bake as above.

Welsh Cakes

Cooking time: 10 minutes ⊚ Makes approximately 12

These small flat cakes, known as Pice Ar Y Maen, are cooked on a bakestone (the Welsh name for a griddle). They are not only quickly made and cooked, but are also delicious. They should be eaten when fresh, but they do freeze very well.

Metric Imperial { **Ingredients** } American
225 g/8 oz { **self-raising flour, or plain flour sifted with 2 teaspoons baking powder** } 2 cups
pinch { **salt, optional** } pinch
110 g/4 oz { **butter or margarine** } 1/2 cup
110 g/4 oz { **caster or granulated sugar** } 1/2 cup
110 g/4 oz { **currants** } 3/4 cup
1 { **egg** } 1
a little { **milk** } a little
To decorate: { **caster or granulated sugar** }

Sift the flour, or flour and baking powder, and salt. Rub in the butter or margarine, add the sugar and currants. Blend with the beaten egg and just enough milk to make a fairly firm rolling consistency.

Roll out the dough until just under 1.5 cm/1/2 inch in thickness, cut into small rounds. Preheat and lightly grease the bakestone. To test if the heat is correct for these cakes shake on a little flour, it should turn golden in 1 minute – no less a time. Place the cakes on the bakestone, cook for 4 to 5 minutes, or until golden brown on the bottom. Turn over and cook for the same time on the second side.

Lift the cakes on to a wire cooling tray and dust with sugar.

Rock Cakes

The recipe for these small and economical cakes is similar to Welsh Cakes (see above) except that the mixture should be a sticky consistency, so the mixture needs a very little more milk. It should stand in peaks when stirred with a knife. Use mixed fruit instead of all currants, increasing the amount to 175 g/6 oz (1 cup). Preheat the oven to 200 to 220°C/400 to 425°F, Gas Mark 6 to 7.

Put small spoonfuls of the mixture on to lightly greased baking trays, or on the baking parchment on the trays. Cook for 12 to 15 minutes, or until golden and firm.

Variations:
- ⊚ The cake mixture can be flavoured with mixed spice or with finely grated lemon or orange zest.Use a little fruit juice in mixing instead of all milk.
- ⊚ **Cornish Saffron Cakes:** are made in the same way but sift a good pinch of saffron powder with the flour. To use saffron strands see page 77.

⊙ Shortcrust Pastry

Cooking time: as specific recipes

Metric Imperial { **Ingredients** } American
225 g/8 oz { **plain white flour** } 2 cups
pinch { **salt** } pinch
110 g/4 oz { **fat – all butter, all margarine, or**
    half butter or margarine and half cooking lard } 1 cup
2 to 3 tablespoons ice cold { **water** } 2½ to 4 tablespoons

Sift the flour and salt into a mixing bowl. Cut the fat(s) into pieces and drop into the flour. Lift some of the fat and flour with your fingertips, or forefingers and thumbs, and rub together. Do this well above the top of the bowl, so you are incorporating air into the mixture and keeping it cool. Continue until all the mixture looks like fine breadcrumbs. Do not over-handle the fat and flour, if you do it becomes sticky. This is particularly important when using a food processor.

Gradually add the liquid and blend with the dough, using a flat-bladed knife. Different makes of flour vary in the amount of liquid they absorb but you have used sufficient when the mixture is easily formed into a ball and leaves the bowl clean.

Dust the pastry board and rolling pin with a little flour, roll out the dough to a neat shape. Like all kinds of pastry, shortcrust is better if it is allowed to rest (relax) for a time. Shape and bake as specific recipe.

⊙ Wholemeal Pastry

While you can use all wholemeal flour, you produce a lighter pastry, and one that is easier to handle if it is made with half plain white flour and half plain wholemeal flour. When sifted together some of the bran may be left in the sieve. Retain this and sprinkle over the pastry when it is rolled out.

⊙ **The modern touch:** Soft polyunsaturated fats of today require a different technique in handling. It is better to cream the fat with a little of the flour and the amount of liquid recommended on the packet then incoporate the rest of the flour.

⊙ Sweet Shortcrust Pastry

It is better to use butter in this pastry but the proportions are the same as for the classic shortcrust pastry above with the addition of 25 to 50 g/1 to 2 oz (2 tablespoons to ¼ cup) caster sugar or sifted icing sugar. Blend into the pastry before adding the liquid.

Flaky Pastry and Richer Pastries

These depend upon incorporating air into the dough by rolling and folding. Flaky pastry has 3 rollings and 3 foldings. Chill the pastry between rollings and wrap it, so it does not develop a hard outer surface.

Use butter or hard margarine, or half butter or margarine and half lard. Some old recipes used half finely diced suet and half butter. The fat should be firm but not too hard. If using more than one fat, blend these together. Strong (bread-making) flour is recommended as it helps the pastry rise and keep a good shape.

Sift 225 g/8 oz (2 cups) strong or plain flour and a pinch of salt into a bowl. Divide 175 g/6 oz (3/4 cup) of your selected fat(s) into 3 portions. Rub a third into the flour, exactly as though making shortcrust pastry. Add ice cold water plus a squeeze of lemon juice to make an elastic and pliable dough; softer than shortcrust pastry. Roll out to an oblong shape.

Cut the second third of the fat(s) into small pieces and dot over the top two-thirds of the dough.

Bring up the fatless section, as if to make an opened envelope.

Bring down the top third of the dough, so making a closed envelope.

Turn the dough at right angles so you have the open end towards you, seal this and the other open end firmly with the rolling pin. Depress the pastry at intervals, known as 'ribbing' the pastry. Roll out the dough to an oblong again.

Add the last of the fat in exactly the same manner as before, fold the dough, seal the ends and 'rib' the pastry. Give the final rolling and folding without fat.

Rough Puff Pastry

Use the same proportions as flaky pastry, above. Sift the flour and salt into the bowl. Cut the fat into pieces the size of a walnut. Add to the flour. Use two knives to cut the fat into the flour until it has formed small pieces, do not rub it in. Blend the dough with cold water and lemon juice. Roll to an oblong and follow the directions for folding, sealing the ends and 'ribbing', as above.

Give this pastry 5 rollings and 5 foldings.

Puff Pastry

Use 225 g/8 oz (1 cup) butter to 225 g/8 oz (2 cups) flour. Sift the flour and salt into a bowl, add sufficient water and lemon juice to give an elastic dough. Roll to an oblong, place all the butter in the centre. Fold the dough and seal the ends etc., as above.

Give puff pastry 7 rollings and 7 foldings.

- **Frozen puff pastry:** The texture and flavour of frozen puff pastry is greatly improved if the pastry is defrosted until sufficiently firm to roll out to an oblong – or use a sheet of just defrosted pastry.

◉ Banbury Cakes

Cooking time: 20 minutes ◉ Makes 12 to 15

'Ride a cockhorse to Banbury Cross' is the first line of a nursery rhyme. The cross to which it refers was destroyed in 1602 by Puritans but rebuilt again in 1859. This Oxfordshire town is famous for its ale and these cakes.

Metric Imperial { **Ingredients** } American
For the puff pastry: 175 g/6 oz { **flour, etc.** } (see page 296) 1¹/2 cups
For the filling:
Ingredients as { **Eccles Cakes** } (see page 298)
plus 50 g/2 oz { **plain sponge cake crumbs or Macaroon crumbs** } (see page 305) 1 cup
To glaze: { **egg white and caster sugar** }

Roll out the pastry as described under Eccles Cakes, but cut into oval shapes, not rounds. Blend the filling ingredients together then proceed as Eccles Cakes.

◉ Coventry Godcakes

These cakes were presented to godparents by their godchildren and also given by the godparents to the children in celebration of New Year's Day.

Metric Imperial { **Ingredients** } American
For the puff pastry: 175 g/6 oz { **flour, etc.** } (see page 296) 1¹/2 cups
For the filling: 300 g/10 oz { **mincemeat** } (see page 314) 1¹/4 cups
To glaze: { **egg white and caster sugar** }

Roll out the pastry as for Eccles Cakes. Cut into 24 to 30 large triangles. Top half the triangles with mincemeat, moisten the edges of the pastry with water and top with remaining triangles. Glaze and proceed as Eccles Cakes.

⊙ Eccles Cakes

Cooking time: 20 minutes ⊙ Makes 12 to 15

Up to the time of Queen Elizabeth I, 'wakes' – the Lancashire name for holidays – were celebrated in the town of Eccles. The Queen abolished these holidays but they were reinstated in the reign of her successor, King James I, and they continued for some centuries. These cakes were undoubtedly sold to celebrate the 'wakes'.

Metric Imperial { **Ingredients** } American
For the puff pastry: 175 g/6 oz { **flour, etc.**} (see page 296) 1¹/2 cups
For the filling:
50 g/2 oz { **butter** } ¹/4 cup
50 g/2 oz { **caster or light brown sugar** } ¹/4 cup
50 g/2 oz { **sultanas** } ¹/3 cup
50 g/2 oz { **currants** } ¹/3 cup
2 tablespoons { **finely chopped mixed crystallized peel** } 3 tablespoons
1 teaspoon { **finely grated lemon zest** } 1 teaspoon
¹/2 teaspoon { **mixed spice** } ¹/2 teaspoon
¹/2 to 1 tablespoon { **lemon juice** } ¹/2 to 1 tablespoon
To glaze: 1 { **egg white and caster sugar** }

Make the puff pastry (see page 296). If using ready-prepared puff pastry you need 350 g/12 oz (3/4 lb). Wrap and chill home-made pastry while making the filling.

Soften the butter slightly then mix with the other ingredients for the filling. The amount of lemon juice used is a matter of personal taste.

Roll out the pastry until about 3 mm/¹/8 inch in thickness. Cut into rounds about the diameter of a saucer. Place a little filling in the centre of each pastry round, moisten the edges of the pastry with water and gather together to form neat balls, completely enclosing the filling. Turn the balls over, so the joins are underneath.

Roll out gently to form flattish rounds 6 to 7.5 cm/2¹/2 to 3 inches in diameter. Make several slits on top of the cakes, then place the pastry on ungreased baking trays. Brush the top of the cakes with unwhisked egg white and coat with the caster sugar. It helps to keep the cakes a good shape if they are chilled for a short time before baking.

Preheat the oven to 220 to 230°C/425 to 450°F, Gas Mark 7 to 8. Bake the cakes for 20 minutes, or until crisp and golden brown. Check the baking after 12 minutes and reduce the heat slightly if the pastry is becoming too brown.

Variation:
⊙   You can use milk to glaze the pastry instead of egg white.

◉ Shropshire Cakes

These cakes are made as Eccles Cakes (see page 298) but the filling consists of 25 g/1 oz (2 tablespoons) softened butter with 175 g/6 oz (1 cup) currants, 25 g/1 oz (1½ tablespoons) chopped mixed crystallized peel, 50 g/2 oz (¼ cup) soft light brown sugar and about 1 tablespoon finely chopped mint leaves.

◉ Maids of Honour

Cooking time: 30 minutes ◉ Makes 12 to 15

This recipe is believed to have originated during the reign of King Henry VIII. It is thought that his second wife, the ill-fated Anne Boleyn, and her maids of honour produced the cakes to please the King. Most chemists, as well as good grocers, sell orange flower water.

Metric Imperial { **Ingredients** } American
For the puff pastry: 175 g/6 oz { **flour, etc.** } (see page 296) 1½ cups
For the filling:
1 { **egg** } 1
1 { **egg yolk** } 1
50 g/2 oz { **caster sugar** } ¼ cup
½ teaspoon { **finely grated lemon zest** } ½ teaspoon
1 teaspoon { **orange flower water or lemon juice** }1 teaspoon
1 teaspoon { **brandy** } 1 teaspoon
100 g/4 oz { **ground almonds** } 1 cup
25 g/1 oz { **fine cake crumbs** } ½ cup
To decorate: little { **icing sugar** }

Make the pastry, roll out until about 3 mm/⅛ inch in thickness. Cut into 12 to 15 rounds to fit into fairly good-sized patty tins. Chill well before filling.

Preheat the oven to 220 to 230°C/425 to 450°F, Gas Mark 7 to 8. Put the egg and egg yolk into a bowl with the sugar, whisk until thick and creamy. Add the rest of the ingredients. Spoon into the pastry cases.

Bake the cakes for 10 minutes at this heat, then reduce to 160°C/325°F, Gas Mark 3 and bake for a further 20 minutes, or until pastry and filling are firm. Cool and top with sifted icing sugar.

◉ Jam Puffs

These are a splendid way to use a small amount of left-over puff pastry. Flaky or rough puff pastries could be used instead.

Roll out the pastry until very thin, then cut into 12.5 to 15 cm/5 to 6 inch squares. Put a good teaspoon of jam in the centre of each square. Moisten the pastry edges then fold to form triangles; seal the edges well and then flake them. This means making tiny cuts horizontally which encourages the pastry to rise.

Place the triangles on to a baking sheet then brush them with a very little lightly whisked egg white and sprinkle a small amount of caster sugar over the surface. Bake at the temperature given for Maids of Honour (page 300) for 15 minutes.

⊙ Rich shortbread

Cooking time; 40 to 50 minutes ⊙ Makes 1 round

Although this Scottish biscuit is enjoyed at all times of the year and by all nationalities, it originated as another speciality for Hogmanay (New Year's Eve). It is essential to use the best quality butter to achieve a fine flavour.

Metric Imperial { **Ingredients** } American
150 g/5 oz { **unsalted butter, weight when moisture removed, see method** } 5/8 cup
175 g/6 oz { **plain flour** } 1 1/2 cups
50 g/2 oz { **rice flour, cornflour or ground rice** } 1/2 cup
75 g/3 oz { **caster sugar** } 3/8 cup

Put slightly more butter than given above in a cloth; squeeze very hard to extract all the moisture, then weigh out the right amount. Sift the flour and rice flour, or alternative, together. Mix half the sugar with the flours; rub in the butter until like fine breadcrumbs. Add the last of the sugar and knead the mixture well.

If using a wooden shortbread mould: brush the 19 cm/7 1/2 inch mould with 2 to 3 drops of oil, then coat in a little flour. Carefully press the dough into the mould. Allow to stand for 15 minutes, then invert on to greaseproof paper or baking parchment on an ungreased baking tray.

Without a mould: form the dough into a neat round on an ungreased baking tray, which can be lined with greaseproof paper or baking parchment. Flute the edges.

Meanwhile, preheat the oven to 150°C/300°F, Gas Mark 2. Prick the shortbread with a very fine skewer. Bake for 40 to 50 minutes until firm and very pale golden. Cool for 5 minutes, then mark into 6 to 8 portions. Remove from the tray when quite cold.

The shortbread can be dusted with caster sugar before serving. Store in an airtight tin, away from other biscuits which might affect the delicate taste.

⊙ Ayrshire shortbread

Reduce the amount of butter in the Rich Shortbread recipe (see above) to 110 g/4 oz (1/2 cup) and increase the sugar to 110 g/4 oz (1/2 cup). Bind the mixture with an egg yolk and 1 to 2 teaspoons cream. Either form into a large round and bake as above or roll out until 1.5 cm/1/2 inch in thickness and cut into 5 cm/2 inch rounds. Prick and bake these for 15 minutes in a preheated oven set to 160°C/325°F, Gas Mark 3.

◉ Fruit Shortbread

Use either the Rich Shortbread or Ayrshire Shortbread recipe. Work 25 g/1 oz (1¹/₂ tablespoons) chopped glacé cherries, 25 g/1 oz (¹/₄ cup) blanched and chopped almonds and 25 g/1 oz (1¹/₂ tablespoons) finely chopped mixed crystallized peel into the dough. Form into a large round, place on a lightly greased baking tray or on baking parchment on the tray. Flute the edges, prick and bake as Rich Shortbread (see page 301).

◉ Petticoat Tails

Cooking time: 15 minutes ◉ Makes 8

Metric Imperial { **Ingredients** } American
As Rich Shortbread (see page 301)
a little { **extra flour** } a little
To decorate: { **caster sugar** }

Make the Rich Shortbread dough (see page 301) but work in a little extra flour, so the dough can be rolled out to 6 mm/¹/₄ inch in thickness. Form into a large round. Place this on a lightly greased baking tray. Cut a 5 cm/2 inch circle from the centre of the round then make the band around this lightly into 8 wedges. Do not cut right through the biscuit mixture.

   Preheat the oven to 160°C/325°F, Gas Mark 3 and bake the round for 15 minutes or until crisp but still very pale in colour. Allow to cool on the baking tray then carefully separate the sections. Dredge with sugar before serving.

◉ Shrewsbury Biscuits

Cooking time: 12 to 15 minutes ◉ Makes 10 to 12

Often these biscuits were called Shropshire Cakes. They were made for All Saints Day, on November 1st each year. The seeds can be omitted and replaced by essences or grated lemon zest.

Metric Imperial { **Ingredients** } American
100 g/4 oz { **plain flour** } 1 cup
100 g/4 oz { **rice flour** } 1 cup
100 g/4 oz { **butter** } ¹/₂ cup
100 g/4 oz { **caster sugar** } ¹/₂ cup
1 to 2 teaspoons { **caraway seeds** } 1 to 2 teaspoons
1 { **small egg** } 1

Preheat the oven to 160°C/325°F, Gas Mark 3. Blend the two flours, rub in the butter until the mixture is like fine breadcrumbs, add the sugar and the seeds. Mix well. Separate the egg and add the yolk to the mixture. If it is too stiff to make a firm rolling consistency, add a little of the white but keep the mixture as dry as possible.

Roll out firmly until 6 mm/1/4 inch in thickness. Cut into rounds. Place on ungreased baking trays and cook for 12 to 15 minutes. Allow to cool for 5 minutes then remove from the trays to a wire cooling rack.

◉ Gingernuts

Cooking time: 15 minutes ◉ **Makes 16 to 18**

Like Brandy Snaps, these are among the oldest British biscuits. Ginger, in various forms, was particularly popular during the nineteenth century.

Metric Imperial { **Ingredients** } American
110 g/4 oz { **plain flour** } 1 cup
1/2 teaspoon { **bicarbonate of soda** } 1/2 teaspoon
1/2 to 1 teaspoon { **mixed spice, or to taste** } 1/2 to 1 teaspoon
1/2 to 1 teaspoon { **ground cinnamon, or to taste** } 1/2 to 1 teaspoon
1 teaspoon { **ground ginger** } 1 teaspoon
55 g/2 oz { **butter** } 1/4 cup
2 tablespoons { **golden syrup** } scant 3 tablespoons
25 g/1 oz { **caster or soft brown sugar** } 2 tablespoons

Preheat the oven to 200°C/400°F, Gas Mark 6. Grease 2 or 3 baking sheets. Sift the dry ingredients together. Put the butter, syrup and sugar into a saucepan and heat until just melted. Remove from the heat and add the dry ingredients. Mix thoroughly and allow the mixture to cool sufficiently to handle.

Roll into 16 to 18 small balls and put on to the baking trays. Allow plenty of space for the biscuits to spread out and flatten. Bake for 5 minutes, then reduce the heat to 160°C/325°F, Gas Mark 3 and bake for a further 10 minutes. If using an electric oven which holds the heat for a long time, you could switch it off and let the biscuits continue cooking in the residual heat.

Cool on the trays for 10 minutes then remove to a wire cooling tray. Store in an airtight tin away from other biscuits.

◉ Flapjacks

These have been one of the favourite biscuits of most children over many generations.

Put 75 g/3 oz (3/8 cup) butter, 50 g/2 oz (1/4 cup) sugar, either caster or light brown, and 2 tablespoons (21/2 tablespoons) golden or maple syrup into a saucepan, heat gently until the ingredients have melted. Add 175 g/6 oz (2 cups) rolled oats. Mix the ingredients together very thoroughly.

Preheat the oven to 180°C/350°F, Gas Mark 4. Grease an 18 cm/7 inch square sandwich tin, add the oat mixture and press down firmly with a flat-bladed knife.Bake for 25 minutes or until golden brown. Mark in fingers while still hot but remove from the tin when nearly cold. Store away from other biscuits.

⊙ Gingerbread Men

Cooking time: 12 to 15 minutes ⊙ Makes 10 to 12

These have delighted children for centuries. They were made for fêtes and fairs. In the old days honey would have been used instead of golden syrup or treacle.

There are many recipes for these but these crisp biscuit shapes store well.

Metric Imperial { **Ingredients** } American
85 g/3 oz { **golden syrup or black treacle, or use a mixture of the two** } 1/4 cup
85 g/3 oz { **butter** } 3/8 cup
85 g/3 oz { **caster or light brown sugar** } 3/8 cup
225 g/8 oz { **plain flour** } 2 cups
1 to 2 teaspoons { **ground ginger, or to taste** } 1 to 2 teaspoons
a little { **milk** } a little
To decorate: { sweetmeats and icing, see method }

Preheat the oven to 180°C/350°F, Gas Mark 4. Grease baking trays or line with baking parchment. Put the syrup or treacle into a saucepan with the butter and sugar. Heat gently until the ingredients have just melted. Allow to cool. Sift the flour and ground ginger, add the melted ingredients with just enough milk to make a firm rolling consistency. Knead the mixture well, then roll out very firmly.

Cut into shapes with a cookie cutter or, failing this, make a shape in cardboard and cut around it. Bake for 12 to 15 minutes or until firm to the touch. Do not allow to become too firm for these biscuits harden as they cool.

When cold, decorate with small pieces of sweetmeat and a little glacé icing (see page 292). These store well in an airtight container, away from other biscuits.

⊙ Whispers

This was a name by which meringues were once known – because they were as delicate as a whisper.

The proportion of sugar to egg white is important. To each egg white, use 55 g/2 oz (1/4 cup) caster sugar or half caster and half sifted icing sugar. Whisk the egg whites until stiff, but not dry and crumbly. Add a few drops of vanilla essence. You can beat in all the sugar gradually or beat in half the sugar and fold in the remainder.

Spoon or pipe the mixture on to a lightly oiled baking tray or a silicone parchment-covered tray. Bake very slowly in an oven preheated to 140°C/275°F, Gas Mark 1. Medium-sized meringues take about 2 hours to dry out.

Almond Macaroons

Cooking time: 20 minutes ⊙ Makes 12 to 18

Macaroons have been a favourite in Britain for a very long time, as almond trees have flourished in this country and the better quality Jordan almonds were imported. In the old days the almonds would have been blanched, dried and pounded until fine. Modern ground almonds make this task unnecessary. If you like a slightly sticky texture to the macaroons place a dish of water in the oven during the baking time.

Metric Imperial { **Ingredients** } American
2 { **egg whites from small eggs** } 2
few drops { **almond or ratafia essence** } few drops
175 g/6 oz { **caster sugar** } 3/4 cup
150 g/5 oz { **ground almonds** } 1¼ cups
1 teaspoon { **rice flour or cornflour, optional** } 1 teaspoon
few sheets { **rice paper** } few sheets
To decorate: 12 to 18 { **blanched almonds** }

Preheat the oven to 180°C/350°F, Gas Mark 4. Whisk the egg whites until just frothy. Add the essence, then the sugar and ground almonds. The mixture should be of a consistency that you can roll into 12 to 18 soft balls. The rice flour or cornflour makes a slightly firmer texture but is not essential.

Place rice paper on baking trays. Arrange the biscuits on the paper, allowing a good space between these. Top with the almonds and bake for 20 minutes or until golden in colour. Cool then cut around the rice paper. Serve freshly made.

Coconut Macaroons

Follow the recipe above but use half ground almonds and half desiccated coconut.

Do not use rice flour or cornflour. Top with halved glacé cherries. Bake as above.

Ratafias

These tiny macaroons are used in desserts. Make the mixture into about 65 small balls. Place on well greased baking trays. Bake for 10 minutes, or until very firm, at the temperature above. When cold store in an airtight container.

Rout Biscuits

These were a speciality of the Regency period. Blend 110 g/4 oz (1 cup) ground almonds with 110 g/4 oz (1/2 cup) caster sugar, a few drops of almond essence and 1 egg yolk. Roll into about 50 small balls. Brush with lightly whisked egg white. Bake in a preheated oven set to 200°C/400°F, Gas Mark 6 for 6 minutes only.

◉ Brandy Snaps

Cooking time: 8 to 12 minutes for each batch ⊙ Makes 16

These have been a feature in Britain for centuries since they were sold at the 'fairings' (fairs) which originally were cattle markets but gradually became amusement fairs as well. Brandy was included in the old recipes.

Metric Imperial { **Ingredients** } American
50 g/2 oz { **golden syrup** } 3 tablespoons
50 g/2 oz { **butter** } 1/4 cup
50 g/2 oz { **caster sugar** } 1/4 cup
50 g/2 oz { **plain flour** } 1/4 cup
1/2 to 1 teaspoon { **ground ginger** } 1/2 to 1 teaspoon
1 teaspoon { **brandy** } 1 teaspoon

Preheat the oven to 160°C/325°F, Gas Mark 3. Well grease 2 or 3 baking trays.

Place the golden syrup, butter and sugar in a saucepan, stir over a moderate heat until the ingredients melt. Remove from the heat. Sift the flour and ginger, blend with the melted ingredients then add the brandy.

Put teaspoons of the mixture on the trays, allowing plenty of room for the mixture to spread. Put in the first tray of biscuits, bake for 8 to 12 minutes, or until the edges become firm. Cool for 1 or 2 minutes and grease the handles of several wooden spoons. Lift the first biscuit off the tray with a palette knife and roll around the spoon handle. Hold in position for a minute then place on a wire cooling tray. Continue like this until all the biscuits are rolled. During this time place the next tray of biscuits in the oven.

By baking in batches the biscuits should not stand too long and become difficult to roll. If this happens, heat in the oven for a few minutes so they soften again.

Always store these biscuits by themselves in an airtight tin.

Variation:
◉   If the brandy is omitted, remove 1 teaspoon flour from the 50 g/2 oz (1/2 cup).

◉ Honey Snaps

Substitute thin honey for the golden syrup and use mixed spice instead of ginger or flavour the mixture with a little finely grated lemon zest.

◉ Coconut Pyramids

Cooking time: 10 to 15 minutes ◉ Makes 15 to 20

Metric Imperial { **Ingredients** } American
2 { **egg whites from small eggs** } 2
110 g/4 oz { **caster sugar** } 1/2 cup
175 g/6 oz { **desiccated coconut** } 2 cups
2 teaspoons { **cornflour, or as required** } 2 teaspoons
few sheets { **rice paper, optional** } few sheets

Preheat the oven to 160°C/325°F, Gas Mark 3. Whisk the egg whites until just frothy. Add the sugar and coconut and blend well. The mixture must be a consistency that can be formed into neat shapes, so add the cornflour slowly to give the right texture. Mould into 15 to 20 pyramid shapes with slightly damp fingers.

Put the rice paper on to baking trays, or grease these or line with baking parchment. Arrange the pyramids on the trays. Bake for 10 to 12 minutes, or until tipped with golden brown. Cool sufficiently to handle, then cut around the rice paper or lift off the trays. These keep for several days in an airtight container.

◘ Afternoon Tea

This is one of the best ways of entertaining friends and family, or even business acquaintances, for all the cooking is done ahead, so everyone can relax and enjoy this leisurely meal.

A typical teatime menu would be something like this:

> **Assorted Sandwiches**
> **Scones with cream and jam**
> **Fruit Tarts**
> **Iced Sponge Cake**
> **Dundee Cake**
> **Shortbread Biscuits**
> **China or Indian Tea**

The sandwiches can be prepared ahead, covered in foil and kept in the refrigerator until required. The recipes for potted foods on pages 8 to 17 give a number of savoury ingredients that would make excellent fillings for some sandwiches. Other fillings could be smoked salmon, salad ingredients, soft cream cheese or scrambled egg.

The recipes for the scones, tarts, cakes and shortbread are in this chapter.

Festive Fare

Like most countries, in Britain we have special dishes to celebrate festivals. At Easter there are decorated eggs and hot cross buns for Good Friday and chocolate eggs and simnel cake for Easter Sunday. The recipes are on pages 309 and 310.

The traditional foods at Christmas time include mince pies, Christmas pudding and Christmas cake. Recipes for these are on pages 311, 312 and 316. Turkey has become the most popular choice for Christmas dinner and there are interesting classic stuffings and sauces to accompany this bird in the relevant chapter. Some people, however, prefer to serve goose or other poultry or meat and ways of cooking these are given in detail.

In Scotland Hogmanay (New Year) is considered as important as Christmas and the Black Bun (Scotch Bun) on page 318 is the traditional cake for that night, although some people do serve it at Christmas time too.

When making these recipes based on dried fruits, choose the best quality available and buy whole pieces of crystallized peel, rather than the ready-chopped variety.

Black Bun

This consists of a rich dried fruit cake baked in a thin pastry layer. Years ago a bread dough was used to encase the filling instead of pastry. Make the cake well ahead, so the flavour can mature. Store in an airtight tin or freeze this.

Christmas Pudding

This is the most famous of all British steamed puddings, however it cannot be said to be one of our oldest dishes. Before the seventeenth century in Britain we celebrated Christmas with a type of porridge, not unlike that known in Nordic countries.

This was gradually replaced by the rich blending of dried fruits and the other good ingredients we know today. Although Christmas Pudding is so often associated with England, it is served during the festive season by the rest of Britain and countries overseas that have a link with us.

Most Christmas puddings are fairly similar and it is virtually impossible to say that any recipe is the classic one. Many households have a family recipe that has been handed down through the generations. The recipe on page 311 has been 'tried and tested' over the years. It has won great praise, it is rich without being too heavy, and it is full of flavour. It is not suitable for microwave cooking.

The fat used in the past was suet and this can still be chosen. Today it is often replaced by butter (or vegetarian fat) and these make a more delicate pudding.

It is not essential to make the puddings weeks ahead; the long cooking process means the flavours mature well, even when the pudding is freshly made.

◉ Simnel Cake

This has become the cake for Easter time but originally it was made by maids to take home to their parents on Mothering Sunday. It is a rich fruit cake with marzipan through the centre and on top.

◉ **For the cake:** as Dundee Cake (see page 291) but omit the almond topping.

◉ **For the marzipan:** mix together 8 oz/225 g (2 cups) ground almonds, a few drops of almond essence, 110 g/4 oz (1/2 cup) caster sugar and 110 g/4 oz (1 cup) sifted icing sugar. Add 2 egg yolks to bind, or the whites of the eggs if you prefer a white marzipan. Take just under half the marzipan and roll it out on a sugared board to make a round very slightly under 20 cm/8 inch in diameter.

Preheat the oven and prepare the tin, as on page 291. Make the cake mixture and spoon half into the tin, add the round of marzipan and then the rest of the cake mixture. Bake as for Dundee Cake, but because of the marzipan layer it will take about 10 to 15 minutes longer to cook. Allow the cake to become cold, then brush the top with a little sieved apricot jam. Roll out most of the remaining marzipan to a 20 cm/8 inch round and place on top of the cake. With the last of the marzipan, form 11 small balls (these represent the disciples – Judas is not included). Press around the edge of the cake. Brush the marzipan with a little egg white and place under a preheated grill for a few minutes to glaze.

◉ Hot Cross Buns

Cream 15 g/1/2 oz (1/2 cake) fresh yeast. Add 150 ml/1/4 pint (2/3 cup) warm milk, or milk and water, and blend with the yeast.

Sift 1 teaspoon ground cinnamon and 1/2 teaspoon grated nutmeg into 350 g/12 oz (3 cups) strong (hard wheat) flour. Rub in 50 g/2 oz (1/4 cup) butter, add 50 g/2 oz (1/4 cup) caster sugar and 100 g/4 oz (2/3 cup) mixed dried fruit. Add the yeast liquid to the flour together with 1 egg and mix well.

Knead, then prove the dough (see page 267). When the dough has risen to twice the original size knead it again.

Divide into 12 portions and form into neat balls. Place on a greased baking tray. Make deep crosses in the dough with a knife. Allow to prove again for about 20 to 25 minutes or until well risen. Preheat the oven to 220°C/425°F, Gas Mark 7. Bake the buns for 12 minutes.

Mix 2 tablespoons (2 1/2 tablespoons) sugar with 2 tablespoons (2 1/2 tablespoons) boiling water. Brush over the buns when they come out of the oven.

Reheat these gently to serve at breakfast on Good Friday.

Variation:

◉ The cross on the buns can be made with narrow strips of economical pastry or thin strips of crystallized peel. Add the cross and then allow the bun shapes to prove.

☉ Easter Biscuits

Cooking time: 15 to 18 minutes ☉ Makes 10 to 12

These are traditionally made for Easter Sunday. Their special features are their size and spicy flavour.

Metric Imperial { **Ingredients** } American
150 g/5 oz { **butter** } 5/8 cup
110 g/4 oz { **caster sugar** } 1/2 cup
225 g/8 oz { **plain flour** } 2 cups
1 teaspoon { **mixed spice** } 1 teaspoon
100 g/4 oz { **currants** } 2/3 cup
1 { **egg yolk** } 1

Preheat the oven to 160°C/325°F, Gas Mark 3. Grease 2 baking trays.

Cream the butter and sugar until soft and light. Sift the flour and spice. Add to the creamed mixture with the currants and egg yolk. Mix well with a knife then gather the mixture together and knead until smooth.

Roll out on a lightly floured surface and cut into 8.5 to 10 cm/3½ to 4 inch rounds, or even a little larger. Place on the trays and bake for 15 to 18 minutes until firm. Cool on the trays for 5 minutes then remove to a wire cooling tray.

☉ Decorating Cakes

Decorated rich Christmas cakes are comparatively modern. There are no recipes for this cake in old cookery books. A Christmas cake is usually coated with marzipan and then with royal icing, made as the recipes below. Sugar paste, which can be bought ready-made, has taken the place of royal icing in many cases, but this cannot be used to give the snow effect which is so suitable for Christmas time. The recipes below give sufficient marzipan and royal icing to cover the sides and top of the Christmas cake on page 316.

☉ **For the marzipan:** to give a fairly thin layer you need 350 g/12 oz (3 cups) ground almonds, a few drops of almond essence, 175 g/6 oz (3/4 cup) caster sugar, 175 g/6 oz (1⅓ cups) sifted icing sugar and 3 egg yolks, or 3 egg whites for a white marzipan. Mix the ingredients together and knead lightly then roll out on a sugared surface.

☉ **For the royal icing:** lightly whisk 4 egg whites then add 1 tablespoon (1¼ tablespoons) lemon juice and 900 g/2 lb (7 cups) sifted icing sugar. Beat until smooth and shiny. This gives a fairly thick layer with enough for piping the edges.

◉ Christmas Pudding

Cooking time: 5 to 6 hours plus time on Christmas Day ◉ Makes 2 large puddings, each serving 6 to 8 people

Metric Imperial { **Ingredients** } American
110 g/4 oz { **suet or butter** } 1/4 lb or 1/2 cup
110 g/4 oz { **glacé cherries, optional** } 1/4 lb
110 g/4 oz { **mixed crystallized peel** } 1/4 lb
110 g/4 oz { **uncooked dried apricots, optional** } 1/2 cup
110 g/4 oz { **uncooked dried prunes, optional** } 1/2 cup
110 g/4 oz { **almonds** } 1 cup
1 { **medium carrot** } 1
1 { **medium cooking apple** } 1
75 g/3 oz { **plain flour** } 3/4 cup
175 g/6 oz { **soft breadcrumbs** } 2 1/2 cups
1/2 teaspoon { **ground cinnamon, or to taste** } 1/2 teaspoon
1/2 teaspoon { **grated or ground nutmeg, or to taste** } 1/2 teaspoon
1/2 teaspoon { **ground allspice, or to taste** } 1/2 teaspoon
110 g/4 oz { **dark moist brown sugar** } 2/3 cup
175 g/6 oz { **currants** } 1 cup
175 g/6 oz { **sultanas** } 1 cup
350 g/12 oz { **raisins** } 2 cups
1 teaspoon { **grated lemon rind** } 1 teaspoon
1 teaspoon { **grated orange rind** } 1 teaspoon
1 tablespoon { **lemon juice** } 1 1/2 tablespoons
1 tablespoon { **orange juice** } 1 1/2 tablespoons
1 tablespoon { **black treacle** } 1 1/2 tablespoons
250 ml/8 fl oz { **beer, stout or milk** } 1 cup
2 { **large eggs** } 2

Grate or finely chop the suet or melt the butter. Chop the cherries, peel, apricots and prunes. Blanch and finely chop the almonds. Peel and grate the carrot and apple. Mix all the ingredients together. Stand in a covered bowl overnight.

Grease two 1.5 litre/2 1/2 pint (6 1/4 cup) ovenproof basins and spoon in the mixture. Cover the puddings with well greased greaseproof paper and foil. Put a central pleat in both covers so the pudding will not split the covering.

Steam each pudding over boiling water for 5 to 6 hours, making sure the pans do not boil dry. Top up with boiling water if necessary. When the puddings are cooked, remove the damp covers at once. When cold, cover with fresh dry greaseproof paper and foil. Store in a cool dry place, away from the steam from cooking.

On Christmas Day: steam the pudding for 2 hours. Serve with cream custard sauce, Brandy Butter or Cumberland Rum Butter (see pages 257 and 315).

◉ Mince Pies

Cooking time: 20 minutes ◉ **Makes 18 to 20**

Old recipes mention making oval-shaped mince pies, to recall the shape of the manger. If you decide to return to this old custom, cut out oval shapes for the bases and tops and fill these with mincemeat. Place these oval pies on flat baking sheets or tins to cook. Nowadays most people prefer to use round patty (bun) tins. Various kinds of pastry can be used to make the mince pies.

It is an old belief in Britain that one must eat at least 12 mince pies over the Christmas period to ensure 12 happy months in the year ahead.

Metric Imperial (**Ingredients**) American
450 g/1 lb (**puff, rough puff, flaky, shortcrust or sweet shortcrust pastry**) 1 lb
            (weight of pastry when made) (see pages 295-6)
350 to 450 g/12 oz to 1 lb (**mincemeat, this varies according to depths of tins**) 3/4 to 1 lb
To glaze: (**egg yolk or white, optional**)
To decorate: (**icing or caster sugar**)

Make the pastry as the specific recipe. Roll out just over half of the dough and cut into rounds (or ovals if following the old tradition described above). Use the rest of the pastry to cut out slightly smaller rounds or oval shapes. Press the larger rounds into patty tins or place the ovals on to flat baking sheets or trays. Spoon mincemeat into the pastry bases. Moisten the edges of the pastry. Put the top lids in position and seal firmly.

You can make two slits on top for the steam to escape, but this is not essential. The pastry can be brushed with beaten egg yolk or unwhisked egg white before cooking to give a shine to the pastry.

Preheat the oven to 220°C/425°F, Gas Mark 7 if using puff, rough or flaky pastry. Preheat it to 200°C/400°F, Gas Mark 6 for shortcrust and 190°C/375°F, Gas Mark 5 for sweet shortcrust.

Allow approximately 20 minutes cooking, but reduce the heat slightly after 10 to 15 minutes if the pastry is becoming a little too brown. This is particularly important when using the richer pastries, which need a really hot oven at the start of the cooking time so the pastry rises well.

Top the mince pies with sifted icing sugar or caster sugar before serving. Cooked or uncooked mince pies freeze well.

⊙ Mincemeat

No cooking ⊙ Makes 900 g/2 lb

Most of the old recipes for mincemeat included minced beef as an ingredient, so one had the unusual mixture of meat and dried fruits flavoured with spices. Yet another very old recipe, however, was rather like a thick marmalade, for the dried fruit and other ingredients were blended with cooked and shredded lemons. Today, most mincemeat recipes are fairly similar – a rich mixture of fruits, apple, spices, etc. The addition of brandy, whisky or rum with the fat and sugar acts as preservative. Butter gives a more delicate flavour to the mincemeat than suet.

Metric Imperial { **Ingredients** } American
110 g/4 oz { **mixed crystallized peel** } 1/4 lb
1 { **medium cooking apple** } 1
110 g/4 oz { **suet or butter** } 1/4 lb or 1/2 cup
450 g/1 lb { **mixed dried fruit** } 1 lb
110 g/4 oz { **brown sugar, preferably Demerara** } 2/3 cup
1 teaspoon { **finely grated lemon zest** } 1 teaspoon
2 tablespoons { **lemon juice** } 2 1/2 tablespoons
1/2 to 1 teaspoon { **ground mixed spice** } 1/2 to 1 teaspoon
1/4 to 1/2 teaspoon { **ground cinnamon** } 1/4 to 1/2 teaspoon
1/4 to 1/2 teaspoon { **grated nutmeg** } 1/4 to 1/2 teaspoon
4 tablespoons { **brandy, whisky or rum** } 6 tablespoons

Chop the crystallized peel finely, peel and grate the apple. Grate or finely chop the suet or melt the butter. Mix all the ingredients together. Spoon into dry jars and seal down firmly. Keep in a cool, dry place. Do not reduce the quantities of sugar, suet and alcohol. It is possible to freeze the mincemeat. Always allow 1 to 2 weeks out of the freezer before using, so the flavour matures.

⊙ **To give additional flavour:** Add 50 to 100 g/2 to 4 oz (1/4 to 1/2 cup) finely chopped glacé cherries and 50 to 100 g/2 to 4 oz (1/2 to 1 cup) blanched and chopped almonds.

In addition to the cherries and almonds, add 100 g/4 oz (2/3 cup) very finely chopped tenderized dried apricots to give the mincemeat a very refreshing flavour.

⊙ **Mincemeat without Alcohol:** Replace the alcohol with orange juice, a mixture of orange and lemon juice, or apple juice. Use only 3 tablespoons (4 1/2 tablespoons).

Brandy Butter

No cooking ● Serves 6

This is the recognized accompaniment to Christmas Pudding in most parts of Britain. The mixture should be made ahead and chilled so it is very firm. For this reason it is also known as Hard Sauce. It makes a splendid contrast to the hot Christmas Pudding. Do not freeze, for this lessens the brandy flavour.

Metric Imperial { **Ingredients** } American
150 g/5 oz { **icing sugar** } generous 1 cup
100 g/4 oz unsalted { **butter** } 1/2 cup
few drops { **vanilla essence, optional** } few drops
2 tablespoons { **brandy, or amount desired** } 3 tablespoons

Sift the icing sugar. Cream the butter with the vanilla essence until soft and light, then add the icing sugar and beat until soft and white. Gradually beat in the brandy. This must be added slowly so the mixture does not curdle. Spoon or pipe into a dish, cover and chill well.

Variation:
● Omit the essence and add 1 teaspoon finely grated orange zest, and use curaçao instead of brandy.

Cumberland Rum Butter

No cooking ● Serves 6

This is an excellent alternative to Brandy Butter. It is so popular in Cumberland that it is made throughout the year and served on bread, in sponges and in pancakes. Chill, but do not freeze. Soft brown sugar makes a smoother mixture.

Metric Imperial { **Ingredients** } American
110 g/4 oz { **unsalted butter** } 1/2 cup
175 g/6 oz { **Demerara sugar** } 1 cup
pinch { **ground cinnamon, optional** } pinch
pinch { **grated or ground nutmeg, optional** } pinch
2 tablespoons { **rum, or amount desired** } 3 tablespoons

Cream the butter, add the sugar and beat well. The mixture never becomes smooth, but rather granular with Demerara sugar. Gradually beat in the spices and the rum.

Rich Fruit Christmas Cake

Cooking time: approximately 3½ hours ⊙ Makes 1 cake

Most European countries have some special cake for Christmas. In Britain gingerbreads (see page 281) were made for Christmas or cakes filled with crystallized fruits (see page 317). Nowadays a dark fruit cake, with a coating of marzipan and icing, is considered the perfect cake for this festival. This mixture would also be suitable for a wedding cake.

Metric Imperial { **Ingredients** } American
110 g/4 oz { **mixed crystallized peel** } 1/4 lb
110 g/4 oz { **glacé cherries** } 1/4 lb
110 g/4 oz { **uncooked dried apricots, optional** } 1/2 cup
110 g/4 oz { **almonds** } 1 cup
450 g/1 lb { **currants** } 2²/3 cups
350 g/12 oz { **sultanas** } 2 cups
350 g/12 oz { **raisins** } 2 cups
300 g/10 oz { **butter** }1¼ cups
300 g/10 oz { **moist brown sugar** } 1²/3 cups
1 teaspoon { **finely grated lemon zest** } 1 teaspoon
1 teaspoon { **finely grated orange zest** } 1 teaspoon
1 scant tablespoon { **black treacle** } 1 tablespoon
300 g/10 oz { **plain flour** } 2½ cups
50 g/2 oz { **ground almonds** } 1/2 cup
1 teaspoon { **ground cinnamon** } 1 teaspoon
1/2 to 1 teaspoon { **mixed spice** } 1/2 to 1 teaspoon
5 { **large eggs** } 5
2 tablespoons { **rum, brandy, sherry or milk** } 3 tablespoons

Preheat the oven to 160°C/325°F, Gas Mark 3. Line the bottom of a 23 cm/9 inch square or 25 cm/10 inch round cake tin with brown paper, then with greaseproof paper or baking parchment. Tie a deep band of brown paper around the outside.

Chop the peel, cherries and apricots. Blanch and chop the almonds. Blend all the fruits together. Cream the butter and sugar with the fruit zest and treacle. Sift the flour with the ground almonds and spices. Beat the eggs.

Gradually beat the eggs into the creamed mixture, add the flour mixture then the fruit and finally the small amount of liquid. Spoon into the tin and smooth flat on top, then press with damp knuckles, this keeps the top of the cake moist. Bake for 1½ hours, then lower the heat to 140 to 150°C/275 to 300°F, Gas Mark 1 to 2. Choose the lower setting if your oven is on the hot side. Bake for a further 2 hours or until the cake is quite silent (see page 317). Cool in the tin.

⊙ Crystallized Fruit Cake

Cooking time: approximately 3½ hours ⊙ **Makes 1 cake**

This cake has much the same proportions as the one on page 316. The oven setting, preparation of the cake tins and baking time are similar but it is important to test rich fruit cakes carefully, see below. Here are the changes in ingredients:

Metric Imperial { **Ingredients** } American
Increase the **chopped crystallized peel** to 175 g/6 oz (1 cup)
      the **glacé cherries** to 175 g/6 oz (1 cup)
      the **chopped, uncooked dried apricots** to 175 g/6 oz (1 cup)
Omit the currants and raisins
Instead use:
175 g/6 oz (1 cup) **chopped crystallized pineapple**
175 g/6 oz (1 cup) **chopped crystallized apricots**
110 g/4 oz (²/3 cup) **chopped angelica**
110 g/4 oz (²/3 cup) **chopped crystallized ginger**
Omit the ground cinnamon and mixed spice.
Instead use: ½ to 1 teaspoon **vanilla essence.** Cream this with the **butter.**
Substitute: golden syrup for the **black treacle**

◘ Testing Rich Fruit Cakes

It is very difficult to give the exact baking time for rich fruit cakes as ovens vary a great deal and this shows more with this type of cake than any other. It is important to check on the baking progress the first time you make this type of cake. After one-third of the total baking time the cake should hardly have changed colour; if it is becoming brown then lower the heat immediately. After two-thirds of the baking time it should be pale golden and nearly firm. If becoming rather dark in colour cover the top of the cake tin with a sheet of foil and lower the heat slightly. Just before the total cooking time test the cake.

A rich fruit cake can be tested by inserting a fine wooden skewer in the centre and seeing if this comes out clean, but with a high proportion of sticky dried or crystallized fruits as in the cake above, or the one on page 316, that is not always reliable. The best way to test the cake is to listen. An uncooked rich fruit cake makes a distinct humming noise. When completely cooked it is silent.

Never turn a rich fruit cake out of the tin while hot as it could break.

⊙ To Add Moisture To The Cake

Prick the cake on top with a fine wooden skewer then spoon a little rum, brandy or sherry over the top and allow it to soak in. Turn the cake over and do the same thing on the bottom. Moistening the cake in this way can be done several times before icing or serving the cake.

⊙ Black Bun (Scotch Bun)

Cooking time: 2¹/₂ hours ⊙ Makes 1 cake

Metric Imperial { **Ingredients** } American

For the filling:

175 g/6 oz { **plain flour** } 1¹/₂ cups

¹/₂ level teaspoon { **bicarbonate of soda** } ¹/₂ teaspoon

¹/₂ level teaspoon { **cream of tartar** } ¹/₂ teaspoon

¹/₂ to 1 teaspoon { **ground cinnamon, or to taste** } ¹/₂ to 1 teaspoon

¹/₂ to 1 teaspoon { **ground cloves, or to taste** } ¹/₂ to 1 teaspoon

¹/₂ to 1 teaspoon { **allspice or ground ginger** } ¹/₂ to 1 teaspoon

good pinch { **freshly ground black pepper** } good pinch

110 g/4 oz { **mixed crystallized peel** } ¹/₄ lb

225 g/8 oz { **almonds** } ¹/₂ lb

110 g/4 oz { **moist brown sugar, Barbados if possible** } ²/₃ cups

550 g/1¹/₂ lb { **currants** } 4 cups

450 g/1 lb { **raisins** } 2²/₃ cups

1 { **egg** } 1

4 tablespoons { **milk or buttermilk** } 6 tablespoons

2 tablespoons { **brandy** } 3 tablespoons

For the pastry:

300 g/10 oz { **plain flour** } 2¹/₂ cups

pinch { **salt** } pinch

110 g/4 oz { **butter** } ¹/₂ cup

To bind: { **water** }

To glaze: 1 { **egg with 1 tablespoon water** }

Sift the flour with the dry ingredients. Chop the peel, blanch and chop the almonds. Mix all the ingredients for the filling together. The flavour is better if the filling is covered and kept overnight in the refrigerator.

Preheat the oven to 160°C/325°F, Gas Mark 3. Grease a 20 cm/8 inch cake tin. Sift the flour and salt, rub in the butter then add sufficient water to make a firm dough. Roll the pastry out very thinly. Use two-thirds of the pastry to line the base and sides of the tin, make sure there are no folds in this.

Put in the filling, moisten the top edges of the pastry and place another round of pastry on top. Seal the edges but do not press this pastry cover down as the fruit filling swells in cooking. Beat the egg and water, brush over the pastry. Make a number of small holes in the top pastry with a fine skewer to allow the steam to escape during cooking. Bake the cake for 2¹/₂ hours, reducing the heat to 150°C/300°F, Gas Mark 2 after 1¹/₂ hours. Cool in the tin for 1 hour, then remove.

Sweets and Candies

There are many sweetmeats that can be made at home with great success. Like most home-made foods they have a better flavour than those made commercially in vast numbers and they are based upon really wholesome ingredients. For many of us, our first experience of cooking was helping grown-ups make fudge or toffee for a special present or event. We have a number of classic British sweetmeats that have been popular for centuries and a range of these are given in this chapter.

The majority of sweets have to be cooked, and the temperature to which the sugar mixture is brought is very important. If you plan to make sweets regularly it is well worthwhile investing in a sugar thermometer, for this makes it easy to assess the temperature. The same thermometer is invaluable when making preserves.

It is possible to gauge the temperature of the sugar mixture by testing a little in cold water, as explained on the next page. In order to make sweets successfully, it is essential to appreciate the importance of the following points.

1   The sugar mixture has to be brought to a very high temperature. In order to do this successfully use a strong saucepan with a thick base, this helps to prevent the possibility of the mixture burning. Use a sufficiently deep pan so there is no fear of it boiling over. Make sure the pan is placed safely on the cooker.
2   As the ingredients cook there is a tendency for some of the mixture to splash against the sides of the saucepan; it could harden and crystallize and so spoil the texture of the sweet, so keep a basin of cold water with a pastry brush beside the cooker and brush down the sides of the pan from time to time.
3   Always stir the ingredients to make sure the sugar has dissolved, then stir as little as possible, for this hinders the mixture reaching the right temperature. With sweetmeats like fudge, where there is a high percentage of milk or cream, stirring is more important than in some other recipes as the cream burns easily.
4   Choose the best quality ingredients. Butter is the fat suggested in recipes but strict vegetarians can substitute high-quality vegetarian margarine.

Equipment for sweetmaking

If you make sweets rarely your ordinary kitchen equipment will suffice. You will need strong saucepans; a long handled wooden spoon, so your hands are kept well away from the hot mixture when stirring; tins on which to put the finished sweets; pastry brushes for brushing down the sides of the saucepan and coating tins with oil or butter; basins of cold water for use in brushing down the inside of the saucepan and for testing the sweetmeats; sharp knives for cutting sweets.

If you plan to make a lot of sweets, you should invest in a sugar thermometer; rubber moulds; small metal moulds; dipping forks and spoons; a small sweet hammer for breaking hard toffee into smaller pieces; a small funnel to enable you to fill moulds with the liquid sweet mixture; a plastic scraper which makes it easy to remove the sugar mixture from the slab or board.

Temperatures to Which the Sugar Mixture is Boiled

These are the temperatures referred to in this book. Always test early during the sweetmaking process, for if the temperature in that particular recipe is exceeded the sweets could be spoiled.

Gently move the thermometer around in the mixture, so you have a true overall reading – the mixture always tends to be hotter in the centre of the pan. Take the pan off the heat while checking the temperature with a thermometer or testing a little of the mixture by dropping it into a basin of cold water.

◉ **Soft ball stage:** 114.4 to 115.5°C/238 to 240°F. When a little of the mixture is dropped into cold water it can be moulded into a soft ball with the fingers. In most recipes 115°C is given but in others 115.5°C gives a better result.

◉ **Firm ball stage:** 118.3 to 121.1°C/245 to 250°F. When a little of the mixture is dropped into cold water it forms a pliable, but firm, ball.

◉ **Light crack stage:** 126.6 to 132.2°C/260 to 270°F. When a little of the mixture is dropped into cold water it is broken easily and makes a slight cracking sound.

◉ **Crack stage:** 138 to 143.3°C/280 to 290°F. When a little of the mixture is dropped into cold water it makes a distinct crack when broken.

◉ **Very hard crack or brittle stage:** 154°C/310°F. When the mixture is dropped into cold water it is extremely brittle and snaps at once.

◙ Melting point of chocolate

On page 341 are the ideal melting points for various kinds of chocolate. By using these recommended temperatures you make sure the chocolate is not over-heated and that it retains both texture and shine. Move the thermometer around in the melted chocolate to ascertain the overall heat.

◉ Fondant

Cooking stage: 115 to 118°/240 to 245° ◉ Makes a generous 450 g/1 lb

A fondant, whether cooked or uncooked, is a versatile sweetmeat. It can be tinted and flavoured in many ways and used as a filling or addition to other ingredients.

Metric Imperial ﹛ **Ingredients** ﹜ American
450 g/1 lb ﹛ **granulated sugar** ﹜ 1 lb
225 ml/7¹/₂ fl oz ﹛ **water** ﹜ scant cup
40 g/1¹/₂ oz ﹛ **glucose** ﹜ 3 tablespoons

Put the sugar and water into a strong saucepan, stir over a moderate heat until the sugar has dissolved then add the glucose. Boil rapidly, with little, if any stirring, until the mixture reaches the 'soft ball' stage for soft fondant or continue boiling until it reaches a slightly higher temperature, i.e. 118°C/245°F for a firmer fondant. Do not beat the fondant mixture in the saucepan, for this makes it slightly granular. Allow to cool and stiffen slightly before handling.

Dampen a slab or working surface with a little warm water. Turn the fondant out of the saucepan and allow to stand for a short time to stiffen slightly. Work the fondant up and down with a spatula or flat-bladed knife until it becomes very white and firm in texture. Portions of the fondant can than be tinted and flavoured as desired for the sweets. Fondant can be stored; wrap in waxed paper then foil.

Variations:
- ◉ Omit the glucose in the recipe above and use 2 tablespoons (2¹/₂ tablespoons) golden syrup instead.
- ◉ **To reheat fondant:** remove the required amount of fondant from the wrapping, place in the top of a double saucepan, or basin over hot water. Heat until soft.

◉ Uncooked Fondant

There are two simple ways to make this.
1   Put 450 g/1 lb sifted icing sugar into a bowl. Add 2 unwhisked egg whites, ¹/₂ tablespoon lemon juice and any flavouring or colouring required. Beat to a stiff smooth mixture. If using an electric mixer choose a low speed. For a slightly softer fondant, blend in 2 teaspoons liquid glucose or glycerine.

2   Put 450 g/1 lb sifted icing sugar into a bowl, add 5 tablespoons (7 tablespoons) canned full-cream sweetened condensed milk and blend together. Add any flavouring or colouring required. This fondant is softer and slightly stickier than others.

⊙ Flavouring Fondant

The quantities given in the recipes below refer to either the cooked or uncooked fondant, for each are made with 450 g/1 lb sugar.

Flavouring essences and colourings should be added slowly and carefully, so the fondant is not over-flavoured or made too bright in colour. The best way to do this is to dip a metal skewer into the bottle of essence or colouring and allow just a few drops to fall into the sweetmeat. Blend thoroughly and taste the mixture, if flavouring it, then continue to add more colour in the same way. Bottled colourings and flavourings should be added when the fondant is ready to handle. It is very easy to work them into the sweetmeat mixture.

⊙ Chocolate Fondant

There are two ways to flavour fondant with chocolate.
1   Melt 100 to 175 g/4 to 6 oz (4 to 6 squares) plain chocolate, then allow to cool until it becomes the consistency of a thick cream. Add to the cooked fondant when it has reached the 'soft ball' stage.Add to either of the uncooked fondants when the sugar has been blended with the other ingredients in the recipe.
2   Sift 25 g/1 oz (1/4 cup) cocoa powder or 50 g/2 oz (1/2 cup) chocolate powder with the icing sugar in the uncooked fondant recipes or add to the cooked fondant just before it reaches the 'soft ball' stage.

⊙ Coffee Fondant

Either add 2 to 3 teaspoons instant coffee powder to the sugar in any of the recipes or use 225 ml/71/2 fl oz (scant cup) strong coffee instead of water in the recipe for cooked fondant.

⊙ Lemon or Orange Fondant

Add 2 to 3 teaspoons very finely grated lemon or orange zest to the sugar in any of the fondant recipes and enhance the flavour with a few drops of lemon or orange essence. The colour of the fondant can be emphasized with a few drops of yellow or orange colouring if desired.

In the cooked fondant, a little of the 225 ml/71/2 fl oz (scant cup) water can be replaced by lemon or orange juice.

⊙ Maple Fondant

Follow the variation for cooked fondant on page 321. Substitute maple syrup for the golden syrup. This gives an excellent taste to the sweetmeat.

◉ Fondant Fruits

These sweets do not keep, for the fresh fruit deteriorates quickly, even when coated with fondant. It is essential to use the cooked fondant recipe (see page 321).

Prepare dessert fruits, such as stoned firm cherries, hulled strawberries, skinned and sliced or diced fresh peaches and pineapple.

Make the fondant as the recipe. Boil only to 115°C/240°F. Lower the fruits into the hot mixture and turn around with a long spoon, then lift out on to a tin moistened with a little warm water. Allow the fondant to set.

These make a good accompaniment to coffee.

◉ Hazelnut Creams

These are better made with the cooked fondant but the uncooked fondant on the same page could be substituted.

Make the fondant with 450 g/lb sugar, etc. (see page 321). When this has reached the correct temperature in the saucepan, stir in just 1 tablespoon (1¼ tablespoons) double cream. This makes sure the fondant retains a softer texture. The cream can be blended with the uncooked fondant.

Hazelnut creams are usually pale pink in colour, so add a few drops of culinary colouring.

To mould hazelnut creams: place hazelnuts into fairly deep rubber sweetmeat moulds. Remove the fondant from the pan and work until firmer in texture, as described in the recipe, then spoon over the hazelnuts in the moulds and allow to set or press small portions of uncooked fondant over the nuts in the moulds. When the fondant is firm remove from the moulds and store in airtight tins.

To produce the sweets without moulds: tint and work the fondant, then take very small pieces and form these into neat conical shapes. Press a hazelnut into the top of each shape. Place on a tin and allow to set.

◉ Fondant Peppermint Creams

Make either the cooked or uncooked fondant (see page 321). Add a few drops of oil of peppermint or peppermint essence to the sweetmeat together with 1 tablespoon (1¼ tablespoons) double cream. Work the fondant, as described in the recipe.

Dust a working surface or slab and a rolling pin with sifted icing sugar. Place the fondant on the sugar-coated surface and roll out until 6 mm/¼ thick, cut into small rounds. Leave in the air to harden, then pack in airtight containers.

Rich Vanilla Fudge

Cooking stage: 113 to 114°C/236 to 238°F ● Makes nearly 800 g/1¾ lb

Good fudge is one of the most traditional of all British sweetmeats. This particular recipe is very soft and creamy.

Metric Imperial (**Ingredients**) American
75 g/3 oz (**butter**) ⅜ cup
3 tablespoons (**water**) 4½ tablespoons
450 g/1 lb (**granulated sugar**) 1 lb
300 ml/½ pint (**double cream**) 1¼ cups
150 ml/¼ pint (**milk**) ⅔ cup
1 teaspoon (**vanilla essence, or to taste**) 1 teaspoon

Use a little of the butter to grease a 20 cm/8 inch square tin. Put the remainder of the butter and the water into a strong saucepan, heat until the butter has melted, then add the rest of the ingredients. Stir over a very low heat until the sugar has melted then boil steadily, stirring most of the time, until the mixture reaches 'very soft ball' stage if you like a really soft fudge or the 'soft ball' stage for a slightly firmer sweetmeat.

Beat the mixture until it just begins to thicken and turns opaque or cloudy. Pour into the tin and leave until almost set. Mark into squares with a sharp knife. When quite firm pack in an airtight container.

Family Fudge

Cooking stage: 114°C/238°F ● Makes 800 g/1¾ lb

This recipe gives a very good creamy fudge, which is relatively economical.

Metric Imperial (**Ingredients**) American
50 g/2 oz (**butter**) ¼ cup
450 g/1 lb (**granulated sugar**) 1 lb
1 x 397 g/14 oz can (**full-cream sweetened condensed milk**) 1¾ cups
150 ml/¼ pint (**water**) ⅔ cup
1 teaspoon (**vanilla essence, or to taste**) 1 teaspoon

Use a little of the butter to grease a 20 cm/8 inch square tin. Put the rest of the butter and all the other ingredients into a strong saucepan and continue as the recipe above. This particular fudge is better cooked to the 'soft ball' stage.

⊙ Flavoured Fudge

Cooking stage: 113 to 114°C/236 to 238°F as in the fudge recipes on page 324.

The following recipes are based upon either the Rich Vanilla Fudge or the Family Fudge above. Additional ingredients should be added at just the right stage.

⊙ Alcohol Fudge

2 to 3 tablespoons rum or brandy or 1½ to 2 tablespoons of a liqueur, such as crème de menthe or curaçao, should be added to the mixture when the sugar has dissolved. Omit this amount of water in either of the recipes.

⊙ Cherry Fudge

Cut 100 g/4 oz (½ cup) glacé cherries into neat pieces, add to the fudge just before the mixture reaches the 'very soft ball' stage.

⊙ Chocolate Fudge

Chop 100 g/4 oz (4 squares) plain chocolate into small pieces. Stir into the mixture when the sugar has dissolved. 25 g/1 oz (¼ cup) cocoa powder or 50 g/2 oz (½ cup) chocolate powder could be used instead.

⊙ Coffee Fudge

Omit the 150 ml/¼ pint (⅔ cup) milk in the Rich Vanilla Fudge or the 150 ml/¼ pint (⅔ cup) water in the Family Fudge. Substitute 150 ml/¼ pint (⅔ cup) really strong coffee instead. You could use 3 teaspoons, or to taste, of instant coffee powder and dissolve this in the milk or water in the recipe.

⊙ Fruit Fudge

This can be dried fruit, such as sultanas or raisins, or diced crystallized fruit such as pineapple or apricots. Allow approximately 100 g/4 oz (¼ lb). Stir into the mixture just before it reaches the 'very soft ball' stage.

⊙ Nut Fudge

Coarsely chop approximately 100 g/4 oz (1 cup) nuts, such as blanched almonds, pecans, peanuts, walnuts. Add to the mixture just before it reaches the 'very soft ball' stage.

⊙ Vanilla Candy

Cooking stage: 115°C/240°F ⊙ Makes nearly 800 g/1¾ lb

The recipes for candy and fudge are very similar, in fact you can take any fudge recipe and turn it into candy by boiling the mixture to a slightly higher temperature. While the ideal stage for fudge is 113 to 114°C/236 to 238°F the mixture for candy should be boiled until it reaches 115.5°C/a good 240°F. The difference in these sweetmeats is the texture. Perfect fudge should be soft and creamy; good candy slightly crisp.

Metric Imperial { **Ingredients** } American
good 50 g/2 oz { **butter** } good ¼ cup
450 g/1 lb { **granulated sugar** } 1 lb
397 g/14 oz can { **full-cream sweetened condensed milk** } 1¾ cups
397 g/14 oz can { **of water, see method** } 1¾ cups
1 teaspoon { **vanilla essence, or to taste** } 1 teaspoon

Use a little of the butter to grease a 20 cm/8 inch square tin.

Put the sugar and the condensed milk into a strong saucepan. Fill the empty can with water, stir well to absorb any milk left in the can, then add the water to the saucepan with the rest of the butter and vanilla essence. Stir until the sugar has dissolved, then boil steadily, stirring quite frequently, until the mixture reaches the 'soft ball' stage. For a soft candy remove the pan from the heat immediately, but for a crisper candy cook very slowly over the heat for another 1 to 2 minutes. This slow cooking will not allow the temperature to rise.

Pour the unbeaten mixture into the tin. Leave until quite cold then mark into squares. There is no need to wrap candy.

⊙ Flavoured Candy

Because candy is slightly more robust than fudge, it enables a number of different ingredients to be added. All the suggestions on page 326 for flavoured fudge can be used for the flavourings, such as chocolate, when the sugar has dissolved or as directed in the specific recipe.

⊙ Butterscotch Candy

Use the recipe above but substitute 350 g/12 oz (2 cups) Demerara sugar and 100 g/4 oz (6 tablespoons) golden syrup for the granulated sugar.

⊙ Apricot Candy

Follow the recipe for Vanilla Candy (see above) but omit the vanilla essence. Use ½ to 1 teaspoon very finely grated lemon zest and 100 g/4 oz (¼ lb) dried apricots, preferably the tenderized type, known as 'ready to eat'. Chop the apricots into very small pieces and add to the mixture with the lemon zest when the sugar has dissolved.

◎ Coconut Candy

Follow the recipe for Vanilla Candy (see page 327). The vanilla essence can be retained or omitted and ¹/2 to 1 teaspoon finely grated lemon zest used instead. Add the zest and 175 g/6 oz (1 cup) either finely grated fresh coconut or desiccated coconut when the sugar has dissolved.

◎ Fruit Candy

Although currants are rarely used in sweetmeats they are particularly good in a crisp candy. Follow the recipe for Vanilla Candy (see page 327). Add approximately 100 g/4 oz (¹/4 lb) currants to the mixture just before it reaches the 'soft ball' stage. Raisins, sultanas, chopped tenderized prunes could be used instead.

◎ Fig Candy

Dried figs give a particularly interesting flavour for candy. Follow the recipe for Vanilla Candy (see page 327), retaining the vanilla essence. Chop 100 g/4 oz (¹/4 lb) dried figs very finely and add to the mixture when the sugar has dissolved.

◎ Mint Candy

Follow the recipe for Vanilla Candy (see page 327) but omit the vanilla essence. Use a few drops of peppermint essence instead or 1 to 2 tablespoons crème de menthe.

A peppermint flavour blends very well with dried fruit, especially with raisins, see above.

◎ Pecan Candy

Pecans give a particularly good flavour to candy but all other nuts can be used instead.

Follow the recipe for Vanilla Candy (see page 327). You can retain the vanilla essence if using pecans, walnuts or hazelnuts, but use almond essence for almonds and peanuts. Chop 100 to 175 g/4 to 6 oz (1 to 1¹/2 cups) pecans. Add to the candy mixture just before it reaches 115°C/240°F, i.e. the 'soft ball' stage.

⊙ Creamy Coconut Ice

Cooking stage: 115°C/240°F ⊙ Makes nearly 675 g/1½ lb

Metric Imperial { **Ingredients** } American
For the cooked fondant:
450 g/1 lb { **sugar, etc.** } (see page 321) 1 lb
2 tablespoons { **double cream** } 2½ tablespoons
175 g/6 oz { **desiccated coconut** } 2 cups
few drops { **pink colouring** } few drops

Lightly oil an 18 to 20 cm/7 to 8 inch square tin.

Make the fondant (see page 321). When it reaches the 'soft ball' stage add the cream and coconut. Spoon half the coconut sweetmeat into the tin. Colour the remainder pale pink and spoon on top of the white layer. Leave until set then cut into squares or bars. Remove from the tin and wrap when firm.

⊙ Sugar Mice

Cooking stage: 115°C/240°F ⊙ Makes about 8

Sugar mice have always been one of the sweetmeats placed in children's stockings for Christmas Day. The fondant is usually left white for these sweetmeats.

In addition to the ingredients for the fondant you need a little very fine string, for the tails, and a small amount of glacé icing (see page 292) for decorating the head. Leave the moulded sweetmeats in the air for 24 hours to dry.

Use the first recipe for the cooked fondant (see page 321) and boil the ingredients to the 'soft ball' stage only. This makes quite sure the fondant is easy to mould.

There are two methods of making the mice:

1   Use small animal moulds (the kind often sold for making jellies). Press the warm fondant into the ungreased moulds, add a small piece of string for the tail. When firm remove from the moulds and pipe on the eyes, nose and mouth with glacé icing.

2   If you do not have any moulds, divide the fondant into even amounts. Wrap the ones you are not handling in cling film so they do not dry out. To shape the first mouse, pull off a small amount of fondant and shape the head. Form an oval shape for the body, press the head against the body while the two portions of fondant are still soft enough to adhere together. Press the string into the end of the body for the tail and decorate the head as before.

Treacle Toffee

Cooking stage: 143°C/290°F ⊙ Makes 1 kg/2¹/₄ lb

Although treacle toffee is popular throughout Britain, it has always been recognized as the favourite sweetmeat of the Welsh.

Metric Imperial { **Ingredients** } American
175 g/6 oz { **almonds, optional** } generous 1 cup
75 g/3 oz { **butter** } ³/₈ cup
450 g/1 lb { **black treacle** } 1¹/₃ cups
450 g/1 lb { **Demerara sugar** } 1 lb

Blanch the almonds, if using, dry well and chop. Use a little of the butter to grease a 23 to 25 cm/9 to 10 inch square tin. Put the remainder of the butter into a strong saucepan, heat gently, then add the treacle and sugar. Stir until the sugar has dissolved, then boil steadily until the mixture reaches the 'hard crack' stage. Stir only occasionally.

Add the nuts at this stage and stir well to blend with the toffee. Pour into the prepared tin. Leave until almost cold, then mark into small squares with a heated knife. When cold, remove from the tin and wrap in waxed paper.

Everton Toffee

Cooking stage: 143°C/290°C ⊙ Makes 500 g/1¹/₄ lb

This has a pleasing, creamy taste.

Metric Imperial { **Ingredients** } American
100 g/4 oz { **butter** } ¹/₂ cup
450 g/1 lb { **granulated sugar** } 1 lb
1 teaspoon { **lemon juice or white malt vinega**r } 1 teaspoon
150 ml/¹/₄ pint { **water** } ²/₃ cup

Use a little of the butter to grease a 20 cm/8 inch square tin. Put the rest of the butter and other ingredients into a strong saucepan, stir over a heat until the sugar has dissolved. Boil steadily until the mixture reaches the 'hard crack' stage, stirring only occasionally.

Pour into the tin and leave until lightly set then mark into squares with a heated knife. When quite cold, remove from the tin and wrap in waxed paper.

Variation:
⊙ Use half golden syrup and half Demerara sugar instead of all granulated sugar, and omit the water and the lemon juice or vinegar.

◉ Toffee Selection

The following toffees are based upon Everton Toffee (see page 330) or Golden Toffee (see page 336). The amount of extra ingredients is suitable for either recipe. The stage to which the toffee should be boiled is 143°C/290°F.

◉ Almond Toffee

Blanch up to 175 g/6 oz (generous 1 cup) whole almonds, dry well and chop them rather coarsely. The toffee can also be flavoured with just a few drops of almond essence, but this is not essential. Add the essence with the water.

Add a generous half of the nuts to the toffee just before it reaches the 'hard crack' stage. Mix well. Pour the toffee into the tin, then scatter the rest of the nuts on top of the soft mixture. Press gently into the toffee with a metal spoon, so they are half-covered and will not fall off when the toffee is cut.

◉ Brazil Toffee

Chop about 100 g/4 oz (1 cup) Brazil nuts fairly coarsely. Cut another 100 g/4 oz (1 cup) in halves lengthways. Add the chopped nuts to the toffee just before it reaches the 'hard crack' stage. Mix well. Pour the toffee into the tin and arrange the halved Brazils on top, at regular intervals. Press these gently into the soft toffee. When cold mark in squares, each square should have a Brazil on top.

Variation:
◉   Use hazelnuts, pecan nuts or walnuts instead of Brazils.

◉ Chocolate Coconut Toffee

This combination of flavours is very pleasing.

Add 100 g/4 oz (4 squares) plain chocolate and 75 g/3 oz (1 cup) desiccated coconut to the toffee mixture just before it reaches the 'hard crack' stage. Stir very well to blend.

◉ Maple Syrup Toffee

Follow the recipe for Golden Toffee (see page 336) but substitute maple syrup for the golden syrup. Everton Toffee (see page 330) is less suitable for this variation.

◉ Rum and Raisin Toffee

Soak 150 g/5 oz (scant 1 cup) raisins in 2 tablespoons (3 tablespoons) rum before making either of the toffees, but in each case use 2 tablespoons (3 tablespoons) less water. Add the rum-flavoured raisins to the mixture just before it reaches the 'hard crack' stage. Mix well.

◉ Pulled Taffy

Cooking stage: 131°C/268°F ◉ Makes nearly 550 g/1¼ lb

Taffy was the original name for toffee, but the word is now used to describe a Welshman. Taffy, the ingredients for which are boiled to a considerably lower temperature than most toffees, was frequently a pulled sweet, as described below.

Metric Imperial { **Ingredients** } American
225 g/8 oz { **Demerara sugar** } 1⅓ cups
175 g/6 oz { **golden syrup** } ½ cup
100 g/4 oz { **butter** } ½ cup
2 tablespoons { **water** } 3 tablespoons
2 teaspoons { **glucose** } 2 teaspoons

Grease a slab or metal tin with a few drops of oil. Put all the ingredients into a strong saucepan and stir until the sugar has dissolved, then boil steadily until the mixture reaches the 'light crack' stage. Pour the mixture on to the slab or tin. When cool enough to handle pull gently until there are long strips of an even thickness. If the mixture is inclined to stick to your fingers, dampen them. Brush kitchen scissors with a few drops of oil, and cut the strips into even lengths. Wrap in waxed paper.

◉ Pulled Black Treacle Taffy

For a mild treacle taste use the recipe above but with half golden syrup and half black treacle.

Variation:
◉ For a less buttery taste but stronger flavour of treacle, reduce the amount of butter from 100 g/4 oz (½ cup) to 25 g/1 oz (2 tablespoons). Omit the glucose and add 1 teaspoon vinegar instead. Put the sugar, black treacle, butter, water and vinegar into a strong saucepan. Stir until the sugar has dissolved then boil steadily until the mixture reaches the 'light crack' stage. Stir ¼ level teaspoon bicarbonate of soda into the ingredients. Mix well then proceed as the recipe above.

◉ Pulled Peppermint Taffy

Follow the basic recipe above, but add a few drops of oil of peppermint or peppermint essence. Proceed as the recipe.

Brittle Toffee

Cooking stage: 154°C/310°F ◉ Makes 450 g/1 lb

This toffee mixture is boiled to the very highest temperature, thus making it very crisp. Take care to remove the pan from the heat the moment it reaches the temperature required, so the mixture does not burn.

Metric Imperial { **Ingredients** } American
225 g/8 oz { **granulated sugar** } 1 cup
225 g/8 oz { **golden syrup** } scant 1¹/₂ cups

Put the ingredients into a strong saucepan. Stir over a low heat until the sugar has dissolved then allow to boil rapidly until the 'very hard crack' stage is reached. Use for making Toffee Apples (see page 334), or as below.

Nut Brittle

Prepare about 225 g/8 oz (approximately 2 cups) nuts. These can be all the same type or a mixture of almonds, Brazils, cashew nuts, hazelnuts, peanuts, pecan nuts and walnuts. Chop the nuts. Grease a 20 to 23 cm/8 to 9 inch square tin with a little butter. Make the Brittle Toffee as the recipe above.

   Add the nuts just before the mixture reaches the 'very hard crack' stage. Spoon into the tin. Leave until it is cold. Break into pieces and wrap in waxed paper.

Mint Humbugs

Cooking stage: 143°C/290°F ◉ Makes a generous 450 g/1 lb

Metric Imperial { **Ingredients** } American
450 g/1 lb { **Demerara sugar** } 1 lb
150 ml/¹/₄ pint { **water** } ²/₃ cup
50 g/2 oz { **butter** } ¹/₄ cup
¹/₂ to ³/₄ teaspoon { **peppermint essence or a few drops oil of peppermint** } ¹/₂ to ³/₄ teaspoon
pinch { **cream of tartar** } pinch

Grease a slab or baking tin with a few drops of oil. Put all the ingredients into a strong saucepan. Stir over a moderate heat until the sugar has dissolved, then boil steadily until the mixture reaches the 'hard crack' stage. Allow the mixture to cool for a short time in the saucepan until it becomes slightly sticky.

   Pour on to the slab or into the tin. Leave until cool enough to handle then pull into long strips. When cold cut these into small pieces. Store in an airtight tin.

⊙ Toffee Apples

Cooking stage: 143°C/290°F ⊙ Coats 8 to 10 apples

Toffee apples have been one of the treats enjoyed by children for generations. They are often made for Guy Fawkes Night, on 5th November. This celebrates the foiling of the plot to blow up the Houses of Parliament in 1606. It is not as easy to coat apples with toffee as one might imagine and the points given in the recipe are important.

Metric Imperial { **Ingredients** } American
Everton Toffee or Golden Toffee made with:
450 g/1 lb { **sugar, etc.** } (see pages 330 and 336) 1 lb
8 to 10 { **small dessert apples** } 8 to 10
8 to 10 { **long wooden sticks for toffee apples** } 8 to 10

Choose ripe dessert apples, free from blemish and those with a crisp texture. Wash the apples well to get rid of the natural oils; dry thoroughly.

Assemble the extra equipment required. In addition to the ingredients, saucepan for making the toffee, the sugar thermometer and/or bowl of cold water for testing the toffee, you need:
1   a lightly oiled flat baking tin, upon which to stand the coated apples;
2   a large container, which should be filled with boiling water. The saucepan of hot toffee has to be placed in this container, to prevent the toffee hardening in the saucepan too soon. It must be kept liquid to coat the apples;
3   a bowl of cold water in which to dip the coated apples, so the toffee around the apples sets quickly;
4   waxed paper for wrapping the apples, if they are not to be eaten soon after preparing them.

Make the toffee as the recipe. Insert the sticks in the apples. Dip the first apple into the hot toffee, swirl it around so it has a good layer of toffee on all sides. Lift from the pan and then plunge into the bowl of cold water. Do this with all of the apples. Repeat the coating process at least once more, so the apples have a thick coating.

Stand the coated apples on the oiled tin and allow the toffee to set. Wrap the apples in squares of waxed paper.

⊙ Brittle Toffee Apples

Both the toffees suggested in the recipe above have a soft creamy texture. For a crisp brittle toffee use the recipe on page 333.

Honeycomb Toffee

Cooking stage: 143°C/290°F ⊙ Makes 350 g/12 oz

This recipe and Golden Toffee are two of the easiest of toffees to make. In the first recipe use a large and deep saucepan, for the mixture rises dramatically when the bicarbonate of soda is added. As the name suggests, this toffee has a texture like a honeycomb. Make only small quantities of this toffee; it becomes sticky in storage.

Metric Imperial { **Ingredients** } American
40 g/1½ oz { **butter** } 3 tablespoons
250 g/9 oz { **granulated sugar** } 1 cup plus 2 tablespoons
3 tablespoons { **golden syrup** } 4 tablespoons
3 tablespoons { **water** } 4 tablespoons
6 drops { **white malt vinegar** } 6 drops
1½ level teaspoons { **bicarbonate of soda** } 1½ level teaspoons

Grease a 15 to 18 cm/6 to 7 inch square tin with a little of the butter. Put the remainder of the butter with the sugar, golden syrup and water into a strong saucepan. Stir over a moderate heat until the sugar has dissolved, then boil briskly until the mixture reaches the 'hard crack' stage, stir in the vinegar and then the bicarbonate of soda. Keep your hands well away from the hot mixture as it rises in the pan. Stir briskly then pour into the tin. Leave until quite cold and hard then break into pieces.

Golden Toffee

Cooking stage: 143°C/290°F ⊙ Makes a generous 450 g/1 lb

Metric Imperial { **Ingredients** } American
50 g/2 oz { **butter**} ¼ cup
450 g/1 lb { **Demerara sugar** } 1 lb
200 ml/7 fl oz { **water** } scant cup
2 tablespoons { **golden syrup** } 3 tablespoons
1 teaspoon { **white malt vinegar** } 1 teaspoon

Grease a 20 cm/8 inch square tin with a little of the butter. Put all the ingredients into a strong saucepan and stir over a moderate heat until dissolved. Boil briskly until the mixture reaches the 'hard crack' stage. Pour into the tin and allow to become quite cold, then break into pieces. Wrap in waxed paper.

⊙ Creamy Caramels

Cooking stage: 121°C/250°F but see method ⊙ **Makes nearly 800 g/1³/4 lb**

Good caramels should have very much the same creamy taste as fudge but be much firmer in texture. They are not easy to cut, the best method is explained below.

Metric Imperial { **Ingredients** } American
450 g/1 lb { **granulated sugar** } 1 lb
397 g/14 oz can { **full-cream sweetened condensed milk** } 1³/4 cups
2 tablespoons { **water** } 3 tablespoons
100 g/4 oz { **butter** } ¹/2 cup
25 g/1 oz { **golden syrup** } 1¹/2 tablespoons
1 teaspoon { **vanilla essence** } 1 teaspoon
pinch { **cream of tartar** } pinch

Grease a 20 cm/8 inch square tin with a very little butter.

Put all the ingredients, except the cream of tartar, into a strong saucepan. Stir over a low heat until the sugar has dissolved, then boil for 2 to 3 minutes.

Add the cream of tartar, stir well. Continue boiling steadily, stirring now and again, until the mixture reaches the 'soft ball' stage. This gives a soft caramel. For a harder sweetmeat boil to 129.4°C/265°F, the 'very firm ball' stage. For a really hard caramel boil to 132.2°C/270°F, the 'light' or 'soft crack' stage.

Do not beat the mixture, it must not be cloudy. Pour into the prepared tin.

To make the caramels easy to cut mark very firmly into squares when half set then cut with a very sharp knife when firm. Wrap in waxed paper.

⊙ Chocolate Caramels

Cut 175 g/6 oz (6 squares) plain chocolate into small pieces. Add to the mixture after the cream of tartar. Boil only to 121°C/250°F – the 'soft ball' stage.

⊙ Coconut Caramels

Blend 175 g/6 oz (1 cup) desiccated coconut into the mixture just before it reaches 121°C/250°F – the 'soft ball' stage.

⊙ Flavoured Caramels

Omit the vanilla essence and add 1 to 2 teaspoons ground ginger or mixed spice to the mixture. You can also add 100 g/4 oz (¹/4 lb) diced preserved ginger just before it reaches 121°C/250°F – the 'soft ball' stage.

⊙ Nut Caramels

Chop 150 g/5 oz (1¹/4 cups) any nuts. Stir into the mixture (see above) at the 'soft ball' stage.

⊙ Butterscotch

Cooking stage: 138°C/280°F ⊙ Makes 500 g/1¼ lb

Both butterscotch and barley sugar are among the best of all home-made sweets. The recipe below uses a generous amount of butter and this is apparent in the flavour of the butterscotch.

Metric Imperial { **Ingredients** } American
450 g/1 lb { **granulated sugar** } 1 lb
150 ml/¼ pint { **single cream or milk** } ⅔ cup
3 tablespoons { **water** } 4¼ tablespoons
75 g/3 oz { **butter** } ⅜ cup
pinch { **cream of tartar** } pinch
To coat the tin: little { **melted butter** }

Grease a 23 cm/9 inch square tin with the butter. Put all the ingredients, except the cream of tartar, into a strong saucepan. Stir over a low heat until the sugar has dissolved then allow the mixture to boil steadily until it reaches the 'crack' stage. Stir several times to prevent the mixture sticking to the pan. Add the cream of tartar and stir well.

   Pour the mixture into the tin. When nearly set, mark into squares with a heated knife. Leave until quite cold then separate the squares and wrap in waxed paper.

⊙ Barley sugar

Cooking stage: 156°C/312°F ⊙ Makes 450 g/1 lb

Metric Imperial { **Ingredients** } American
450 g/1 lb { **loaf or granulated sugar** } 1 lb
150 ml/¼ pint { **water** } ⅔ cup
few drops { **saffron yellow colouring** } few drops
1½ teaspoons { **lemon juice** } 1½ teaspoons
To coat the tin: few drops { **oil** }

Grease a 20 cm/8 inch square tin with a very little oil. Put all the ingredients into a strong saucepan, stir over a moderate heat until the sugar has dissolved. Boil steadily, without stirring, until the mixture reaches the 'brittle' stage. Pour the mixture into the tin and leave until half-set, then mark in squares with a heated knife. Leave until quite cold, then remove the squares and wrap in waxed paper.

Variation:
⊙   Use half liquid glucose and half sugar. This makes a very crisp sweetmeat.

Edinburgh Rock

Cooking stage: 129°C/256°F ◉ Makes 450 g/1 lb

This Scottish sweetmeat is flavoured and coloured to taste as described in the ingredients. All culinary colourings should be used sparingly to give pale tints.

Metric Imperial { **Ingredients** } American
450 g/1 lb { **loaf or granulated sugar** } 1 lb
200 ml/7 fl oz { **water, but see Variation** } 7/8 cup
pinch { **cream of tartar** } pinch
to taste { **raspberry essence and pink colouring,**
      lemon essence and yellow colouring,
      peppermint essence and green colouring } to taste
To grease the tins: few drops { **oil** }
To dust the rock: little { **icing sugar** }

Put the sugar and water into a strong saucepan, stir until the sugar has dissolved then boil steadily until the mixture reaches the 'light crack' stage. Add the cream of tartar, stir well. Allow the mixture to cool in the pan until it stiffens slightly. Brush baking trays with the oil. Divide the mixture into 2 to 3 portions and put on the trays.

Work a very few drops of essence and colouring into the first portion; do the same with the other portions. You can of course use just one essence and colour, or simply flavour the mixture and not use colour.

Dust the work surface and your fingers with sifted icing sugar and pull and knead each portion of rock until it becomes opaque. Make very long thin sticks, then cut into lengths of about 12.5 cm/5 inches. Leave in the air for 24 hours, or until the mixture becomes powdery and soft. Pack in boxes.

Variation:

◉ For a softer version of this rock use 300 ml/1/2 pint (11/4 cups) water and 1/4 teaspoon cream of tartar. In very cold weather, boil only to 121°C/250°F; in very hot weather to 127°C/260°F.

Barley sugar sticks

Follow the recipe for Barley Sugar (see page 338). Brush a slab or baking tin with a little oil. Pour the mixture on to this. When cool enough to handle take portions and pull and knead into long sticks. Twist these. When firm wrap in waxed paper.

Acid Drops

Cooking stage: 156°C/312°F ⊙ Makes a scant 450 g/1 lb

When making boiled sweets that should have a clear texture it is important to remove any scum that floats to the top of the mixture during boiling.

Metric Imperial { **Ingredients** } American
450 g/1 lb { **loaf or granulated sugar** } 1 lb
150 ml/¼ pint { **water** } ⅔ cup
1 level teaspoon { **tartaric acid** } 1 level teaspoon
To coat (optional): icing sugar

To produce good shaped sweets it is better to have small moulds. If not available, then lightly oil a baking tray.

Put the sugar and water into a strong saucepan, stir over a moderate heat until the sugar dissolves then boil the mixture until it reaches the 'brittle' stage. Allow the very hot mixture to cool slightly in the saucepan, then, while it is still a pouring consistency, carefully blend in the tartaric acid. Mix thoroughly.

Pour into the tiny moulds and allow the mixture to set, or pour into the tray and leave until sufficiently cool to handle, then form into long rounded bars. When cold, cut into small pieces. These could be rolled in a little sifted icing sugar.

Fruit Drops

Follow the recipe above but use various flavoured essences, such as blackcurrant, raspberry, lemon or orange. Look for those products that are labelled 'natural essence' for these give a far better taste to the sweets. Extra colouring can be added if desired. If using just one flavour then this can be added at the same time as the tartaric acid.

To produce a selection of flavours from just the 450 g/1 lb sugar etc. in the recipe above, add the tartaric acid and mix with the syrup then pour the unflavoured mixture into the oiled tray. Leave until sufficiently cool to handle.

Take a small portion of the mixture, allow a few drops of flavouring and of colouring, if using this, to drop on to the surface of the sweetmeat then work in by pulling and stretching the warm sweetmeat.

Repeat this process with different flavourings and colourings.

To Add Flavouring And Colouring

Insert a fine skewer into the bottle and turn it around until it is well coated then hold the skewer over the food to be flavoured, or coloured, and allow just a few drops of the liquid to fall from the skewer.

Chocolate for Coating

Chocolate itself is not easy to make – it is really a job for experts, for it depends upon the right ingredients and correct temperature, humidity and other conditions. It is quite satisfactory to buy chocolate and melt it to coat various filling. Tempering is less important when coating sweet with chocolate. The ideal melting temperatures are below.

Coverture chocolate: this is of high quality and obtainable in both dark (plain) and light (milk) flavours. It keeps its shine well if melted correctly. Heat to 46 to 47°C/115 to 117°F for plain couverture and 43°C/110°F for milk couverture. For some people chocolate couverture lacks sufficient sweetness.

Plain and bitter chocolates: buy the best quality possible. Heat to 53 to 54°C/128 to 130°F.

Milk and white chocolates: take great care these are not overheated in melting. Heat to 41°C/106°F.

To Melt Chocolate

Break the chocolate into small pieces, or grate it to make it easier to melt evenly. Remove the chocolate from the heat as soon as it looks slightly melted and check the temperature; it continues to soften in the heat of the container.

If melting over hot water: make sure the water does not touch the base of the basin in which the chocolate is placed. Heat the water under the chocolate to 82°C/180°F, this is well below boiling point, but hotter than your hands could bare.

If melting in a saucepan: stir over the lowest possible heat; remove the pan from the heat as soon as the chocolate shows signs of softening. If melting in a microwave: use the DEFROST setting and check progress regularly. Remove from the microwave as soon as the chocolate shows signs of melting.

To Coat Sweets With Chocolate

Prepare the fillings before melting the chocolate. Arrange foil or waxed or greaseproof paper on flat trays.

Melt the chocolate then stir this to ensure you have an even texture and heat. Jellied sweets must be coated in cool liquid chocolate. Use a long-handled spoon or fork; there are proper dipping spoons and forks available.

Put the first sweet into the chocolate, turn around until evenly coated then lift out and hold over the chocolate, so any drips fall back into the container. Place the coated sweet on the foil or paper then continue coating the rest of the sweets, making sure the chocolate remains at the right temperature.

Allow the chocolate coating to stiffen slightly then top the chocolates with nuts, crystallized roses, violet petals or other decorations.

◉ Stuffed Dates

Dessert dates look most attractive if stuffed with marzipan. Carefully remove the stones from the fruit so their shape is not spoiled. Fill each date with a little marzipan. This can be tinted, or mixed with chopped nuts or chopped glacé fruits. Roll the coated dates in a little sifted icing sugar.

◉ Uncooked Peppermint Creams

No cooking ◉ **Makes 450 g/1 lb**

This recipe is very similar to royal icing (see page 310). In fact, left-over icing can be used to make the sweetmeats by adding peppermint flavouring.

Metric Imperial { **Ingredients** } American
2 { **egg whites** } 2
450 g/1 lb { **icing sugar** } scant 4 cups
2 teaspoons { **glycerine** } 2 teaspoons
few drops { **oil of peppermint or peppermint essence** } few drops
To roll the sweets: extra { **icing sugar** }

Put the egg whites into a bowl and whisk until just frothy. Sift the icing sugar into the egg whites, add the glycerine and flavouring. Beat with a wooden spoon, or use an electric mixer on low speed, until the mixture is very white and smooth.

Dust a slab or pastry board and a rolling pin with more sifted icing sugar. Roll out the sweetmeat until 6 mm/1/4 inch in thickness, cut into small rounds. Leave in the air for some hours to harden, then pack in airtight containers.

◉ Chocolate Peppermint Creams

Make the sweets as the recipe on this page, or on page 323. Allow the sweets to harden slightly and then coat in chocolate (see page 341).

◉ Coating Sweets In Chocolate

Most sweets can be coated in chocolate (see page 341). The most successful are:
◉ **Caramels and Toffees:** make these sweets as the recipes on pages 330 to 337. Cut into neat squares when cold and coat with chocolate as soon as possible, so the sweets do not become sticky.
◉ **Fondant:** make the fondant as the various suggestions on pages 321 to 323. Leave until firm before coating.
◉ **Fudge and Candy:** make these as the recipes on pages 324 to 328 and allow to become cold, then cut into neat shapes. Do not leave in the air for too long or the sweets will become over-hard before coating.
◉ **Peppermint Creams:** see pages 323 and above.

Appendices

▣ Measurements

Metric, Imperial and American measurements are given throughout the book. Always follow one list of measurements; they are not interchangeable.

Metric measurements shown in the majority of recipes are the accepted equivalent of Imperial measurements, i.e. 25 g/1 oz; 150 ml/1/4 pint, etc. In some recipes a slightly different metric measurement is given, e.g. in Shortcrust Pastry, page 290, you will find: 225 g/8 oz plain flour and 110 g/4 oz butter.

The alteration from the usual measurement is because you need half fat to flour. Obviously it is difficult to add 10 g to the usual 100 g on the scales, all it means is you weigh out a generous 100 g.

A metric 15 ml spoon/Imperial 1 tablespoon is equivalent to 11/4 American tablespoons. In a few recipes, where several times 11/4 tablespoons is difficult to measure I have 'rounded off' the tablespoons slightly.

▣ Ingredients

Butter: this is a book of British classic recipes and butter would have been the choice of fat with the exception of pure dripping (now far from easy to obtain).

Nowadays there are many kinds of margarine, including the polyunsaturated type. These can replace butter in recipes, unless stated to the contrary.

Lemons: two terms are used – 'finely grated lemon rind' and 'finely grated lemon zest'. If you see the latter it means you must be extra careful to take absolutely no white pith from the fruit.

▣ Cooking Temperatures

All recipes have been carefully tested in both gas and electric ovens. Individual ovens do vary and you may have to adjust the settings slightly in the light of your own personal knowledge of your cooker. If you own a fan oven it is wise to reduce all settings by 10°C or 25°F. With solid-fuel cookers, follow the advice given by the manufacturer of your particular model as to which oven to use.

◨ British Cheeses

We have a wonderful range of cheeses in Britain, many of which rank among the finest in the world. Today more and more dairy farmers are producing new varieties of cheese. A selection of both well-known and less well-known is given below. Be adventurous and sample any new varieties you discover including smoked cheeses.

Pubs today make a feature of their Ploughman's Lunch, which consists of crusty fresh bread with butter and a selection of cheeses. Washed down with beer, or a favourite drink, and served with chutney or pickled onions, plus a ripe tomato, you have a simple but excellent meal. The following are just a small selection of our cheeses, with brief suggestions as to the way they are best served. They are all excellent with bread or biscuits; those particularly good for cooking are mentioned.

Arran – from Scotland, not unlike a Cheddar, excellent for cooking.

Ayrshire Cream – a wonderful creamy Scottish cheese, ideal for sandwiches.

Blarney – a semi-soft cheese, particularly good in salads or for cooking.

Caboc – a Scottish cream cheese coated with oatmeal, excellent with fruit.

Caerphilly – an outstanding Welsh crumbly cheese, good in salads, cooks well.

Cheddar – one of the best known English cheeses, there are many variations, and it is made throughout Britain as well as in its true home – England's west country. A truly mature Cheddar has a wonderful taste; good eaten raw and first class for cooking.

Cheshire – another excellent hard cheese, has the same virtues as Cheddar.

Crowdie – a Scottish crumbly cheese that cooks well and is excellent raw.

Derby – a slightly tangy flavour, often flavoured with sage. Excellent raw.

Double Gloucester – this has a strong taste when mature and a delicate one when young. Excellent in cooking (see Welsh Rarebit on page 226) or to eat raw.

Lancashire – a crumbly cheese, which develops a sharp flavour when mature. Cooks well and is good served raw with an apple pie or a rich fruit cake.

Leicester – a mild cheese with a somewhat flaky texture, good in sandwiches.

Stilton – often described as the greatest cheese of all. Blue-veined, although you can obtain a white Stilton. It must be mature, but not over-ripe, to have a really full flavour. Cooks well, although most people prefer it uncooked.

Wensleydale – a creamy soft texture and a mild taste, with a faint saltiness. Ideal to have with salads or with fruit.

◧ Lesser Known British Cheeses

The list below gives a small selection of British cheeses. Be adventurous and sample any new varieties you discover including smoked cheeses.

◉ English

Appleby's Red – one of the oldest cheeses made, an excellent crumbly cheese with a fresh tangy flavour.

Smoked Appleby's – oak-smoked to give a full, smoky flavour with a crumbly texture.

Berkswell – named after the Saxon chief, Bercul. It has a firm ivory paste with a fabulous flavour.

Cornish Blue – matured for 12 weeks to develop a full flavour and blue veined character.

Cotherstone – popular with drinkers of stout. A moist tangy cheese.

Elgar Mature – firm but slightly open texture and a rich flavour.

Harbourne Blue – white, firm and crumbly with a distinctive aromatic flavour. It is still the only goat's milk blue made in Britain.

Lynher Valley Dairy Yarg – based on a 13th century recipe. This cheese, from a Duchy of Cornwall estate farm is wrapped in nettle leaves, is moist and has a tangy flavour.

Stinking Bishop – is washed in perry which is made from the Stinking Bishop variety of pear. A pungent and spirited aroma.

◉ Irish

Ardrahan – a distinctive earthy aroma. Beneath the washed rind, the deep yellow interior is firm and slightly chalky. The finish is reminiscent of a young Gruyère.

Cooleeney – a Camembert-style Irish cheese. Full flavoured and grassy, with a distinct aroma of mushrooms when ripe. It has a rich, semi-liquid interior.

Cashel Blue – a medium-flavoured blue with a melt in the mouth creaminess, is less salty than the majority of blues.

Desmond – hard granular cheese. Deep-cream coloured with a thick, hard rind, the flavour is intense and spicy. Can be used like a Parmesan.

Durrus – produced in the style of Tomme de Savoie. The humid, warm, salty conditions of the south-west tip of Ireland are ideal for making this creamy washed rind cheese.

Gabriel – made on the same farm as Desmond, this is a hard, granular cheese with a deep fruity flavour and a mellow aftertaste. Can be used like a Parmesan.

Gubbeen – the salty sea air is perfect for this type of cheese which has a silky, pliable texture and a fresh, milky flavour.

Smoked Gubbeen – oak-smoked. The smoked flavour does not swamp the natural flavour of the cheese.

⊙ Scottish

Bishop Kennedy – full fat soft cheese, rind washed in malt whisky. Runny when ripe.

Dunsyre Blue – lesser known Dunsyre Blue is made using the rich unpasteurised milk of Ayrshire cattle.

Inverloch – pasteurised pressed goat's cheese from Isle of Gigha. Coated in red wax.

Kelsae – unpasteurised pressed cheese made near Kelso from Jersey milk; but creamy in texture and taste.

Lanark Blue – the sheep graze on wild heather pastures which impart their flavours to the Roquefort-style cheese. A very variable cheese with the strength varying from full to fierce. Available June to January.

Lanark White – a white version of famed ewe's milk blue cheese, a smooth texture and nutty salty flavour.

St. Andrews – award winning full fat, washed rind, a mild creamy, full flavoured soft cheese.

Stichill – unpasteurised and creamy made with Jersey milk, Cheshire style, from the Scottish borders.

⊙ Welsh

Brie – has a rich, creamy texture and a distinctively earthy taste.

Celtic Promise – washed in cider. An orange rind, supple texture and spicy aromatic flavour.

Cilowen Organic – rich, creamy flavour, it sets a high standard for other organic cheeses.

Smoked Cilowen Organic – naturally smoked over oak logs, this has a smooth texture with a gentle, smoky tang.

Llanboidy – made using the milk of the rare Red Poll cow. A hard cheese with a firm, creamy texture and a hint of herbs. Laverbread is an edible seaweed found in the Gower. When cooked and dried it is added to Llanboidy cheese.

Saval – washed in cider. It is a larger version of Celtic promise. Sharp and fruity with earthy undertones.

Y-Fenni – a mature Cheddar blended with mustard and ale to give a moist tangy flavour. Excellent melted on toast.

Index

Other books by Marguerite Patten published by Grub Street

The Basic Basics Jams, Preserves and Chutneys Handbook
Paperback
978-1-902304-72-4

The Basic Basics Baking Handbook
Paperback
978-1-904010-11-1

The Basic Basics Soups Handbook
Paperback
978-1-904010-19-7

A Century of British Cooking
Paperback
978-1-902304-69-4

Marguerite Patten's 100 Top Teatime Treats
Hardback
978-1-904943-29-7